ANOTHER FREEDOM

SVETLANA BOYM

ANOTHER FREEDOM

The Alternative History of an Idea

THE UNIVERSITY OF CHICAGO PRESS | CHICAGO AND LONDON

The University of Chicago Press, Chicago 60637
The University of Chicago Press, Ltd., London
© 2010 by The University of Chicago
All rights reserved. Published 2010.
Paperback edition 2012
Printed in the United States of America

21 20 19 18 17 16 15 14 13 12   2 3 4 5 6

ISBN-13: 978-0-226-06973-9 (cloth)
ISBN-13: 978-0-226-06974-6 (paper)
ISBN-10: 0-226-06973-7 (cloth)
ISBN-10: 0-226-06974-5 (paper)

Library of Congress Cataloging-in-Publication Data

Boym, Svetlana
Another freedom : the alternative history of an idea / Svetlana Boym.
p. cm.
Includes bibliographical references and index.
ISBN-13: 978-0-226-06973-9 (cloth : alk. paper)
ISBN-10: 0-226-06973-7 (cloth : alk. paper) 1. Liberty. I. Title.
JC585.B696 2010
320.01'1—dc22

                                                    2009042961

To my parents,
Musa and Yuri Goldberg

Contents

Acknowledgments

Writing a book on freedom proved to be a lonelier exercise than writing a book on nostalgia. I am grateful to my friends, students, and rare colleagues who still pursue intellectual adventure against all odds and the mood of the moment. I would like to thank my first readers and interlocutors: Isobel Armstrong, for her poetic wisdom and belief in radical aesthetics, and Maya Turovskaya, who inspired me to reflect on the banality of evil and the ephemerality of good. I am grateful to Michael Holquist for sharing his intellectual passions for philosophy and philology and for reading the manuscript, to Gregory Nagy for his kindness and intimate knowledge of Greek *technê* and for encouraging me to work on tragedy, to William Mills Todd III for his generous insights into Pushkin and Dostoevsky and for inspiring me not to shy away from honest controversies, and to Benjamin Nathans for reading my chapter on estrangement and dissent and sharing his research on Soviet dissidents.

I began work on this book on a sabbatical leave at Harvard University and during a fellowship of the American Academy in

Berlin. I am grateful to its director, Gary Smith, and to the generous staff. I benefited greatly from sharing friendship and a few "real conversations" ranging from moral masochism to secularism with Michael Steinberg and Susan Stewart-Steinberg. Parts of the book were presented at the Gauss Seminar at Princeton University in 2003, and I would like to thank Caryl Emerson, Michael Wood, Diana Fuss, and others for early encouragement. My thanks also to the editor and the anonymous readers of the *Slavic Review* for the input on my article "Banality of Evil, Mimicry, and the Soviet Subject," which became a foundation of the last chapter. I also benefited from challenging discussion at the University of Chicago with Robert Bird, Jonathan Lear, Robert Pippin, and Loren Kruger. I have gained insight from many other discussions, especially at the University of Pennsylvania, Cranbrook, Stony Brook, Stanford, and the University of Southern California as well as in Madrid, Puebla, Ljubljana, Venice, Bologna, London, and Cambridge.

There is an important etymological connection between freedom and friendship. Friends share worlds and help cocreate them. Thanks to Eyal Peretz for sharing his intellectual vocation and a few joyful phantoms, to Tamar Abramov for shared adventures in free-thinking past and future, to Alexandra Smith for poems and shared nostalgias and anti-nostalgias. My accident and the broken leg ordeal cast a new light on my intellectual and artistic life. Special thanks to the friends of the broken leg days, Kati Orban, Linda Voris, Despina Kakoudaki, Ken Shulman. To my long-term friends, colleagues, and interlocutors who supported me throughout this period: Giuliana Bruno, David Damrosch, Susan Suleiman and Lena Burgos-Lafuente, Greta and Mark Slobin, Tomislav Longinovic, John Hamilton and Larry Wolff, and Nancy Ruttenburg. To my friends who are now far away for whom the shadowplay of freedom really matters: Eugene Yelchin, Vitaly Komar, Dubravka Ugresic, Masha Gessen, Eva Hoffman, and Alexander Etkind. And to my former brilliant students, now writers and professors in their own right, who witnessed the conception of freedom: Cristina Vatulescu, Julia Vaingurt, Julia Bekman Chadaga, and Anna Wexler Katsnelson.

I am enormously grateful to my editor at the University of Chicago Press, Susan Bielstein, who embraced the space of freedom with enthusiasm, wisdom, and caution. Thanks to Christopher Westcott for helping me sculpt the unruly introduction to the book, to Anthony Burton, to Maia Rigas for her meticulous, intelligent, and insightful copyediting and for her graciousness and good humor, and to Teresa Iverson, my first manuscript editor, for her excellent work and poetic insights.

My assistants and friends helped tie the loose ends and find the missing references and supported me throughout: Charlotte Szilagyi, Ana Olenina, and at the end, Joanna Greenlee.

Finally, something more than thanks goes to Dana Villa, who once upon a time introduced me to Hannah Arendt (and the rest is history), and to my parents, who know too much about freedom and its discontents.

Figure 1. Svetlana Boym, chessboard collage combining the Human Statue of Liberty, 1918, and the Goddess of Liberty and Democracy from Tiananmen Square, Beijing, China, 1989.

Beloved by many modern artists and writers from Shklovsky to Duchamps and Nabokov, the chessboard became a model for the zigzag of off-modern creativity. Historically, the chessboard displaces the battlefield allowing gaming to compete with warmongering. The cosmopolitan ornament of black and white squares moved between cultures and didn't lose much in translation. My chessboards are never really black and white, but always a little off with a glare and texture of local materials. The surface of the chessboard plays with perspectives and grids, opening onto the fourth dimension of fiction.

FREEDOM AS COCREATION

Adventure and the Borders of Freedom

At the beginning of the twenty-first century we had difficulty imagining a new beginning. The future appeared frightening rather than liberating, while the past remained a domain of nostalgic utopias. For the first eight years or so our century seemed to have had a false start.

So how to begin again? Let us try to imagine freedom by thinking "what if" and not only "what is." Let us explore missed historical opportunities and highlight alternative spaces of freedom. This book is an attempt to rescue another history of freedom and propose a new vocabulary that goes beyond today's political debates. It explores the experience of freedom as cocreation in the world and as an adventure in political action and individual judgment, in public and private imagination and passionate thinking. The questions that concern me point to the paradoxes of freedom: What, if anything, must we be certain of in order to tolerate uncertainty? How much common ground or shared trust is needed to allow for the uncommon experiences of freedom? Can they be transported across national borders? If so, can we distinguish between firm boundaries and porous border zones and travel lightly between them?

Instead of vetting typologies and definitions we will engage in rigorous storytelling and follow cross-cultural dialogues between political philosophers, artists, dissidents, and lovers who address the very ground of the possibility of freedom and deliberate its boundaries. Many of these encounters took place in the wake of major historical cataclysms, wars, and revolutions, when the dreams of the new beginning and initial moments of liberation were followed by attempts to establish a regime of freedom. In all of them, experiments in thinking and imagination were also connected to life experiments, sometimes producing more contradictions than continuities. These experiments allow us to explore the relationship between *freedoms* in the plural (political freedoms, human rights) and *Freedom* in the singular (religious, artistic, or existential freedom) and look at the moments in which political and artistic understandings of freedom become intertwined. My freedom stories won't take the shape of military epics or romances of independence or martyrdom.[1] Neither will they function merely as cautionary morality tales. At best, they can shed some light on the dilemmas of freedom that are sometimes more difficult to confront than the discreet charms of power.

The experience of freedom has not been valued equally throughout history and across cultures. Even today freedom is out of sync with other highly desirable states of being, such as happiness, belonging, glory, or intimacy. While those states suggest unity and fusion, freedom has an element of estrangement that does not by definition exclude engagement with others in the public world but makes it more unpredictable.

Not only has freedom been a contested value, there has been no agreement as to what freedom would look like. Defining freedom is like capturing a snake: the snake sheds its skin, and we are left with the relic of her trickery as a souvenir of our aspiration. There was no god or goddess of freedom in any ancient mythology, only a belated Roman statue of Libertas, which caused many cultural scandals throughout the centuries. Her "liberty cap" covered the shaved head of a former slave, who acquired rights in the democratic city-states of antiquity, thus making an attribute of Liberty into a simultaneous memento of slavery. As late as 1855 Senator Jefferson Davis of Mississippi, soon to become the president of the Confederacy, objected to the idea of erecting a statue of Freedom wearing a liberty cap on top of the United States Capitol, arguing that this ancient badge of emancipated slaves would offend Southern sensibilities.[2]

The most famous American Statue of Liberty does not wear the memento of slavery either; instead, the traditional liberty cap is transformed into the crown of enlightenment, a beacon for the new modern world. The statue was a gift from a disenchanted Frenchman, who believed that Liberty no longer resided in Europe but only in the United States. To create the goddess of enlightenment, he was inspired, so it is said, by the body of his wife and the face of his mother. But his creation—accepted with great reluctance in the new world—soon shed its skin, metamorphosing into a goddess of immigrants, a tourist attraction, and a security threat. In other countries, like Russia, statues of Liberty were highly unpopular and lacked native iconography. Much preferred was Mother Patria, with classical breasts clad in prudent drapery not dissimilar to those of Lady Liberty.[3] Curiously, the Chinese Goddess of Liberty erected by dissenting students during the Tiananmen Square demonstrations in 1989 referenced both the American and the Russian monuments; it also bore an uncanny resemblance to a Soviet Peasant and Worker statue from the 1930s massreproduced all over the world. Quickly brought down by the government forces, this destroyed Goddess of Socialism with a Human Face had unpredictable multicultural features. Of course, all iconographies have their own pitfalls; in the case of freedom, they only point at the unrepresentable.

Having lived half my life on the westernmost point of Russia and the other half on the eastern edge of the United States, I am forever haunted by the specter of two worrying queens—America's Lady Liberty and Russia's Mother Patria. This kind of personal and historical double exposure prompts me to recognize the fragile space of shared dreams that sometimes must be rescued from both extremism and mediocrity. While examining cultural differences in various dialogues on freedom, I will not focus solely on the clash of cultures or external pluralism but will explore internal pluralities within cultures and trace elective affinities across national borders. The examination of freedom requires a creative logic of its own.

One should not forget that freedom has also been associated with invisible elements like the free air of the city and that this "free air" is hard to export or commodify. Freedom's inherent strangeness or noniconicity finds its best reflection in experimental art. The avant-garde artist Kazimir Malevich preferred a zero degree of representation, an image of the black square, an "embryo of multiple potentialities," while his rival Vladimir Tatlin designed the enigmatic monument *To the Liberation of Humanity*, known also as *Monument to the Third Internationale*, a tower of two mirroring spirals that resembled both a ruin of the Tower of Babel and a utopian construction site of the future. These artists believed that the new architecture of freedom would not require conventional technical drawings but could be built through experimental artistic technology. For many reasons ranging from the technical to the political, the monument to the liberation of humanity was never to be built. It remains a phantom limb of nonconformist art all over the world, an example of the improbable architecture of "what if."

The German American immigrant and political thinker Hannah Arendt described the experience of freedom as something fundamentally strange, a new beginning and a "miracle of infinite improbability" that occurs regularly in the public realm.[4] Since freedom is one of the most abused words in present-day politics, I will explore it as something "infinitely improbable" and, nevertheless, possible.

The new beginning marked by the experience Arendt describes is neither a return to nature and myth nor a leap into the "end of history." For better or worse, freedom is an ongoing human miracle. Arendt finds a new space for the experience of freedom—not inside the human psyche or in the domain of the will but in human action on the public stage. She traces the first positive appreciation of freedom back to ancient Greece, to the conception of public or political freedom. For her, "care for the common world" becomes a measure and limit of such freedom. The experience of freedom is akin to the theatrical performance that uses conventions, public memory, and a common stage but also allows for the possibility of the unprecedented and particular. Such experiences constitute our "forgotten heritage," which is frequently written out of the conventional historiography and therefore is something that every generation must discover anew.

The improbable element in the discussion of the experience of freedom is the word "infinite." Freedom is only possible under the conditions of human finitude and with concern for boundaries. In fact, since Aristotle, thinking of freedom begins with the disclaimer that freedom does not mean doing what one wishes, abolishing all boundaries and distinctions. Before thinking of "freedom from" and "freedom for" or negative and positive freedom we have to map the ground of possibility of the experience of freedom. Dreaming of borderlessness, we become aware of our fences and passages, bans and banisters, border zones and bridges where double agents are occasionally exchanged. But how do we understand a boundary: as a barrier or a contact zone, as a limit point or a horizon from which the world can be reimagined? Which boundaries are more important? Boundaries between cultures or between the individual and the state? Between private and public or within the self? Can there be a

Russian freedom, an American freedom, a hyphenated freedom? Is one man's tyranny another man's national community of freedom? Touching upon contemporary debates around liberalism and its critics, around negative and positive conceptions of freedom, freedom of imagination and freedom of action, as well as of national and universalist understanding of rights of individuals and nation-states, this book will explore the border zones between political, religious, and cultural spheres, between economics and moral sentiments, between human rights and human passions.

The experience of freedom is akin to adventure: it explores new borders but never erases or transcends them. Through adventure we can test the limits but also navigate—more or less successfully—between convention and invention, responsibility and play. German sociologist Georg Simmel proposes an experimental spatial and temporal structure of adventure that in my view exemplifies the paradoxes of freedom. Adventure is an event, which both interrupts the flow of our everyday life and crystallizes its inner core.[5] Examples of adventure can vary: from the experience of foreign travel to the exploration of one's native modern metropolis, from a political action to an erotic experience or any life-transforming encounter. The concept will be further expanded to refer to the adventures of thinking, judging, of love and dissent. In adventure we "forcibly pull the world into ourselves," but at the same time allow a "complete self-abandonment to the powers and accidents of the world, which can delight us, but in the same breadth can also destroy us."[6] Thus the relationships between inside and outside, foreign and native, center and periphery, core and everyday practice are constantly reframed. Adventure is like "a stranger's body" which foregrounds the most intimate.[7] Through the experience of adventure we enter into a dialogue with the world and with the stranger within us.

Adventure literally refers to something that is about to happen, *ad venire*, but rather than opening up into some catastrophic or messianic future, it instead leads into invisible temporal dimensions of the present. The temporal structure of adventure echoes the spatial one: it can be described as a time out of time, yet it also changes our everyday conception of what it means to be timely. Adventure might work against the linear conception of time, the time of modern progress or human aging; it challenges the implacable irreversibility of time without recourse to nostalgia. In the experience of adventure we can deflect the vectors of past and future and explore potentialities of the present, reenchanting modern experiences.[8] The adventurer pushes "life beyond the threshold of its temporal boundaries," but this "beyond" is never beyond this-worldliness. Neither transcendence nor transgression, adventure is a kind of profane illumination, to use Walter Benjamin's term. It pushes human possibilities but doesn't break them. It involves an encounter with the incalculable that forces us to change life's calculus and explore the dimensions of "what if."

Adventure opens up porous spaces of border zones, thresholds, bridges, and doors. It is not about experiences of the sublime but of the liminal that expand our potentialities. Adventure is described by Simmel as "a third something," neither an external incident nor an internal system. Similarly, the experience of freedom can be understood as "a third something," which calls for an adventure in thinking. I use "neither, nor" here to approach the sliding structure of adventure, but one can also describe it as "and, and" or "yet, and still" or "against all odds."

Albert Camus, a writer of working-class origins, French Resistance fighter, and one of the practitioners of existentialism, echoed Simmel's conception of adventure in his discussion of modern and ancient adventurers and rebels forging the idea of radical moderation. In *The Rebel*, Camus explores modern rebellion ranging from regicide and terror to resistance and artistic creativity. According to Camus, the ultimate adventure aims beyond the passionate romantic thirst for liberation toward the creative experience of freedom that might come with radical moderation. Moderation, in his unorthodox definition, is "a perpetual conflict, continually created and mastered by the intelligence," while "intelligence is our faculty not to develop what we think to the very end, so that we can still *believe* in reality."[9] "Intelligence" in this sense means something closer to "wisdom," a torturous but honest road between imagination and lived experience, between contemplation and action, that pushes the limits but does not destroy the space of the common trust or what Arendt called "the care for the world."

Many political thinkers have thought that defining freedom is as "hopeless" as trying to square a circle by simply inscribing one inside the other, yet forging into those asymptotic spaces of the adventurous and incalculable is a fundamental enterprise for the human condition.[10] It seems better to locate the experience of freedom in such asymptotic spaces than to square the circle once and for all. Recognition of such hopelessness is a sine qua non for my thinking about freedom. It is always a form of thinking out of or from within an impasse—an aporia, that is—turning obstacle into adventure in the broad sense of the word.

The adventure of freedom in this understanding is about reframing but not breaking and removing all frames. The word "frame" itself has had an adventurous past. "Frame" originates in "from," which suggests that it is made of the same timber as the object that it surrounds or that the two become codependent. Originally, "from" also had a meaning of "forward," "ahead," and "advance." I don't know how and why it evolved into the unfortunate direction of nostalgic introspection. Freedom frames can be unstable and unforeseen.

Eccentric Modernities and Third-Way Thinking

Defying the occasional mood of hopelessness, I view the contemporary moment in history as particularly timely for rethinking freedom from a broader interdisciplinary and cross-cultural perspective, recovering its forgotten heritage. We live with destruction, wars, and injustices, just like at the beginning of the twentieth century. Wars take place in Europe, Asia, the Middle East, the Americas—and unfortunately, not on the Internet. Yet in my view, the contemporary moment is not characterized by a pure "clash of cultures" but rather by a clash of cultures of modernization. It can be described as a conflict of asynchronic modernities, of various projects of globalizations or globalizations that are often at odds with one another. I distinguish between *modernization*, which usually refers to industrialization and technological progress as a state policy and social practice, and *modernity* (the word coined by poet Charles Baudelaire in the 1850s), which is a critical reflection on the new forms of perception and experience and which often results in a critique of modernization and an unequivocal embrace of a single narrative of progress without turning antimodern, postmodern, or postcritical. This modernity is contradictory and ambivalent; it can combine fascination for the present with longing for another time, a critical mixture of nostalgia and utopia. Most important, reflection on modernity makes us critical subjects rather than mere objects of modernization and includes the dimension of freedom as well as the recognition of its boundaries.

This is why I want to get away from the endless "ends" of art and history and the prepositions post-, neo-, avant-, and trans- of the charismatic postcriticism that tries desperately to be "in." There is another option: not to be out, but off—as in off-stage, off-key, off-beat, and occasionally, off-color. Off-modern does not suggest a continuous history from antiquity to modernity to postmodernity, and so on. Instead, it confronts the radical breaks in tradition, the gaps of forgetting, losses of common yardsticks, and disorientations that occur in almost every generation. Off-modern reflection does not try to cure longing with belonging and a refabrication of traditional yardsticks. Rather, it produces off-spring of thought out of those gaps and crossroads, opening up a third way of intellectual history

Figure 2. Victor Shklovsky, diagram of the knight's move, from the cover of *Khod konia* (Berlin: Gelikon, 1923).

of modernity. It involves exploration of the side alleys and lateral potentialities of the project of critical modernity. In other words, it opens into the "modernity of what if" rather than simply modernization as it is. Victor Shklovsky proposes the figure of the knight's move that follows "the tortured road of the brave," preferring it to the official teleology of the revolution or the master-slave dialectics of dutiful pawns and kings (fig. 2). The politics and aesthetics of the lateral moves that combine estrangement from the world with the estrangement for the world will be examined in chapter 5, opening into another political history of modernism that is barely known.

An off-modern approach works both temporarily and spatially. It allow us to think about alternative genealogies and histories of modernity and at the same time invites us to look at the different shapes and forms of the modern experience all over the world beyond the presumed Western center, as well as the complex reactions that modernity elicits.

For many postmodern thinkers freedom was one of many simulacras, but for the off-modern, freedom is an existential imperative. The "off" in off-modern designates both the belonging (albeit) eccentric to the critical project of modernity as well as its excess, the second emphatic "f." In some way off-modern reflection returns to the unfinished business of critical modernity. It exemplifies both the edginess and the urgency of the reflection on freedom and offers an antidote to antimodern ideologies of all kinds.[11]

In order to rescue the experience of freedom from historical oblivion, one has to "brush history against the grain," to use Walter Benjamin's expression. Sometimes, the more monuments to the freedom-fighters there are the more forgotten is the individual experience. Some of those monuments are a part of *ars oblivionalis*, the art of enforced amnesia that creates false synonyms to conquer the space of memory. At first glance, freedom seems to be the opposite of memory; it is prospective rather than retrospective and travels along the unpredictable forks in the paths of the future. Unlike burdened memory-mongers with their overweight carry-on luggage, lovers of freedom travel light and enjoy the occasional shock of the new. But this is only at first glance; a more thorough examination reveals that the two share common frameworks and a common ground of possibility. What is this common ground, and how may one expand its limits and horizons?

Contemporary economist and philosopher Amartya Sen proposes in *Development as Freedom* a distinction between economic development and the expansion of freedom, which might overlap but never entirely coincide. This echoes the distinction between modernization and reflective modernity. In Sen's view, larger concerns for human well-being might slow the flow of capital but ultimately what matters is the expansion of freedom, not a free global expansion of capital or economic development for its own sake.[12] In other words, freedom is not a byproduct of economic development but an alternative form of human development in its own right, which should be the end in itself.

To understand the idea of development *as* freedom and the expansion of freedom that pushes but does not abolish boundaries and distinctions, I question the divisions of labor that exist between different areas of study. In contemporary debates, freedom has been chopped into pieces, compartmentalized, and packaged in different domains that sometimes do not communicate with one another: economic, political, legal, existential, and artistic. An understanding of freedom as adventure that tests the limits and as a cocreation in the public world trespasses such divisions of labor and forces us to think differently about the progress of freedom and to explore the reservoirs of our cultural memory and imagination to recover a broader understanding of the political. An occasional nostalgia for past dreams of freedom might offer a creative way of addressing the current situation and a way around an impasse in the future.

It is striking that the early twenty-first century has so far not produced anything comparable to the early twentieth-century flourishes of artistic innovation that often anticipated and paralleled innovations in science. Yet the study of freedom is to a large degree a humanistic endeavor that requires an alternative artistic logic of understanding. It challenges all-encompassing systems of thoughts and a superhuman understanding of freedom as manifest destiny, an invisible hand of the market, the laws of history, cunning of nature, or cunning of reason. The experience of freedom is about the encounter with uncertainty that exceeds the "calculated risk" of the latest mathematical formulae and therefore cannot be safely repackaged into the future "derivative product" together with our toxic historical debt—to use the metaphors of contemporary financial crisis.

The idea of cocreation requires rethinking the role of human agency and the architecture of the public stage. Thinking and acting creatively in this case does not mean thinking in the state of sovereignty. The concept of freedom as cocreation defies the idea of sovereignty—both communal and individual—suggesting instead complex interactions between the individual and the world. At the same time, the "co-" of cocreation should not be seen in opposition to individual creativity, responsibility, or independence. The experience of freedom is not managed by some committee on freedom; it probes the limit of minoritarian democracy rather than satisfying "the tyranny of the majority" and tests the trust in the common world and a possibility of a new ethics—an ethics of worldliness.

The Public World and the Architecture of Freedom

Hannah Arendt offers a cautionary tale of the appearance and disappearance of the public world: "To live together in the world means essentially that a world of things is between those who have it in common, as the table is located between those who sit around it, the world like every in-between relates and separates men at the same time. What makes mass society so difficult to bear is not the number of people involved, or at least not primarily, but the fact that the world between them has lost is power to gather them together, to relate and to separate them. The weirdness of this situation resembles a spiritualistic séance where a number of people gathered around a table might suddenly, through some magic trick, see the table vanish from their midst, so that two persons sitting opposite each other were no longer separated but also would be entirely unrelated to each other by anything tangible."[13]

The "world" here appears uncanny, like a flickering ghost in a gothic tale. Yet it is also the measure and framework of human interaction, an everyday ground of common ethics and trust, obvious as the old dining table and not always visible due to its obviousness. In present-day terms, the "world" is rarely used without qualifiers: third world, second world, first world, old world, new world. To describe "the world" we have to come up with something like a *retronym*—a word introduced because an existing term has become inadequate, like "snail mail" in the era of e-mail. Has public worldliness become an endangered subject in contemporary thought? "Worldliness" refers neither to biological life nor to economic globalization; it is the realm of human artifice where the plurality of humanity manifests itself in its distinctiveness and multidimensionality, not merely in its agonistic otherness. Usually associated with the public sphere, which "gathers us together but prevents us from falling over each other,"[14] worldliness can be regarded more broadly as a realm of action and storytelling that speaks of fragility and finitude but also grants an extensive duration to the world beyond individual life-span or even the life-span of several generations. What is at stake here might not be the "immortality of the soul" or the mark of eternal life, but the survival of the manmade world. At its best, architecture and art can offer a "premonition of immortality," a "non-mortal home to mortal beings." Contrary to the poetic dictum that philosophy is about homecoming, there could be a different way of inhabiting the world and making a second home, not the home into which we were born but a home that we freely choose for ourselves, a home that contains a palimpsest of world culture.

Worldliness is often discussed together with architecture, material and metaphorical. Architecture inhabits philosophy just as much as philosophy inhabits architecture. Plato's *Republic* contains a mutual codependence between architectural and philosophical thinking. But Plato's protocinematic cave, where humans caught in the "world of appearances" watch the shadows of their existence on the screen, offers us a subterranean and unworldly metaphor for human existence. And this is not the only architectural possibility. Architecture is, after all, a form of *poesis*—a creative making of world culture that does not merely reify hierarchies but commemorates human labor and artifice and exceeds its immediate utilitarian function.[15] It is not by chance that myths of language and architecture overlap: the Greek labyrinth, the Biblical Tower of Babel, the Native American "world house" whose mistress is the playful serpent dancing with sympathetic humans. Most of these projects were unfinished works in progress, not unlike the avant-garde *Monument to the Third International* or the *Monument to the Liberation of Humanity*. The architecture of freedom is a kind of transitional architecture traversed by storytelling that opens up spaces of desire and possibility.

The architecture of freedom frequently presents a combination of ruins and construction sites that reveals the fragility of manmade worlds. Architecture is not architectonics; it does not give to the world a system or a superstructure but rather a texture of concepts and common *yardsticks*.[16] To understand the forms of local cosmopolitanism and grassroots politics that provide insight into larger political structures in any country, it is most useful to examine the disputes around urban sites, monuments, and architecture, which can take the form of deliberation, oppositional demonstration, or orchestrated violent protest. Recent examples might include debates over the ground zero site in New York City, the discussions about public spaces and "the commons" threatened by corporate privatization in other American cities, mafia wars over real estate in the center of Moscow, or fights around squatters and "free states" like Christiania in Copenhagen or new "model" favelas and reorganized shantytowns in Latin America. Or, to think closer to home, during the financial crisis of 2008–2009 formerly middle-class Americans squatted in their own "foreclosed" suburban homes, expropriating like imposters the simulacra of their American dream. Debates around architecture provide a form of civic education based on care for the built environment, public memory, and forms of social justice.

"Worldliness" is not synonymous with "globalization." The word "globalization," first registered in 1959 at the beginning of space exploration, operates with an aerial picture of the Earth from outer space, or in contemporary terms, with a Google map view of the global flows of capital and populations. Worldliness suggests a different form of engagement with the world based not on virtual distance but on the interconnectedness and messiness of the human condition. Rethinking the concept of worldliness pushes us beyond the opposition between nature and culture, culture and civilization, or global and local; it is about thinking this-worldliness over other-worldliness. Fortunately, paradise has already been lost, so we have to start loving our less-than-paradisiacal world and accept the freedom of exile. The experience of freedom requires a renaming and remapping of *this* world and a challenge both to the metaphysics and to the notion of globalization.

The discovery of this-worldliness in the history of political thought is directly connected to a new appreciation of public freedom. It stemmed from a double perspective of slaves turned citizens in the Athenian city-state and was later developed by religious heretics, dissenters, and immigrants. Sociologist Orlando Patterson connected the positive conception of freedom to the particular circumstances in the Greek city-states. He observed that in most ancient and modern civilizations the native word synonymous with freedom does not necessarily carry a positive meaning. In ancient Egyptian the word for freedom signified "orphanhood."[17] Similarly in contemporary Chinese and Japanese, the native word for freedom was originally negative, suggesting privation or nonbelonging. This, of course, doesn't mean that there are other contemporary terms that reflect a more hybrid thinking. What was specific to the ancient Greek city-states was the fact that slavery was not necessarily a permanent condition; nor were captives murdered or sacrificed, as was the practice in many other ancient civilizations. Instead, in Athens slaves could be emancipated into citizens. Hence the negative term (*a-douleia*, simple noncoercion) developed into *eleutheria* (freedom). Of course, the first step after enfranchisement is a liberation from want and the satisfaction of basic human needs: shelter, food, minimal protection from violence, and liberation from immediate coercion. Freedom is the next step, but the relationship between freedom and liberation is never quite linear. My hypothesis (explored in chap. 1) is that the space of freedom was colonized from the space of the sacred and centered on the redefinition of sacrifice both in politics and in theater. The Athenian polis was supported by democratic practices and theatrical performances of tragedy and comedy. Tragedy educated democracy not only by providing the cathartic experience of a violent spectacle but also by showing the dangers of mythical violence through the twists of theatrical plots. At the center of Athenian tragedy is the issue of "corrupted sacrifice," which from its beginning as a sacred ritual becomes a deliberated act, opening into a space of negotiation and reflection in worldly theater.[18] Questioning violence and transforming the practice of human sacrifice into a space of deliberation would also be important in the later struggles for freedom of religion and freedom of consciousness that are fundamental for the early modern understanding of the idea.

The primal scene of the Greek *eleutheria* is public, not private; its setting is the public square (*agora*), not the inner citadel of the human psyche. *Eleutheria* was a combination of play and duty, an obligation and a potential for creative civic action. Ancient cultures did not have our contemporary understanding of the notion of individual freedom. Considerably later, the Greek Stoic philosopher Epictetus (c. 55–c. 135 CE), himself a freed slave who experienced many misfortunes in his life including physical handicap and exile, developed the doctrine of inner freedom as the individual's only refuge, an "inner polis" and an "acropolis of the soul." Uncannily, inner freedom mirrored the public architecture of the lost polis of the Greek city-state in the age of the Roman Empire.

If we look for the origins of the word "freedom" in several Indo-European languages, using etymologies broadly and poetically, we find some surprising results. The Greek word *eleutheria* and the Roman *libertas* have a common linguistic base in *leudhe/leudhi*, signifying "public" or common space.[19] The Latin word for play, *ludere*, linked to illusion and collision, also goes back to this common base, as do *libidia*, love, and possibly Greek *elpis*, hope. The English word "freedom" is also connected to joy and friendship. Even the most explicitly antiarchitectural contemporary rhetoric of the "*removal* of barriers," off-shoring, and superhuman flow of capital also point back to a certain shared design and topography. "Trade" comes from *treadth*, a path, and "market" refers to a building where negotiations took place. Law, too, especially in the Greek conception of *nomos*—the boundary—was connected to a certain topography of cultural memory and was frequently used in the plural.[20]

Many historians have noted that the ancient Greek polis offered a limited space of self-realization that was available only to male citizens, but the polis gave shape to an aspiration, an ideal of freedom that spread beyond its walls. An understanding of spiritual freedom delineated by Epictetus reveals cross-cultural connections between East and West, between Indian, Persian, Hellenic, and Hebrew cultures. What is originally Greek is the concept of political freedom. Yet from the Middle Ages to the Enlightenment, debates on freedom, both spiritual and political, and on the preservation of the Greek philosophical heritage, became a cross-cultural affair. Among the first early medieval interpreters of Aristotle were Persian Muslim scientist, physician, philosopher, poet, and statesman Abu Ibn Sina (Avicenna [980–1037]) and the Spanish Egyptian Jewish philosopher, physician, and rabbi Moshe ben Maimon (Mussa bin Maimun or Moses Maimonides [1135–1204]; the enumeration of adjectives and occupations is in itself amazing). In modern times, one might recall the passionate philosophical dialogue between Moses Mendelssohn and Immanuel Kant on the nature of progress and freedom of conscience beyond the Christian conception of universalism, and in the twentieth century the deliberation of civil disobedience and dissent from Gandhi to the American civil rights movement and East European, East Asian, Latin American dissidents. There is no exclusive cultural patrimony of freedom; the concepts circulate and interact. The history of freedom is what Anthony Kwame Appiah calls "the case for contamination." Worldliness is not the same as cosmopolis, but the two notions overlap.[21] There are many vernacular cosmopolitans coming from different localities (with memories of inequality, but not entirely defined by a colonial or postcommunist or any other particular history) but sharing the preoccupation with worldly architecture.[22] Freedom is never about purity—ethnic or otherwise—but about contacts, contaminations, and border crossings. And so is what I would call "fascinating unfreedom," which takes different shapes but shares an eros of power and paranoic antimodern or post-postmodern ideology.

Agnostic Space: Freedom versus Liberation

To investigate the relationship between self and other and to explore the otherness inherent in the experience of freedom itself, I propose a distinction between *agonistic* and *agnostic* understandings of the public realm. This distinction once again highlights the connection between valorization of political freedom in ancient Greece and the emergence of tragic theater. The relationship between agonistic and agnostic is not in itself antagonistic but suggests a shift in the frame of reference and epistemological orientation. In ancient Greece, *agon* referred to action in an athletic contest, in politics, and in theatrical performances with its masked "protagonists." But the poetics of drama was based not only on *agon* but also on *mimesis* (imitation/performance), which, among other things, dramatized the encounter with luck, fate, uncertainty, and the everyday mysteries of the human condition (chap. 1). An agnostic understanding of the public realm puts more emphasis on the tragic and the comic aspects of human life that are not reducible to competitions, struggles, and contests that open into the space of the improbable and new. One can either dedicate the whole book to the distinction between agonistic and agnostic conceptions of the space of freedom or leave it to one extensive footnote and future deliberation.[23]

Agnostics (in my unconventional understanding of the term) do not think of political action as merely strategic or instrumental, but also as a form of public performance and encounter with the unpredictable beyond the political theology of the moment. If there is an *agon* among agnostics, it manifests itself as passionate opposition to antiworldliness or as charismatic advocacy for ultimate emancipation from worldly concerns (from Saint Paul to Saint Lenin). Possibly the only way to discover or rescue alternative frameworks of freedom for the twenty-first century is through thinking freedom neither as the means for an end nor as an end that justifies the means but simultaneously as means and ends, or as something that defies the mean-and-ends rationale altogether.

Poet and thinker Friedrich Schiller proposed a similar understanding of freedom in his work *On the Aesthetic Education of Man*, written two hundred years ago in the wake of the French Revolution. In response to revolutionary terror and postrevolutionary political disillusionments, Schiller argues that the political, aesthetic, and life realms are best mediated through the practice of play, which should be a foundation of a citizen's education. Only through serious play can one experience freedom both as a means and as an end of human existence because freedom is not merely an abstract goal but also an educational experience in shared humanity. Recognition of worldly play allows us to negotiate between chaos and cosmos, radical uncertainty and hopeful action, and also to acknowledge the multiple roles of others instead of typecasting them as friends or foes.[24] Aesthetic education is accomplished not merely through making art and teaching moral values but also through a variety of creative practices in the world. The word "aesthetics," like the word "politics," has been much maligned and too frequently used as an insult. I understand aesthetics in the original sense of the word, neither as an analysis of autonomous works of art nor as a connoisseurship of the beautiful but as a form of knowledge that proceeds through a particular interplay of sense, imagination, and reason and "the distribution of the sensible," to quote Jacques Rancière.[25] I will distinguish between aesthetic practice of the "total work," which strives to aestheticize politics and affirm total authorial control and aesthetics of estrangement, which is open to experiences of freedom, wonder, and renewal in art and politics (chap. 5).

It is not by chance that the moment of valorization of public freedom in the political realm coincided with the birth of theater in Western culture (chap. 1). As a parallel with the distinction between the agonistic and the agnostic, I will examine the culture of liberation and the culture of freedom, what in Greek tragedy began with the distinction between *mania* (madness, inspiration) and *technê* (skills, arts). Liberation (which might be a necessary first step in many struggles for independence) strives for dissolution of boundaries. Liberation can be of short duration but involve broad expansion and destruction. Freedom, on the other hand, requires a longer expanse of time but less expansion in physical space; it builds a creative architecture of political institutions and social practices that opens up virtual spaces of consciousness. Liberation is often engaged in a master-slave power struggle while freedom has many heterotopic logics. Liberation is antiarchitectural and at the end can become antipolitical as well, while the experience of freedom requires an unusual architecture of public memory but also spaces where desire can reside. The experiences of liberation and freedom also carry very distinctive moods, if we understand moods not as the transient ups and downs that color our daily life but instead as more fundamental experiences of modern temporality and of our interaction with the surrounding world (chap. 4). The mood of liberation might begin with anger, a thirst for justice and enthusiasm. The constant drive of liberation, however, might result in a form of paranoia and resentment and a need for an agonistic enemy in ever changing masks. The mood of freedom is what follows the enthusiasm of liberation. It starts with anxiety, which is then counteracted by a certain self-estrangement and curiosity, an openness to play but also care for the world. It may occasionally crash in despair but never stops at hopelessness.

Scenography of Freedom: Political Optics and Phantasmagoria

The architecture of freedom has a particular scenography. Neither brightly lit nor completely enlightened, it is a scenography of luminosity, of the interplay of light and shadow. Walter Benjamin, with his inimitable oblique lucidity, wrote about the importance of short shadows. They are "no more than the sharp black edges at the feet of things, preparing to retreat silently, unnoticed, into their burrow, their secret being."[26] Short shadows speak of thresholds, warn us against being overly short-sighted or long-winged. When we get too close to things, disrespecting their short shadows, we risk obliterating them, but if we make the shadows too long we start to enjoy them for their own sake.

Short shadows urge us to check the balance of nearness and distance, to trust neither those who speak of the essences of things nor those who preach conspiratorial simulation. Søren Kierkegaard spoke of "shadowgraphy" as a form of Platonic writing in this world. My shadowgraphy of freedom includes spaces of luminosity commemorating the fragile world of appearances. Writing about Walter Benjamin's life and art and that of other "men and women in the dark times," Arendt observed that in the circumstances of extremity, the illuminations come not from philosophical concepts but from the "uncertain, flickering and often weak light" that men and women kindle and shed over the lifespan given to them. This luminous space is the space of "humanitas," where "men and women come out of their origins and reflect each other's sparks"; by doing so they embrace social theatricality, not introspective sincerity.[27] The darkness of the human heart is not to be fully revealed in public; freedom is not about inquisitorial denunciation or smug claims of authenticity.

The demand of transparency defines political scenography in the contemporary media. But how transparent or realistic is such a demand? In the totalitarian regimes of the twentieth century, the private lives of individuals were supposed to be fully transparent for the authorities (at least in theory) while political life (bright colors of the parades and movies notwithstanding) was, in fact, completely obfuscated. In democratic societies, one would think that we can demand transparency from our political leaders and financial institutions, in which case transparency stands for accountability. At the same time, individuals' private lives must be protected from the demands of transparency, which in this case become synonymous with surveillance. In other words, what distinguishes democratic societies from authoritarian regimes, at least in theory, is the protection of nontransparency and privacy as personal rights, the public demand for political transparency and accountability, and the complex architecture that distinguishes one from the other. Today this story is complicated by both new technologies and media. The popular media's insistence on the public's right to know about politicians' private lives encourages mass voyeurism instead of democratic reflection, reselling the desire for transparency at a high price. At the same time, ordinary citizens' privacy is being invaded from every digital orifice, often under less-than-transparent guise. Thus, the moralism of complete transparency and authenticity can obscure the distinctions between public and private and distract attention from economic and public issues while indulging in the private indiscretions of politicians that appear to be more "media-friendly."

Even in modern architecture the uses of transparency are ambivalent: they hark back to the modern dreams of a technological progress that would transform architecture into a form of social engineering and the edifice of the new utopian collectivity. But we know that the architecture of transparency was used for both utopian communes and corporate structures, for both utilitarian and decorative reasons, for openness and for surveillance. In the end it appears that an understanding of transparency requires a complicated cultural optics. Transparent surfaces have become reflective and refracting mirrors and screens of our history and our technology, exposing the cracks and the patina of the medium itself.

The space of luminosity does not offer complete transparency or absolute clarity but might provide occasional lucidity. It helps to avoid the

most stark delusions and to nurture a flickering hope in the preservation of the common world. Reflective chiaroscuro can be more reliable
than blinding illumination in providing broad perspectivism and worldly
insight.

Political philosophy—from Plato's cave to Thomas Hobbes's ana-
morphs, from Denis Diderot's theater of paradox to Marx's phantasmagoria of revolution—engaged with optical and theatrical metaphors that
were integral to its arguments about freedom. To take one striking example, one could juxtapose Hobbes's *Leviathan* (1651) and Diderot's "Paradox of an Actor" (1770), since both share the Renaissance conception of
the world as a theater in which all people are actors. Hobbes writes at
the time of the English revolution of 1649 while Diderot foreshadows the
events of the French Revolution and the Terror; both connect political
and artistic judgment to theatrical spectatorship and to the recognition of
artifice it entails.

Hobbes's *Leviathan*, the treatise on the "matter, form and power of
commonwealth," opens with a famous reflection on the "art of man"—
man's ability to imitate nature and create artificial monsters of Biblical
proportions: "For by art is created that great Leviathan called a Commonwealth or State which is but an artificial man, though of greater stature
and strength than the natural, for whose protection and defense it was
intended, and in which the sovereignty is artificial soul."[28]

Such a baroque image represents a curious double figure of the body
of the sovereign, made of his people (fig. 3). It/he is at once an artificial
animal and the people who created him and obey him. Moreover, in the
emblem the men greeting the sovereign happen to be wearing hats, less
a sign of prostration before the divine monarch than a behavior of spectators, suggesting a peculiar form of political theatricality. The figure of
the Leviathan or the state is not a political symbol but an ambiguous emblem, technically, a "catoptic anamorph" that actively engages the spectators and plays on their double vision. Hobbes was very interested in the
theories of illusion making and perspective through "interactive optics"
that revealed how a spectator can alter the event.[29] Catoptic optics—a precursor to the modernist revolution in vision—went beyond the study of
three-dimensional perspective that can be politically manipulated by forc-
ing the viewer to project empathetically and identify with a packaged illusion. By contrast, catoptic double play celebrated a theatrical artifice and
creative perspectivism that combined invention and judgment.[30]

In other words, Hobbes represents not merely a theocracy based
on fear, but also a *theatocracy* with an active spectator who consents to

Non est potestas Super Terram quæ Comparetur ei Iob. 41. 24

LEVIATHAN

Figure 3. Leviathan, engraving by Abraham Bosse, frontispiece of Thomas Hobbes, *Leviathan*, 1651.

delegate some of his powers to the sovereign as part of a political pact, not as a divine entitlement. The emblem desanctifies the sovereign and at the same time endows it with contractual obligations. This is an example of an early modern theatrical body politics.[31]

Hobbes offers a special optics for looking at Diderot's "Paradox of an Actor" as a form of political art. It also connects the Renaissance and baroque to a certain strain of Enlightenment thought through the conception of play and the perception of the world as a theater. Diderot was working on "The Paradox of an Actor" while literally crossing the borders of Europe—on his way to see Catherine the Great, the "enlightened despot" of the Russian Empire. The text survived in the library of the Hermitage and was not made public for fifty years after it was completed, decidedly failing to enlighten the Russian court.

Unlike Hobbes, Diderot does not offer a treatise but a dialogue between the "men of paradox" using the Socratic method. The paradox is that a "natural actor," "a man or a woman of sensibility" who suffers on stage, gives a performance that is inferior to an "imitative actor" who recreates the scene from past observations. The best actor doesn't weep on stage but makes us weep, for the illusion is ultimately ours, not his. Diderot explains: "I want him [a great actor] to have a lot of judgment, for me there needs to be a cool, calm spectator inside this man, so I demand sagacity and no feeling, the power to imitate anything," says the "man of paradox."[32] This kind of actor who identifies with the "phantom," the spirit of theater itself, rather than of a particular character, is not unlike the Hobbesian anamorph, a figure of double vision, a performer and spectator at once, except that his doubleness is not only spatial or visual but also temporal. The great actor combines memory and imagination, observed moments of sublimity in the past with performance in the present.

Judging contemporary theater, Diderot advocates for tragedy and not for a "moving story" or tearful comedy. The best theater redefines the boundaries of the stage through movement and action; it transports us back and forth, beyond and inside, but it never obliterates the stage. Sense and sensibility are developed through e-motions that involve movements and peripeteias. From the perspective of the twentieth century, Diderot is arguably closer to the physical and intellectual theater of Vsevolod Meyerhold and Bertolt Brecht (minus the didacticism) than to Antonin Artaud. The answer to hypocrisy and injustice is not in emotion and sensibility but in the paradoxical politics of engagement and estrangement embodied in the actor's identification with the "phantom" and a certain existential irony.

In this respect Diderot's vision of the theater and more broadly of freedom is the opposite of Jean-Jacques Rousseau's, and their dialogue is at the core of debates for centuries to come. Rousseau and many generations of cross-cultural Rousseauists from all over the world share an antitheatrical prejudice and view the theater as the evil of insincerity and unfreedom. Is it possible that, being an insightful if somewhat resentful observer, Rousseau might have suspected that he was only a "natural actor" and not a natural man and thus wanted to ban theater so that nobody might judge his poor performance?

For Diderot, the advocacy of extreme sincerity on the social or political stage is in itself insincere and hypocritical if not downright manipulative and dangerous. Sincerity and empathy alone do not account for the exercise of free judgment that arises from mediation between experience and reflection, emotion and cognition.

Yet in the true spirit of paradox, Diderot doesn't offer an agonistic battle between the natural and the imitative actor. The experience of freedom comes when the actor surprises himself. Sometimes the imitative actor stops acting and forgets himself and is "overcome with sensibility," open to natural wonder and amazement. And the "natural man" begins to praise nature for being picturesque and for looking like a beautiful landscape, as if imitating art. So in the moment of freedom each actor exceeds himself, discovers the other within, and confronts his or her paradoxical inner plurality.[33]

But the real paradox involves transferring theater into life—not only through identification with feeling but also through estrangement and free play.[34] The paradoxicalist becomes a model personality for Diderot's version of playful Enlightenment unconstrained by scientific reason; he is an adventurist in a Simmelian sense, a wanderer, a peripatetic conversationalist who enjoys the shadow play and luminosity of existence. The paradox of an actor becomes the paradox of a good citizen, not necessarily a revolutionary, but always a player on the world stage who embraces the phantom of world theater.

In the nineteenth and twentieth centuries the discussion of modern freedom is accompanied by the theater of phantasmagoria, which offers another kind of scenography, with specters of communism haunting Europe (and beyond) challenged by the ghosts of history. Marx, Baudelaire, and Dostoevsky pondered the phantasmagorias of modern urban life and their use in poetry, revolution, and terrorist movements of the nineteenth century (chap. 3). Arendt too described the memory of public freedom and public happiness in the twentieth century as a *"fata morgana"* and the return of worldliness as an uncanny postphantasmagoric realization.

The word "phantasmagoria" was invented for the theater of optical illusions, which were produced chiefly by means of the magic lantern or similar devices. One of the pioneers of phantasmagoria, Etienne-Gaspar Robertson, opened his spectacle in the Capuchine cloister in Paris in 1799 to a French audience haunted by the Revolution and Terror. Revolutionaries Jean-Paul Marat, Georges Danton, and Maximilien Robespierre as well as King Louis appeared as specters and skeletons in the phantasmagoric shows. In the words of Tom Gunning, "Phantasmagoria literally took place on the threshold between science and superstition, between Enlightenment and Terror."[35] It was also a combination of mystification and demystification, of new technology and historical violence, of haunting images and scientific explanations. While watching phantasmagoric presentations, the viewers could focus on the uncanny and mysterious haunting of the past, and their scientific elucidation, or on the ambivalence and play of such juxtapositions. Throughout the nineteenth century phantasmagorias haunted artists and political thinkers, offering many different optics and plots for dealing with the new experiences of modernization—from gothic romance to modernist allegory. Karl Marx uses phantasmagoria to describe the farce of the revolutions of the "Eighteen Brumaire" and the policies of Louis-Bonaparte (chap. 3). Marx's phantasmagoria evokes a gothic novel or a mystery play of the "world-historical conjuring of the ghosts of the dead."[36] The figure for phantasmagoria in Marx is the urban crowd, which for him is a great dissimulator. The crowd is a space where classes mix and where spontaneous and unpredictable associations beyond class struggle can emerge. Phantasmagoria in Marx is used negatively as a model of distorted perception, the "smoke and mirrors" behind which one can find the real and the undistorted. Theatrical metaphors are used similarly in a sarcastic fashion. The opposition is between the theatricalization of history and phantasmagoric optics and the higher vision of historic reality into which Marx had special insight. Marx, like Dostoevsky, disliked the everyday theater of modern life and was ready to sacrifice it for the future liberation of mankind. If many political thinkers and writers from Diderot on often used the metaphor of theater in speaking of revolution, Marx spoke of "the birth pangs" of the revolution as if revolution was a labor of nature or historic necessity. But phantasmagoria plays unforeseen tricks with Marx's dialectics and continues to haunt it. In the "Eighteenth Brumaire" as well as in "The Manifesto of the Communist Party," the ghost of the past is opposed not by living beings or existing social entities but by the "specter of communism" and the "spirit" of the revolution. The uncanniness of this resides in the fact that sometimes it is difficult to distinguish good ghosts from bad ghosts, the ghosts that should be with us and the ghosts that are against us.

Similarly in Feodor Dostoevsky's novel *The Possessed* (chap. 3), the phantasmagoria of Russian life created by terrorist conspirators must be eliminated, and yet it is shown as seductive and powerful. Dostoevsky, too, is fascinated by the gothic novel and the melodrama. While exorcizing some of the demons of terror and revealing the banality of actual terrorists, the novelist occasionally demonizes the experience of modern public life, demanding freer freedom and truer truth instead of the masquerade of modern appearances. Dostoevsky understands the power of charismatic seduction, which can never reveal its modus operandi and explain the inner working of its phantasmagoric fascination.

For the poet Charles Baudelaire, who coined the term "modernity" in his essay "The Painter of Modern Life," phanstasmagoria is no longer a bad word. It is constitutive of the experience of modern urban life, which cannot be merely unveiled and abolished. The poor, the injured, the war veterans, and the prostitutes are all present in the Baudelairian urban crowd, which is no longer cast as some gothic tale. The experience of urban phantasmagoria demands new plots, prose poems, and experimental essays that are open to chance encounters with unpredictable outcomes. Baudelaire's antiheroic modern wanderer is himself a phantasmagoria addict. Phantasmagoria contributes to the atmosphere of human liberty and cannot be completely destroyed for the sake of future liberation. The debates on theatricality and phantasmagoria are echoed a century later in Theodor Adorno's correspondence with Walter Benjamin, in which he accuses Benjamin of becoming a phantasmagoric writer. Phantasmagoria for Adorno is once again the enemy of the revolutionary spirit: "A profound and thorough liquidation of phantasmagoria can succeed only if it is conceived as an objective category of the philosophy of history."[37] For Benjamin, phantasmagoria is an integral part of the dialectical image through which the past manifests itself in the present. Adorno's protestation notwithstanding, he refuses to disavow his phantasmagoric modern wanderer, the flâneur, who acts out the paradox of the actor on the city streets. Phantasmagoric ambivalence is a way of cohabiting or even cocreating with the ghosts of the past and the technologies of the present without the predictable agonistic plots of horror and romance. Phantasmagoric ambivalence is not a subjective fancy but a part of the phenomenology of modern experience that cannot be exorcised entirely—neither in the name of the objective laws of history nor in the name of the truer religion of the people (as in Dostoevsky). If approached critically and creatively, phantasmagoria ceases to be an obstacle for the everyday arts of freedom and instead becomes its manifestation; it opens up nonlinear potentialities of action and imagination by allowing us to recognize rather than exorcize our inner strangers.

Passionate Thinking, Judging, and Imagination

What, then, is the shape of free thinking, and how can we develop an eccentric methodology of "freedom studies"?

Many writers explored in this book were rigorous thinkers who participated in several systems of thought but chose not to belong to a single one. They were experimental essayists in the Socratic tradition of dialogue and peripatetic deliberation that questioned closed systems of thought, the exclusivity of analytical logic, and the scientific method. "Essay" meant at once a trial and an experiment. More than a genre, it was a mode of thinking and acting, an attitude towards truth. The essay is a reflection not merely of a style of thinking but also of thought's substance; the quest for freedom here is not a theme, not a form of writerly experience. In other words, Schiller's notion of play is a way of exploring freedom by way of freedom, for freedom must not be a betrayal of the imagination.

At a certain point in their lives, almost every "freedom thinker" went through a crisis of judging, a mind change or paradigm shift. A change of mind or change of heart was not considered by them to be a sign of weakness but a necessary right of passage for a free thinker. In the cases of Dostoevsky and Kierkegaard, this crisis of conscience resulted in a religious conversion or a "leap of faith," while for Tocqueville it provoked a turn away from institutional religion and toward a contradictory embrace of the "new political science" and critical and spiritual reflection for the sake of "educating democracy." Similarly, camp survivors and writers such as Primo Levi and Varlam Shalamov appealed to creative estrangement, curiosity, and imagination as a route of minimal self-liberation rather than to political or religious beliefs. So the paradigm shift involved in the exploration of freedom doesn't follow a predictable arc from atheism into religion or the other way around and can take the shape of either a conversion or an open conversation.

Arendt proposed a distinction between "nonprofessional," or passionate, thinking that searches for meaning based on reason's "concern with the unknowable," and "professional thinking," which searches for truth and is based on the intellect's concern with cognition. The origin of nonprofessional or "passionate" thinking is wonder and astonishment vis-à-vis the cosmos and the world. Professional thinking, on the other hand, has its existential root in unhappiness and "arises out of disintegration of reality and the resulting disunity of man and world, from which springs the need for another world, more harmonious and more meaningful."[38] Passionate thinking does not withdraw from "the world of appearances" into an interior invisible citadel or ivory tower. It bridges both *vita activa* and *vita contemplativa*, sometimes crisscrossing back and forth between the two.

A note of caution: the phrase "passionate thinking" could be misconstrued. It is *not* about sloppy and unrigorous thinking through suffering, passion, or identification. Rather, "passionate" here means yielding to the "nearness" of life, to everyday experience, relying upon one's curiosity and listening to worldliness. Passionate thinking is not thinking through mastery; it is fundamentally about understanding, not control. Understanding means yielding to the uncomfortable and incalculable.

Passionate thinking contains both adventure and humility, and a combination of thinking and *thanking* (life, being, existence), of reflection and
"gratitude for being": "We will remember in Lethe's cold waters / That
earth for us has been worth a thousand heavens," wrote Osip Mandelshtam
in 1918.[39] Passionate thinking has to be versatile and mobile, since it mediates between philosophical knowledge and everyday experience, between
politics and poetics.

The Russian poet Joseph Brodsky, once a prisoner and an underground
poet in the Soviet Union, later an immigrant to the United States and a
Nobel laureate, writes about his own difficulty in evolving from a "freed
man to a free man": "Perhaps our [immigrant writers'] greater value and
greater function are to be unwitting embodiments of the disheartening
idea that a freed man is not a free man, that liberation is just the means of
attaining freedom and is not synonymous with it. However, if we want
to play a bigger role, the role of a free man, then we should be capable of
accepting—or at least imitating—the manner in which a free man fails.
A free man, when he fails, blames nobody."[40] The exiled writer stops being a victim perpetually in search of scapegoats. He can no longer resort
to the culture of blame, or even of identity politics, as an ethnographic
excuse.[41]

The "freed man" becomes free when he tries to break the chain of violence and coercion, of victim becoming a victimizer or slave becoming a
master, when there is something other than revenge that drives him. A
free man or woman is someone who has an uncanny double within them
and cohabits with these foreigners within like Socrates with his talkative
daemon. They have to be able to laugh at themselves but never stop at
this moment of laughter. Conscience can be described somewhat dramatically as a neighbor or stranger who makes one feel at home or *chez soi*:
"Conscience is the anticipation of that fellow who awaits you if and when
you come home."[42] It is unclear whether the fellow daemon is your host
or your guest as long as the home visit is not too unsettling. Such a conception of conscience resembles Diderot's vision of the imitative actor and
adventurer at once. Inner plurality might force us to question the conception of the self as a fortress of sovereignty and autonomy, but such plurality is not a threat to individual integrity, quite the contrary: only a person
who can change his or her mind can be a free thinker. Inner plurality is
not the same as external pluralism; while not mutually exclusive, they are
inherently contradictory. This relationship between inner plurality (of individuals and cultures) and external pluralism (encounter with the other,
monolingual or polyglot) will be explored throughout this book.

Judging is the most urgent form of passionate thinking, which mediates between universal and particular, theory and practice; it is neither
a systematic rationalism nor groundless decisionism but a border zone
deliberation between precedent and unprecedented. The process of judging is not an applied art; one uses some existing laws and conventions
and discovers others in the process. It requires a double movement—
defamiliarizing experience through the practice of thought and defamiliarizing habits of thought in response to changing experience. The space of
reflective judgment is like a Möbius strip that moves seamlessly inside out
from the known to the unknown, from the familiar to the unpredictable,
from the reliable to the improbable. Judgment orients itself from within
and without using imagination.

The mysterious category of imagination has been crucial for the philosophical conception of freedom since the early modern era. With the help
of imagination we can conceive of what our senses do not perceive, as if
connecting the invisible within us to the invisible in the world, discovering the inner cosmos that enables us to confront the cosmos beyond
our reach.[43] Imagination bridges the gulf between visible and invisible,
or—to go beyond the metaphors of sight—also between the overheard
and silenced, the well-thought-through and the unthinkable. It devises all
kinds of "transports" through metaphors (which derives from the Greek
metaphorein, to transport), similes, anamorphoses, allegories and symbols.
Imagination entertains the hypothetical, moves through leaps, lapses, and
ellipses and engages in double vision. Only through imagination does one
have the freedom to picture otherwise, of thinking "what if" and not only
"what is." Imagination navigates the space between emotional and rational, defying any single law but often developing laws of its own. Romantic
and modernist artists believed that the capacity to imagine is the human
way of imitating the act of creation itself, not merely the created world.
Imagination is not entirely free of cultural common places but is not bound
by the borders of a single system of coordinates; it is heteronymous and
moves from one country to another without visa restrictions. Imagination
bridges not only spatial but also temporal discontinuities, connecting "no
longer" and "not yet" as well as "could have been" and "might become."
It is not by chance that Kant considered imagination to be a "schemata"
for cognition, the faculty that underlies different forms of human understanding and relations to the world. Imagination is a capacity to move
beyond individual psychology into the common world and includes a capacity for self-distancing. In this sense I have defined imagination as what
is in-human in humans, "in-" here being a polysemous prefix that refers to

the inherently human capacity of self-distancing, the recognition of inner plurality in oneself and in the other.

But still, what is the relationship between the laws of imagination and the laws of the world? Thinking imaginatively and not proposing an analogy, Arendt suggests that the measure for those disparate, individual, imaginative judgments, the *"tertium comparationis,"* is the care for shared worldliness, the *"sensus communis"* that is the foundation of cosmopolitan architecture. With this in mind, we might distinguish different tendencies in the act of imagination which are once again not antagonistic. A certain degree of self-distancing or estrangement is imperative in the act of imagining but here we can evoke different kinds of estrangement (which will be explored in chap. 5), estrangement *from* the world and estrangement *for* the world. (This is not the opposition between estrangement and belonging, or alienation and its overcoming, but between different horizons and trajectories of self-distancing.) One form of imagination might be associated with the intense experience of inner freedom and introspection and the other with a continuous double movement between the sheer energy of imagination and concern with the common world. We can provisionally call them "introspective" and "worldly" imagination. The potential danger of the introspective imagination based on estrangement from the world is that its laws might acquire a life of their own and occasionally take a form of rational delusion and develop a paranoic causality, which severs the connections between the private and public world. This might produce a dungeon imagination that walls itself against the world like Dostoevsky's Underground Man. The danger of the second kind of imagination, based on estrangement for the world, is that it would become too cautious and moderate and abandon the adventure of individual creativity.

Worldly imagination is theatrical, it works with phantoms of the world, restaging them with many overlapping shadows. It engages phantasmagorias but also, like Diderot's paradoxical actor, changes masks and angles of vision. Such imagination works through peripeteias rather than simply jump-cutting from one ecstasy to another. In this sense of the experience of freedom we are not looking at ineffable, sublime, or mystical illumination, which can produce terror and silence but for the aesthetic or creative practice that is agnostic and adventurous but not ineffable. In other words the most important characteristic of the worldly imagination is its perspectivism, an ability to change the systems of coordinates and reframe ideas, images, and grids for life.

Imagination might not be the panacea for building up the public realm, which also relies on collective solidarities, political rights, and flexible institutions. However, flights of imagination are not as unsafe as they are often made out to be; in fact, they are necessary in order to imagine the world anew, to make life worth living.

Arendt never ceased to repeat that, after the Second World War and the unimaginable scale of inhuman destruction in the twentieth century, we lost the yardsticks with which to measure our common world. The answer, however, is not in restorative nostalgia, the reinvention of national tradition, or the resacralization of the disenchanted modern world. We cannot simply restore the broken vertebrae of common communication, covering up the scars and gaps. So what is to be done? Arendt uses an architectural metaphor: she proposes to "think without a banister." What is the relationship between those two kinds of measure and support—excessively fragile yardsticks and excessively solid banisters? Could the banisters of social convention be the remainders of the lost yardsticks of tradition?

In the extreme circumstances of twentieth-century history, the banister of social common places and familiar clichés can turn into a *scandala*, an obstacle that leads to a moral scandal and foundation for the "banality of evil." One has to think through these radical breaks in the twentieth-century tradition that alter the way we measure things; otherwise one person's banisters can turn into another's barbed wire.

And yet, thinking without a banister does not mean thinking without foundations, but rather thinking without familiar props. In literal terms, banisters refer to the railing on a staircase. While occasionally skipping along a flight of stairs in a dancing gait, we have to preserve our bearings on the staircase (our home is shared, after all) and balance somehow between flying and falling. The experience of freedom occurs in this liminal space, and it is up to us to prevent the worst disasters from becoming a regular occurrence.

In light of twentieth-century history, the lost yardsticks of a living tradition cannot be replaced by comforting readymade banisters of a neoclassical style. We have to "think without a banister" in order to understand a world that can no longer be measured with familiar yardsticks. The larger-than-life collective inhumanity of twentieth-century mass movements requires a counterpoint: a creative and singular "in-humanity" of human imagination that can push the temporal and spatial limitations of the present moment.[44] Judgment and imagination negotiate the space of "between" and "beyond," collective and individual, precedent and unprecedented. Judging keeps imagination in check, imagination enlarges the possibilities of judgment, and so the process goes, back and forth. "Between" is never completely bounded by familiar yardsticks, but neither

is "beyond" synonymous with boundlessness. The "beyond" opens unforeseen horizons; but the moment these horizons are transgressed
or transcended, we lose the perspective of wonder. Freedom might be
dangerous, but it is always interesting—in the literal sense of the word,
inter-esse—suspended in between.

Shape of the Book

The book was conceived at the turn of the twenty-first century in reaction to narratives proclaiming the end of history, politics, and art and the
triumphalist celebration of technology and the free market, which did not
necessarily include concern for political freedoms.

On a more personal level, after writing *The Future of Nostalgia*, I wanted
to think of the existential space that was a space not of memory or longing
but of adventure and the unpredictable. Or perhaps, there was no way to
think about the future of nostalgia without thinking about freedom. This
was also a challenge to not reduce history to memory, and to rediscover
the heritage of freedom. I realized that while there is a large body in the
philosophical canon and political theory that deals with freedom, there
is little written on the subject in the contemporary context of arts and
humanities. As for the social sciences, they often operate on the level of
collective structures and mythologies and tend to be less concerned with
the role of individual agency, issues of judging and freedom. While exploring cultural differences, I was also interested to combine pluralism with
plurality and heed the internal dissent and diversity within a culture that is
necessary for rethinking a broader public architecture.

This book examines the moments in which political and artistic understandings of freedom are intertwined, from Greek tragedy to contemporary culture. Instead of consolidating the rigid separation between
aesthetics and politics and cultural distinctions, we will look at freedom as
a fluid "social art" that occupies a broad sphere between political, social,
and artistic practices.[45] We explore the narrative and spatial configuration
of "third way" thinking that includes architecture, theory, literature, philosophy, and other forms of eccentric and experimental theoretical storytelling that often fall in the cracks between intellectual genres, systems of
thought, and academic disciplines. The writers to be discussed here offer
unconventional and paradoxical figures for this kind of adventure in thinking: Alexis de Tocqueville's circle of the individual space in the stream of
progress, Benjamin's dialectic at a standstill, Victor Shklovsky's knight's
move, zigzag, and lateral extension, the spirals of Vladimir Nabokov and

Tatlin, Aby Warburg's *figura serpentina* in the architecture of the world house of the Native Americans from the Pueblo region and the iconology of the interval, and Arendt's diagonal of freedom that she deciphers in Franz Kafka's enigmatic parable. They contribute not to system building but rather to a way of thinking about life and art as a sort of work in progress, an agnostic project that does not reveal absolute truth or authenticity but highlights the borders and the edges of things.

The book does not proceed in strict chronological order; instead, each chapter focuses on a particular aspect in the deliberation on freedom, including the relationship between artistic and political freedoms, violence and terrorism, love and the freedom of the other, political dissent and estrangement, the totalitarian experience, and the possibility of individual judgment. Each encounter and experiment in freedom has an element of unpredictability, that margin of error or elusive shadow that escapes the frame, offering us a final surprise, if not always a happy ending.

The expression "another freedom" comes from a virtual debate between Alexander Pushkin and Alexis de Tocqueville over democracy in America. Tocqueville's book has a notorious history of misinterpretation; while in the United States it was considered extremely complimentary to the American political system, in Russia Tocqueville's book was read as an indictment of democracy or, in Pushkin's view, a form of "tyranny." Pushkin defines "the other freedom" in the poem "From Pindemonti," written after he read Tocqueville's first volume of *Democracy in America* in 1836. The poet mocks the defense of constitutional rights and democratic freedoms, including freedom of the press and freedom of expression, calling them merely "words, words, words." "Another, better freedom" praised in the poem is not merely a-political but antipolitical; it consists in a voluntary exile "from the tsar and the people" and a nomadic exploration of natural and artistic beauty that supposedly knows no borders. Ironically, Pushkin declares his support for moderate censorship and at the same time takes the necessary precaution of protecting himself from a watchful censor, attributing his verses to the Venetian poet Ippolito Pindemonti and posing behind the mask of a humble translator. The "other freedom" becomes a license for poetic translation, revealing the paradoxes and precariousness of any form of freedom fighting that insists on a radical separation of art and politics.

The other, better freedom is not defined by Pushkin in national terms at all, but Pushkin's followers and worshippers, Dostoevsky among them, would define it as a Russian radical liberation, or a "freer freedom" that Dostoevsky first dreamed about in the penal colony. At the same time, in his later novels Dostoevsky offers a depiction of terrorism in nineteenth-century Russia, revealing how easily the dream of absolute freedom can turn into absolute despotism and how a hero-liberator might be at the same time a banal impostor.

I will explore different forms of otherness in the discussion of freedom, not limiting myself to cultural difference. Often the problem with sweeping discussions of cultural differences is that they tend to ignore differences within and the internal plurality of cultures and individuals. In my understanding, otherness is constituent of the very experience of freedom, of discovering potentiality or inner plurality, of our capacity to cocreate in a world that might still surprise us. Otherness is not located in any Saint Elsewhere or otherworldliness, but in this-worldly architecture, in the unpredictability of human cocreation with the world.

Chapter 1, " Freedom versus Liberation: Corrupted Sacrifice from Tragedy to Modernity," examines the foundations of the space of freedom that is conquered from the space of the sacred and later from the space of historical determinism. I will focus on the opposition between *telos*, end, goal, and *elpis*, hope, that opens up the space of human finitude and between *technê* (Promethean skills and arts) and *mania* (Dionysian madness or divine inspiration) that would distinguish arts of freedom and liberation. In the ancient conception, freedom was not always a "gift of the gods" but more often a theft from the gods. Thus the Titan Prometheus cheated Zeus by offering him a perfumed package with the bare bones of the sacrificial animal and leaving the flesh for the humans. Did Prometheus trick Zeus or the other way around? What happens in tragedy when the nature of sacrifice and its value for the polis are in doubt? What started the Trojan War: Helen's unfaithfulness or Agamemnon's war propaganda that included the sacrifice of his daughter Iphigenia, an act that remains contested? Was his sacrifice done out of piety or as a tool of persuasion? The second part of the chapter traces this tragic heritage in modernity across cultures, including Kafka's parable "Prometheus," Mandel'shtam's "Stalin's Ode" (a reworking of the Prometheus myth in the circumstances of totalitarianism), and Aby Warburg's lecture "The Serpent Ritual of the Pueblo Indians," written in the sanatorium that transports the reflection on sacrifice and deliverance from European to Native American culture and back again.

Chapter 2, "Political and Artistic Freedoms in a Cross-Cultural Context," offers a framework for the debates around liberalism and aesthetics in the international context, focusing on democratic freedoms and artistic freedom, or public and inner freedoms, modernity and reinvention of national tradition. After reading Tocqueville's *Democracy in America*, Pushkin was horrified by what he called the "tyranny of democracy" and wrote a polemical poem about "another, better freedom." Some hundred years later, on the eve of the Cold War, liberal philosopher Isaiah Berlin spent a night (talking) with the Russian poet Anna Akhmatova and evoking an imaginary encounter between Tocqueville and Pushkin. Through these two encounters the chapter develops further the distinction between cultures of liberation and cultures of freedom and examines responses to the classical liberal tradition by eccentric political thinkers, philosophers, and poets from the "margins of the West."

Chapter 3, "Liberation with a Birch Rod and the Banality of Terrorism," focuses on the issues of terror, sacrifice, and corporal punishment (including Dostoevsky's national philosophy with a birch rod, Sacher Masoch's contract, and Marx's conception of revolution). The discussion of the "malignant pleasure" of violence moves from Dostoevsky's prison memoir to his novel *The Possessed*, which centers on a terrorist plot and offers the figure of the terrorist instigator as a "petty demon," a man of clichés rather than a romantic martyr. The chapter explores the logic of phantasmagoria and the banality of terror, the rhetoric of conversation and conversion, modernism and anti-Occidentalism as manifested through the foreign travel and encounters with the modern city. In 1859–1861 Feodor Dostoevsky, Karl Marx, and Charles Baudelaire brushed past each other on the streets of Paris. While Baudelaire found the experience of urban crowds electrifying and invented the word "modernity," Dostoevsky decried the modern city, calling it the "whore of Babylon." Marx saw it as the inauthentic masquerade of capitalist exploitation. These encounters focus on a radical critique of liberalism, a debate about national identity, revolution, and different forms of "reenchantment" of the modern experience. Sometimes the reaction to foreign travel, urban modernity, and new political institutions resulted in anti-Occidentalism and conversion to the religion of the native soil, other times it led to the creation of a radical philosophy of liberation, and yet other times it elicited the prefiguration of artistic modernism.

Chapter 4, "Love and the Freedom of the Other," questions the mutual codependence of love and liberty and the erotic architecture of porous walls and unsurpassable shadows. After the end of her secret love affair with Martin Heidegger, Hannah Arendt wrote that romantic love for a single one is "a totalitarianism for two" that threatens to exclude the world between and around them. The chapter focuses on philosophers' love letters and invites us to rethinks existential aspects of freedom through the experience of the "modern Eros" and the difficulty to imagine the freedom of the other. Reading Kierkegaard's *Diary of the Seducer* and his actual correspondence with Regine Olsen, and more in depth, the letters and notebooks of Hannah Arendt and Martin Heidegger, who first met to discuss Kierkegaard and subsequently developed contrasting conceptions of freedom and worldliness. It turns out that parables and double entendres, sacrifices and acts of questionable judgment, creative misreadings and mood swings, don't destroy the space of tenderness that survives against all reasonable odds in the lives of the philosophical lovers.

Chapter 5, "Dissent, Estrangement, and the Ruins of Utopia," examines different forms of nonconformism, heresy, and dissent in the twentieth century, from artistic experimentation of the avant-garde to existential rebellion and civil disobedience. Instead of utopianism and its failures, the focus is on the creative survival of estrangement and its transformation into dissent. Reflecting upon the lessons of the Russian revolution, writer and literary theorist Victor Shklovsky claims that only the tortured zigzag road is the "road of the brave" and one needs to find the "third route" of thinking about art and politics through estrangement. His ideas about the architecture of freedom and the third space echo the ideas of Camus and Arendt, who develops her notion of the asymptotic diagonal of freedom with the help of an unlikely freedom fighter, Franz Kafka. The chapter goes on to examine the trials of dissident writers and artists from the 1960s to 2000 in Russia (who use the theory of estrangement for their defense) and on the tension between dissent and national mythologies that contribute to the rewriting of history and exclusion of the experience of freedom.

Chapter 6, "Judgment and Imagination in the Age of Terror," continues with the examination of estrangement, the banality of evil, and the relationship between thinking, judging, and the ethics of responsibility in the age of terror. At its center is the philosophy of the banality of evil and judgment and the memoirs and literature of the Soviet Gulag that reflect on the possibility of paradigm shifts and eccentric judgment even within the closed system. Theodor Adorno in a famous statement questioned the possibility of writing lyrical poetry after the Holocaust. It is less well known that in the second part of the quotation Adorno asserted that only a certain kind of modern art has an ability to speak about contemporary horrors without "betraying" them. Similarly, Varlam Shalamov, the survivor of seventeen years in the Soviet labor camps, writes about the importance of "intonation" and imagination in documenting Soviet terror and estranging the happy ideology of the Soviet utopia. The chapter also reflects on the arrests and a radical change of conscience experienced by two women thinkers and writers, Evgeniia Ginzburg and Arendt. Why is there a persistent "glamorization" of the culture of terror and authoritarianism? What kind of fantasy does it engage and tamper with? How does one change one's mind and judge against the prevailing ideology? How does judging and imagination help undo the fascinating unfreedom that is still with us?

Figure 4. Svetlana Boym, chessboard collage combining an author's photograph of a Venice antique store, one of the last known photographs of Osip Mandelshtam from the files of the NKVD, and a fragment from the photography of Aby Warburg's archive.

ONE

FREEDOM VERSUS LIBERATION
CORRUPTED SACRIFICE FROM TRAGEDY
TO MODERNITY

Hope or Fate?

In Aeschylus's tragedy *Prometheus Bound*, the Chorus asks the Titan to recount his "crimes":

> *Chorus*: Is there not some further wrong you did?
> *Prometheus*: Yes, I caused humans not to fear their deaths.
> *Chorus*: What cure have you offered for that fear?
> *Prometheus*: I seated a blind hope in their hearts.[1]

Hope, *elpis*, cannot help humans overcome their finitude, only to survive it. Yet it lays an elusive foundation for the space of human freedom, *eleutheria*. In fact, during the thousands of years following Aeschylus's play, the drama of freedom will play out between *elpis* and *telos* (goal, purpose, end). *Telos* is a necessity that will take different guises, from religious fate to the invisible hand of the market or the spirit of history, while *elpis* offers hope and also a wonder that opens toward that incalculable and unpredictable element in the adventure of humanity.

Prometheus, the great trickster, does not tempt humans with the promise of eternal salvation or an otherworldly paradise. Nor does he demand blind faith, power, or love for himself. He decides to empower humans for their own sake, not offering them gadgets but rather immaterial gifts, out of pity (*eleos*) and fear (*phobos*). Prometheus's gifts, *technê* and *elpis*, are ambivalent: *technê* (craft, art) refers not to tools or objects but to arts and skills, and *elpis* brings not immortality or security but the broadened horizons of human existence beyond immediate necessities. Like any art of freedom, they are imperfect and hardly risk-free. While the stories of liberation from captivity abound in every tradition, the dramas of living in freedom are much harder to come by and more difficult to survive. The relationship between liberation and freedom is explored in the early works of theater—Greek tragedy. There is not a god of freedom or goddess of liberty in the Greek pantheon. Instead of the *myths* of freedom, we find here *plots* of freedom; instead of gods and goddesses who personify this new concept of *eleutheria*, we discover imposters, demigods, and dissident Titans mediating between human and divine realms and exploring new thresholds of possibility at the edges of the polis.

Greek tragedy enacts the ambivalences that surrounded the foundation of the space of freedom. "In tragedy the city must both recognize itself and bring itself into question," argued French historian Pierre Vidal-Naquet.[2] Coeval with the development of the democratic city-state, classical tragedy blossomed and ceased to exist within a single century, a crucial development in the history of the West. The material of tragedy is the stuff both of myth and of the social and legal thought particular to the city-state, yet tragedy stages their conflicts in the unprecedented space of the theater. Each tragedy depicts one system of justice, or *dikē*, in conflict with another, showing humanity at the crossroads and dramatizing the relationship between religion and civic life, questioning what it means to act and to be human.

My focus is not on what is called "tragic" in the everyday sense of the word, referring, that is, to an unfortunate occurrence often beyond one's control and the lack of a Hollywood-style happy ending. Nor is the problem of fate and the "tragic flaw" (*hamartia*) of the hero possessed by hubris and excessive self-confidence central to my argument. Morality tales hardly ever feature in stories of freedom. The concept of *hamartia* is notoriously ambiguous and is translated as "accident," "mistake," "flaw," or literally, a "missed mark" (in the context of a shot arrow). It is unclear whether *hamartia* originates from inside or outside, from the ethos or the character of the protagonist, or from his *daimon* (that stranger that cohabits with us within and without—or the unfortunate collision of the two). At first glance the plot of tragedy defeats any conceivable modern understanding of freedom of action and will. However, what interests me is not a *drama of fate* but a *fate of drama*, which delineates the space of deliberation, imitation, and play, mediating between the rules of the polis and the rituals of religion. The difference between a god and a deus ex machina is huge; gods on stage are much more dialogical than the ones in the temple. The space of *hamartia*, the mystery of the missed mark and the ambivalence around its interpretations, marks that asymptotic margin of freedom that differentiates tragedy from a religious ritual.

Even the word for freedom, *eleutheria*, is related to the border zone town of Eleutherae between Athens and Thebes, to art and religion, the history of the festival of the Dionysia and the emergence of classical tragedy. Pausanias reports that "the reason why the people of Eleutherae came over was not because they were reduced by war, but because they desired to share Athenian citizenship and hated the Thebans." They carried with them the wooden statue of Dionysus, who initially was not accepted in Athens. According to the legend, the god from the borderlands became infuriated and brought plague to the city of Athens. This is how the festival of the Dionysia came into being. Subsequently this collective festival opened a space for individual creativity, transforming ritual into theater—a space where political and artistic *eleutheria* opened dialogues about the boundaries of the polis. *Eleutheria* is a freedom of the border zone—a freely chosen "immigration" and incorporation of local and foreign gods—that also gives birth to poetry and theater.

The literal meaning of the word *tragedy*, "goat-song" from *tragos*, "goat," and *odi*, "ode, song," also bears traces of the transformation of sacrificial practices. Goats were associated with satyrs but also, on the days of the Dionysia when the tragedies were performed, one could hear the sounds of the goats being sacrificed. The "song of the goat" or its scream might be heard at a distance during the theatrical performances, like the sound of a distant violin of discord in Chekhov's *Cherry Orchard*. Thus the animal sacrifice cohabited with tragedy; yet in many texts of classical tragedy we find parodic or rhetorical use of ritual practices and language. Moreover, tragedy spoke about violent scenes but did not represent them in a sensationalistic manner. Unlike contemporary horror movies, classical tragedies kept violence out of the scene and did not rely on it for theatrical effect. There was a special cart, an *ekkyklêma*, which could be rolled out to reveal the aftermath of a violent event that had happened offstage, out of sight of the audience. The space of the theater was about the transfiguration of violence into deliberation, of spectacle into performance.

While following some aspects of Aristotle's analysis of tragedy, my reading belongs to a *lateral* poetics. In my view, the parables of freedom develop laterally vis-à-vis the central plots of tragedies; they spring from the moments of nonrecognition between men and gods, between laws and actions, potentialities and realizations. The margin of freedom is that excess that was neither banned nor resacralized. I focus on two works that meditate on the bonds and boundaries of freedom and mark the beginning and end of classical tragedy: Aeschylus's *Prometheus Bound* and Euripides' *Bacchae*.

It is customary among scholars of tragedy to contrast the tale of two cities, Athens and Thebes. The story of Athens is about building roads to civilization, developing the architecture of the polis with its boundaries and measures, claiming a limited victory against undifferentiated nature. The story of Thebes is the road away from civilization, the return of the slain (repressed) dragon. Cadmus, founder of the city of Thebes, slays the serpent, only to be turned into a serpent at the end of the story in an act of Dionysian revenge. In both works the protagonists of the plots of freedom are neither mortals nor gods, but the mediators and go-betweens whose identity crisis and borderline predicament help creative mortals (the tragedians) to explore their own, newly discovered and mysterious freedom. Both tragedies deal with "corrupted sacrifice" and result in an ambivalent or even "corrupted" catharsis opening on the theater of reflection and wonder.[3]

Prometheus's story is about *technê*, the human arts of freedom that develop out of blind hopes, while the Dionysian one is about *mania*, the blinding, orgiastic madness that would liberate mortals from the human condition itself. The former is about humanization and its discontents and the latter about dehumanization (or divine animality) and its no less troubling complications. Aeschylus's Prometheus is a powerful Titan, a master of *mêtis* (cunning) who tries to help humans and finds himself temporarily powerless and "bound" up with the human condition and its pains. Euripides' Dionysus is no less cunning, but he is also a resentful "upstart god" who comes disguised as a mortal and attempts to corrupt and unmask the very nature of human justice for the sake of divine revenge and power, and to bring about the destruction of civilization.

Nietzsche observed that Prometheus is but a mask behind which lies Dionysus. In some way Prometheus and Dionysus might uncannily be echoing one another as liminal heroes /gods, "resident aliens" in the human world that mark the geographic frontiers of the Greek universe. Prometheus's brother Atlas is a burdened global border guard, carrying the world on his shoulders; Dionysus himself is a wanderer between East and West, a cross-dresser and a border crosser.[4] For Greeks he is both a stranger and a native, a returning exile claiming to be more native than the natives. Perhaps they can also combine to form the two faces of the god of the threshold, Janus? What matters for us, however, are not characters but actions and plot, and the actions of Prometheus are the inverse of those of Dionysus. Prometheus wishes to make humans coauthors of their existence and unwittingly finds himself sharing human pain; Dionysus woos mortals with a promise of shared divinity that results in animalization. The Promethean promise is a heroic version of "human, all too human," while the Dionysian one is that of a superhumanity with instant gratifications. Prometheus is a good dissident but a bad politician, as Plato observed. He would not function well in ancient or modern bureaucracy. Dionysus is an orgiastic liberator who becomes a vengeful despot. In other words, the Promethean *technê* leads to *deliberation* while Dionysian *manias* promise *deliverance*.

Of course, the relationship between *technê* and *mania* is hardly that of an agonistic binary. Both concepts are ridden with ambivalences that become manifest through history. The Greek conception of *technê* emerged in opposition to nature (*physis*) and chance (*tyche*) and engaged human creativity and play as well as the art of making (*poiesis*). *Technê* came to mean both art and craft, theoretical and practical skills becoming a foundation of antiutilitarian (theoretical) and utilitarian (and technological) knowledge.[5] In his desire to discredit both democracy (beautiful and multifarious like female fashion, but transient and leading to despotism) and poetry (an imitation of imitations), Plato believed that, for politics, utilitarian crafts and medical techniques are more important than art or imagination. In my understanding, *technê* by no means encompasses a mere technological prosthesis or a foundation of technical or technocratic knowledge. Rather, it is a foundation of the arts of freedom, offering a horizon of meanings as if before and beyond a binary difference between productive and unproductive practices, between *arts* in the plural and *art* in the singular. The arts of freedom produce an imaginary architecture of the border zone space, not a walled boundary.

Like *technê*, *mania* is double-edged and refers simultaneously to insanity and divine inspiration: in the first instance the manic transcendence of boundaries destroys civilizing forms while, in the second, it can contribute to the adventure of creativity and experimentation, an invention of new forms and play. *Mania* is about being beside oneself, out of one's mind, with one's demons. The issue in our examination is what kind of plot results from Dionysian transcendence or Promethean transgression and whether one can return to the space of shared humanity. In other words, what matters is how it all ends: whether in a mythical *deliverance* from worldly conditions or in a *deliberation* about them. The ambivalences and interplay of *technê* and *mania* will be explored throughout the book.

In my version of the myth, male demigods and go-betweens are protagonists in this drama; however, when it comes to mere mortals, female protagonists are often more distinguished freedom fighters who occasionally challenge both. While deprived of explicit political rights, even in Athenian democracy, women were among the audience in the tragic theater. In tragedies female protagonists often take more risks, experimenting with different systems of justice (Electra, Antigone), with cruelly executed "parodies" of ritual sacrifice (Clytemnestra), or with prophecies and warnings about impending catastrophes (Cassandra). As for the heroes of *technê* and *mania*, there is a paradoxical link between the *mania* of inspiration and the *technê* of theatrical creation, which is a landmark of Promethean-Dionysian artistic "coproduction": they are both at once actors and authors of their plots of freedom and liberation.

With reference to experiments in freedom, the legendary biographies of the tragedians themselves offer an uncanny twist on Promethean and Dionysian predicament, and a tension between *technê* and *mania*, as well as between theater, politics, and religion. Aeschylus was born in 525 BCE at Eleusis, the home of the cult of Demeter and the birthplace of the famous Eleusinian mysteries. According to legend, one day after consuming delicious local wine, Aeschylus fell asleep and Dionysus himself appeared to him in a dream inspiring him to compose for the Dionysian celebration. Aeschylus creatively interpreted his dream and instead of participating in cultic celebrations transformed them to create the first authored theater. He had his fair share of *mania*—in his case not madness, but divine inspiration, which he put to creative use. However, the epitaph on Aeschylus's tombstone, possibly his own composition, celebrates his life as a citizen and a soldier, participant in the Battle of Salamis, with no mention of his literary glory. Aeschylus knew the laws of the biographical genre of his time.

Aeschylus witnessed the rise of Athenian democracy and remained its admirer. Yet he was accused of impiety for revealing the secret rites of his native city Eleusis, the Eleusinian mysteries, to foreigners. The charge may have been a political fabrication, and Aeschylus was acquitted on the ground that he was not "initiated," in other words, he used the elements of the rituals for his poetic and tragic storytelling, not for religious or mystic purposes. Legend also has it that Aeschylus met his death in Sicily when a large eagle mistook his bald head for a rock and dropped a turtle on it. Uncannily, in this legend we find the motifs of the Promethean story—the rock and the eagle, as if the mortal creator of the first literary version of the Prometheus story had died from the Promethean curse. And contrary to his epitaph, he is remembered most today for his tragedies, not for his military exploits.

Euripides' life, like that of Aeschylus, is filled with legends and motifs from his tragedies. He was born on the day of the Battle of Salamis and lived in a cave in Salamis much of his life, mostly reading and composing tragedies. As a child, Euripides served as a cupbearer to the guild of dancers who performed at the altar of Apollo, and later he may have served as a priest of Zeus. He was also exposed to the great thinkers of the day and was admired by Socrates. Like Aeschylus he was put on trial for impiety, in his case, on the accusation of Aristophanes, the conservative comedian. Supposedly Euripides, too, used his literary skills to argue that his characters, not he himself, exposed dangerous views. Euripides was a subject of frequent ridicule and at the end of his life abandoned Athens to live in Macedonia at the court of King Archelaus. In less than eighteen months, a tragic accident occurred in which, as if mistaken for hunting prey, the playwright was torn to pieces by the king's hounds. The legend of his death evokes the death of Pentheus in the *Bacchae*, torn to pieces as if he were an animal. It seems that tragic plots migrated into life—especially when it came to the death of these early authors of tragedy. And yet their works survived, and so did the legendary stories of their lives, early experiments in writing and living in the fragile democracy.

Technê: Plotting Freedom

At the opening of *Prometheus Bound*, the Titan protagonist describes the miseries of the human condition: "They had eyes but couldn't see, had ears but couldn't hear; they stumbled the length of their lives through a purposeless blur like the rugged shapes of dreams."[6] Any discussion of freedom must be accompanied by a consideration of slavery. In this version, humankind itself lives in slavery with little hope for emancipation. In such a condition, humans are neither authors nor interpreters of their own dreams, but only weak dream objects of a resentful and insecure Olympian god living in dark caves.

It is important that Prometheus brings to humans not *insight* but *fire*. Fire is overburdened with cultural symbolism that bridges Eastern and Western religions. It offers illumination as well as heat, metamorphosis of vision as well as better cooking.[7] Why is it so dangerous to play with fire?

The theft of fire is linked to ritual sacrifice and the intercourse between gods and men. As Hesiod recounts the story, after the war between the gods and Titans, the Titan Prometheus seeks peace with the new masters and offers his services to the new Olympian ruler, Zeus. He becomes a moderator between gods and humans. To determine what belongs to Zeus and what belongs to mortals, he plays his first game of justice, hiding two portions of a slain ox, one beautifully packaged and the other appearing to be repellent. Zeus, who gets to choose his portion first, falls for the attractive packaging (this might be the first instance, but not the last, of the seduction of wrapping). Inside he finds only the white bones of the ox, aromatic but inedible. From now on the bones of a slain animal were to be burned on his altar, perfumed with incense and offered to the gods. The humans in turn are given the fatty portion of the ox, containing its flesh and entrails necessary for their nourishment. While this seems only fair, since ambrosia-eating gods are not known to be fond of steak, Zeus feels cheated by Prometheus and refuses to share his celestial fire with humans. Prometheus, the just mediator, steals some of the divine fire to help humans cook their portion of the ox.[8]

We remember that Prometheus (foresight) has a brother Epimetheus (hindsight), and Zeus matches Prometheus's treacherous gift of corrupted sacrifice with his own treacherous gift of the beautiful Pandora and her own beautiful package, or box. Pandora's box, however, does not cancel the Promethean accomplishment exemplified by Greek tragedy, which reflects the changing understanding of sacrifice.[9] From a sacred ritual that requires no justification, it becomes a contested act, a result of negotiation, or even of bargaining and trickery. Sacrifice is a form of communication between gods and men, a gift exchange that occasionally turns treacherous. The specter of a corrupt sacrifice haunts tragedy like a Trojan horse.

In Aeschylus's tragedy, Hermes appears as a "slavish" mediator while Prometheus is a liberating and creative one. He is a messenger who shares responsibility for the message. Or rather Prometheus tricks the message sender (Zeus), cocreates the message (the sacrifice), and instructs its addressees (humans) in how best to use it. In this sense, Prometheus is indeed a mask of Dionysus; he is a master of theatrical ceremonies, a coauthor of the drama of negotiated sacrifice that takes place "behind the scenes."

The opening up of *agnostic space* and distinguishing it from the realm of the sacred is necessary for the foundation of the polis, which establishes the ground for an appreciation of human freedom. The relation between religion and politics has been anxiously contested from ancients to moderns. For the ancient Greeks, the political realm was not coincident with the atheistic, but history shows that the space of freedom emerges with the desacralization of some areas of human existence, changing the architecture of human space. The development of Greek literature reveals how the space of ritual sacrifice begins to leave room for the exchanges of gifts and for deliberations between humans in the agora, in the theater, and in the symposium. The problem is that we lack a vocabulary rich enough to designate the gradations of the secular, a kind of gray zone of asymptotic desacralization that is never complete.

Where do we find the architecture of freedom in *Prometheus Bound?* The place of action is the "rock of enslavement," but all the dialogues and monologues are about liberation. The polis is not explicitly represented in the tragedy but is its implied audience. And the theater audience is reminded of the exotic geography of the prepolitical world. Here freedom emerges from deliberations, from the common places (*topoi*) of storytelling that transform myth into literature. The word "freedom" is first associated with Zeus, the possessor of the thunderbolt: "Only Zeus is free," claims the Chorus. The freedom of Zeus, Olympian freedom, is known to all cultures, even those without any notion of political freedoms. This is the case of the exception in which freedom is synonymous with tyranny, just as Orwell would have it. This kind of freedom does not create more freedom; rather, it enslaves others. For a space of human freedom to exist, it has to be shared. Prometheus and Zeus represent different understandings of justice, power, and freedom. Prometheus challenges Zeus's authority by calling him "an upstart god." Necessity is more powerful than Zeus. The three Parcae weave their textiles of human fate behind the stage. Prometheus, however, is no Spartacus, who led a slave rebellion; he is neither an outcast nor an outsider, but rather a representative of a previous aristocracy, to use anachronistic language. Moreover, in the art of trickery Prometheus and Zeus are comparable, only, unlike Zeus, Prometheus uses the gifts of cunning and beguilement for the purpose of justice. Prometheus is a kind of noble thief, stealing from the rich and powerful. Freedom for Prometheus resides in shared illuminated space and shared skills.

The action in tragedy is neither agonistic nor antagonistic; rather, it is about recognitions and nonrecognitions, about deliberating distinctions and ways of judging choices and action. Prometheus is surrounded by various alter egos and doubles who mirror some aspects of his action, fate, or character. Zeus is a competing legislator (a tyrant), Hermes a rival messenger (mental slave to the tyrant), Io (the only human in the play) a fellow victim of tyrannical divine revenge. If Prometheus is deprived of the most primary freedom, freedom of movement, Io is punished with the extreme unfreedom of enforced, constant movement. Interestingly, *Bia* (Violence) and *Kratos* (Power) are personified while freedom and memory are not. It is Prometheus's story itself that as it unfolds offers a plot of freedom to the others in the play, including the cautious Chorus. "Time on its ceaseless path that teaches all things," Prometheus tells Hermes (192). "Time" here is neither the time of the immortals nor the time of mortals but perhaps a time of a storytelling, a time of choices, actions, and literary tales that immortalized them, staking the space of common culture. Prometheus no longer "speaks in riddles" and prophesizes. Instead he acts like a fallen angel who enters into human time. To paraphrase Hannah Arendt, this is a time of hopes (and not all of them blind) and promises (not all of them prophetic) that makes common worldliness possible. Prometheus's act of "corrupting" sacrifice and stealing fire (that happens behind the scenes) was an act of liberation, a theft and a gift (*doron*) at once. The staging of the story about the consequences of this act, about pain of punishment and persistent unrepentance, becomes a deliberation on the art of freedom.

Slavishness in the play is not associated with physical coercion or impediment to movement. Nor is it connected to the social status or historic condition of slavery. In tragedy the only one called "slave" is Hermes, because he acts slavishly: "I'd not trade my misfortune for your slavery, be sure of that," Prometheus says to Hermes when the latter accuses him of foolishness and lack of reason. Prometheus defends his "foolishness" as a conscious choice and bravery. Slavery is not an in-born condition but a form of action and behavior; it is a part of Hermes' ethos. Prometheus is physically unfree and "cannot free himself from pain" but still is free in his choice of action. This is not a Stoic model of inner freedom but rather a form of internal self-liberation for the sake of sharing in freedom. In the tragedy Prometheus is a doctor who has fallen sick, an enslaved liberator, but his story does not end there. Prometheus insists on his version of the story and redefines its terms and its ethos: he would like to persuade his audience that the rule of those in power should not be equivalent to "abject enslavement," that sometimes "madness" and foolishness (of which Hermes accuses him) is a form of bravery and common sense, and that the status quo is a legitimation of cowardliness. Most importantly, in the end the tragedy is not about an agonistic power struggle, violence, pain, and redemption. Ultimately Prometheus's tale is about injustice. There might be some poetic justice in the fact that *Prometheus Unbound* was not preserved. It is precisely the lack of redemptive, didactic, or purifying denouement in this first tragedy that inspired deliberations on it and poetic rewritings.

One of the best-known versions belongs to Goethe, who rewrote Prometheus's monologue addressed directly to Zeus:

> Or did you think perhaps
> That I should hate this life,
> Flee into deserts
> Because not all
> The blossoms of dream grew ripe?
>
> Here I sit, forming men
> In my image,
> A race to resemble me:
> To suffer, to weep,
> To enjoy, to be glad—
> And never to heed you,
> Like me!

Not all dreams and hopes come true, but this does not mean that we should stop dreaming and making stories. In the twentieth century in response to many optimistic and utopian versions of the Promethean story in which Prometheus's foresight becomes equivalent to progress, we have parables that challenge the survival of Promethean memory.

Prometheus and Dionysus have acquired many additional masks in the past thousand years. While Prometheus has become a Faustian modern man, a Romantic, a Marxist, a Socialist Realist hero, and Picasso's modern artist, Dionysus has metamorphosed into an Orphic poet, an anarchist, and an avant-gardist exposing the spirit of the most radical music. Both deal with the delegitimization of power and competing claims to justice, with madness and wisdom, with sacrifice and sacrilege.

Mania: Plotting Liberation and Tyranny

From Nietzsche's perspective, Euripides was the great master tragedian even as he killed tragedy and posed a grave threat to "the theater of Aeschylus."[10] The word for "drama" (from the Greek verb *dran/prattein*) signifies both ritual and theater, acting in the world and acting on stage.[11] One of Euripides' last tragedies, the *Bacchae*, in which Dionysus takes bloody vengeance on and destroys the house of Cadmus of Thebes, shows that extreme rituals of liberation can do away with the theater of the polis, making all claims to political freedom and justice obsolete. In other words, taken to its logical extreme, Dionysian *mania* might obliterate the *technê* of freedom and threaten the survival of tragedy and tragic poets.

The main protagonist of the *Bacchae* is Dionysus himself, at once the god of a mystic cult and a patron of tragedy. He is a master of disguise, a power-hungry protector of the disempowered, a cunning and controlling prince of orgiastic liberation. Both a "character" and an "author," in the *Bacchae* he orchestrates the plot of the unintentional (corrupted) sacrifice of Cadmus's grandson, the young and arrogant ruler of the polis, Pentheus. The sacred taboo of many ancient religions precluded a face-to-face encounter with divinity. Those who spy on divinity and sacred rites would be burned to ashes, consumed not by creative Promethean fire but by the fire of divine vengeance. So how was it possible for Euripides' audience to confront Dionysus and not be blinded by the vision? Does the play make the audience more immune to Dionysian cult worship or stage the inevitable return to religious autocracy? What does it mean to return to *manias* of liberation, to resacralize, belatedly, the agnostic space of freedom?

Pentheus challenges the "upstart god" as well as his orgiastic initiates and opportunistic followers. "You want still another god revealed to man, so you can pocket the profits from burnt offering and bird watching?" he asks the city elder Teireisias (165).[12] Euripides' Dionysus has none of the romantic or revolutionary glamour. He is a resentful and unforgiving authoritarian creature, who, like mortals, cannot control his emotions. He is not a *Dionysus Liber*, whose cults emerge during the later Hellenic period throughout the Roman empire, becoming a pariah religion of slaves, outcasts, and the disempowered, all those without hope and thus susceptible to promises of happiness in an otherworld. Euripides' tragedy itself was interpreted in many different ways, sometimes as a reluctant conversion and acceptance of divine justice on the part of an exiled and disenchanted playwright and sometimes as a stark warning about the fragility of any civilized order.

According to political theorist Peter Euben, "Dionysus's punishment of the house of Cadmus is the undoing of the civilizing act." By transforming Cadmus into a serpent, the god is reversing the civilizing act because the founding act of Thebes is the slaying of the serpent. Not only does the god thereby remove the foundation of the city, he robs Cadmus of the one thing he has left: the visible signs of great deeds, reputation and identity. Denying the possibility of imperishable glory (*kleos aphthiton*), Dionysus rejects the idea of worldly immortality that had been the spur to wisdom. The end of Cadmus's house is the end of Thebes, the end of heroism, and the "dismembering of civilization itself."[13]

Euripides' tragedies stage the ambivalences of *mania*—madness and divine inspiration, and the conflict between freedom and liberation, human and divine justice, *ethos* and *daimon*, within human beings. The figure of Dionysus in the *Bacchae* invites an exploration of limits but also challenges the worship of the liminal.

The historic and geographic origins of Dionysus are uncertain. He was long considered to be a foreigner, whose cult of mystical psychic liberation undermined the civic religion of the Greek polis. Dionysus claimed to be the child of Zeus himself, and most likely he was a "hyphenated" Greek, a resident alien in the Greek Pantheon. According to one of the myths of his origins, Semele, the daughter of Cadmus, ruler of Thebes, charmed insatiable Zeus, who, disguised as a mere mortal, lay with her every night to avoid Hera's wrath. Like Psyche, Semele wished to see her divine lover and paid dearly for it. She gazed at Zeus and was "midwifed by fire, delivered by the lightning's blast" (155), as Euripides describes it. Once again, the quest for the true identity of one's god or one's lover leads only to dramatic destruction. Semele became pregnant with the future Dionysus, but having violated the primary taboo of confronting and viewing the god, she was burned to ashes. As she burned, Zeus lifted his unborn child from her, slashed his own thigh and used it as a female womb. Thus Dionysus was "twice born." (A dream of paternal pregnancy, a "maternity envy" complex, permeates the mythology of Zeus.) After his birth Dionysus goes into exile, to Thrace and then to Lydia, to the steppes of Persia and to rich Arabia where he established his *thiassoi* (groups of initiates, mystical collectives) of Bacchae.[14]

Dionysus has been described as a god of ambivalence and master of *manias* in the double meaning of sickness and divine inspiration. Dionysian religious experience does not integrate individuals into the social life of the polis but projects them outside, beyond the status quo into the ecstatic. In the *Bacchae* we see the city of Thebes invaded by vagrant

women from Asia, followers of the Dionysian cult. They live in the forests, nurturing the wild beasts, singing and dancing at the outskirts of
civilization. They do not seek worldly immortality through the pursuit
of virile glory and civic virtues. They do not long to possess but to be
possessed by the god himself and to belong with him at any cost. Public freedom and material belongings pale in comparison with orgiastic,
Dionysian self-abdication.[15]

At first glance it seems that the conflict of the *Bacchae* is between the
god Dionysus and Pentheus, the ruler of the polis: they represent two different forms of authority, the mystical and the political. Pentheus in fact is
Dionysus's cousin, a son of Agave, the sister of Semele who was skeptical
of the divine nature of her sister's lover. Pentheus is a virile young Greek,
of no particular talent or imagination but with a strong belief in the rationality of political institutions. According to Pentheus, Dionysus comes to
Thebes as one "of those charlatan magicians with long yellow curls smell-
ing of perfumes"; thus Dionysus is an epidemic god who spreads the virus
of antisocial *mania* around his domain. Even Pentheus's mother, Agave, is
not immune to powerful orgiastic longing.

The problem is that *mania* in the play has no clear counterpart, no heroic antagonist. Civic courage, worldly wisdom, practical reason, love—
all those virtues and human emotions reveal their manic side at one point
or another.[16] Pentheus and Dionysus are cousins in more ways than one;
they recognize each other's trickery and weakness. Their encounter is
a reciprocal exchange of gifts and threats. The Chorus and the elders of
Thebes—Cadmus, Teiresias, Coryphaeus—claim that Pentheus himself
suffers from a *mania* of arrogance, unable to recognize the legitimacy of
Dionysus. Dionysus, for his part, uses logical reasoning and persuasion to
lure Pentheus into his trap. He finds the ruler's Achilles heel, a youthful
curiosity. Dionysus persuades Pentheus to come and witness his secret
mysteries in the mountains where Pentheus's mother, Agave, worships
together with other Bacchae. His arguments are cunningly political rather
than religious, promising political reconciliation and the end of civil
strife and bloodshed in Thebes. The price for this political peace is cross-
dressing. Once Pentheus ridiculed Dionysus's effeminate ways and tried
to cut his yellow curls; now he himself must don a wig and disguise his
masculinity to join the female Bacchae.

Possessed by boundless curiosity and self-righteousness, Pentheus
follows Dionysus into the mountains and, perched in the branches of a
tree, manages to eavesdrop on the secret life of the women of Thebes.
But one cannot be a voyeur of orgiastic mysteries without becoming a

participant, or worse, the sacrificial object. In a state of ecstatic possession Pentheus's mother mistakes him for a wild beast and brutally murders her own son. Pentheus ends up in his mother's lap, returning to the womb of the Earth.

The end of the play takes us from the wilderness to the heart of the polis; Agave is confronted by her father Cadmus, regains her sobriety and confronts the consequences of her orgiastic possession. The "recognition" is filled with uncanny horror: she has hunted her own son. Her act, moreover, is not treated by Dionysus as a redeeming sacrifice to his cult: he is a young and unforgiving god. Agave's *mania* is god's punishment, not an initiation. She is declared "unclean," and no purification ritual is offered for her. Her sacrifice cannot even redeem the blasphemies of her family, making her doubly excommunicated—banned from the community of the Bacchae as well as from the new Thebes ruled by Dionysus. Dionysus is not satisfied with the recognition in his own community of initiates, the *thiassos* of the faithful Bacchae; he wants to be recognized by the polis, which he swears to resacralize at any price. Dionysus is a cunning "stage manager" of the "the unclean" slaughter of Pentheus by his mother, Agave. Yet he does not accept it as a redemptive sacrifice on account of her impurity, turning her act into the sacrilegious blasphemy of nonrecognition, and he takes radical revenge on the city. "Pentheus himself becomes the bearer of the city pollutions, the symbolical *pharmakos* (both poison and cure), put to death by the very rite of stoning with which he threatens the allegedly polluting god."[17] The confusion of hunting with human sacrifice threatens civilized codes and distinctions.

The corruption of sacrifice functions differently in the case of Prometheus and Dionysus. Prometheus cheats Zeus—not for his own gain but to spread freedom. Dionysus orchestrates a terrifying murder as an act of revenge to terrorize the polis. Agave's accidental murder of her son becomes a cruel and bloody parody of the sacrificial rite that the god himself refuses to accept. Just as her sacrifice was corrupted, so is the tragedy's catharsis, which remains incomplete, not offering the spectators a comforting liberation from their fears and emotions. There is a sense of belatedness to both Dionysus and Pentheus; one is the new god who has something of a cult following of born-agains about him, the other is a dim replica of the Greek democratic ruler, power-hungry and turned mediocre. If in *Prometheus Bound* the Titan aspired to endow humans with skills and blind hope, in the *Bacchae* mortals belatedly realize that they are "only humans." As Cadmus puts it, "I am a man, nothing more. I do not scoff at heaven." Teireisias supports him: "We don't trifle with divinity."

In fact, in the *Bacchae* the secondary characters are of greater interest. The elders, Teireisias and Cadmus, also disguise themselves, but do so without orgiastic aspirations. Their disguise is more of a pro forma uniform, on the chance that Dionysus might be a god. They do not really believe in him, but neither do they have the courage of disbelief or belief in anything else for that matter. Theirs is the cynical reason of the late tragedies. Their fatalism is psychological defensiveness, not a cosmic understanding. Ultimately, their reason is pragmatic. Cadmus advices Pentheus: "Even if this Dionysus is no god, as you assert, persuade yourself that he is; the fiction is a noble one, for Semele will seem to be the mother of a god, and this confers no small distinction on our family."[18] Instead of embracing the orgiastic, they embrace the opportunistic, offering us early examples of how "wise men" survive tyrannical regimes and religious or political fundamentalism, persuading themselves that some fictions are more noble (and more convenient) for survival than others.

Like *Prometheus Bound*, the *Bacchae* is about sacrifice, disguise, and the delegitimization of power. According to the Greek concept, the human being was conceived as existing in tension between *ethos* (character) and *daimon* (a soul, an inner demon); the two are in conflict, but also uncannily are doubles of one another. As Heraclitus put it, man's character is his *daimon*. "For there to be tragedy, it must be possible for the text to simultaneously imply two things: it is his character in man that one calls *daimon* and, conversely, what one calls character in man, is in reality a *daimon*."[19] The adjective *Promethean* refers to the ethos of coresponsibility for human actions, in spite of all the pain and struggle involved in those actions, while *Dionysian* is about a surrender to one's *daimon*, enjoying it, however briefly it lasts.

Nietzsche may have been right that Euripides performed a ritual murder of tragedy, thus becoming an early predecessor of modern literature. There are no properly tragic heroes in his play: Dionysus and Pentheus appear as their own parodies or secondhand replicas; Cadmus as cautious Flaubertian bourgeois *avant la lettre* or as a protagonist in Czeslaw Milosz' psychology of survival under authoritarianism. No shared civic ideals or passions remain, only pragmatic psychologism and extreme possession that lead to religion and psychological drama, away from political art in the ancient sense of the word.

According to French classicist Jean-Pierre Vernant, *Bacchae* shows that the polis cannot protect itself from its own mystical "underworld" but must instead recognize it. But the play does not end in voluntary recognition, rather in a resacralization of the polis by force. This is not the Dionysian spirit of music, not the liberational potential of the orgiastic or of escape from time, but a colonization of the polis. Its goal is revenge, not justice. The Dionysus of the *Bacchae* has neither generosity nor imagination; he is neither a hedonistic philosopher nor a joyful Pan nostalgic for the lost Arcadia. A sense of joy, or even of humor, is alien to him. He is not portrayed as a carnivalesque fool or a playful artist. In Euripides, Dionysus is human, all too human, in a Nietzschean sense. The elderly tragedian reaffirms his control of the stage; in the world of his drama, Dionysus, who appeared to be a master of ceremonies, remains enslaved to his own resentment and other violent emotions. Dionysus is, after all, only a character who, in fact, lacks character (in the Greek sense of *ethos*). Is Dionysus a god himself (a *"daimon autos"*) or an impostor possessed by his own unrecognized *daimons*? The tragedy leaves both options open. Not having enough *ethos* to take command over the tragic form, Dionysus succumbs to his own *daimons*.

In the end, the sword is double-edged; the polis jeopardizes its system of justice by excluding the marginal, the ecstatic, the undisciplined. But once the master of the mystical ceremonies takes over the polis, he too loses his liberational appeal and promises to be a tyrant of the worst kind. The practices of what seems like a radical liberation at the end confirm radical authoritarianism. Instead of *Dionysus Liber* we end up with *Dionysus Rex*, who obviates the fragile memory of political freedom. Seeing the liberator face-to-face and worshipping him as a god can burn to ashes the grounds of the political.

Euripides oversees his orchestration of the brutal sacrifice and the corrupted catharsis that results from it, leaving his audience in a state of awe as well as thought-provoking ambivalence. The only Dionysian rite he salvages is the rite of tragedy itself; he shows the radical effect of violence and at the same time while avoiding its display, preserves the fragile architecture of the tragic form.

Peter Euben sees tragedy as the conflict between membership and dismemberment. One could add that it is also between dismemberment and remembrance. Dionysus might have been a god of oblivion, but Euripides the tragedian makes us remember the forgetting and learn something from it.

Catharsis: Freedom or Liberation?

So *how* do we learn from tragedy? Do we share in its *mania* or its *technê*, or else do we, as its distant audience, reenact a more "civilized" version of violent sacrifice through catharsis?

Jakob Bernays, Sigmund Freud's uncle, said that the word "catharsis" is a "pompous expression that the educated person has at hand but that no thinking person will know precisely what it means." In fact there is only a single mention of catharsis in Aristotle's *Poetics*, in a clumsy turn of phrase in the original Greek: "Tragedy is an imitation of an action that is admirable, complete (composed of an introduction, a middle part, and an ending), and possesses magnitude; in language made pleasurable, each of its species separated in different parts; performed by actors, not through narration; effecting through pity and fear the purification [catharsis] of such emotions."[20] The theory of catharsis that Aristotle promises in his *Politics* is not delivered in his *Poetics*. Unless, of course, just like his treatise on comedy, Aristotle's treatise on catharsis has been lost, in a library of Babel operated by Jorge Luis Borges and stage-managed by Umberto Eco.

Etymologically catharsis refers to purification and seems to bring together theater, hygiene, and ritual. Catharsis can be seen as a form of "homeopathy," a release of violent emotion. Yet through centuries it remains a mysterious concept in which nothing can be taken for granted, neither the meaning of "pity and fear" nor its function for the audience. There were those who, like Saint Augustine, put pagan catharsis in the service of Christianity and saw the experience of sympathetic pity as a enjoyable path to redemption. Others, like David Hume, resisted subsuming Aristotle's *Poetics* into Christian ethics and asserted that if we enjoyed experiencing sympathetic pity, a hospital would be preferable to a ballroom. Hume believed in the paradox of tragedy that transforms violent emotions into a form of emotional wisdom and calm aesthetic feeling.[21] German philosopher and playwright Gothold Ephraim Lessing saw in tragic catharsis a mediation between public and private feelings; through affect comes moral emotion, at once tempering passionate experience with reflection and moderation and making public morality wiser and more imaginative.

Later in the nineteenth and twentieth centuries the distinction can be made between those who believed in the importance of the metamorphosis of violent emotion into aesthetic experience and those who wished to medicalize and psychologize "pity and fear." Bernays put catharsis in the service of medicine, seeing in it a cure for hysteria and other forms of neurosis. In popular culture, catharsis was transformed into a genre formula for an emotional quick fix, and in political propaganda it became a form of manipulation for a cause. On the other hand, Lev Vygotsky, a Russian psychologist of art and a friend of Formalist critics and poets, proposed a radical interpretation of catharsis as an antagonism between form and content that is at the core of literature and art. It "slows down violent

emotion" and transforms it into a form of emotional wisdom, play, toleration and pleasure.[22]

But the story of catharsis doesn't end in the puzzle of competing interpretations. Contemporary philological scholarship took a fantastic detective turn. In 1954 in Skopje, then in Yugoslavia, ruled by Marshal Tito,
distinguished classicist M. D. Petrusevski proposed a thesis that Aristotle
never used the word "catharsis" in the definition of tragedy in the *Poetics*.
This daring but meticulously argued interpretation did not receive much
resonance in contemporary scholarship, perhaps on account of the eccentric place in which it was published or the provincialism of classical "centers" of research. The thesis is that the actual wording in the definition
is not *pathematon katharsin* ("catharsis of feeling") but *pragmaton sustasin*
("action brought together").[23] So the line from Aristotle would be more
elegant and grammatically correct placing emphasis upon the tragedy's
composition that "through action brings together fear and pity." Catharsis
as purification was in Petrusevski's view the domain of music, not tragedy.

Can catharsis be a misprint, or a hypercorrection of an overzealous
copyist who tried to cover up the "tragic flaw" in Aristotle's text?

Whether this theory is true or not, I cannot judge. It is not surprising
that this conjecture of a censorious copyist and the erasure of the rational art of composition (in favor of an audience's passions) took place in
the former Yugoslavia. In my view, such a palimpsestic reading of Aristotle's *Poetics* is very thought-provoking, for emotional reaction can go
together with the art of composition. Tragedy deliberates deliverance and
turns manic liberation into one twist of the plot, showing the dangers of
an unreflected upon enthusiasm. Ultimately, the architecture of freedom
delineated in the tragic art is based on this fantastic palimpsest of *cathar-
sis/sustasis*, a coexistence of emotional purification and a compositional
play that does not erase but transforms violence and sacrifice into an ambivalent space of storytelling.

I want now to transplant the deliberation on theatrical *technê* and *mania*
into the twentieth century and amplify it through three unconventional
tragic experiments, those of Aby Warburg, Franz Kafka, and Osip Mandelshtam. Each brings the discussion of the Promethean and Dionysian
into another genre—Warburg's critical account of the journey of the Native American villages in New Mexico (composed and performed as a form
of cure), Kafka's parable of Prometheus Forgotten (that leaves in the rock
of remembrance) and three of Osip Mandelshtam's poems about the theater of Aeschylus and the tragedy of survival in Stalin's time. "Tragedies

cannot return," writes Mandelshtam, but each experiment demonstrates a
curious persistence of the tragic imperative and a dream of another space
for theater in an alternative modernity.

Warburg or the Architecture of Deliverance

> The deliverance from blood sacrifice as the innermost ideal of purification
> pervades the history of religious evolution from East to West. The serpent
> shares in this process of religious sublimation.
>
> Aby Warburg

Historian of Renaissance and pagan antiquity and experimental anthro-
pologist Aby Warburg (1866–1929) believed that the serpent and its rich
iconological history deserve a page in the philosophy of "as if." "As if" in
this case represents a third way of thinking and imagining the road to modernity that sidesteps the opposition between progress and nostalgia. Or
rather, if there is a modicum of nostalgia here, it is imbued with a longing
for the primitive as something neither pure nor violent. And if it includes a
belief in progress, it is defined not as a triumph of technological rationality
but as a creative organization of chaos and human dignity.

Warburg's own experiment in living and thinking about the snake ritual continues with his reflection on the architecture of freedom in a cross-
cultural context. In a moment of personal crisis, Warburg reflects on his
personal and intellectual biography at the crossroads of East and West:

> When I look back on my life's journey, it appears to me that my function has
> been to serve the watersheds [*Wetterscheide*] of culture as a seismograph of
> souls. Posited from my very birth in the middle ground between Orient and
> Occident, driven by force of elective affinity to Italy, where in the fifteenth
> century the confluence of pagan antiquity and Christian Renaissance caused
> an entirely new cultural persona to emerge, I was also driven to travel to
> America in the service of extrapersonal causes in order to experience life
> there in its polar tension between pagan, instinctual forces of nature and
> organized intelligence.[24]

A "seismograph of souls" is a creative instrument of alternative *technê*.
Warburg's space is that "middle ground" and "watershed," not a line but
rather a zigzag and an interactive boundary. Warburg doesn't see himself
as a member of the group of "others" but rather as a double stranger within
the dominant culture and within the German Jewish community as well,

estranged from but also embedded in his own religious and cultural tradition and not completely accepted into the German academic establishment.

In 1923 Warburg found himself suffering from psychic illness in the Kreuzlingen Sanatorium under the direction of the existential psychiatrist Dr. Ludwig Binswanger. At the time Binswanger was searching for a complex understanding of human subjectivity beyond biologically determined instincts and exploring various phenomenological and artistic approaches to "self-realization."[25] He offered the ailing Warburg an interesting deal, promising to release him from the hospital if he composed and delivered a scholarly lecture of his choosing. Warburg chose to reflect upon the serpent rituals of the Native Americans from the Pueblo region and their ritual "deliverance from [the] bloody sacrifice," which draws unexpected connections "between Athens and Oraibi," as well as between "primitive humanity" and modernity. He returned to his journey of almost thirty years earlier to the settlement in the Native American Southwest, displacing Dionysian *manias* and Promethean *technê* onto a very different time and place and looking for a personal but also "extrapersonal" catharsis in the middle ground between cultures.[26] As we shall see, in his analysis *mania* and *technê* are no longer tragically incommensurate but rather copresent and synchronous in that peculiar in-between space created by public performance.

At the center of Warburg's examination is the representation of the snake in drawing, architecture, and ritual. If other modernist writers and anthropologists tended to focus upon the more violent culture of the Aztecs, who practiced blood sacrifice, Warburg is fascinated by the indigenous transition to the language of mediation and symbolization that represents an alternative to violence. The lecture followed several synchronic journeys inward and outward in time and space, through language and image, motion and emotion, delineating a new serpentine architectonics of mediation between various multicultural demons. Warburg developed his own version of passionate or even "pathic" thinking going back to Greek antiquity and, following the iconology of pathos, dynamic crystallizations of emotion and ritual. The delivery of the lecture became for Warburg a kind of deliverance from psychic pain and an avenue for a broad reconsideration of the connections between East and West. Yet deliverance in this case is neither an ecstasy of identification nor an exorcism of difference, but a recognition of "spiritual distance taking" and a space of reflection (*Denkraum*) in which some version of freedom can appear. In his diary of that period Warburg uses the word "catharsis," but what kind of catharsis is he speaking about—an exorcism of *daimons* or a dance with them organized into a creative composition? The figure for this homeopathic mimesis is the zigzag; the gestus is the pagan snake dance, the architectural embodiment is the stair-shaped roof of the world house. But to demonstrate this, I will recount Warburg's story from the beginning.

In 1895 the young Aby Warburg left Florence to attend a family wedding in New York. Disenchanted by the "gilded modernity" he found there, Warburg traveled to the American Southwest, passing by the cliffs of Mesa Verde, which he called "the American Pompeii." Then in 1896 he continued his journey to New Mexico and Arizona, where he visited the pueblos of San Juan, Laguna, Acoma, and Ildefonso. There he met the tribe elders, observed their ritual dance, and worked with the Hopi schoolchildren. He followed up with creativity experiments with the children, asking Hopi children to draw illustrations for his tale and explain them. He wanted to see how the children represented storm and lightening and whether they used traditional Hopi symbols of the snake, the weather deity in the form of zigzags and an arrow, or whether they would make more naturalistic representations. To his amazement, under the influence of American public education, twelve of the fourteen children who made drawings depicted lightning "realistically," while only two drew the snake symbols. Later, observing the ritual dances, Warburg came to the conclusion that the culture of the Native Americans from the Pueblo region shows an "evolution from instinctual magical interaction to the spiritualized taking of distance."

The synchronicity of the mythic and the logical allows for the creation of a symbolic in-between space and study of the "iconology of the interval," one of Warburg's most interesting discoveries. Whereas nostalgic attempts had been made by some foreign ethnographers to reconstruct indigenous cultures, Warburg was not trying to salvage Native American purity; rather, he acknowledges their hybrid (or even, in his words, "schizoid") nature. What in his view needs rescuing is not only the "mythological soul" of the Native Americans but also their particular way of organizing chaos in the natural world through a "spiritual distancing" from violence, which offers an alternate route to human dignity. In the Hopi and Walpi rituals, Warburg sees the elements of Greek tragedy. The common topos is deliverance, only the Native American rituals follow symbolic plots rather than peripeteias. The road to dignity doesn't move toward the formation of political institutions in the Western sense of the word but to a staging of elective affinities between human, animal, and the divine through symbolic practices and the creation of common space.

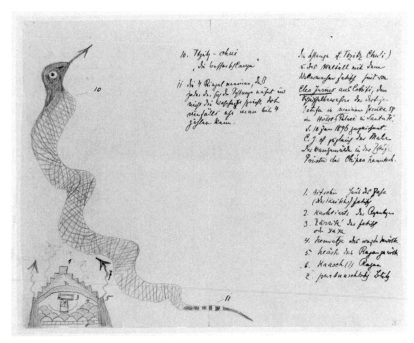

Figure 5. Drawing by Cleo Jurino of the serpent and the "world house" of Pueblo Indians with annotations by Aby Warburg. Courtesy The Warburg Institute.

Underlying the worldview of the Native Americans of Hopi and Walpi descent is the architectonics of the "world house," which is at once a cosmological concept and a foundation of the practical architecture of their dwellings. Warburg observed that the stair-shaped roof and the diagonal (rather than perpendicular) stairs of Hopi houses, which can be found both in everyday Hopi architecture and in their spiritual and ritual drawings, are still reminiscent of their tree origins, and that both echo the zigzag movement of the serpent.

The world house is a less pessimistic alternative to the Tower of Babel. It is not a ruin, but a fragment, a space of hope and wonder. The world house appears like an inverted amphitheater from which one can observe the cosmos. Diagonal stairs repeat the movement of the snake, the zigzag: neither purely vertical nor horizontal, suggesting not complete transcendence but mediation and openness. If the legend of the Tower of Babel speaks of the desire to communicate with God and the subsequent failure of a universal language, the world house with its zigzag shapes

Figure 6. Acoma. Stair-shaped roof ornamenting the church wall. Photograph by Aby Warburg. Courtesy The Warburg Institute.

opens into the space of hieroglyphic mediation between word and image. It is built neither on an opposition between them nor upon a prohibition against images; different modes of representation are not in an agonistic but rather in a sympathetic relationship.

Warburg's own photographs of the architecture of the world house are quite remarkable in the way they deviate from the conventions of ethnographic photography with their strange, off-centered compositions and multiple shadows (figs. 6–7). They resemble those of early twentieth-century photographers, especially Jacques-Henri Lartigue and Eugène Atget; they capture movement and transience itself and also a modernist sensibility. We look at one photograph and recognize an image of the world house in a minimal shack made out of trees in the background; in the foreground there is a dog running away from the photographer, as if it is looking for a hiding place amid the long shadows of the late afternoon. Three of the photographs taken by Warburg haunt us with their empty spaces, which are often in the foreground of the image: the cracked dark background of the church wall that separated the zigzag-shaped painting of the world house from the faces of the Hopi women, the shadow play on the cathedral floor. Rather than markers of melancholia, they become

Figure 7. Stair ornament carved from a tree. Photograph by Aby Warburg. Courtesy The Warburg Institute.

spaces of reflection, a recognition of dignity and difference as well as of the shared modernity commemorated by the photographic snapshots. Warburg adds his own images to the pictures of the Native Americans, coauthoring their representations of the world house.

Yet Warburg warns us against seeing the world house as a site of tranquil cosmology: for the mistress of the world house remains the uncanniest of creatures, the serpent. The serpent becomes a cultural mediator. For Warburg, the snake dance is hardly an example of primitive wildness unique to the Pueblo culture. He observes that two thousand years earlier "in the very cradle of our own European culture, in Greece, cultic habits were in vogue," and in the orgiastic cult of Dionysus the Maenads danced with snakes. The dance of the Maenads would culminate in a bloody sacrifice in a state of frenzy while in the Moki dances the sacrifice becomes a ritual mediation. In this way, through the serpent's dance Warburg pushes beyond a Nietzschean Dionysian / Apollonian opposition or even Orphic mysteries, looking for a space of mediation, a common place. In this space Goethe's Prometheus and Nietzsche's Dionysus can cohabit with Renaissance nymphs and the Native American hero Ti-Yo, creating an intertwined topography of world culture. It was Ti-Yo, accompanied by his guide, the female spider (an animalistic version of Dante's Beatrice, to extend Warburg's comparison), who goes on a subterranean journey to discover the source of water. He returns from the underworld with two serpent maidens, who bear him serpentine children and force the tribes to change their dwelling place and abandon their habitats. "In this snake dance the serpent is not sacrificed but rather through consecration and suggestive dance mimicry is transformed into a messenger and dispatcher, so that returned to the soul of the dead it may in the form of lightning produce storms from the heavens."[27]

What is the logic of the serpent ritual? For Warburg, "the masked dance is a danced causality." "Causality" here is that of "as if," of another kind of "sympathetic logic" of synchronicity that doesn't exclude contradictions the way the Western system of logic does. It doesn't matter so much what the serpent stands *for*, what matters is that it stands *with* the dancer and, to quote William Butler Yeats, you cannot tell the difference between "the dancer and the dance." Causality and mimesis cohabit the space of the dance, allowing it to perform deliverance.

The serpent is a figure of many contradictions and of inner and outer *daimon*s: she is a mistress of the world house and a mercurial goddess-messenger who crosses borders and sheds skins. She moves between heaven and earth, between East and West, between hieroglyph and dance.

The snake can be found in most ancient cultures, from ancient Babylon to Greek antiquity, Judaism and Christianity. The snake embodies oppositional forces within both pagan antiquity and Judaism. In Greek mythology, the Maenads and the snakes punishing Laocoön are redeemed by the curing snakes of Asclepius, whom Socrates refers to before his death. In the Old Testament, Moses had commanded the Israelites in the wilderness to heal snakebites by setting up a brazen serpent for devotion. Because it was ambivalent enough to foster multiple interpretations, the snake is the main image surviving in the culture of the ancient Hebrews, which prohibited the veneration of images and idols. Finally, in contemporary philosophy, Jacques Derrida engaged in his own deconstructive serpent dance in his reading of poetry and philosophy together, Plato combined with Stéphane Mallarmé. The space of the serpentine dance is not destroyed in dissemination; rather, it is embodied in the aporia of difference in the *"pharmacon"* that is at once a poison and a cure, just like a snake bite. In Plato's account the *pharmacon* refers to the art of writing itself, at once a destroyer and preserver of cultural memory.[28] So if we were to choose an animal of liberty, it would have to be the dancing, zigzag-shaped, only partially domesticated rattlesnake.

Among the world religions, Christianity is the most unkind when it comes to serpentine ambivalence. In the Christian tradition the snake became unambiguously linked to the figure of the tempter devil, responsible for the expulsion from paradise. The snake tempts innocent humans to commit original sin. (Of course, if we don't hold prejudicial views about the "tree of knowledge," we might see the snake as an educator of the first couple and not only as a tempter, but this would not be a canonical reading). In his cross-cultural snake study, Warburg circumscribed the dominant Christian treatment of the serpent, which denies ambiguity, offering instead an unconventional modernist interpretation that brings together in a sympathetic fashion Hellenic and Renaissance paganism with Haskala, the humanistic tradition of Judaism, and the account of the rituals of Native Americans at the turn of the nineteenth to the twentieth century.

In this instance modernity is different from mere "modernization"; it is a critique of modernization, not from the antimodern but from a certain modernist humanist perspective, which allows for synchronicity, mediation, the coexistence of different temporalities and symbolic systems. In fact, the zigzag is also a familiar figure of modern art and literature—the shape of Vincent Van Gogh's strokes, of Victor Shklovsky's movement of the knight, which embodies his affection for the third way, the tortured oblique roads of unresolved paradoxes. In Warburg's alternative genealogy, the space of nonviolent ritual is "the space of devotion that evolves into the space of reflection." Warburg transforms Hopi "spiritual distance" into his central concept—a modern *Denkraum*, a space of thinking, a space of dignity, a circle around the individual that allows freedom for judging and acting. The synchrony of "fantastic magic" and "sober purposiveness" appears as a symptom of a cleavage; for the Native Americans this is not schizoid but rather a liberating experience of the boundless communicability between man and environment.[29] Thus the zigzag demarcates the agnostic space where freedom can make an appearance. At one point in his diary notes for the lecture, Warburg speaks about "artistic" practices of the Native Americans but then erases the word "artistic," catching himself using an anachronism. Modern art, rather than modern logic or technology, might be the only space where these ambivalences of synchronicity and sympathy are poetically preserved. In fact, the actual involvement with surviving pagan cultures gives Warburg an insight into European modernity and also an interesting method of self-inscription, which we observe in his photographs of the Native Americans and in his autobiographical diagrams of family migrations from the Middle East to Spain, Germany, and Turkey, and his own travels to New Mexico, which resemble the drawings of Hopi children.[30]

Warburg's autobiographical diagrams, full of zigzags and border crossings, suggest another mapping of cultural distinctions and discourses on freedom and liberation. Liberation for him is not liberation *from* civilization and its discontents, but *for* another kind of understanding of civilizational possibilities. Warburg doesn't glamorize the purity or the violence of the primitive because he doesn't see himself as completely "other" in relation to them, and he shares their desire to organize (but not subjugate) the chaos of emotion. The opposition of Nietzsche and Kant, or the rational versus the irrational, civilized inhibitions versus a liberation of instincts, is not on Warburg's map. In fact, he locates the "irrational" within European culture in his autobiographical account of German anti-Semitism and in the return of the Dionysian *manias* in the garb of the theatrical authoritarianism of Benito Mussolini and later Adolf Hitler. Historian Michael Steinberg describes Warburg's witnessing of the Mussolini rally as an uncanny "repaganization of Rome."[31] Such a revival of the mass ritual was for Warburg a dangerously nostalgic invention of tradition that would revive the furies of world domination in the garb of *Dionysus Rex*.

Warburg's lecture does not end on a hopeful note. He leaves us with a frightening prophetic image of the American Prometheus, who has placed his *technê* indiscriminately in the service of technological progress. The "spiritual distance" and the space of reflection are threatened both from violent Dionysian *mania* and the new Faustian-Promethean technology:

> The American today is no longer afraid of the rattlesnake. He kills it in any case, he doesn't worship it. The lightening imprisoned in wire—captured electricity—has produced a culture with no use for paganism. What has replaced it? Natural forces are no longer seen in their biomorphic guise, but rather as infinite waves obedient to the human touch. With these waves, the culture of the machine age destroys what the natural sciences born of myth so arduously achieved: the space for devotion, which evolved in turn into the space required for reflection. The modern Prometheus and Icarus, Franklin and the Wright brothers, are precisely those ominous destroyers of the sense of distance, who threaten to lead the planet back into chaos.[32]

In his dramatic take on American technological progress, Warburg creates his own version of Pueblo hieroglyphics. He sees in electricity's waves the alternative to the zigzag. The zigzag mediated between the human and the divine; the wave is a human representation of a physical phenomenon. In Warburg's story the Pueblo people are "schizoid" while the scientific believers in progress and cheerful modernizers are almost barbaric. Electricity, like the snake's poison, can be seen both as "a poison and a cure" of modernization. In fact, around the same time that Warburg was decrying the destructive omnipotence of electric power, Vladimir Lenin was celebrating electrification as the weapon of the World Communist Internationale, which strove ceaselessly for the newest advances in technology—from the radio to electrification, the conquest of space, and then the nuclear arms race. The writers were to be "engineers of the human soul" in the service of the industrializing state. Warburg was highly pessimistic about this kind of techno-utopia. The electrified or digitized "world house," in his view, would hardly guarantee cosmic communicability between cultures. And yet we remember that at the beginning he defined himself not as an "engineer" but as a "seismograph" of the soul, not shying away entirely from modern technology. Ultimately, Warburg's version of modern seismography turned out to be his atlas of memory, which preserved the fossilized map of modern affects.

Warburg developed his own version of passionate thinking, becoming one of the first scholars of "pathos formation" in the fields of Greek antiquity and the European Renaissance, as well as in non-Western cultures.[33] Studying snakes and Maenads, nymphs and melancholic scholars, Warburg developed his concept of the "fossilization" of affect, the transmission of emotion and pathos through cultural memory. The folds in the sculptured robes of the American Statue of Liberty preserve the pathos of the pagan nymphs and goddesses in the process of perpetual metamorphosis. "Pathos formation" was Warburg's way of preserving ambiguity and the space of the interval, seeing form in the formless and the pathetic in the aesthetic.

Freud believed that neurosis had its origin in the inability to tolerate ambiguity. For Warburg, as for Socrates before him, dancing with his own *daimons* was a way toward self-liberation, a recognition of dangerous inner plurality and toleration of cultural pluralism. Self-liberation was a necessary first step toward living in freedom, which can take place in the agnostic and asymptotic space of life's adventure.[34] The catharsis that Warburg was seeking in preparing to deliver his lecture became a *catharsis-sustasis* that offered an insight into schizoid humanity through the art of composition and the creative organization of chaos.

Kafka or the Ground of Truth

In response to many optimistic and utopian versions of the Promethean story in which Prometheus's foresight becomes equivalent with progress, the twentieth century offered parables that challenged the survival of Prometheus's memory. In Kafka's parable there is no longer Prometheus bound or unbound but Prometheus forgotten.

> Prometheus
> There are four legends concerning Prometheus:
>
> According to the first he was clamped to a rock in the Caucasus for betraying the secrets of the gods to men, and the gods sent eagles to feed on his liver, which was perpetually renewed.
>
> According to the second, goaded by the pain of the tearing beaks, Prometheus, pressed himself more and more deeply into the rock until he became one with it.
>
> According to the third, over the course of thousands of years his treachery was forgotten by the gods, by the eagles, forgotten even by himself.
>
> According to the fourth everyone grew weary of the affair, which had become meaningless. The gods grew weary, the eagles grew weary, the wound closed wearily.
>
> There remains the unelucidated mass of rock.
>
> The legend tries to elucidate the unelucidated. Since it comes out of the ground of truth, in turn it has to end in the unelucidated.[35]

Kafka's parable is about modern ennui, the weariness that covers up wounds, erasing distinctions between *techné* and *mania*. We are in the modern era when, as Hannah Arendt points out, the common yardsticks of tradition can no longer be taken for granted. At first reading, the parable appears to have a circular structure—beginning and ending with the inexplicable, or literally, "unelucidated." It hardly speaks about freedom at all, rather about the oblivion that points beyond the dialectic of memory and forgetting.

For why are there four different legends here and not a single, definitive one? Each version of the legend offers us a different temporality: the first one has the circular temporality of myth, the eternal return of punishment, not in the Nietzschean version but rather in the Dostoevskian version of "bad infinity." The second version develops a mythical plot of metamorphosis. Prometheus, like a persecuted nymph, turns into the rock to escape the pain. The third and fourth versions of the legend are about modernity: the post-Enlightenment modernity presses in on tradition, like Prometheus pressing into the rock. The story of Prometheus becomes a parable about storytelling.

Kafka blurs the boundary between the Greek myths, which exist in multiple versions, and the Jewish tradition of Midrash and Hassidic tales. Their storytellers compensate for centuries of a lack of actual political freedoms with a relative freedom in interpretation. The tragic plot of liberation and freedom migrates in time and place and becomes a cross-cultural fable.

Before we surrender in haste to the commonplaces about the Kafkaesque and the inexplicable, let us try to elucidate what is there that produces stories: the remnants of truth and light, and a memorable piece of rock.

Upon rereading we begin to notice repetitions pertaining to roots: the "groundless affair" contains the "ground of truth"; by analogy what remains "unenlightened" is what demands enlightenment. In other words, the parable urges us to confront our limits and understand what we don't understand. The "ground" here is not explicitly a theatrical stage but a space of long-term cultural interpretations. But how does the truth shine through it?

Insight into the relationship between truth, light, and theater comes from one of Kafka's aphorisms:

Our art consists in being dazzled by the truth: The light upon the grotesque mask as it shrinks back is true and nothing else. (*Unsere Kunst ist ein von der Wahrheit Geblendet-Sein: Das Licht aufdem zurückweichenden Fratzengesicht ist wahr, sonst nichts.*)

Kafka had a lifelong interest in modern Yiddish theater, which makes use of masks and shadow play. Here the masks of Yiddish theater and Greek tragedy collide. The theatrical mask refracts the light of truth, casting short shadows. The light dazzles but does not provide complete illumination: it would be an authoritarian lie in Kafka's world to claim total possession of the truth. At best, we can cherish the space of luminosity and chiaroscuro, for truth is relational, not relative. Promethean fire continues to burn here, obliquely, forging cross-cultural parables into existence. What remains is the shadow play of agnostic truth—the only one we have in the world of parables. The rereading of the parable shatters its "pessimistic" circular structure, revealing a parabolic spiral in which every interpretation re-marks the previous one, foreshadows the next but also remains singular. Whether he wishes it or not, Kafka continues

Prometheus's labors of storytelling in a world that thrives on obsolescence and oblivion. His Promethean storyteller and Camus's Sisyphus are twin brothers.

Mandelshtam or the Theater of Terror

The other twentieth-century parable of Prometheus haunted by *mania* comes from Osip Mandelshtam (1892–19?) and transports us to the Soviet Union of the 1930s. The tragic space is occupied here by a dialogue between the poet's texts and life and his own corrupted sacrifice. The site of Prometheus's rock—in the faraway Caucasus—is now an actual place in the world, the birthplace of the "great leader of the people," Joseph Stalin, and also the site of exile of the Roman poet Ovid. In 1937, Mandelshtam could not afford the parable of forgetting and weariness because he lived in the land of radical forgetting, where Kafka's vision had become a fact of life.[36]

Authoritarian and totalitarian regimes favor a resacralization of the public realm. This is why literature and the arts must be controlled, because they offer rival discourses and values of those "unofficial legislators of the people," writers and artists. Their unsanctioned performances in life and art would question the newly sacralized boundaries of the grandiose but undifferentiated state-space that constitute the "totalitarian sublime," cemented by intoxicating mass festivals and the secret spaces of fear. Under such circumstances, the elucidation of the ground of truth is an improbable yet necessary imperative.

Osip Mandelstam never planned to become a martyr who carefully calculated his sacrifices, whether for the sake of a paradise in which he didn't believe or for posterity. In fact, he wanted to be a poet "without a biography," a poet whose biography would be a bibliography "of the books he read" and who would be remembered—unlike Aeschylus, for military glory—for his poetry and his nostalgia for world culture. For fellow writer Joseph Brodsky, Mandelshtam was a Russian Jewish "homeless poet" who dreamed of a "world culture" in which Dante and the Dadaists could share the same space.

He was an unlikely candidate for direct confrontation with the Soviet leader. Yet the first mention of the "Kremlin man from the mountain" appears in his poem "Epigram to Stalin" as early as 1933. Mandelshtam, who had a reputation as a poet's poet withdrawn from the political sphere, turned out to be one of the very few who were civic-minded enough to write a lucid epigram about Stalin's era:

We live not knowing the country beneath us
At ten feet away you can't hear the sound
Of any words but "the wild man in the Kremlin,
slayer of peasants and soul-strangling gremlin."
Each thick finger of his is as fat as a worm,
to his ten-ton words we all have to listen
His cockroach whiskers flicker and squirm
and his shining thigh-boots shimmer and glisten.

. . . .

At each execution he belches his best.
This Caucasian hero with his broad Ossetian chest.[37]

"We" here is the civic "we" of the polis audience, not that of the mythi-cal "people" from socialist posters. Mandelshtam's poem hardly has a single Soviet expression; it combines the time-honored tradition of the political epigram with folkloric animal imagery and criminal camp jar-gon.[38] To use a Promethean metaphor, Mandelshtam "stole his fire" and mischievously read the epigram to five of his close friends. The rest is a familiar story: one of the friends informed on him, and Mandelshtam's persecution began. First came the home search, then arrest, interrogation, and exile to Voronezh, where Mandelshtam lived in miserable conditions, desolate and isolated, suffering from asthma and heart disease and fear-ing another denunciation and rearrest. There in 1937, at the height of the great purge, he wrote "The Ode to Stalin," a poetic hymn in the tradition of the Pindaric ode to the great leader of the Soviet people, the father Zeus from the Caucasus. This was hardly an unprecedented act in the his-tory of the relationship between the tyrant / emperor / great leader and the poet, and not a unique act even in those circumstances. Initially when the poem appeared in print, submitted anonymously to an American journal in 1976, it seemed to violate the poet's image as a dissident martyr, but that was due to an unreflective approach to history on the part of its read-ers. In my view, there is no need to venerate martyrologies, which usu-ally take the overtones of Christian redemption; it is more important to understand the tragic dimension of freedom and appreciate the nuances of history and gradations of courage and responsibility. In her memoirs, the poet's wife, Nadezhda Mandelshtam, describes the unusual process of the poem's composition. Contrary to Osip Mandelshtam's habit of compos-ing verses while walking and reciting lines aloud, he secluded himself and "deliberately gave way to a general hypnosis, putting himself under the spell of liturgy which in those days blotted out all human voices. Working himself up into the state needed to write the 'Ode,' he was in effect deliberately upsetting the balance of his own mind."[39] The poem, however, is not to be read either as extraneous to Mandelshtam's opus or as a coherent and integral part of his hidden mythology. Rather, I propose to read it as a tragic offering to the leader and to the Russian civic tradition that took grotesque form at the time of Stalin's purges. The poem concludes with the corrupted sacrifice of the poet, not dissimilar in structure to those of the Greek tragedy that he knew and loved.

> Were I to take a charcoal for the sake of supreme praise—
> For the sake of the eternal joy of drawing—
> I would divide the air into cunning angles
> Both carefully and with alarm.
> To make the present echo in his features
> (My art bordering on audacity),
> I would speak about him who has shifted the world's axis
> Honoring the customs of one hundred and forty peoples.
> I would lift a small corner of his brow
> And lift it again, and redraw it differently:
> Oh, it must be Prometheus blowing on his coal—
> Look, Aeschylus, how I weep as I am drawing.
> . . . .
> I would take a few thunderous lines,
> His youthful millennium entire,
> And would bind his courage with his smile,
> And let it loose again, illuminated softly.
> And in the friendship of his wise eyes, I shall find for the twin
> (I won't say who he is) that expression, drawing close to
> Which, to him—you suddenly recognize the father
> And gasp, sensing the proximity of [world].
> And I want to thank the hills
> That have shaped this bone and this hand:
> He was born in the mountains and knew the bitterness of jail.
> I want to call him, not Stalin,—Dzhugashvili!

In this "manic" state Mandelshtam composes a strange text—an ode in the subjunctive in which the poet hopes to achieve—even more than a reconciliation—an intimacy with the Great Leader himself. The charcoal of the poem is a Promethean instrument: Mandelshtam confesses that he couldn't draw, he could only dream. So here the master-poet presents himself as a painter-beginner. He is summoning Aeschylus himself, who understood so well the fragility of the tragic theater and the boundaries of political freedom, as his distant addressee to bear witness to his tears.

If these verses sound awkward and not entirely comprehensible in English, it is not due to awkwardness in translation: Mandelshtam's Russian is even stranger than any English can make it. At times, it resembles a "trans-sense" language used in Mandelshtam's earlier odes and in the poetry of Velimir Khlebnikov. Paradoxically the strangeness resides in the fact that the poet tries not to be a stranger. He wishes to abandon estrangement; with a last asthmatic gasp he makes the ultimate effort to "get close" to the leader and to the Soviet world, to move from longing to belonging. There is a sincere desperation here. The words related to "closeness" are repeated excessively so that they begin to sound like incantation (blizost [intimacy, proximity], bliznets [close twin], blizias [getting near, closer]). The poet attempts to conjure up closeness—to the point of asymptotic tautology. It is customary to lament dramas of alienation, but here we have a horrific example of a drama of belonging, an attempt at intimacy with a leader.

The riddle of the mysterious "close twin" (bliznets) whose identity the poet won't reveal occupies a strange place in the middle of the ode. There are many uncanny doubles throughout Mandelshtam's text: Prometheus-Zeus, Mandelshtam-Stalin, Stalin-Dzhugashvili (Stalin's real name), Stalin and his double created by the "Ode." Mandelshtam questions his own paternity as the author of the ode and asserts that the true epic singer of the epic leader should be a "people-Homer" (narod-Gomer). Such a predicament would be a writer's suicide, rendering obsolete the role of the individual poet using Promethean technê; he would be a mere "author-producer" who could be banned at any time from the not-so-Platonic republic.

Can it be that Mandelshtam's mysterious "close twin" (bliznets) is the impostor-ode writer, a Frankensteinian offspring of this impossible poetics of closeness? In the end, the ode failed to secure the intimacy of the poet with the leader, but it generated doubles and monsters, like Goya drawings in which the poet barely recognized himself. Yet, this is not merely a hack poem written for the occasion. Through a tragic mimesis, the poem mimics the manias of the time and reenacts the hypnotic state described by Nadezhda Mandelshtam, which was a precondition for the mass incantation and euphoria of belonging. Mandelshtam tried to push the boundary of mere sincerity to touch what he calls a "truer truth" that could obliterate the need for poetry altogether: "There is no truer truth than the sincerity of a fighter" (Pravdivei pravdy net chem iskrennost' boitsa). The problem is that almost every "sincere" sentence is a quote either from the Russian poetic tradition or from Stalin's slogans. Every "truer truth" recalls a truism of the time.

It is as if by putting himself into a hypnotic state Mandelshtam becomes a Socialist Realist poetic machine that recites, crying and gasping for air, ready-made sentences, permanent epithets, and rhymes like *kliatva* (oath) and *zhatva* (crop) without any coherent causal relationship between them, giving us an amazing insight into the orgiastic poiesis of Socialist Realism. Incongruity or even logical absurdity is just as characteristic of Socialist Realist aesthetics as the teleological master plot.[40] It was incongruity based on fear. So at times "The Ode to Stalin" reads like a mediocre Mandelshtam poem, and at other times it becomes a shamanic oath or mantra, consisting of the clichés of the "banality of evil." We recall Kafka's aphorism about the refraction of the light of truth on the grotesque mask of the tragic or comic actor. At the end of the "Ode," Mandelshtam's "truer truth" and extreme sincerity remain as mysterious as Kafka's.

The landscape of the poem is epic and Soviet, remade in the image of a larger-than-life leader who can move mountains. In fact, there is hardly anything separating the leader and the people. This type of sweeping landscape was described by Hannah Arendt as a destruction of the theatrical architecture of the public realm. In Arendt's view, totalitarianism begins by abolishing the space of public freedom with all its little walls, partitions of civil society, and multiple channels of communication: "To abolish the fences of laws between men—as tyranny does—means to take away man's liberties and destroy freedom as a living political reality."[41] Totalitarianism, in Arendt's description, "substitutes for the boundaries and channels of communication between individual men a band of iron which holds them so tightly together that it is as though their plurality had disappeared into One Man of gigantic dimensions."[42] This results in a peculiar *intimacy with terror.*[43]

It is useful to evoke here Arendt's distinction between loneliness (a state of isolation in which an individual finds himself in the modern totalitarian or late imperial society, which devastates the individual's inner plurality and does not allow one to engage in dialogue with oneself) and solitude, which is a necessary state for the engagement of the life of the mind and the confrontations between conscience and consciousness and one's other inner *daimons.* This is the drama of the poem: in trying to repair isolation with intimacy and belonging, the poet risks his poetic solitude, inner plurality, and dialogues with world culture. This is how desire for extreme belonging leads to extreme alienation.

J. M. Coetzee wrote insightfully about a particular kind of alienation that Mandelshtam's "Ode" produces: "Mandelshtam's performance was to fabricate the body of the Ode without actually inhabiting it."[44] According to Coetzee, the poet attempted against all odds "not to yield the tool"—the Promethean charcoal—trying to hold onto his *techné* in spite of his *mania*. Coetzee evokes Shklovsky's estrangement, but in my view, the form of alienation we are dealing with here is the very opposite of a poetics of estrangement, which stands for the world's wonder. The homeless poet is at home in artistic estrangement and the cosmopolis of world culture. Psychic and existential alienation is caused by the fear of losing the space for poetic estrangement.

Tragedy is not merely another subtext of the "Ode"; it brings in a different space of memory of world culture, which debated the limits of the polis and of the leader's power. The space of tragedy is delineated by the poems of 1937 and by the events of the poet's life and death in 1937–1938. The tragic hero here is not Prometheus, but the poet himself, who in spite of his sacrificial zeal in the "Ode" misses the mark. His "tragic flaw" resides neither in the poet's character nor in the poem but in the relationship between the individual and the state and in the totalitarian predicament, which tries to abolish any possibility of nonstate theater. The poet used all his Promethean skills, the *techné* of charcoal, and all the hypnotic powers of Dionysiac *mania*, but failed to achieve his goal. Nadezhda Mandelshtam said prophetically (she was, after all, called Cassandra) that the poem hadn't saved Osip Mandelshtam but might have helped to save her. She preserved the "Ode," although she might have destroyed it, in order to speak about the tragic lives that people led and the multiple deaths that threatened them.

In retrospect we are not surprised that the "Ode" did not save Osip Mandelshtam. It seems that the whole idea of Mandelshtam's attempting to persuade the totalitarian leader of his love for him could not prove effective because there were always other "thin-necked leaders" more Stalinist than Stalin himself. Upon returning from exile to Moscow, Mandelshtam went to many writers' apartments and to the Writers' Union offices performing his "Ode to Stalin" and asking for rehabilitation and help, or at least the possibility to lead a relatively normal life. He managed to convince very few people. The official writer Pavlenko thought that there were a few good and sincere lines in the poem, but this was not enough. The general secretary of the Writers' Union, Nikolai Ezhov, denounced him to the head of the NKVD (secret police), claiming that he was "stirring up discussions in the Writers' Union." Mandelshtam was rearrested. Stalin called Pasternak personally asking if Mandelshtam was "a master," but Pasternak was so transfixed by the phone call that he asked Stalin to discuss life and death in general rather than the life and work of Mandelshtam in particular. It might have been better for Mandelshtam to have hidden somewhere in the deep provinces, as Mikhail Bakhtin did, and just keep out of the public eye during the purges. But neither the poet nor many in his circle had that kind of foresight. Osip Mandelshtam died in the transit camps of the Gulag in 1938, one of approximately eighteen million people who passed through the camps. The poet is immortalized in a Gulag folk song: "A good fellow Os'ka Mandelshtam is reciting Petrarch to us by heart here, by the campfire."

Totalitarian regimes did not tolerate tragic genres and preferred moralistic novels and cheerful musicals. "Life has become merrier, life has become better." The sacrifices were real but happened behind the scene of the spectacular theater of Socialist Realist representation.

Nadezhda Mandelshtam believed that Mandelshtam's alienating experiment in the poetics of Soviet intimacy was not entirely wasted. She observed that, "out of the womb of the Ode other poems sprang that moved its themes in opposite directions. This Ode did not fulfill its purpose—to save his life—but it gave rise to a whole series of other poems which were not only unlike it but also flatly contradicted it. Rather like the uncoiling of a spring, they were a natural response to it."[45] Nadezhda Mandelshtam's metaphor of the uncoiling of a spring reminds us of Warburg's zigzags and dancing serpents and of Nabokov's image of the spiral that is a "spiritualized circle" that produces co-creations instead of repetitions. For Nabokov the spiral is a key figure for understanding mimicry, not as a collaboration or tautology but as a cryptic disguise and creative cheating of the laws of nature and history.[46] In his other poems of 1937, Mandelshtam transports his mimicry and *manias* into the landscape of world culture. The poem "Where Is That Bound and Fettered Groan?" written at the same time as the "Ode," speaks about what remains of Prometheus's voice.

> Where is that bound and fettered groan?
> where's Prometheus, the rock's buttress and support?
> And where is the kite and yellow-gazing slash
> of talons flying out from beneath its brow?
> It cannot come again; tragedies have no return,
> But these forthcoming lips bring us to the very kernel
> of Aeschylus, the load carrier, and Sophocles, the wood chopper.
> He is the echo and the greeting; the milestone, no, the plough

The air-and-stone-built theater of our growing times
Has risen to its feet; and we all want to glimpse all—
Those born, destroyed, and dispossessed of death.[47]

At first we seem to be in Kafka's world of oblivion, but the dialogical form of the poem itself brings back the poet's own inner conversations as well as the shadows and the gestures from another, non-Soviet, tragic theater. The imperative of the "forthcoming lips" doesn't allow the poet to fall silent. The Soviet rhetoric and the "people-Homer" are absent from the poem. Rather we are back to the fragile architecture of the world culture made of air and stone that is present in much of Mandelshtam's poetry. The "air" reminds us of another Mandelshtam metaphor, that poetry under the authoritarian regime is either "abomination" (*merzost'*) or "stolen air" (*vorovannii vozdukh*), the air of the free city or republic of letters. The theater of Aeschylus persists in the stolen air of the poet's imagination in the last year of his life. Mandelshtam's commemoration of tragedy is, strangely, more optimistic than Kafka's. He admits that tragedy "has no return," but does not concede the destruction of its fragile theatrical stage. The dialogical voices of the poem recreate the space of resounding echoes and tragic afterimages. More than a mere rock, a memory of the theater remains as the only place where the "ground of truth" can be glimpsed through suggestive shadows.

Mandelshtam's last poem about Promethean memory is not about stealing fire but about stealing air for poetry. Looking through Mandelshtamian prisms back to Camus's Sisyphus and Kafka's Prometheus, we come up with the fifth version of the parable: in the "dark age" the unelucidated is not merely dark; it could be a space of luminosity and imaginative shadow play as long as it generates stories. To recite this version over and over again, like a labor of Sisyphus, might be the only hope for the poet inhabiting a Kafkaesque world of Stalin's imagination. Perhaps, we owe it to Mandelshtam to imagine Sisyphus happy.

Figure 8. Svetlana Boym, chessboard collage using fragments of the only existing snapshot in which Isaiah Berlin and Anna Akhmatova appear together, taken in Oxford by an anonymous photographer in 1962.

TWO

POLITICAL AND ARTISTIC FREEDOM
IN A CROSS-CULTURAL DIALOGUE

Plurality or Pluralism? *Svoboda/Volia/*Freedom

What makes the stuff of our dreams and helps us to survive: spiritual, artistic, or political freedom? Are beauty and freedom ever compatible? Do they always demand national qualifiers, like *Russian* beauty and *American* freedom, or do they defy those adjectives and gain in translation?

"One must not . . . imagine the realm of culture as some sort of spatial whole, having boundaries but also having internal territory. The realm of culture has no internal territory: it is entirely distributed along the boundaries, boundaries pass everywhere, through its every aspect," wrote Russian philosopher and literary critic Mikhail Bakhtin.[1] Here Bakhtin invites us to understand our own cultural soil as a border zone, a space of cocreation and a living medium, not a closed, self-sufficient system. For here is a difference between a border understood as a line of separation and a boundary that is more of a contact zone. The art of freedom is to transform border into boundary but also to acknowledge the architecture of internal bans that cannot merely be dismissed. This chapter approaches the issues of cultural pluralism and internal plurality through deliberations on Russia and America, raising a broader issue concerning the critique of the Enlightenment and the relationship between freedom and liberation.

Almost a hundred years before the outbreak of the cold war, French philosopher and politician Alexis de Tocqueville made a prophetic statement about the two great nations that would determine the course of modern history and the fate of freedom.

> There are at the present time two great nations in the world . . . I allude to the Russians and the Americans. The American struggles against the obstacles that nature opposes to him; the adversaries of the Russian are men. The former combats the wilderness and savage life, the latter, civilization with all its arms. The principal instrument of the former is freedom, of the latter, servitude. Their starting point is different and their courses are not the same; yet each of them seems marked out by the will of Heaven to sway the destinies of half the globe.[2]

Responding to Tocqueville directly or indirectly, Russian writers and thinkers articulated a discourse on Russia's "other freedom," which was to be found not in the country's political system but in its artistic and spiritual heritage. This expanded into a reflection on the relationship between public freedoms and inner freedom and freedom and liberation, as well as between classical liberalism and national culture; with broad international implications.

Russian cultural mythologies of national identity are often based on words that were deemed untranslatable. For example, in Russian there are two words for truth: *pravda*, which is linked to righteousness and law, and *istina*, a truer truth, linked to the innermost being that, in the words of Vladimir Nabokov, does not rhyme with anything. Similarly, there are two words for freedom, *svoboda* and *volia*. *Svoboda* appears to resemble the Western word "freedom," while it is claimed that *volia* connotes a radical liberation and "a freer freedom" rhyming with the boundlessness of the steppe and the ruthless dreams of rebels and bandits. Actual etymologies do not conform to such cultural oppositions and reveal transnational histories and common cognates. *Svoboda* can be used in the plural while *volia* (the term used to signify freedom for the Russian serfs) is always singular.[3] According to one of the first historians of the Russian conception of freedom, George Fedotov, *svoboda* can include what John Stuart Mill called "the freedom of the other," while *volia* is usually a liberation from social ties for oneself only. In this sense, *"volia* is not opposed to tyranny, for the tyrant is also a creature of *volia."*[4] It often happens that the *volia* of the radical bandit (who in Russian history occasionally posed as an impostor-tsar) mimics the radical voluntarism of the absolute monarch for whom everything is permitted. There is a curious codependence of the outlaw and the autocrat in Russian cultural mythology: "The bandit and the rebel are ideals of *volia* in old Muscovy, like Ivan the Terrible is the ideal tsar," writes Fedotov.[5] In other words, the powerless often imitated the folkways of the powerful, sharing their dreams of control and domination of the masses.

Writing at the end of World War Two and on the brink of the cold war, Fedotov posed the question of continuity in the theories and practices of freedom in the Russian empire and the Soviet Union. Would Russia become a "rightful participant in the most free and happy society in the world," or would it return to its geopolitical destiny of a gigantic threshold nation between Europe and Asia?[6] Some Russian and Soviet patriots of the time as well as Eurasianists saw in this unique destiny the key to Russian stability, greatness, and international recognition, while others decried the national "inclination towards despotism" and "demotic" or protofascist tendencies that recur throughout its modern history.

There are obvious historical and geographic factors that explain differences between Russian and Western European attitudes toward freedom. Geographically, Russia lay on the threshold between Europe and Asia and occupied huge and scarcely populated territories of forests and steppe that had to be controlled and protected from foreign invaders. With regard to religion, medieval Rus' took eastern Christianity from Byzantium, which was theocratic and without separation between church and state. Historically, Russia had to ward off foreign invasions—from Mongols, which lasted over the course of three centuries, to Adolf Hitler, which lasted for four years. Politically, Russia was an absolute monarchy and empire for a long period of its history, with barely eleven years as a constitutional state (mostly spent in declarations). Serfdom was abolished in Russia in 1861, only a year before slavery was abolished in the United States, but the effects of serfdom on the Russian population persisted well into the twentieth century. The Russian propensity toward authoritarian political organization—often perceived as natural, inevitable, and nearly sacred—permeated every tenet of life: from social hierarchies, to attitudes toward law and property, to personal relationships and conceptions of the individual and community. There was little historical memory of an independent judiciary or equality before the law. Legal consciousness has never been strong in Russia, neither before nor after the Revolution. In Russian politics and in the Russian artistic imagination, the way to right wrongs was by way of radical rebellion, not reform, often through cultivation of personal charisma and prophetic ideology.

The political culture of the "threshold nation" promoted all kinds of double agents, impostors, and hybrid identities. During the Middle Ages the grand princes of Muscovy collaborated most with the Mongol and Tatar invaders, often betraying other Russian princes and consolidating and centralizing power through ruse and ruthlessness, a strategy that would be perfected in the late nineteenth century by internal double agents—individuals who were both members of revolutionary secret societies and collaborators with the Tsar's secret police. The history of the Gulag in Soviet times and the survival of the Soviet secret police infrastructure in post-Soviet Russia is a testimony to the livelihood of this model of Muscovite power (which can be found in Leningrad / St. Petersburg as much as in Moscow, and by now is not a property of place but a form of mentality).

And yet, Russian history hardly conforms to the conception of Russian destiny and Russian soul as imagined by Slavophile and Eurasian philosophers from the nineteenth to the twenty-first century. According to Fedotov, medieval Kievan Rus' "had all the same foundations for freedom as did the West where the first springs of freedom were taking root."[7] The Novgorodian republic in the north of Russia was a form of the free city-state with a popular assembly before it was brutally conquered by the Muscovite state. Russian culture has its other heroes, dissenters, writers, reformers, dreamers, third-way thinkers and radical innovators, and "impure Russians" who are often either sanitized or written out of Russian history. Fedotov suggests that only as late as the reign of Ivan the Terrible did there develop a particular Muscovite type of "heaviness," a combination of cruelty, lawlessness, and liberationism that dominated but hopefully did not define Russian history. To equate the cultural mythology of a country with its actual history means to turn mythology into a self-fulfilling prophesy.

If the Russian political heritage is not admirable, Russian artistic heritage is. Writers offered a different kind of double agency, cultural mediation, and translation. If there is a single indisputably positive outcome of Russian-Western cross-fertilization, it is the birth of classical Russian literature. Writers were often regarded as "foreigners in their own land," and yet, since Alexander Pushkin, they were also unofficial legislators of the people, in Russia more than anywhere else.[8]

Pushkin was called "our everything" by the generations of his enthusiastic followers. According to literary critic Vissarion Belinsky, Russian national identity emerged as a community of readers of Russian literature, of Pushkin in particular. (This inclusive concept of national culture unfortunately did not survive for long.) It comes then as no surprise that in Russia the critique of serfdom as well as ideas of freedom and liberation developed more subtly in literature than in philosophy, political theory, or law. So the border between Russia and the "West" reflects also on the relationship between art and politics.

Yet the cross-cultural encounters and travel across the border often confirmed cultural stereotypes instead of undermining them. Russians traveling to Europe in the late eighteenth century through to the twenty-first century often perceived Western political freedoms, as well as the whole idea of the social contract rooted in political institutions, as inauthentic theatricality if not hypocrisy and constraint. For their part, Western commentators were frequently struck by the uncanny coexistence of Russian literary dreams of liberation with authoritarian political regimes, which some great writers treated with a certain fatalistic inevitability, like bad Russian weather. At the same time the Russian tradition of social, artistic, and occasionally political dissent offered powerful creative strategies and uses of "negative freedom" that inspired Western philosophers of freedom, including Isaiah Berlin.

Do we accept the argument of cultural difference as a powerful alibi for what a foreigner might perceive as a lack of freedom? What are cross-cultural dialogues based on: recognition and toleration of the tragic incommensurability of cultures and individuals or the belief in a common border where deliberation can still take place?

At the center of the chapter will be the relationship between *freedoms* in the plural and *freedom* in the singular, with a focus on an "other freedom," a unique poetic and spiritual art first articulated in verse by Alexander Pushkin. I will confront cross-cultural dialogues on freedom between Russian poets and Western liberal thinkers, focusing on Pushkin and Tocqueville, both writing in the wake of the French Revolution, the failure of the revolution of 1830, and the Decembrist rebellion, and on Berlin and Akhmatova, who met on the eve of the cold war. Akhmatova took the poetic license to claim that their nightlong conversation had started the cold war, indirectly alluding to Tocqueville, whose work was of interest to her. Each writer and political thinker offers their own architecture of freedom and a distinct conception of the dialogic encounter that fosters free speech: a poetic play with the "words, words, words" of other writers (Pushkin); the practice of deliberation and "educating democracy" (Tocqueville); extemporaneous and forbidden intimacy with "guests from the future" in a closed society (Akhmatova); and cultural pluralism and free conversation against all odds (Berlin).

"Another Freedom" and the Art of Censorship

A proud grandson of Ibrahim / Abraham Hannibal, an Abyssinian taken by Peter the Great from the seraglio of the Ottoman emperor and educated to become an exemplary "man of Enlightenment," Pushkin was known as the Russian poet of liberty. In his youth he was a friend of the Decembrist revolutionaries, who staged a heroic but failed rebellion against the Tsar in 1825, and he was the author of the famous "Ode to Liberty," for which he was exiled to the south of Russia. However, by 1830, the freethinker and libertine was a married man, a chamber Junker in the court of the tsar Nicholas I, obliged to bring his young wife to the royal balls, and a writer of historical prose. The year before his tragic death in a duel, Pushkin offered a poetic manifesto of an "other freedom" in a short poem that he presented as a modest translation from the Italian, entitled "From Pindemonte" (1836):[9]

> I do not greatly value [those] famous rights
> Which give vertigo to so many minds.
> I do not mutter at the gods' having denied me
> Sweet participation in disputing taxes
> Or interfering with kings at war with one another;
> And it's small grief to me whether the press is free
> To mystify the numbskulls, or a sensitive censorship
> Does cramp some wag in journalistic schemes;
> All this, you see, are *words, words, words*.*
> Other [and] better rights are dear to me;
> Another, better freedom do I need:
> Be subject to a king, be subject to a people—
> Is it not all the same to us? Let them be.
>   To no one
> To be accountable, oneself alone
> To serve and please; to power, to a livery
> Not [to have to] bend either conscience, ideas, nor one's neck;
> By one's own whim to wander here and there,
> Marveling at Nature's godlike beauties,
> And before works of art and inspiration
> Joyfully tremulous in transports of emotion:

There [is] happiness! There [are] rights! . . .
[* Hamlet (*footnote in the original*)][10]

The poem begins with a series of negations, suggesting that the road to the "other freedom" is a *via negativa*. It charts the commonplaces of European discourse on freedom, from political slogans of the French and American revolutions to the Stoic and elegiac notions of artistic freedom.[11] At first glance it appears to be based on the opposition between freedoms in the plural, that is, democratic rights, and freedom in the singular, the poetic ideal defined as "another freedom" (*inaia svoboda*). The first part of the poem is written as a moral satire against all those infatuated with democratic rights, especially the "literary entrepreneurs" who abuse freedom of speech. While ridiculing the new journalism, Pushkin himself uses the language of the political feuilleton with its colloquialisms, use of the present tense, and polemical form of communication. The second part of the poem offers a personal declaration of independence and an elegiac manifesto of the "other freedom."[12] It transports us into the virtual space and time of a poetic dreamland. The landscape here is hardly Russian but rather idealized Greco-Roman or Italian, evoking places to which Pushkin was not allowed to travel. Ironically, the poet who had returned from exile, punished for his excessive practices of the arts of freedom and later pardoned by Tsar Nicholas I, desires another exile, this time of his own choosing. In the phrase *inaia svoboda*, the word *inaia* is connected to foreignness—in one's origins, faith, or way of thinking.[13] Contrary to Dostoevsky's later vision of Pushkin, this "other freedom" is not anything quintessentially Russian. In fact, its ideal is peripatetic; the Arcadia where the poet can practice his arts of liberation is not rooted in the native soil or even in the native artistic imagination dating back as to the poetry of Horace from the golden age of the Roman empire.

The dream of this "other freedom" is presented through a series of infinitive constructions, revealing a virtual dimension of the "other freedom" as a form of "other existence" (*inaia svoboda* as *inobytie*).[14] This kind of "happiness *sub specie infinitiva*" suggests a suspension of the conventional temporality of political discourse, opening up other vistas where wandering and wonder go together beyond the pragmatic present and the bright future.

In line with Pushkin's later poetics, "From Pindemonte" is composed in fairly prosaic language, without much recourse to metaphors or other poetic tropes. Its nerves are the rhymes: they crystallize the poem's central conflict between words and rights, *slova / prava*. In the first part of the poem the two concepts appear equally discredited—only to be defamiliarized and recaptured in the dream of the other freedom. If at first the political rights appear as "mere words," at the end the poet's words seem to offer the poet his inalienable human right—the promise of happiness. Constitutional freedoms, parliamentary systems that might influence the wars of kings, input into public policies, and other forms of "contractual" relationships appear as a conventional hypocrisy; the poet's declaration of independence proclaims a liberation from the tsar and the people and a celebration of the unique freedom of exilic delights in nature and culture.

But the poem is not as simple as it appears at first glance. There is a detective story there in the tension between the poem and its many contexts and intertexts that offers clues to the drama of freedom in Russia for centuries to come.[15] The first part of the poem reads as a transvaluation of the poet's own earlier project of liberty. Pushkin in his early poems celebrates in a rather playful manner the charms of the Greek goddess of liberty Eleutheria and her hedonistic entourage of Bacchus and Venus. Liberty in Pushkin's early poetry is a social art in the eighteenth-century sense of the word, an interplay of eroticism, friendship, leisure, and dreams of civil liberty. In one poem, *Eleutheria* rhymes with *Rossiia*, but semantically the pairing constitutes a negation. The poet invites his goddess of liberty to live with him in the south because both have difficulty surviving in the cold Russian climate.[16] In "From Pindemonte" Pushkin becomes something of an apostate of the goddess of liberty that he had celebrated before. Using the discourse of both the American Declaration of Independence and the French Revolution Pushkin turns the democratic project into a parody, placing a wider political debate in the literary public sphere.

Precisely at the time he wrote the poem, Pushkin was reading the first volume of *Democracy in America* in the French original. (Tocqueville's book on American democracy was prohibited in Russia during the reign of Nicholas I, as was the text of the American Constitution.) In a letter to Piotr Chaadaev, Pushkin reveals his deep-seated fear of the providential march of democracy: "Have you read Tocqueville? His book has had a strong effect on me, and I am thoroughly frightened by it."[17] Instead of writing directly about the book, however, Pushkin chose to review the memoirs of John Tanner, which sides with Tocqueville's critique of slavery and the conditions of the African Americans and Native Americans. This is a matter close to Pushkin's heart since he greatly admired his own African grandfather, Ibragim / Abraham Hannibal, whom Tsar Peter the Great helped educate to become a new kind of enlightened Russian aristocrat. Yet it seems that democracy scared Pushkin almost as much as slavery: "With amazement, we saw democracy in its disgusting cynicism, its cruel prejudices, its unbearable tyranny. Such is the portrait of the American states recently offered to us."[18]

If we knew nothing about Tocqueville, we might conclude from Pushkin's observation that the French traveler offered a scathing critique of America. It is ironic that Tocqueville's ambivalent and complex book is seen as praise for America in the United States and as a scathing critique of America in Russia. Occasionally it seems that Pushkin read a different book from his American contemporaries, never paying attention to Tocqueville's lengthy discussion of American town meetings and political institutions.

Alarmed by Tocqueville's description of democratic life, Pushkin proposes to divorce artistic freedom from political and social liberty, embracing the dream of inner freedom in its Stoic and Romantic conception.[19] The Stoic notion of the "inner polis" mirrors the decline of the public polis; the conception of freedom is internalized, placed into the "inner citadel" of one's self. The philosophy of "inner freedom" developed in a time of empire, when Greek democratic ideals were in decline. As in the case of the Roman Stoics, the dream of inner liberty cohabits with a fatalistic acceptance of political absolutism. When it comes to the political situation, the poet of inner freedom follows Epictetus's advice and embraces the status quo of absolute monarchy. According to Epictetus, that meant wishing and accepting "what is" and, I might add, occasionally conflating *what is* with *what ought to be.*

It is in this context of gradually accepting the status quo of the political life of the Russian empire that one can examine Pushkin's evolving views on censorship in Russia and Western Europe, which changed significantly between the 1820s and the 1830s.[20] To put it bluntly, Pushkin was hardly ever an advocate of the "First Amendment"; rather, he believed that Russia (unlike Western Europe or the United States) must embrace "enlightened censorship." Like other prominent poets of the time, he aspired to become the censor's educator and literary advisor. In his diaries of 1835–1836, Pushkin polemicizes with Russian advocates of the Enlightenment. In the entries from 1836, Pushkin goes so far as to suggest that Alexander Radishchev (whose ode "Liberty," inspired in part by the American Revolution, had influenced Pushkin's own 1817 ode on the subject) practiced freedom of speech to an unfortunate excess. In his defense of political freedoms and his radical critique of serfdom, Radishchev challenged the authority of the (purportedly) enlightened empress Catherine the Great to an unnecessary degree, thus in Pushkin's polemical view, being at least partially responsible for his own political persecution and tragic fate. It is not by chance that the critique of serfdom and the critique of censorship went together in the nineteenth-century Russian empire, as do the critiques of human rights and conditions of life of average people and the suppression of freedom of the press in the twentieth- and twenty-first-century Soviet and post-Soviet Russia. Russian history shows that the debate on censorship has never been merely about the rights of journalistic self-expression. In the eighteenth century Radishchev was one of the first Russian authors to write about the history of censorship, tracing its origins to the Inquisition. Pushkin agrees that censorship might have originated with the Inquisition, but unlike Radishchev he does not regard the Inquisition as a historical aberration:

> Radishchev did not know that the modern European system of jurisprudence is based on the Inquisition (torture, of course, is a separate issue). The Inquisition was a necessity of the age. What is despicable in it is an inevitable consequence of the social customs and the spirit of the time. Its history is not well known and still awaits an unbiased researcher.[21]

Thus, Pushkin regards the Inquisition as a reflection of the "spirit of the age" that must be seen in terms of its historical inevitability. In the end, he casts a shadow on European jurisprudence as one instance of the practices of the Inquisition, which is strikingly in line with the views of Joseph de Maistre and other critics of the Enlightenment conception of law. Needless to say, such a view is hardly historically accurate: while there are intricate links between European jurisprudence and the Inquisition, the European system of law goes back to the Roman empire, which in turn appropriated the legal systems of the Greek city-states and ancient Mediterranean empires. In his belated debate with the bard of liberty, Radishchev, Pushkin goes so far as to question Radishchev's critique of serfdom and the conditions of virtual slave labor in Russia. Much less critical of Russian serfdom in his later years than he was of American slavery, Pushkin observes in his diaries that the conditions of the Russian peasant under serfdom might in the end surpass those of the English or American industrial laborer whom Pushkin never encountered and whose situation he knew only from books.[22]

And yet, before we confirm Pushkin as an apostate of enlightened liberty, we should look back at his poem, which offers us alternative interpretive possibilities. There are at least two instances in the poem that

contradict our previous thematic and contextual reading, and both are located at the limits of the text and in the words of other writers. The first
is the attribution of the poem's "original" to Pindemonte, and the second
is Pushkin's footnote that refers us to Shakespeare's *Hamlet*. These cross-
cultural dialogues complicate the political reading of the text.

Pushkin does not present himself as the author of the poem about an
"other freedom." He poses as a translator from the Italian, a language that
he in fact did not know. There is scholarly consensus that the poem was
not written by Ippolito Pindemonte (1753–1828), especially since in an
earlier version it was attributed to the Frenchman Alfred Musset. Yet this
proto-Borgesian gesture of false attribution allows us to see many interesting ironic echoes between Pushkin and Pindemonte. Ippolito Pindemonte
(by now a virtually forgotten poet from Verona) was known in his time for
his *poesie campestri*, bucolic poetry about freedom and solitude in the lost
Arcadia of dreams. Unlike Pushkin, who was forbidden by the tsar to travel
beyond the Russian border to visit Western Europe, Pindemonte travelled
extensively in his youth and lived abroad. Sismondi, whose book introduced
Pushkin to the Italian poet, commented that Pindemonte's evocations of exotic places would have been more appropriate in the mouth of an American
writer.[23] Pindemonte's poetry, however, is less inspired by wanderlust and
more by nostalgia for his own homeland and its golden age. One of Pindemonte's poems that Pushkin might have known is about the displeasures
of going abroad: "Oh felice chi mai non pose il piede / fuori della nativa sua
dolce terra" (Oh, happy is he whose foot has never strayed over the sweet
threshold of his native land).[24] Here too we observe that the road to happiness requires a series of negations and subjunctives, but instead of opening
horizons they place No Trespassing signs on the borders of the motherland.

Curiously, at present Ippolito Pindemonte is better known as a translator than as a poet. Among other things, he is remembered as a mediocre
translator of the *Odyssey*, this Italian version of the Homeric epic being
almost as difficult to read as the Greek original. In the twentieth century,
it was Antonio Gramsci who invoked Pindemonte when speaking about
the attitudes of the Italian *literati* during the fascist era and their indifference to politics; according to Gramsci, during the rise of Mussolini, many
Italian writers felt closer to Ippolito Pindemonte than to the needs of their
own people.[25] Here "Pindemonte" becomes an example of the "forgotten poet" who wrote escapist poetry, a mediocre version of art for art's
sake. In the Russian context, the poet from Verona was immortalized
by Pushkin's fake translation. The virtual intertextual dialogue between
Pushkin and Pindemonte is more remarkable for its ironies and silences

than for its obvious echoes. For instance, Pindemonte never wrote a word about democratic rights, taxes, or censorship. This part of the poem is an imaginary dialogue with Pushkin's contemporaries and with Tocqueville. Thus, the political (or rather antipolitical) references in Pushkin's poem are free translations from a nonexistent original. Here the poet partially relinquishes the responsibility of authorship. While defending sensitive and enlightened censorship, Pushkin pretends to be a mere translator of the controversial verse to fool his not-so-sensitive censor and less-than-enlightened tsar, Nicholas I.

The issue of translation itself is linked to the history of censorship as well as the history of the Inquisition. In his discussion of censorship, Michael Holquist draws attention to the fact that one inquisition case in Spain was brought against the poet Fray Luís de León, a recent convert to Christianity, for his translation of the Hebrew Bible. Luís de León was punished not for his translation but rather for using a "corrupt original."[26] In Pushkin's case, we are dealing with a corrupt original of a different kind. Pushkin seemed to have internalized censorship, or alternatively, used it as a poetic device, appropriating its constraints to make a space for poetic licenses of his own. In the 1970s, a peculiar Pushkinian neologism was coined and acquired currency in the unofficial language of a new generation of Soviet translators. The translators often spoke about *pindemontias* that they took in their work. In honor of Pushkin's poem, "pindemontia" came to signify a unit of poetic license in the art of translation and a way of speaking indirectly about political issues. Thus, while becoming an apologist of enlightened censorship and absolute monarchy, Pushkin also turned out to be one of the founding fathers of the "Aesopian language" that would flourish in the twentieth century. Hence, beyond the thematic reading, the art of freedom exemplified in the poem is not merely an escape from politics but also a form of play, of mediation between the political and the poetic spheres.

The issue of Aesopian language is also linked to Pushkin's quotation of Hamlet's famous remark about "words, words, words." Does Pushkin cast Hamletian doubt on words, his poetic medium? Does the repetition "words, words, words" devalue the word, putting an end to the dialogue? I would warn against a reading of the poem that would treat it as a metaparody. In fact, such a reading would depend on interpreting Hamlet's expression, "words, words, words," to mean "mere words," that is, untruths or inauthenticities. This would be a "corruption" of the Shakespearian original.

Pushkin refers to act 2, scene 2, of the play, the encounter between Polonius and Hamlet. Seeing that Hamlet is reading a book, Polonius strikes up a conversation.

Polonius: What do you read, my lord?
Hamlet: Words, words, words.

Hamlet here speaks a literal truth (he is reading the words on the page) that at the same time functions as a disruption of social conventions, completely disorienting poor Polonius. Hamlet's dialogue with Polonius, in its interplay of disguise and brutal sincerity, of method and madness, creates an interpretative vertigo. Hamlet refuses to play a part in anyone else's conventional spectacle. "Words, words, words" is at once an affirmation of literal truth and of a right to ambivalence. Hamlet appears as a post-tragic trickster who plays with words and defies imposed conventions to reveal the corrupted sacrifices of early modern experience, which will challenge many codes of language and behavior and expand the space of freedom. Hamlet's "tragic flaw" might be his intimation of modernity to come.

In Pushkin's poem, Hamlet's *words* (*slova*) rhyme with *rights* (*prava*). At first, the rhyming of *words* and *rights* appears to be a satirical comment on the infatuation with democratic discourse, but, in fact, it is also a declaration of the poet's main right—the right to ambivalence. The poem stages its ambivalence with Hamletian virtuosity, not allowing itself to be translated into a political or historical discourse. At the same time, the poem does not let us forget the underlying context of Shakespeare's *Hamlet*, the fact that Denmark is a prison and the things are "out of joint." The figure of Prince Hamlet, viewed as a melancholic dandy trickster, clad in black, a cipher and a hieroglyph, will be a crucial figure of the poet from Mallarmé to Pasternak and Nabokov (*Bend Sinister*).[27] "Words, words, words" affirms both a linguistic skepticism and the poetic right par excellence, representing an antipolitical inner freedom not inscribed in any constitution. It is not by chance that in the final line of the poem Pushkin takes liberty with poetic language itself, truncating the line in the middle and thus disrupting the rhyming pattern. The poem remains an inconclusive fragment, and its dialogues and wanderings are unfinalizable.

Freedom in Russia versus Democracy in America?
Pushkin and Tocqueville

Let us now turn to Tocqueville and follow the path of Pushkin's creative misreading, which can be illuminating for the two writers as well as for the cross-cultural discussion of freedom. Pushkin and Tocqueville both came from old aristocratic families, and both reacted to the French Revolution with admiration and horror. Yet by 1830 their conceptions of the spirit of the time radically diverged. While Pushkin, writing in the wake of the Polish rebellion, believed that the destiny of Russia in the nineteenth century was to preserve the monarchy and the empire, Tocqueville saw a providential force in the development of democracy. He was convinced that not only is democracy inevitable but also that it is the only form of government that corresponds to the demands of justice.[28] However, his early form of liberalism is not to be confused with contemporary neo-liberalism: Tocqueville never advocated a *laissez-faire* commercial republic; instead he harbored a (somewhat) utopian aspiration to "educate democracy" through practices of participatory citizenship and the preservation of a pluralism of cultural values, as opposed to the growing commercialism that he observed in America. While offering a detailed description of American *mœurs* and institutions, Tocqueville admits that he saw in America not just America, but "the shape of democracy itself." His was a journey through the fears, ideals, and phantoms of Europe's potential future as much as a journey through America's present. Tocqueville hoped to save democracy from itself for its own sake by revealing both its blessings and its ills. Hence Tocqueville finds for himself a peculiar vantage point somewhere between nostalgia and progress, between the ruins of the past and the abyss of the future: "Placed in the middle of a rapid stream, we obstinately fix our eyes on the ruins that may still be descried upon the shore we have left while the current drags us backwards towards the abyss."[29] To avoid both the nostalgic gaze of Lot's wife pining for the ancien régime and an uncritical embrace of the "wild instincts" of democracy, Tocqueville offers at the end of the book a poetic image of the geometry of freedom: "Providence had not created mankind entirely independent or entirely free. It is true that around every man a fatal circle is traced beyond which he cannot pass; but within the wide verge of the circle he is powerful and free."[30]

To further amplify the cross-cultural dialogue, one could say that the best interpreter of the French intellectual context against which Tocqueville is reacting was the Russian revolutionary thinker and émigré Alexander Herzen, who wrote about French post-Revolutionary culture after the dissolution of the 1848 revolutions:

> There is no nation in the world that shed so much blood for freedom as did the French and there is no people that understands it less. . . . The French are the most abstract and religious people in the world; the fanaticism of ideas with them goes hand in hand with a lack of respect for persons. . . . The despotic *salus popoli* and inquisitorial *pereat mundus* and *fiat justitia* are engraved equally in the consciousness of royalists and democrats.[31]

Herzen, like many Russian thinkers, is not averse to generalizations about and conventional stereotypes of the entire French nation, yet he points to the major intellectual failure of French Revolutionary thinking: its reliance on abstractions about freedom for humanity without concrete cultural reflection or respect for experience in the world. To counteract this, Tocqueville proposed to launch "a new political science for a world itself quite new" to explore this verge of the circle of human freedom. This new humanistic science of politics combined analysis of the political system of decentralized democracy with a cultural anthropology of contemporary America (on the example of the Northern United States), thus anticipating by at least half a century the development of many future disciplines and interdisciplinary studies.[32] Tocqueville was a prebourgeois thinker who wrote before the scientific division of labor and the separation of the spheres of inquiry. Tocqueville spoke about the "art of being free" as a kind of eighteenth-century social art that examines political laws and social "*mœurs*" together. It is precisely this innovative genre of French Enlightenment writing on the art of freedom that translates badly both in Russia and in America. While early American interpreters of Tocqueville casually disregarded the cultural side of his description of democracy, treating it as a "soft science" of the old Europe and focusing on the study of New England townships and other forms of political culture, the Russian poet saw in Tocqueville's writings an expression of anthropological disgust, overlooking Tocqueville's discussion of the successful system of American laws and civic participation, which for Pushkin was synonymous with democratic mediocrity and social conventionality. In fact, a recent examination of Pushkin's copy of Tocqueville's *Democracy in America* in his library revealed that the pages dealing with political institutions of democracy were never cut open; the poet didn't bother, or perhaps didn't get a chance, to read them before his premature death.[33]

This omission might not be accidental. While Pushkin saw his own diminishing role in educating monarchy, Tocqueville believed in "educating democracy"; his ideal, in other words, was enlightened democracy, not enlightened despotism. Moreover, as if uncannily responding to Pushkin, Tocqueville distinguished between selfishness and individualism, which were frequently conflated in nineteenth-century Russian thought. Individualism is not a bad word for Tocqueville: "Selfishness is a passionate and exaggerated love of self, individualism is a mature and calm feeling which disposes every member of the community to sever himself from the mass of his fellows and to dream apart with his family and his friends so that after he has thus formed a little circle of his own, he can willingly leave society at large to itself."[34] Here the circle appears again, but in this case, it is "individualism."

At the same time, Pushkin's reading points at one of Tocqueville's insights in his discussion of the "tyranny of the majority," revealing some paradoxes of "the daily business of democracy" that might impede on reflective judgment and individual creativity. Tocqueville writes: "I know of no other country in which, speaking generally, there is less independence of mind and a true freedom of discussion than in America . . . In America the majority has enclosed thought within a formidable fence . . . We need seek no other reason for the absence of great writers in America so far; literary genius cannot exist without freedom of spirit, and there is no freedom of spirit in America."[35]

The metaphor of the fence echoes Locke's definition of liberty (as a "fence" around our property), yet here the fence is a confining frontier, not an enabling boundary. Tocqueville was among the first to reveal the American paradox, an advanced and liberal political system in the northern United States combined with social conformism. (In the twentieth century, Arendt and Nabokov would both reflect on this.) In America, notes Tocqueville, people are not prone to speculative reflection; "they do not read Descartes; they find the source of authority in themselves."[36] This insight might be read as praise of American self-reliance. Indeed, Tocqueville appreciated the "free *mœurs*" he observed in New England; however, he saw the limits of such self-reliance in the way that it could weaken public deliberation and the collective imagination. Tocqueville proceeds to unfold his paradox: "There is, on the one hand, freedom of the press, and on the other hand, great superficiality of opinions and a great stubbornness with which people cling to them, not because of belief and conviction, but because of a single belief that 'my opinion is no worse than yours.' Human opinions are reduced to intellectual dust, scattered on every side, unable to collect, unable to cohere."[37] Tocqueville was one of the first thinkers to reflect upon the dangers of the "privatization of opinion" that leads to divestment from public life and from deliberation and creative solidarity across political lines. Thus he anticipated twenty-first-century debates about the blogosphere and advanced technologies of self-expression that often lead to preaching to the converted and to narrowing circles of public communication into a self-aggrandizing echo chamber. For reflective thinkers, in Tocqueville's view, dialogue with others is a "salvatory servitude" that leads to a fuller enjoyment of freedom. It is in this habit of "privatizing opinions" that Tocqueville saw "the soft despotism of democracy." (This is developed in the second volume, which

Pushkin could not have read, and we shall not presume, as Chaadaev did in his time, that Tocqueville "plagiarized" Pushkin's insight.)

At the root of this problem and at the heart of its solution for Tocqueville lies the American conception of freedom as the "daily business of democracy." Tocqueville admired it when it led to daily participation in political life but also feared it when it meant taking freedom for granted, reducing democracy to economy and the "wild instincts" of individual needs. Even in the twentieth-century conception, the American dream as opposed to a French or Russian dream is a strange everyday affair, a utopia achieved here and now.[38] Once freedom is taken for granted, it loses its inherent otherness and inspirational improbability, becoming a mere habit of social practices and political institutions. Of course, these habits are indispensable for the practices of public freedom, yet public freedom is not reducible to such customary practices. The challenge of freedom that consists in the expansion of the potentialities of human imagination and action seems to be absent there.

While Pushkin and Tocqueville depart from the same eighteenth-century conception of the social art of liberty, observe some similar aspects of the democratic predicament, and share a deep disgust of slavery, they come to opposite conclusions about the relationship between democracy and freedom. For Pushkin, *freedom* in the singular is antithetical to *freedoms* in the plural; the poet was against extending the rights of citizenship to the emergent middle class and equated democracy with mediocrity and philistinism and freedom of press with journalistic license. Moreover, Pushkin was hardly sympathetic to Tocqueville's support for decentralized government and a federalist system of power; Pushkin could not care less for the democratic and civic political institutions and the everyday practices of democracy. In fact, he gave support to the tsarist policies of imperial centralization, including the suppression of the Polish rebellion, which became a watershed in Russian political consciousness in the 1830s. Pushkin was opposed to the Polish struggle for independence from the Russian empire. In contrast, for Tocqueville, the two conceptions of freedom, democratic rights and freedom of spirit, had to complement one another. In this respect Tocqueville is in agreement with Camille Demoulin's statement made at the height of the French Revolution that the license of the press should be cured by a true freedom of press, not by its suppression. According to Tocqueville, America's problem was not the excess of liberty but the lack of protection against tyranny that should come from both political participation and the education of a free mentality.

This aspect of Pushkin and Tocqueville's cross-cultural dialogue exceeds personal idiosyncrasies and points at the different cultural and political conceptions of freedom in Russia, Europe, and America, as well as to a larger distinction between cultures of liberation and cultures of freedom. Caryl Emerson made the insightful observation that Russian intellectuals were often more concerned about feeling free than about acting in freedom.[39] Hence, in Russia freedom is seen as a dream of escape and radical liberation of the noble-bandit or ex-con who poses as a pretender to the throne, like Sten'ka Razin or Emelian Pugachev, whose revolt was one of Pushkin's favorite subjects of exploration. It is an object of a nostalgic or futuristic desire, not a set of rules for everyday behavior in the present. Liberation presents itself often as trespassing, transgression, or transcendence, not as a balancing act between play and responsibility at the boundary of the law. At the same time, an uncritical practice of *freedoms* in the plural, when conflated with the tyranny of the majority, might breed conformism and limit imagination. American democracy cannot become a form of manifest destiny for the world. Freedom needs its otherness, its creative individual dimension reflected in literature, philosophy, and unconventional arts of living. Thus, the imaginary dialogue between Pushkin and Tocqueville reveals political aspects of Pushkin's thought and poetic aspects of Tocqueville as well as intricate connections between the freedom of personal imagination and political frameworks that shaped artistic myths.

Perhaps what scared Pushkin most about democracy in America was not the fact that it did not work but the fact that it could. It was as if he foresaw with horror his own disappearance beyond physical death, in the desacralization of poetry itself. In the land of the "equality of conditions," there would be no need for a poet to be "the second government." The immortal monument that Pushkin was erecting for himself would have no place in the new world.

Two Concepts of Liberty beyond the Cold War: Berlin and Akhmatova

Now if this were a film and not a text, there would be a fade-out and a title card: *A century later* . . . In 1946, another encounter took place that dramatized further the dialogue between *freedoms* in the plural and *freedom* in the singular, between aesthetics, heroism, and democratic imperatives. The protagonists are Isaiah Berlin and Anna Akhmatova: he is a student of the liberal tradition, of Constant, Mill, and Tocqueville, and she is a great twentieth-century poet and unconventional Pushkinist, who responded to many of his poems, including "From Pindemonte."[40] More important, as if echoing Tocqueville's famous prediction of the future opposition of Russia / USSR and America, their meeting took place at the very outbreak of the cold war. Akhmatova, who, in Berlin's words, always saw herself as an actress on the world-historical stage, believed that their meeting ushered in the cold war. "What he and I will accomplish will confound the twentieth century," wrote Akhmatova in a passage of *Poem without a Hero*, dedicated to her meeting with Berlin.[41] Berlin stated that the encounter with Akhmatova was one of the most important events in his life. They talked about life, art, and everything in between. Political, artistic, and existential freedom might not have been spelled out as their main subject but haunted everything that was said and what remained unsaid. I would suggest that this encounter (among other things) inspired Berlin to shape his own theory of positive and negative freedom as well as his notions of cultural pluralism.

The meeting with Berlin had tragic consequences for Akhmatova; she was under constant surveillance, and her spending the night in conversation with Berlin unleashed Stalin's fury. "So our nun is receiving British spies?" Stalin was reputed to have asked A. A. Zhdanov, whom he had charged with Soviet cultural policy. In Zhdanov's famous resolution, Akhmatova was called a "half-harlot, half-nun," condemned as a representative of the old Petersburgian, not Leningradian, culture.[42] Soon after the resolution appeared, her son was rearrested and sent back to the Gulag. The year 1946 marked a major change in Soviet politics, the beginning of the cold war and the last wave of the purges, this time against the Jewish doctors who were referred to as cosmopolitans and "Zionist Fascist" collaborators. Berlin's relatives, whom he visited in Moscow, were arrested as well. Obviously, no one could have predicted the whims of Stalin's late politics, and Berlin's visit was most likely only one pretext among many for the political paranoia of the late 1940s in the Soviet Union.

Berlin recollects that the Soviet Union in the winter of 1945–1946 was a tragic "fools' paradise," in a state of limbo between the victory over fascism that promised a new openness toward Russia's war allies, the British and the Americans, and an impending cold war. Berlin found himself in the Soviet Union in 1945 as a translator and secretary at the British Embassy in Moscow, which had a shortage of Russian interpreters. This was Berlin's first return to the country where he grew up and to the city of Leningrad–St. Petersburg where he had witnessed as a boy the unfolding of the Russian Revolution. In Berlin's account, published in 1980, he wandered into a writers' bookstore on Nevsky Prospect and by sheer accident was invited to the "Fontanka House" of Anna Akhmatova for a meager feast of boiled potatoes. She lived in a remarkable mansion on the Fontanka that had been subdivided into a dozen communal apartments, constituting a sort of collective panopticon. In the middle of the conversation, a strange incident occurred. Berlin recalled hearing his name called from the yard of Akhmatova's house. It was Randolph Churchill, Winston Churchill's son and a fellow student at Oxford, who wanted to buy caviar in Leningrad and needed Berlin to translate for him. Randolph Churchill acted like a "tipsy undergraduate completely oblivious to the circumstances." Yet the appearance of Churchill's son in Akhmatova's yard was responsible for the onslaught of persecution that came upon Akhmatova.

The encounter has some curious theatrical aspects that have a direct bearing on the question of freedom and its social staging. In his own description, Berlin acts as a timid, slightly repressed Englishman cast in a play whose script he does not fully understand. The meeting is marked by a deep intimacy and also a disjuncture, an incommensurability of sorts. The first transgression that occurs is that of the conventions of time and space. Berlin thinks of Akhmatova as Christina Rossetti or as an "exiled queen," while for her he is "a guest from the future" and a link to the past. Cut off from the rest of the world, with her only son under arrest, Akhmatova could not help but feel that the meeting was her link to the outside world, an Ariadne's thread out of her claustrophobic existence. The evening extends into late morning, defying all conventions of small talk—this was not a love affair, but something much more interesting.

Moreover, Russian and English conceptions of public and private clearly differ. Akhmatova appears regal in her confinement. She is a prisoner of her communal space and a queen of a phantom world of her imagination. Berlin is for her at once a stranger and a native. At first, she recites Byron's *Don Juan* in an incomprehensible English with an intensity that embarrasses him. Berlin looks out the window in order not to meet her eye. Akhmatova's declamatory style, as if before a stadium of people, is incongruous with their chamber setting. It is as if only in the private sphere, in the off-hours, can she recreate her ideal public world where nostalgia for world culture rules.

No conventional understanding of cultural difference would be able to account for this unconventional encounter. Akhmatova speaks to Berlin about the Renaissance and about the world culture of which she and Mandelshtam have dreamed. She imagines them playing on the stage of the world's theater. Akhmatova does not make a distinction between Russia and England, but rather tells Berlin that he comes from the "world of human beings" to which Russia used to belong. In other words, no national or Herderian model of culture applies here. If he first thinks of her as a Russian/Soviet poet, she does everything to undermine that, speaking of the pagan and "un-Russian" world of her childhood in the Crimea and her commitment to the cosmopolitan ideal of what Goethe understood as "world literature." Isaiah Berlin for her is an ideal addressee, a fellow citizen of the free world of culture. Akhmatova reads to Berlin her *Poem without a Hero*, which he finds mysterious and evocative and asks her to annotate, explaining the intertextual references, hints, and personal allusions. She refuses to do so. She wrote it, in her view, for "eternity." Her conception of dialogue goes beyond contemporaneity, paying tribute to Osip Mandelshtam's poetic notion of *sobesednik*, the ideal cosmopolitan and poetically hermaphroditic addressee.[43] Akhmatova writes for readers without borders, temporal and spatial, not for future fact finders.

The night-long conversation between Akhmatova and Berlin turns occasionally intimate. For her, it is almost a love affair *via negativa*, a platonic love—not at first sight but first conversation.[44] The moment of intimacy comes when he compares her to Donna Anna in *Don Giovanni*, moving his Swiss cigar to and fro and tracing Mozart's melody in the air between them. She would later evoke this moment in a poem about the visit of Aeneas to Dido in war-wracked Carthage. Berlin was rather embarrassed by this comparison and even complained to Joseph Brodsky about it. "Indeed, he was no Aeneas," commented Brodsky.[45] Yet Brenda Tripp, Berlin's colleague on the trip, recalls that after seeing Akhmatova Berlin threw himself on the bed in his room with the words "I'm in love, I'm in love."[46] (Many years later, when Akhmatova learned that Berlin had gotten married, she commented in her usual acerbic manner that "the bird is now in a golden cage.") So retrospectively, their conversation is an impossible encounter between the captive queen and the liberal in a golden cage. He is only a bourgeois professor, after all, a little too cautious in his liberal arts. Thus, in the social art of freedom both succeed and fail. She risked more, paid a higher price, and had more at stake.

In discussing literature, they both agree and disagree. He loves Turgenev and Chekhov, the most "British" of Russian writers, known for subtlety, nuance, and moderation, rather uncharacteristic in Russian culture in general. She prefers Pushkin, Kafka, and Dostoevsky, whom he could hardly stomach.[47] (Could it have been a flirtation on her part, a plea against moderation and for a more risky intimacy, which he missed?) In his tastes, Berlin is ultimately a nineteenth-century man, who reads literature either as a twin sister of intellectual history or as a morality tale of creative personalities. Berlin's thinking harks back to that moment in the nineteenth century when liberals and Romantics shared the values of creative and self-transforming individuality. As a poet, Akhmatova does not subscribe to Romantic aesthetics; it is not by chance that in her youth she was close to one of the most anti-Romantic literary schools of the twentieth century, the Acmeists. While writing in the form of a personal diary, she did not conflate life and text. As Victor Shklovsky wrote in an early review of her work, when elements of life become art, they are estranged, they become devices of literature, not of biography; but Berlin is not concerned with the modernist literary imagination.

For Berlin, Akhmatova is a model of the integrity that he noted in Russian thinkers; she never utters a single anti-Soviet word, rather, appears patriotic, yet her literary work is an indictment of the Soviet system. By no means a political dissident, Akhmatova was a model of Pushkinian inner freedom, which in the circumstances of the Soviet Union acquired political significance. One of Akhmatova's early poems exemplifies a striking conception of personal freedom: "In the intimacy of two people there is an inviolable line that can be crossed neither in tenderness, nor in passion."[48] This line, like that verge in the circle of providence and freedom, does not destroy but rather enables both love and poetry. Akhmatova's own behavior somehow embodied the poem and challenged it.

In my view, the meeting with Akhmatova was fundamental for Berlin's conception of liberty and pluralism of "the ends of life." In an interview with Steven Lukes, Berlin describes himself as a supporter of Roosevelt's New Deal policy and certain forms of European socialism rather than of Hayek's libertarian and economic definition of freedom. Yet, he is profoundly anti-Marxist and anti-Hegelian. His visit to the Soviet Union confirmed his deep antipathy to any form of deterministic ideology that regards human beings as instrumentalizable human material for building a bright future. While Berlin is more sympathetic than other liberal thinkers to the aspirations of national recognition, in the encounter with Akhmatova the discussion of freedom does not follow national or cultural boundaries. If anything, the participants reveal differences within themselves, their multiple ways of belonging and occasionally their foreignness to themselves.

In his essay "Two Concepts of Liberty," Berlin offers a critique of "positive freedom." His conception, however, is far from binary. Positive freedom is associated with the notion of self-discipline and self-mastery that leads to a collective mastery over the "crooked timber of humanity" so dear to Berlin. Negative freedom is defined at first as freedom from coercion and from government interference into an individual's private life, but it is not limited to this Anglo-American conception and is imbued with positive creative potential. Another cross-cultural dialogue takes place between the lines of Berlin's often paradoxical description. Berlin states that negative freedom is not the sine qua non of democracy. Here Berlin continues the critique of the tyranny of the majority carried on by Tocqueville, Mill, and Herzen.

For Berlin, the greatest Russian thinker of freedom was not Pushkin, but Alexander Herzen, whom he places somewhere between Tocqueville and Marx. Herzen develops further the creative dimensions of the individual freedom that in his view should never be sacrificed for the sake of either democratic conformity or revolutionary brotherhood. This was one of Berlin's favorite quotes from Herzen: "Why is liberty valuable? Because it is an end in itself, because it is what it is. To bring it as a sacrifice to something else is simply to perform an act of human sacrifice."[49]

Herzen is caught between two shores: the Russian wealth of personality and imagination without political rights and the growing "philistinism" and middle-class conformity that he witnesses in the more democratic regimes in the West. In the end, in spite of his insights into Russian history and disillusionment with Romanticism, Herzen admires the Russian peasant commune much more than Western civic middle-class associations celebrated by many Western liberals. As for Berlin he prefers not to choose between his beloved Herzen, whose Romantic personality and lucid thinking he cherishes, and a more sober Mill, whose political views might be closer to his own.

Berlin does not agree with Mill that genius can only survive in a democratic society.[50] Akhmatova and other Russian artists are ample proof of the opposite. They have the highest appreciation of minimal personal liberty for its own sake. Berlin's negative freedom has a dimension that is not reducible to political rights; it also has to be a freedom of potentialities (not merely rational choices) and of those infinite improbabilities that constitute the best moments of a human life. Some thirty years after writing "Two Concepts of Liberty," Berlin gives a revealing explanation of his vision: "Negative freedom is about how many doors are open to you, positive freedom is about who governs you."[51] Here we witness an interesting reversal: Berlin's negative freedom is described as enabling and "positive" in its potential, while positive freedom is about power that restricts human beings and keeps them in their place. Moreover, the metaphor of the open door comes directly from Akhmatova's poetic cycle "Cinque," the last part of which was dedicated to their meeting: "You, living, and not in my dream, do you hear my calling? / That door that you cracked open, I have no strength to close."[52] In Akhmatova's poem the door is only half-opened, but she courageously refuses to slam it. Berlin's "negative freedom" does not automatically mean democracy,[53] but at the same time, it becomes clear from a footnote to "Two Concepts of Liberty" that Berlin takes for granted the existence of fundamental political and human rights even if his notion of liberty is not reducible to them. The footnote has a complementary and contradictory relationship to the main body of the text; it makes a clear distinction between the choices in totalitarian and democratic societies and does not reduce possibilities to consumer choices.

> Negative liberty is something the extent of which, in a given case, is difficult to estimate. It might, prima facie, seem to depend simply on the power to choose between at any rate two alternatives. Nevertheless, not all choices are equally free, or free at all. If in a totalitarian State I betray my friend under the threat of torture, perhaps even if I act from fear of losing my job, I can reasonably say that I did not act freely. . . . The mere existence of alternatives is not, therefore, enough to make my action free . . . in the normal sense of the word. The extent of my freedom seems to depend on (*a*) how many possibilities are open to me . . . ; (*b*) how easy or difficult each of those possibilities is to actualize; (*c*) how important in my plan of life, given my character and circumstances, these possibilities are when compared with each other; (*d*) how far they are closed and opened by deliberate human acts; (*e*) what value not merely the agent, but the general sentiment of the society in which he lives, puts on the various possibilities.[54]

Berlin's conception of negative liberty is not a continuation of Pushkinian "inner freedom." While Berlin loved Pushkin's poetry, he did not see the poet's centrality in Russian intellectual history in the way that many Russian thinkers and writers do. In his essay on Belinsky, Berlin describes Pushkin's attitudes toward the emerging, increasingly democratic literary culture and speaks about the poet's "snobbery, his intermittent attempts to pretend that he was an aristocratic dilettante and not a professional man of letters at all, and his avoidance of meeting Belinsky, deeming him 'unpresentable' and embarrassing to his aristocratic sensibility."[55] In "Two Concepts of Liberty" Berlin does not identify negative freedom with inner freedom. Rather, he seems to regard the Stoic and Christian model of the inner citadel as a form of radical self-mastery and the other side of the positive freedom that could coexist with political unfreedom. Berlin reverses Epictetus's statement about internal liberation. In response to Epictetus's statement that his leg can be chained but his will cannot be chained even by Zeus, Berlin proposes his own parable: "I have a wound in my leg. There are two methods of freeing myself from pain. One is to heal the wound, but if the cure is too difficult and uncertain, there is another method: I can get rid of my wound by cutting off my leg . . ."[56] Epictetus, the former slave, might have felt freer than his master, but the conception of self-liberation that he had created was an antithesis to political freedom. Rather, it was an unfree man's way of surviving with dignity in the imperial age. Similarly, the inner freedom and personal integrity cultivated by Akhmatova was a form of resistance in extremely oppressive circumstances, but to idealize or romanticize it would be to disrespect her and to perpetuate the oppression. Berlin does not share the pernicious belief that censorship is always conducive to good poetic metaphors.

What Berlin learns from Akhmatova is both the need for pluralism of the ends of life and its limitations. The limitation is a question of political rights, without which a romanticization of inner freedom (when it is not the only choice or a matter of absolute necessity, as was the case for Akhmatova) can turn into a tacit acceptance of political servitude. While Berlin amplifies the notion of *freedoms* in the plural, including poetic freedom, he does not collapse the distinction between *freedom* and *freedoms*. When the word *freedom* claims the singular, whichever beautiful qualifying adjective precedes it, it becomes a threat to pluralism. Moreover, in his conception *freedom* and *system* are antonyms. (This definition comes from Brodsky, who saw Berlin's essay not as a philosophical piece but as "a gut reaction" to the disasters of the twentieth century.) Nevertheless, Berlin does not propose like Tocqueville or even Mill to educate democracy. Sometimes Berlin's agonistic liberalism, his concept of incommensurability of different cultures and of individual "ends of life," leaves us with more questions than answers, yet his own dialogical form of writing and speaking always invites further deliberation.

The encounter between Berlin and Akhmatova, notwithstanding its tragic consequences for the poet, had another dimension that was dear to both of them. It was a great adventure, infinitely improbable in the Leningrad of 1945. As such, it pushed the thresholds of time and space, and in spite of its many incommensurabilities, became one of those perfect moments of human spontaneity and conversation, a night of freedom. In one of his rather positive, in my view, definitions of negative freedom, Berlin offers us another version of the open-ended cross-cultural dialogue with many potentialities, not imagined as cultural incommensurabilities. Freedom is obviously not happiness, often quite the opposite of it, yet occasionally the two coincide in a lucky moment of encounter and of *"bon-heur."* It is, in Berlin's poetic description, a moment of unplanned *"douceur de vivre,"* of "loose texture and toleration," of "idle talk and idle curiosity without authorization and without any conscious hope for success that is worth more than the neatest and the most delicately fashioned imposed pattern."[57]

Figure 9. Svetlana Boym, chessboard college combining photographs of the Dostoevsky monument in Omsk, Russia, and the Marx monument in Moscow, Russia, with a nineteenth-century caricature on Sacher-Masoch and the "master-slave dialectic."

THREE

LIBERATION WITH A BIRCH ROD
AND THE BANALITY OF TERRORISM

Modern/Antimodern: Dostoevsky's Dialogues

Political liberty is a sham liberty, the worst possible slavery; the appearance of liberty and therefore the reality of servitude.[1]

Friedrich Engels

Shortly after his *liberté, egalité, fraternité* was proclaimed. Liberty. What liberty? Equal liberty for everyone to do anything he wants to within the limits of the law. When may you do anything you want to? When you have millions. Does liberty give each person a million? No. What is the person without a million? The person without a million is not the one who does anything he wants to. . . . Understand me: voluntary, completely conscious self-sacrifice . . . is, in my opinion, a sign of . . . the highest form of self-mastery, the greatest freedom of one's own will."

Feodor Dostoevsky[2]

What happens when we think of political liberty as disguised servitude and consider modern experience itself to be a carnival of inauthenticity and phantasmagoria? How far are we prepared to go in search of radical liberation, and how much violence and sacrifice are required for that goal? What is the price of uncorrupted sacrifice, and does the end justify the means? And finally, how does this struggle for radical liberation and against democratic political freedoms and the public sphere link seemingly unlikely bedfellows on the radical left and radical right, those messiahs of socialist atheism and the prophets of the newfound religion that populate Dostoevsky's work?

While some of these questions appear contemporary, they were already being broadly debated in the middle of the nineteenth century. After the failure of the revolutions of 1848 in Europe there was a sense of disillusionment among many politicians, writers, and intellectuals with the slogans of the French Revolution, *liberté, égalité,* and *fraternité,* and with the idea of liberal reform in general. While major acts of political liberation—the abolition of serfdom in Russia (1861) and abolition of slavery in the United States (1862)—took place only a year apart, there was a new understanding that political freedoms alone don't offer a grid for happiness. From the left to the right, a more radical version of freedom was proposed, a liberation of the human species through ultimate salvation in paradise—on earth or elsewhere. The space of this freedom was no longer a public or private realm but another world altogether. Political rights barely acquired and secured in a few European countries suddenly appeared bourgeois, insufficient, and nearly obsolete; it also appeared that the fences and partitions that constituted the fragile architecture of the public sphere would crumble like a house of cards, the gamble of the bourgeoisie. The case of the Russian empire is particularly striking since there the radical discourses of liberation ranged from anarchism to populism, from socialism to Slavophile utopianism, and all of them developed in the context of the absolute monarchy. If in Europe one can speak about the crisis of liberal thinking, the disillusionment with parliamentary politics, and the development of industrial capitalism, in Russia the critique of democratic freedoms took place in a largely preliberal society (with only very limited citizen rights granted after the reforms of 1862). Yet Russian writers and later some politicians thought of using their belatedness to their advantage and imagined themselves in the vanguard of European liberation. They did so with artistic vengeance and with a characteristic superiority-inferiority complex. Ultimately, they dreamed of catching up and surpassing the West and liberating the West from itself. Such dreams are still alive in the twenty-first century.

In the center of my discussion will be the conception of what Dostoevsky called a "freer freedom," imagined while in the penal colony and developed further in the literary and political underground that included writers, political radicals, and self-described terrorists of the nineteenth century. Sometimes this "freer freedom" appears to be a kind of photographic negative of the architecture of worldliness and public freedom; it is empowered by the authority of divine legislation and the "malignant pleasure" of suffering. The quest for freedom will involve crossing the border between East and West and a reconsideration of cultural difference. Traveling with Dostoevsky, eastward to Siberia and then westward to Europe (by way of the underground), we will encounter strange fellow travelers—Karl Marx, Charles Baudelaire, Leopold Sacher-Masoch, and Mikhail Bakunin, who offered different visions of the modern phantasmagoria, master-slave dialectics, and dreams of liberation. Knowing the cast of characters and their fascinating and explosive tempers, one could only imagine that their actual encounters in the urban crowd or on the train would have produced nothing but mutual irritation. So we will focus on the virtual encounters to help us understand the radical staging of modern freedom from a variety of perspectives.

In the view of the Russian critic and philosopher Mikhail Bakhtin, Dostoevsky's novels offer us a unique literary form and with it a vision of the human condition in which dialogue is not a means to an end but an end in itself, a form of unfinalizable and creative human communication. This dialogue is liberating because it is about being with the other, experiencing joy and wonder together.[3] Multivoicedness, or heteroglossia, in Dostoevsky doesn't occur merely on the level of the character but goes into the deep architectonics of language and communication, revealing an inner plurality of words that is deeply antiauthoritarian.[4] Bakhtin's creative reading of Dostoevsky sounds like a philosophy of freedom. But what is the nature of the philosopher's own dialogue with Dostoevsky? Are Dostoevsky's texts pretexts for Bakhtin's freedom-loving polemics?

Hannah Arendt's observations about the nature of Dostoevsky's dialogical imagination take a different interpretative road. Her fragmented lecture notes on *The Possessed* are all that we know about her reading of Dostoevsky, but they are very suggestive:

Please be aware of the unique form of dialogue in these [Dostoevsky's] novels: it is as though naked soul speaks to naked soul. Intimacy approaching telepathy, i.e., the abolition of all distances; what somebody says is answered by: I knew it; . . . Compared with intimacy of this intensity, Western civilized society is hypocritical, full of lies; here all appearances immediately lead into the interior of the soul. The appearance is never a facade.

Most important however is this: the world, as an objective datum, is somehow absent. No description, it not a topic of dialogue; hence the multitude of perspectives from which you can see it (Balzac) is absent. The topic is not the world but some ultimate concern.

The intimacy can be realized only within one's own people.[5]

Where Bakhtin saw the uniquely creative "architectonics" of dialogue, at whose center is a human being, Arendt found telepathic, intimate communication that might result in the disappearance of worldliness and the public realm. She observed that the two sides of "intimacy" in Dostoevsky, particularly, when it is "within one's own people (i.e., the Russian people, in his case); such intimacy creates intense and powerful relationships between people but it might also jeopardize the worldly architecture of facades, squares, and common spaces for the sake of the "ultimate concern." Telepathic communication might become a monologic projection; by dissolving distances, it can end up dissolving differences, discarding inner plurality and pluralism alike. Her brief remarks challenge a long-standing twentieth-century Western tradition—from existentialists to, more recently, philosopher Emmanuel Levinas—that regards Dostoevsky as a great humanist and ethical thinker. Perhaps the time has come to deliberate the ethics of radical national liberation?

Bakhtin considered Dostoevsky-the-novelist to be a modern Prometheus who set his novelistic heroes free to dialogize with and contradict their creator: "Just like Goethe's Prometheus Dostoevsky doesn't create voiceless slaves, like Zeus, but free people who can stand next to their creator and not agree with him."[6] We remember that the Prometheus of the ancient tragedy and of Goethe's poem teaches humans the transient arts of freedom. The Greek Titan transformed the ritual of sacrifice into a negotiation that challenges divinity rather than blindly submitting to it. Yet in his non-novelistic texts, especially in *The Diary of a Writer*, Dostoevsky attacks the Promethean freedoms of modern man, advocating a voluntary self-conscious submission and a new form of sacrifice that redeems all the corruption of the secular age. Moreover, in his political views, Dostoevsky embraces absolute monarchy and the tsar / Zeus and stages a very different scenario of power. Is there, then, a contradiction between Dostoevsky's multivoiced novels and his explicit ideological positions stated in *The Diary of the Writer*? In other words, is this a productive and thought-provoking dialogue between a (free) literary form and (liberational conservative) politics and religion? Or does a larger dialogue within Dostoevsky's corpus put the dialogical tolerance itself into question? What is the relationship between the rhetoric of *conversation* and the rhetoric of *conversion*, between unfinalizable dialogue and the endless spin of ressentiment, between worldly human theatricality and the higher ideals of ultimate intimacy in the national community?

Moreover, in his novels (especially *The Possessed*) Dostoevsky is more engaged with Dionysian *manias* and orgies than with Promethean skills. Dostoevsky's art and life did not escape their own tragic contradictions: he was one of the most modern nineteenth-century writers, an innovator of the European novel who expanded its physical space and metaphysical range and staged the crisis of modern personality in the disenchanted world of worrying beliefs. He is also an outspokenly antimodern writer, who in the latter part of his life cherished the utopian vision of the Russian community and the unlimited God-given authority of the tsar. Dostoevsky is a modern antimodernist, at once dialogic and authoritarian. He masterfully uses the forms of the European novel to wage war between Russia and Europe to transform the West forever, playing it in and out of the heightened consciousness of his unforgettable protagonists. He can be considered one of the great anti-Occidentalists in the Occidental tradition.

My focus will be largely on Dostoevsky's notes and travelogues, more specifically the trilogy of "notes": *Notes from the House of the Dead*, the writer's fictionalized account of his life in the penal colony in Siberia; *Winter Notes on Summer Impressions*, a theatrical, autobiographical travelogue to Europe via Russian cultural myths; and the *Notes from Underground* (1864), an explicitly fictionalized account of the thoughts of a Petersburg paradoxicalist in his voluntary self-imprisonment.

Mine will be a drama in seven acts with recurring themes. I will focus on the alternative architecture of the "freer freedom" dreamed in prison and in the underground, and the way in which it shapes attitudes toward law, politics, and violence (occasionally erasing differences between corporal punishment and domestic violence, the self-inflicted pleasure of pain, and the penal procedures of the Russian state). As an effect of this architecture, the place of physical violence in Dostoevsky's work will be examined, followed by the transformation of political violence into the philosophy of suffering that becomes a proof of authenticity and a foundation of moral authority. A prominent place in this discussion belongs to the perverse praise of flogging and the "malicious pleasure" of pain that brings together Dostoevsky and Sacher-Masoch. From the inward and upward journey in search of the freer freedom, we will move the journey westwards and examine encounters of Dostoevsky, Baudelaire, and Marx with the modern city as well as their reflections on modern theatricality and phantasmagoria. Finally we will examine the political implications of malignant pleasure and confront the heroes of Dostoevsky's "novel-pamphlet," *The Possessed*, which offers a novelistic reflection on the historical trial of the self-proclaimed terrorist Sergei Nechaev, the disciple of the famous anarchist Mikhail Bakunin, and offers an anatomy of the conspiracy of radical liberation. With echoes of Euripidean *Bacchae*, the novel offers a striking portrayal of the terrorist as a man of inspirational clichés, a "petty demon" and not a glamorous demigod, who is nevertheless capable of wreaking incredible destruction. Such an inspired portrayal of the everyday pettiness of a terrorist instigator might become in turn an inspirational model for a twenty-first-century novelist.

At the end of his life Dostoevsky returns to his beginning and rewrites the freer freedom and his experiences in *Notes from the House of the Dead*, "remembering" his conversion to the Russian religion of the people with the help of the peasant Marei. He promises reconciliation, a cure for modern alienation, and a redemption of the tragic contradictions of modern existence.

Freer Freedom in Prison

> Here is the end of my wandering: 'I am in prison!' I constantly repeated to myself; 'here is my anchorage for many long years' . . . But who knows? Perhaps when, after many years, the time comes for me to leave it, I shall be sorry to go! . . ." I added, not without an element of malignant pleasure which is sometimes almost a craving to reopen one's wounds—as though one could be in love with one's own pain, as though one found true pleasure in the realization of the full extent of one's misery.
>
> In consequence of our day dreaming and our long divorce from it, freedom appeared to us here [in prison], somehow freer than real freedom, that exists in fact, in real life.[7]
>
> Feodor Dostoevsky, *Notes from the House of the Dead*

How is it possible to be homesick for prison and imagine the "freer freedom" from a vantage of deprivation and confinement? The *Notes from the House of the Dead* is a paradoxical text that presents at once a striking condemnation of the Russian prison system and the anatomy of the "malignant pleasure" that transforms the penal colony into a spiritual home of the freer freedom.

Dostoevsky had the particular misfortune to die several deaths. Arrested as a member of the Petrushevsky Circle, the group engaged in a discussion of European socialism, democratic reforms, and the abolition of serfdom in Russia, he was placed in the Peter and Paul Fortress in St. Petersburg and then sentenced by the tsar to a "civil death" (that is, deprivation of all rights as a citizen and a member of the gentry estate) followed by actual death by firing squad. The writer and his comrades were brought out to the Semenov Square in St. Petersburg, where they kneeled in front of their executioners, who proceeded to break the swords over their heads, performing the ritual of civil annihilation. Dostoevsky, standing in the second group of the condemned, saw the soldiers advance toward the stake and raise their rifles in order to execute the prisoners. At that last moment, as the sun was rising over Petersburg, something astonishing happened: the tsar's messenger arrived at the scene of the execution announcing the imperial pardon. The tsar had orchestrated the spectacle of this "unfinished execution" from beginning to end, managing to instill terror and perverse gratitude at once in the hearts of some of his former enemies. Mock execution was followed by a mock resurrection granted by the tsar. The writer's sentence was commuted to forced labor in the penal colony in Siberia.

In his letters to his brother Mikhail, Dostoevsky expresses great anxiety about another possible death following his "civil death"—that is, his death as a writer: "If writing is to be forbidden, I will perish. Better to be locked up for fifteen years but with a pen in my hands." Dostoevsky writes that his head is filled with unconsummated projects and "not yet embodied images" (*ne polnost'iu voploshchennye*). Thus the experience of an unconsummated execution was accompanied by this unconsummated death of a writer. As Nancy Ruttenburg observes, the writer found himself in a state of deep estrangement, or a "conversio interrupta, in which the process of rebirth is protracted and indefinite." *Notes from the House of the Dead* then is an unprecedented literary document that attempts to reverse the writer's civil death through the process of writing and publication of a text. The composition of the *Notes* is a form of self-liberation and a writerly resurrection. They are framed by two fictitious narrators—a polite nobleman who introduces the text, and the author of the prison memoir, Gorianchikov, who, unlike Dostoevsky, is not a political prisoner but a common murderer guilty of killing his wife. Goriachnikov writes in a straightforward, sympathetic yet unsentimental manner, without the paradoxical humor and dialogical experimentation that characterize Dostoevsky's later novelistic style. The ellipses and fragmentation of Gorianchikov's memoir capture the nature of the estrangement and horror of the prison experience. The chronicler is not a man of ressentiment, the way the Underground Man would be; he is a survivor and an estranged observer who cannot afford any additional self-laceration and spite. Twenty years later, Dostoevsky would attempt to bridge this gap of estrangement and rewrite his prison experiences in the light of his conversion to the Russian communal religion that requires suffering and sacrifice. In this original text, there are gaps in the narration and vague dreams and no mention whatsoever of the legendary peasant Marei who brought about the writer's spiritual rebirth. Instead, the work dwells on the contradictions of malignant pleasure, of the double bind of victim and executioner and on the paradoxes of freedom in this "living hell" of Siberian wilderness. Incarceration and the threat of physical violence go together with mental torture, the deprivation of privacy, difficult for everyone but especially for the political prisoners who cannot retreat even into the citadel of one's inner freedom. The architecture of the penal colony becomes internalized, shaping the stuff of prisoners' dreams. A hundred years after Dostoevsky, the prisoners of the Soviet Gulag, from Varlam Shalamov to Evgeniia Ginzburg and Alexander Solzhenitsyn, would look back at *Notes from the House of the Dead* as a foundational fiction of the Russian penal "zone."

In the colony the convicts develop their own techniques of survival and cherish any minor form of temporal liberation. "There was a convict whose favorite occupation, in his spare time, was to count the pales of the stockade. There were about fifteen hundred of them, and he knew them all by their position and characteristics. For him, each one of them meant a day; each day he counted off one pale, and in this way, from the number remaining still uncounted, he could see at a glance how many days he must still spend in the prison before the end of his term of servitude."[8] The convict inhabits the border zone between the colony and the "free world," reappropriating the stockade for his own unofficial game of hope and exercise in patience. Each miniscale corner of unguarded and unregimented space in the penal colony offers a coveted escape into a retreat of solitude from where one can dream of the freer freedom. Utilitarian activities, like smuggling and working, become curious liberational techniques when they are performed for their own sake, defying imposed servitude. Work is seen as a form of escape and smuggling is treated as an art: "The smuggler works for love of it, because he has a vocation. He is in some sense a poet."[9] The moment of grace, the cessation of violence and reconciliation among prisoners, is achieved through shared artistic experience and not through common religious faith. The theatrical performances put together by the prisoners themselves bring forth their human and creative potential. While in his other texts Dostoevsky tends to condemn theater, especially vaudeville and melodrama, here the prisoners' amateur performances appear as an important form of self-realization that offer a gasp of freedom.

In the unwritten Russian prison law, artistic abilities, from storytelling to music playing, are highly valued among prisoners, while utilitarian pursuits are viewed with suspicion. Thus a prisoner could blow all his money in a fit of festive debauchery or violate his promises to return a debt, informing on the pawnbroker instead. What matters is spontaneous sincerity of action, the expression of Russian *volia*, not any formal or informal contracts or pledges. Dostoevsky makes the profound insight that the experience in the penal colony neither cures nor disciplines prisoners: "Prison and penal servitude do not, of course, reform the criminal . . . In the criminal himself, prison and the most strenuous forms of hard labor develop only hatred, a thirst for forbidden pleasures, and terrible irresponsibility . . . Of course the criminal, rebelling against society, hates it and thinks himself innocent and it guilty."[10]

Something else is at stake here beyond the prisoner's rebellion against society and the harsh conditions of penal servitude. In fact, the unwritten law of the penal colony erases the distinction between just and unjust punishment, between political and civil crime, between criminals and innocents as they exist in the outside world. "There was hardly one of the prisoners who in his heart acknowledged his own lawlessness. If anyone who was not one of themselves had reproached a prisoner with his crime or reviled him for it (although it is not in the Russian spirit to upbraid the sinner), there would have been no end to the cursing and swearing."[11] An example of this is that perpetrators of crimes vastly different in degree—a man who was unjustly accused of parricide, a Pole arrested for protesting the Russian partition of Poland, and a man who murdered for pleasure a five-year-old girl—receive similar treatment.

The penal colony is a place where violence of all kinds is perpetrated, and the distinctions between victim and victimizer are sometimes blurred. But what are not blurred are the national and class and estate (*soslovie*) differences. In fact, one of the striking scenes of flogging depicted in the text involves an elderly Polish political prisoner, Ziolkowski. His "crime" is that he inadvertently challenges the rule of the sadistic camp commander and insists on differentiating between the criminals and political prisoners. "The old man was beaten. He lay down under the rods without protest, bit his hand and endured the punishment without a groan or a murmur and without moving a muscle."[12] After the flogging (which was not practiced in Poland and from which the "gentry" prisoners were supposed to be exempt), Ziolkowski goes to the barrack without a word and begins praying. While Ziolkowski gains instant respect from his fellow convicts for not "crying out" under the rod, he and the other Polish prisoners are treated with some suspicion by the Russian narrator. The Poles don't easily forgive their executioners, don't open themselves up, and keep their distance from their fellow prisoners, and in the law of prison, sincerity and open-heartedness are occasionally valued more highly than fairness and courage.

Dostoevsky was one of the first writers in Russia to bring public attention to the conditions of the penal colony. He offered a profound psychological and political analysis of its effects: "The right given to one man to inflict corporal punishment on another is one of the ulcers of society, one of the most powerful destructive agents of every germ and every budding attempt at civilization, the fundamental cause of its certain and irretrievable destruction."[13] The experience forges a bond between the victim and the executioner perpetuating cruelty. Moreover, Dostoevsky considers such a system of corporal punishment to be profoundly "anti-Christian." Once a human being experiences this intoxicating power of humiliating "a human being like himself, a brother according to the Christian law," he becomes addicted to it and is no longer "a master but a servant of his own sensations." In Dostoevsky's analysis of the master-slave dialectic, tyranny becomes an everyday habit and develops into a disease. The practice of the "absolute freedom" of inflicting pain on others doesn't liberate masters but turns them into the slaves of their own sweet "malignant pleasure."[14]

At first glance the *Notes* poses a contradiction between such insightful analysis of the psychological effects of the policies and practices of corporal punishment during the period of the Russian empire and the systematic erasure of political discourse. It becomes clear that the very notion of "political justice" in this text becomes synonymous with a discord between nations and social groups in the writer's later work: or perhaps the very notion of political justice is linked to the Western style of thinking altogether. Gorianchikov is not a political prisoner but a wife murderer, guilty of a crime of passion that allows him to find a common language with other prisoners by listening to their stories of domestic violence and crimes of passion. The experience of violence of any kind—already posited as a road to tyranny and moral servitude—becomes a national bonding experience. The political is domesticated and transfigured into the national. The agency of the executioners and the executed, victimizers and victims, is less crucial than the experience of violence and suffering itself. This way all avoid responsibility for the circle of violence, except for the "irritable and misanthropic" Poles who don't know how to forgive the corporal punishment inflicted upon them and do not seem to comprehend this Russian pleasure toward suffering.

A paradoxical nostalgia for a certain "sincerity" of the prison experience with its clear bars and fetters permeates the text:

> Here is the end of my wandering: I am in prison!' I constantly repeated to myself; 'here is my anchorage for many long years . . . But who knows? Perhaps when, after many years, the time comes for me to leave it, I shall be sorry to go! . . ." I added, not without an element of malignant pleasure which is sometimes almost a craving to reopen one's wounds—as though one could be in love with one's own pain, as though one found true pleasure in the realization of the full extent of one's misery.
>
> In consequence of our day dreaming and our long divorce from it, freedom appeared to us here [in prison], somehow freer than real freedom, that exists in fact, in real life. [15]

At first this reads like a classical description of melancholia: an open wound without an object. The prisoner begins to cherish wounds for their own sake, like his fellow convicts rear up work and art for their own sake. This effort starts out as a way of surviving the trauma of punishment, a form of necessary self-estrangement. Rearing up pain is a way of appropriating it, reauthoring it, taking control of one's deep trauma.[16] Malignant pleasure is more than a mere "affliction of imagination" (which was a classic description of nostalgia and melancholia), for pain is not a metaphor. Dostoevsky easily blurs the difference between physical and mental violence. The political practice of flagellation turns into a psychological habit of self-flagellation that then legitimizes the flagellation of others. The dialectic of the "malignant pleasure" allows the dream of the "freer freedom" that is somehow "freer than real freedom . . . that exists in fact, in real life."[17]

Why do we need a "freer freedom"? Why is freedom not enough? Dostoevsky, usually the critic of eloquence, is fond of superlatives: life has to become livelier, a "living life," freedom has to be freer. A freer freedom is both unprecedented and desperately tautological, transgressive and claustrophobic. It pushes sincerity to the limit, aiming beyond the boundaries of law and civilized conventions. It is manic, and in this mania one recognizes Dionysus the tyrant of Syracuse more than Dionysus the god of wine and tragedy. Dostoevsky's philosophy of freedom underwent a

radical transformation during his years in prison. It was no longer a book-
ishly romantic liberty straight from Schiller's *The Robbers*, the favorite play
of the young Dostoevsky, nor the socialist idealist conception of political
freedom that was at the center of the Petrushevsky circle. The practice of
radical dreaming is at once a strategy for self-liberation and a legitimation
of captivity. A freer freedom embodies lack and excess; the obvious lack
of freedom of movement in captivity produces additional emotion and an
excess of imagination.

Dostoevsky's freedom in prison is quite different from the Pushkinian
idea of aesthetic delights "far away from the tsar and the people." At the
same time, it shares in a disdain for political rights and an insistence on
inner freedom (not in its disciplined Stoic version, but in the unbound-
edness of Russian *volia*). The Stoic conception of inner freedom was "an
acropolis of the soul" that preserved the memories of democracy in an era
of empire. Dostoevsky's model is more the inner steppe, where the bandit, the saint, and the dreamer wander without restriction and exchange
roles. While disavowing politics, both Pushkin's "other freedom" and
Dostoevsky's "freer freedom" depend on the political context of censorship. Pushkin's poem exonerating censorship never passes through the
censor, and Dostoevsky lives in fear of the civil death that could put an
end to his writerly career. However, external censorship is not the main
reason for the antipolitical nature of the freer freedom. At its core is the
dream of national grandeur and reconciliation without boundaries.

Gradually, the survivor's therapeutic fantasy becomes a foundation of
the writer's philosophy. In the end the "freer freedom" perpetuates the
architecture of the prison walls that it tries to escape. Those walls expand
and circumscribe an overwhelming metaphorical camp: prisonhouse of
reason, prisonhouse of language, prisonhouse of the body, prisonhouse
of earthly life.

The One I Love Is the One I Flog: Violence and Enlightenment

> "For goodness' sake, what are you talking about?" another will say. "You in-
> tended to talk about Paris, but you've gone over to birch rods. Where is Paris
> in all this?"[18]

Winter Notes on Summer Impressions, the account of Dostoevsky's first travels to Western Europe, picks up where *Notes from the House of the Dead*
left off, with discussions of civilization and barbarism along with flogging and wife beating. The text belongs to the genre of the paradoxical

antitravelogue: Dostoevsky goes traveling to Europe in order to find a homeland and to alienate his own cultural alienation. Dostoevsky's motto in the account of his European journey is sincerity over accuracy. The stakes of a writer's sincerity are painfully high and are more important than observations of foreign life, exploration, and wonder. This is not a journey of discovery of foreign and unfamiliar lands but of the recovery of one's own native culture. The writer hated guidebooks with their many "places of interest" and self-interest. The guidebook for him is a model of touristic unfreedom that offers only sanitized maps of experience.[19] Dostoevsky's journey to Europe is hardly a journey of exploration or surprise. He travels to Europe to rediscover Russia, a *via negativa*, as it were. He is in dialogue not with any living Europeans but rather with Russian Europeanizers and perhaps with his own younger self.[20]

The first protagonist in the repertoire of the Russian mythology of the West is a typical Europeanized Russian nobleman of the eighteenth century. He wears the costumes of the European Enlightenment in public but preserves patriarchal habits at home, like drinking and occasionally beating his serfs and his wife. Our guide, however, is hardly outraged with the violent behavior of the so-called new Europeans. He argues that the Russian peasants understand this violence as well as the dress code; they prefer that their master wear his hierarchies on his sleeve, so to speak: "So what that they [eighteenth-century landowners] occasionally flogged the peasants to death, they still were dearer to the common people than the gentry of today, they were closer to the people." In this case, flogging is not only a form of state punishment of prisoners in the Russian empire; it turns out to be also a common practice of the courts of people's justice established in the Russian villages after the liberation of serfs in 1861. It becomes then a part of Russian folkways.[21]

Another amusing eighteenth-century anecdote that the narrator relates comes from Denis Fonvizin's comedy *The Brigadier*. Here a folksy widow tells a gentry girl, Sofia, a story about an "oh-so pretty" young captain's wife who was receiving her daily beatings from her dear husband the captain, who hit her so hard that the people in town would hear her screams and see her black-and-blue marks: "In our regiment we had a captain of the First Company by the name Gvozdilov; his wife was such a pretty young thing. Well, it happened he would get mad about something, the more when he was drunk; then as you believe in God, my dear, he nailed her to the wall, beat her, he did, until near nothing but her soul remained." "Please, Madame, cease speaking of what is revolting to humanity!" exclaims the educated and enlightened heroine of the comedy, Sofia. "You see, deary, you don't even want to hear about it. What must it have been for the captain's wife to suffer it?" responds the brigadier's widow.

Here is Dostoevsky's comment: "Thus the well-bred Sofia, with her highly cultivated sensitivity, faded before a common woman . . . But the most striking thing of all is that Gvozdilov still nails his wife to the wall and almost more comfortably than before. It's the truth. They say that it used to be done more from heart and soul. 'The one I love, they say, is the one I beat.'"[22] Once again, the "truth" that comes from heart and soul goes together with heavy beating. After all, the "so pretty" wife of Gvozdilov suffers only in her body, while her "soul remains." Sofia's protestations against wife beating are nothing but hypocrisy that comes from reading too many foreign books. Dostoevsky's sarcasm entices the reader into narrative complicity; it is directed against the civilized taboos of Russian Europeans. Not the captain who beats his wife, but a young Westernizer who dares to voice her indignation is guilty of insincerity.[23] Corporal punishment is an expression of tough love and communal wisdom, which is ultimately more sincere than formal law and the legal practices that come from Western countries, where community is not valued and "nationality is only a system of taxation."[24]

A third story that Dostoevsky relates in *Winter Notes* refers to another "naïve popular custom" dubbed by the "progressive" journalists of Dostoevsky's time the "remnants of Russian barbarism." In Russian (and not only Russian) popular custom, the wedding night would end with a public display of the bride's blood on the sheets, the cause of much merriment and debauchery on the part of inebriated wedding guests. It is worth quoting the paragraph in full to examine Dostoevsky's rhetoric of liberating Russians from the Western conception of freedom:

Indignantly, boastfully, sneeringly the newspaper reported this unheard-of barbarism "which remains even now, despite all the advances of civilization." Gentlemen, I confess to you that I burst terribly with laughter . . . This is vile, this is unchaste, this is savage, this is Slavic . . . although it was all done without any evil intention . . . in the simplicity of the soul, out of ignorance of anything better, higher, European. No, I was laughing at something else. Namely: I suddenly recalled our barin's wives and fashionable shops. Of course, now civilized ladies no longer send dainty garments to their parents, but when, for example, it comes to ordering a dress from a milliner, with what tact, with what fine calculation and a knowledge of their business do they insert padding into certain places in their charming European clothings! What is this padding for? Why, it goes without saying, for elegance, aesthetics, *pour paraître.* . . . The article had a swaggering tone, as though it did not care to acknowledge that the accusers themselves are perhaps a thousand times more vile and worse . . . This is either faith or swaggering over people or, ultimately, unreasoning, *slavish* [*rabskaia*] worship of European forms of civilization; in that case it is even more ridiculous.[25]

The difference between Slavic and European is exemplified here by various pieces of women's clothing—bloody undergarments versus padded clothing. In fact, Slavic is opposed to "slavish," here "slavish worship of European forms of civilization." We have the world of truth, honesty, simplicity of soul, and sincere suffering on the one hand, and the world of appearances on the other. Forget the embarrassment of the young bride, the exposed blood, the drunk and foul-smelling groom, and the guests. Pain and blood function as testimonies of the sincerity and freedom of the Russian character. The presumed "Russian barbarism" works as a litmus test to reveal the hypocrisies of a civilized attitude. The emancipation (of women in this case) is only a masquerade for another enslavement; the writer thus advocates liberation from the European "civilized" notion of freedom.

Dostoevsky employs satire and a rhetoric of persuasion more often than irony. In this case his rhetoric of persuasion works through satirizing the satirizers from the progressive press. He expropriates their devices of civilized discourse and rational argument and radically inverts them: as a result, the young gentry girl (over)dressed in the European fashion is described in much more violent language than the beaten up peasant wife. Could it be worse to be a *slave of civilization* than, literally, to be a *slave / serf*?

Considering the fact that the date of the text is 1862—a year after the abolition of serfdom in most Russian provinces by Tsar Alexander II and at the time of the abolition of slavery in the United States, the word "slave" is undoubtedly very strong. Yet in Dostoevsky's usage it has nothing to do with an actual political and social condition, with cruelty and physical pain, but rather with the enslavement of the soul, with the voluntary subjugation to fashion. Suffering can become a form of redemption and liberation; fashion has no redemptive qualities. Human rights and political freedoms appear in this paradoxical travelogue as nothing more than minor embellishments of the Enlightenment fashion industry.

The dialogue with the reader takes the form not of conversation but rather of conversion; the irony doesn't aim at inverting relationships for the sake of gaining new perspectives but at converting and persuading the reader through what appears to be an entertaining satire. The dynamic of conversation requires the space of unpredictability; the dialogical author could never dream of including all points of view into his text. Instead, the mechanism of paranoia is based on a constant projection of expectations and personal fears and anxieties onto the virtual interlocutor, precluding any form of genuine interaction. "The reader would say" effectively precludes that you might say anything beyond authorial control.

Dostoevsky's critique of the Enlightenment predates that of Michel Foucault by some hundred years, yet one notices uncanny parallelisms there in spite of radical political differences. In *Discipline and Punish* Foucault wrote that the more rational and scientific forms of reeducation and discipline always have the body at issue even when they do not "make use of violent or bloody punishment" and use instead "'lenient' methods involving confinement or correction . . . and have only the secret souls of criminals as their objective."[26] The "rational" and "lenient" forms of discipline aim at creating docile "civil slaves": "the soul is the effect and instrument of a political anatomy; the soul is the prison of the body."[27] While Dostoevsky's and Foucault's conceptions of soul might differ, we notice that Foucault insists that the abolition of corporal punishment does not abolish the subjugation of the body, but in fact, the reeducation of the "soul" might be an even stronger form of discipline that disguises a more direct and honest spectacle of torture (with which Foucault's book begins). Dostoevsky uses a similar argument to claim national difference if not superiority for Russian customs that do not hide the spectacle of bodily pain; only he is speaking in the political and historical context of absolute monarchy in which the "rational" and "lenient" forms of punishment and the judicial system are far from what is actually being implemented. Sites of violence and pain somehow function as sites of authenticity for both authors. Dostoevsky's critique of Enlightenment comes from a counter-Enlightenment rather than from a modern perspective and it has immediate political resonance in the Russian context.

The political aspect of the issue of corporal punishment that was so important for the Russian reformers of the nineteenth century is now carefully blurred by Dostoevsky; corporal punishment is substituted by customary domestic wife beating or naive and well-meaning medieval humiliation of the newlywed bride.

Looking at the reforms of the 1860s, historians are struck by the fact that there was no progress at all made in the area of general human rights, protection of individuals from corporal punishment or infringements of the state. The insistence on the protection of human rights combined with social assistance would ensure in practice improved conditions for the recently liberated serfs. Yet in the writings of reformers, populists, and social democrats we find a striking disregard and even satirization of political freedoms, which are seen as another kind of bourgeois hypocrisy. Nikolai Mikhailovsky, a leading social and literary critic and Dostoevsky's contemporary, explains that the populist revolutionaries in Russia didn't ask for any "rights for themselves because this would seem as a mere expression of egoism. They wished to share what people shared." In this case, such an attitude translated into shared political oppression. Moreover, both Westernizers and Slavophiles believed that Russia should go its own special way. Even such thinkers as Herzen, disenchanted with some aspects of the Western middle-class life that he himself ended up leading, thought that there was a way of development moving from the peasant commune straight to socialism. In this case, political freedoms and human rights would be an unnecessary bourgeois detour. It was in the tradition of Russian radicals to cherish *"la politique du pire"* (the politics of the worse, the better), which means a destabilization of everyday life with the belief that the worse the conditions in the present, the better it would be for future revolution. Nineteenth-century legal historian Bogdan Kistiakovsky observed that the ideas of political and human rights did not appeal to Russian thinkers because there was no absolute value to them. For in Russia both idealistic radicals and idealistic conservatives were looking for absolute values, not for relative rules of improved human coexistence. According to Dostoevsky, only absolute values can create Russian opposition to the seductive but devilishly inauthentic theatricality of Western modern life.

Urban Phantasmagoria: Dostoevsky, Marx, Baudelaire

Generally, foreigners—this was quite striking to me—are almost all incomparably more naïve than Russians.[28]

The sacrifice must be made in just such a way as to offer all and even wish that you receive nothing in return, that no one will in any way be obligated to you. How is this to be done? After all, it is like trying not to think of a polar bear. Try to pose for yourself this task: not to think of a polar bear, and you will see that the cursed thing will come to mind every minute.[29]

Winter Notes on Summer Impressions, a chronicle of Dostoevsky's journey to three European capitals, is a satirical version of a divine comedy. Germany is a philistine purgatory where the petty traders commit the terrible sacrilege of hawking eau de cologne right up against the majestic Cologne Cathedral. Berlin's bad weather contributes to the writer's patriotism and propels him to London, which he likens to a modern version of the city of the biblical Baal and a capitalist hell. London overwhelms him with the misery of industrialization, which is disguised behind the optimistic rationalism of the Crystal Palace. Finally, Dostoevsky goes to Paris, the land of *liberté, égalité, fraternité,* where he finds himself in the paradise of the bourgeoisie. Paris is worse than the other places because it appears to be superior and pretends to be free, thus profaning the dream of true liberation. Paris is the false gospel of Russian Europe.

Dostoevsky would insist that he had not come "to see Paris." The curiosity and wonder of a traveler are alien to him. He spends more time describing the plots of melodramas and vaudevilles that are playing on the Parisian stage than recording actual slices of life or everyday observations. His travelogue is also literary, and like his Russian literary predecessors Dostoevsky goes to Paris in search of Jean-Jacques Rousseau, *l'homme de la nature et de la vérité,* "the man of nature and truth." The very opposition of sincerity and theatricality, so prominent in narrations of Russian journeys to Europe, is not a native invention but a product of international Rousseauism.[30]

What is most insincere is the modern democratic theatricality of Parisian life. Dostoevsky makes a pilgrimage to the Pantheon, where he discovers the tomb of Rousseau and is subjected to another bourgeois ritual, that of a guided tour. "'Ci-git Jean-Jacques Rousseau,' he continued, walking up to the next tomb. 'Jean-Jacques, l'homme de la nature et de la vérité!' It suddenly struck me as funny. The high-flown word debases everything."[31] Paris is presented as the place where nature and truth are entombed like Rousseau. Parisian everyday life is nothing but an artificial stage set for vaudeville or a Platonic world of shadowy appearances. The bourgeoisie "playact" the human condition and invent artificial nature in their little urban picnics, *"les dejeuners sur l'herbe"* (breakfasts on the grass) and their dreams of civilized escape to see the sea, *"pour voir le mer."* Whenever French is quoted or spoken in Dostoevsky's text (even by the French themselves on their own native soil), it becomes an act of insincere phrasemongering. Political deliberations are seen as "eloquence for the sake of eloquence." The expression *liberté, égalité, fraternité,* a slogan that in Dostoevsky's view unites French bourgeoisie and the socialists, is one of those French clichés that has no meaning.

> [It] was shortly after his *liberté, égalité, fraternité* was proclaimed. Liberty. What liberty? Equal liberty for everyone to do anything he wants to within the limits of the law. When may you do anything you want to? When you have millions. Does liberty give each person a million? No. What is the person without

a million? The person without a million is not the one who does anything he wants to. . . . Understand me: voluntary, completely conscious self-sacrifice imposed by no one, sacrifice of the self for the sake of all, is, in my opinion, a sign of the very highest development of the personality . . . the highest form of self-mastery, the greatest freedom of one's own will.[32]

Dostoevsky rages against the theatrical disguises of Western liberty; he doesn't merely lay them bare but pierces them through the heart. Radical sincerity equates the sacrifice of an individual with dissolution into the "general will" of the national community. French *liberté* is a false legal ideal that in his view is ignored by current French legal practice. Jury trials for Dostoevsky represented examples of the utmost theatricality and role-playing and are incapable of discerning truth. *Liberté* is a product of French rhetorical eloquence and insincerity, as is *égalité*. Dostoevsky erases the distinction between democratic freedoms and capitalist exploitation, seeing the former as a disguise for the latter.

The rhetoric of sacrifice involves, first of all, liberation from Western liberty and then resacralization of the disenchanted world. Its utopian quality is intentional since it is meant to be an inspiration for the future and a denigration of the present. Sacrifice is unbounded by law or rationality, since all conventions are a part of the vaudeville of modernity. There is no question about "consenting" to sacrifice, for the very notion of consent is based on the acknowledgment of individual agency. Sacrifice cannot even be "voluntary," since it is beyond will. But of course, the more a modern writer tries to become a sincere advocate of sacrifice, the more he sees the damned "polar bear" of selfhood in Western furs. Unlike Herzen, who believed together with Mill in liberty for its own sake, Dostoevsky sees any form of individual liberty as imprisonment. He asserts that whereas the liberal-minded Western individual sees imprisonment in the coercion of the state, he sees imprisonment in the shell of individualism itself. However, this is not an expression of the people's desire or will, since Russian peasants and townspeople do not have much voice in this text; this is not a return to the actual Russian people who by the 1860s were rather tired of the involuntary hard labor and constant self-sacrifice demanded of them by the state and the landowners. What Dostoevsky offers here is a reinvention of tradition, a resacralization, a modern purification of modern impurities.

The key to Dostoevsky's conception of liberation and sacrifice is contained in the notions of the "Russian soul," "Russian personality," and sincerity, which form a part of a long-standing Russian mythology. While they describe and address particularities of Russian history and culture,

in themselves they are hardly pure national ideas. Even the genealogy of
the Russian soul reveals an international coproduction dating back to the
late eighteenth–early nineteenth century: it was coauthored by enthusiastic foreign travelers to Russia like the Marquis de Vogue and by Russian
visitors to Germany. The Russian soul has an Oedipal relationship to the
German geist; it is at once homeless and rooted in the national home. Soul
and soil are closely connected.[33]

Curiously, Dostoevsky writes about Parisian theatricality and the spectacle of *liberté, égalité, fraternité* in practice at exactly the same time as do
Charles Baudelaire and Karl Marx. For Baudelaire, this kind of theatricality emerges as a major feature of modernity, while for Marx it would be
a phantasmagoria of bourgeois democracy. Sometimes it is difficult to
imagine that the poet of decadence and modernity, Baudelaire, and the
grand master of the novel and radical turned conservative, Feodor Dostoevsky, were contemporaries. Yet they were born in the same year, 1821,
and Baudelaire, like Dostoevsky, had his dose of experimentation in radical politics, art, and alternative spirituality. They shared a critique of capitalism and of middle-class values, embraced antiutilitarian conceptions of
beauty, and loved the same American writer, Edgar Allan Poe. Moreover,
both were influenced by and exerted influence upon writers, thinkers, and
readers on the left and on the right.[34]

Like Dostoevsky, Baudelaire was deeply affected by social-democratic
and socialist thinking in the 1840s and went to the barricades during
the revolution of 1848. This involvement led to a profound disappointment both with socialists and with the bourgeoisie of the reign of Louis
Bonaparte. The coup "has physically depoliticized me," writes Baudelaire.
"There are no more general ideas. If I had voted, I could only have voted
for myself."[35] His "conversion," however, was not from left to right or
from politics into religion, but rather from politics into literature and an
understanding of the modern experience. Baudelaire, like Dostoevsky, is
a postrevolutionary writer, yet his attitude toward modernity could not
have been more different.

Baudelaire finds the "tumults of human liberty" and "promise of happiness" in the landscape of the great city where he spies on the unprecedented and controversial "modern beauty."[36] Thus the poet of the city
coins a new word to account for a new form of experience: "Modernity
is the transitory, the fugitive, the contingent, the half of art of which
the other half is eternal and the immutable." His term, *modernité*, refers
neither to modern-ism nor to modernization. *Modernité* is not an -ism but
a form of experience that breeds a new imagination and a new form of

reflection on the contemporary life. In other words, the Baudelarian imagination of modernity transforms us from mere objects of modernization
into critical subjects who are capable of reflecting on the new experience.
While it is distinct from the modernization that is associated with industrial progress, Baudelaire's project is to "represent the present," to capture the transience, the excitement, the protean qualities of the modern
experience—one cannot hide from it in the underground. Creative melancholia is inescapable but it is not an equivalent of resentment; in fact, it
is within modern urban experience that one could find profane illuminations and love "at last sight," as Walter Benjamin described it.[37] Between
political freedoms in the plural and the artistic ideal of Freedom in the
singular, Baudelaire discovers something else: the social arts of freedom
that reside not only in the extreme experiments of alternative living but
also in the everyday exercises in modern curiosity on the Paris boulevard.
If for Dostoevsky curiosity is not high on the list of values dominated by
sincerity and spirituality, for Baudelaire it is a sine qua non of the modern
adventure.[38] Baudelaire proposes a critique of Rousseau's ethics of sincerity, arguing in defense of the theatrical modern city as a site where "tumults of freedom" can be truly experienced.

Who is the hero of modern life? Neither a bandit nor a saint, neither a romantic poet nor a man of the people, but a *flaneur* and a man of the world.
(Baudelaire gives his own long list of modern dreamers: an actor, a dandy,
a prostitute, a melancholic passerby, a bohemian, a soldier, a lesbian, a
homeless man.) The modern urban wanderer is a "lover of the universal
love [who] moves into the crowd as though into an enormous reservoir of
electricity. He, the lover of life, may also be compared to a mirror as vast
as this crowd; to a kaleidoscope endowed with consciousness which with
every one of its movements presents a pattern of life, in all its multiplicity,
and the flowing pace of all the elements that go to compose life."[39] The
flaneur is a threshold figure who moves in and out of the crowd. His dialogue with the people of the city is not only verbal but also haptic. He has
a different body language, which is inaccessible to the Underground Man.
Unlike a Romantic poet or a dreamer he is not opposed to the crowd. His
estrangement is a part of creative wonder and curiosity, not of terminal
alienation. Unlike a Romantic nationalist, he does not dream of curing
his longing with belonging to a premodern natural community. He is an
urban cosmopolitan, a man of the world, not a man of the soil. Moreover,
while critical of emergent capitalism like Dostoevsky and Marx, and using
money in his poems in the most uneconomical manner, Baudelaire does
not shun entirely the new world of democratic fashions.

For his part, Dostoevsky shuns the foreign urban crowd. His version of the democratic man is a lackey who becomes a parody of the *honnête homme* ("honest man"). Partly due to Russian political and social realities and partly to cultural tradition, Russian writers prior to Chekhov are notoriously uncharitable toward any kind of middle-class hero or democratic man or woman, the "third estate," preferring aristocrats or abject heroes (lumpen aristocrats), blessed fools or nihilists.[40] Dostoevsky writes that for a servant to pretend to have human dignity—that's the worse. "What is *tiers état*? Nothing? What should it become? Everything." Here the Russian writer echoes Karl Marx's *Manifesto of the Communist Party*, observing that the bourgeoisie is so anxious even though they have everything, because now they have everything to lose.

The problem with the bourgeoisie for Dostoevsky is that they have the soul of a lackey. "Why are there so many lackeys among the bourgeoisie, with a very noble appearance? The nature of a lackey penetrates the nature of the bourgeois."[41] "Freedom of conscience, the most important freedom in the world," is regarded as a tool of lackeys, spies, and flatterers. The lackey is a go-between, a travesty both of the image of the common people and that of the nobility; he is a corrupt representative of the people who disguises himself as a man of dignity. Anna Dostoevskaia remembers that her husband had a particularly difficult relationship with servants, waiters, and actual lackeys during his travels in Europe. In her account Dostoevsky demands respect for his status and the observance of certain social hierarchies that the Western "natives" tend to ignore. He found Western European service people endlessly disrespectful toward him even when they did not mean to be and far from obedient servants. They became a projection of his resentment and status anxiety. Political freedoms appear to be freedoms for the lackeys that Dostoevsky despises. Thus for him, Rousseau's ideal, "a man of nature and truth," cannot survive in the West and can only be revived in the mythical Russia of the future.

Like Dostoevsky and Baudelaire, Marx also confronts the theater of Parisian life in the wake of the coup d'état of Louis Bonaparte on December 2, 1852. Yet instead of drinking the Baudelairian "wine of life," he offers us a ghost story. "The Eighteenth Brumaire *of Louis Bonaparte*" begins with one of the most famous restagings of history: "Hegel remarks somewhere that all great world-historical facts and personages occur, as it were, twice. He has forgotten to add: the first time as tragedy, the second time as farce."[42] Where Dostoevsky saw vaudeville, which banishes the spectacle of suffering, Marx saw a farce that mass-reproduces tragedy. The French Revolution appeared in Roman clothes, Cromwell in the garb of the Old Testament, and in turn Louis Bonaparte wears the used clothes of his only mildly more illustrious namesake. On the one hand, Marx offers profound insights into the corrupt political regime of Louis Bonaparte that profanes the dream of the revolution. Bourgeois society is in need of heroic sacrifice to mask its mediocrity. This is a corrupted sacrifice that merely mimics the trappings of the past. On the other hand, Marx's critique goes beyond the particular circumstances of the French republic, offering a critique of the modern condition and a vision of a true heroism and uncorrupted sacrifice for the sake of the "kingdom of freedom."

"The Constitution, the National Assembly, the dynastic parties . . . the civil law and the penal code, the *liberté, égalité, fraternité*, and the second of May 1852—all have vanished like a fantasmagoria . . . It is not enough to say, as the French do, that their nation has been taken by surprise. A nation and a woman are not forgiven the unguarded hour in which the first adventurer that came along could violate them," writes Marx.[43] According to Marx, the task of the proletarian revolutionary struggle does not consist in "making the ghost walk again" but in "finding once more the spirit of the revolution."[44] While farce and vaudeville connect Marx with Dostoevsky, phantasmagoria links Marx and Baudelaire. Yet their understanding of it is radically different. For Marx, phantasmagoria is part of a ghost story, a haunting memory of the unforgiven loss of virginity and the original sin of inauthenticity. Hardly a feminist *avant la lettre*, Marx compares the French nation to an unchaste woman who commits adultery with the ghost from the past, who prefers period-piece costumes to genuine sacrifice.

For Marx, communist liberation will be liberation not only from these ghosts but from politics as such, from the need for political freedoms, human rights, or a deliberative public sphere. Phantasmagoric imagery is usually applied to those who are on the wrong side of history, according to Marx. In some respect his usage of optical imagery is closer to Plato's world of shadows and deceptive appearances.[45] Urban social freedoms are a part of ghostly theatricality and have to be sacrificed for the sake of the future liberation. But phantasmagoria haunts both Marx's dialectics and his metaphors, like a ghost in the gothic tale. In "The Eighteenth Brumaire" as well as in *The Manifesto of the Communist Party* the ghost of the past is opposed not to the living being or existing social entity but to the "specter of communism" and the "spirit" of the revolution. The uncanniness resides in the fact that sometimes it is difficult to draw a line between the good ghosts and the bad ghosts and to distinguish the specters of friends and foes.

For Baudelaire, phantasmagoria cannot be merely "unveiled" and abolished. It is a part of the experience and understanding of modernity, not merely an evil spirit of modernization. The Baudelairian hero, the flaneur, thrives in phantasmagoric exploits that enable a different kind of critical practice of modern life which upsets capitalist assumptions and challenges the lifestyles of both the bourgeoisie and of some of their philosophical critics. Walter Benjamin, performing a balancing act between Marx and Baudelaire, never discards the phantasmagoric lenses and draws attention to their powers. In his description the flaneur himself is a figure of phantasmagoria, going between classes, an embodiment of social mobility in a literal and figurative sense: "The crowd was the veil from behind which the familiar city as phantasmagoria beckoned the flaneur."[46] Benjamin observed a paradox: the philosophers of the modern condition often hated the actual experience of it. Engels writes, "The very turmoil of the streets has something repulsive, something against which human nature rebels." For Benjamin, Engels's description reveals a combination of "unshakable critical integrity with an old-fashioned attitude. The writer came from a Germany that was still provincial; he may never have faced the temptation to lose himself in a stream of people."[47]

Marx perceived urban life as a mere phantasmagoria of capitalism and bourgeois democracy. More sophisticated and elaborate in his critique of capitalism, Marx nevertheless shares with Dostoevsky a distrust of political liberties, equating them with capitalist exploitation. Political liberty is nothing but a part of the hypocrisy and the superficial disguise of capitalist economy. Moreover, by improving some aspects of society, it distracts attention from the revolution. Like Dostoevsky, Marx sees the world in the present, the Baudelairian critical and poetic modernity, as a realm of inauthenticity rather than merely a realm of imperfection that requires improvement and further modernization en route to scientific communism.

All classes are guilty of phantasmagoric distortion: the bourgeoisie engaged in the mediocre farce of borrowed heroism; peasants are compared to sacks of potatoes, conservative and homogeneous; while the bohemians are described as "noisy, disreputable, rapacious" with caricaturesque self-theatricalization.[48] Only the proletariat is pure. The proletariat (Marx's neo-Roman reinvention) appears as a "new Adam" of the future revolution, who attends to her "birth pangs" (endured by the whole society), the angel of messianic liberation. The proletariat is not an actual working class, but rather an ideal spirit of the revolution. A phantasmagoria, perhaps, that Marx doesn't fully account for? The actual laborers or members of the workers' unions who were engaged in everyday politics and policies were involved with political action in the present, not with the liberational march of necessity; they made brave decisions as well as mistakes, side with the bourgeoisie, drink alcohol with the bohemians and profane their good name, becoming the "lumpen proletariat" that Marx so much despised.

Hannah Arendt observed that Marx's most "original discovery," which went beyond Hegelian theory, was that of the proletarian revolutionary potential, but later the scientist in Marx recast revolutionary spirit and violence into a historical necessity: "While he had first seen man-made violence and oppression of man by man where others had believed in some necessity inherent in the human condition, he later saw the iron laws of historical necessity lurking behind every violence, transgression and violation."[49] Violence becomes a necessary part of liberation, a purification of the corrupted sacrifice for the sake of the future freedom. In spite of their many irreconcilable differences, the proletariat in Marx functions like the Russian folk in the late Dostoevsky; while mythical and larger than life, it is exempt from phantasmagoria and is regarded as an angel of future liberation and the kingdom of freedom-to-come.

Underground Man and Venus in Furs: Resentment, Play, and Moral Masochism

> I reached a point where trudging back to my corner on the foul St. Petersburg night, I would feel a certain hidden, morbid, nasty little pleasure in an acute awareness that I had once again committed something vile . . . and I would gnaw and gnaw at myself in silence, tearing and nagging at myself until the bitterness would finally begin to turn into a kind of shameful, damnable sweetness and at the end into definite, positive pleasure! . . . I always wanted to find out: Do other people experience such pleasures?[50]

> It is said that Cleopatra . . . was fond of sticking golden pins into the breasts of her slave girls and enjoyed their cries and writhings. You will say that this was, relatively speaking in a barbarian age, that our age is also barbarian, because (also relatively speaking) pins are also being stuck in people, though man has learned to see more clearly . . . to behave according to the dictates of reason and science . . . And then (all this is being said by you) new economic relations will follow, ready made and also calculated with mathematical precision, so that all possible questions disappear in a single instance, because they will all be provided with an answer. And then the Crystal Palace will arise. . . . . . Of course, it is impossible to guarantee (and this now is myself speaking) that life will not become, let us say, dreadfully boring . . . who can tell what people may think up out of boredom. After all, gold pins are also stuck into bodies out of boredom.[51]

The Underground Man, that nineteenth-century blogger *avant la lettre*, who issues his missives to the world from his tiny room, is a curious inversion of both the Russian European traveler and of the prisoner of the house of the dead. He mocks the European conception of rational liberty and freedom of movement by retiring underground, from where he can stick out his tongue at the monuments of the European Enlightenment. Barbarism is a part of civilization (he asserts this long before Walter Benjamin) and no amount of well-wishing, science, or rational conception of law will be able to eliminate the irrational choices that the individual can make.[52] The goddess of the self-proclaimed underground "paradoxicalist" is Cleopatra, whose whimsical master-slave dialectics embodies the malignant pleasure of modernity and the persistence of barbarism in modern civilization. Cleopatra is no democrat; her "free will" to stick pins into slave girls is hardly an example of the democratic freedom or respect for the freedom of the other advocated by John Stuart Mill. Yet her boredom and irrationalism challenge the whole edifice of rational choice and enlightened science. Cleopatra in modern nineteenth-century clothes (with some of the shoulder padding that Dostoevsky so despised) is a sadistic queen of the Underground Man, comparable only to the *Venus in Furs* immortalized by Leopold von Sacher-Masoch.

The underground is a version of the European theater of freedom *via negativa*. At the same time, the Underground Man unwittingly mocks the prisoner of the house of the dead, for he is not forced to live in fear of flogging surrounded by a stockade in the Siberian wilderness, nor is he unjustly arrested; his confinement in what he calls a "loathsome, stinking underground hole" is entirely voluntary. The "underground" in the text is a site not for revolutionary conspirators but for the solitary existential anarchist and the poet of malignant pleasure. Once again, Dostoevsky takes political metaphors and depoliticizes them.

The Underground Man pokes fun at the Western "democratic" obsession with walls; he disrespects the respect for walls and boundaries of law, imagining a limitless freedom of will. Yet in his dream of boundless freedom beyond the walls of the law he locks himself up in the voluntary confinement of his tiny Petersburg flat. His unlimited, subversive freedom is a freedom in prison, only this time, it is a prison of his own design. His imagination is prolific but not liberating. Ultimately, the space of his freedom is as long as the length of his versatile tongue, which he sticks out at the Crystal Palace of European rationalism.

The Underground Man's encounters with other people are particularly striking. He sees them as if they had already existed in his imagination as his interlocutors. As a result, he is averse to any manifestation of the unpredictability of another person. The "freedom of the other" is an entirely alien concept for him. The world of the Underground Man is the theater of one sole actor; he is a consummate monomaniac, in spite of his skillful use of the dialogical form, who rejoices in his special treat, his "hidden, nasty voluptuous pleasure" of being at once his own executioner and his own victim. The Underground Man parodies discussion and debate in order to control it. His is a superiority-inferiority complex so characteristic of many members of the Russian intelligentsia.

Most interesting are the Underground Man's interactions with his servant Apollon and with Lisa, the young woman he meets in the Petersburg brothel. A representative of the "people" and a self-sacrificial woman are supposed to be ideal sufferers or even ideal "masochists" in the universe of Dostoevsky's later novels and nonfictional writing. Here they do not act according to the Underground Man's scenario and resist his typecasting.

Apollon is an "extremely dignified" elderly man (no relation to the Greek god) who engages in tailoring when he is not called to serve the whims of the self-conscious hero. To remind Apollon of his "will of a master," the Underground Man conducts an experiment on his servant by withholding his wages for a week or two just to teach him a lesson in humility. Instead of acting as a proper servant and begging forgiveness, Apollon responds with a dignified silence, coming into his master's room and staring at him "with the most outrageous composure." The servant's silent stare is regarded as an act of "torture" that throws the master off. 'That isn't it, that isn't it, what I'm asking you, torturer,' I screamed, shaking with rage. I'll tell you, you, hangman, what you've come here for. You see, I haven't given you your wage and you're too proud to bow and ask for it." The roles are suddenly reversed, and in the paranoiac mind of the master, the underpaid servant emerges as a hangman and a torturer. Freud would call such a description an example of paranoiac projection: It is the Underground Man who inflicts some undeserved suffering upon Apollon, but in his mind, Apollon emerges as a torturer and a hangman. Apollon's crime is his independence and dignity; he violates the Underground Man's "dialogical" script by not participating in the master-slave dialectics designed for him.

Lisa, the humble but equally proud prostitute, is seen as even more guilty than Apollon. She embarrasses the master. The Underground Man stumbles into the brothel after a humiliating encounter with his acquaintances. There he finds a new girl, Lisa, who quietly and patiently obliges him, but this does not satisfy our hero. He lectures her about her lost soul and her perdition only to find her embarrassed and still reluctant to open her soul to him. Finally she does just that, confessing to him a rather trivial story without the spectacular suffering that the Underground Man had expected, her love for a student, escape from her family in Riga, her modest hopes. His words at first appear strangely "bookish" to her, but then they break her heart. Lisa too is made of literary stereotypes, but throughout the *Notes* she grows beyond them and the angles of her particular face emerge from behind the mask. From a stereotypical prostitute with the heart of gold, she emerges as an empathetic and sensible human being who is able to accept the Underground Man almost the way he is. She even comes to visit him, embarrassing the Underground Man in the midst of his quarrel with Apollon. She lays bare his bookishness and derivativeness—not by any form of striking originality but by a small but unpredictable gesture of humanity. Lisa is a threshold creature who inhabits the "demi-monde" of Petersburg life. Her visit disrupts the walled architecture of his virtual underground, opening up an entry to the unforeseen adventure of human relationships.

This is a peculiar case of a performance disruption; Lisa fits the role of a good woman a little too well, and this does not fit into the Underground Man's bookish scenario of the saintly whore. He remakes her back into a prostitute and pays her off. Lisa defies him, rejecting his final offer and leaving the wrinkled rubles in his room. A typical Dostoevsky scene of self-inflicted double humiliation ensues. To give justice to the Underground Man, he realizes his inability to love. Loving for him means "tyrannizing the other person and flaunting his moral superiority": "I sometimes think that love consists precisely in the voluntary gift of the loved object of the right to tyrannize over it. I have never conceived of love as anything but struggle, I always began with hatred and ended with moral subjugation, after which I cannot even imagine what to do with the conquered object."[53] In the end, Lisa is left with another broken illusion of human communication, and the Underground Man is left with another rhetorical question: which is better, cheap happiness or noble suffering?

Bakhtin had observed that the Underground Man is all "heightened self-consciousness," and it is hard to say anything about him that he doesn't already know. Such open-endedness and unfinalizability is not only due to the hero's heightened self-consciousness but also to the logic of "malignant pleasure" of self-deprecation and exhibitionism that is continuously in need of an audience. His inability to act is in inverse proportion to his ability to imagine actions. The tantalizing self-conscious monologue from the underground seems to illustrate that "free will" taken to the extreme can indeed be the very antithesis of "public freedom" and freedom to act. It negates the world in between, any public realm in which he can keep his thoughts in check.

The theater of heightened self-consciousness has a potential of "bad infinity," of limitless self-exposure and a diary without end. "Shouldn't I perhaps conclude my Notes at this point? It seems to me that it was a mistake to start them?" He claims that his *Notes* are "no longer literature, but corrective punishment."[54] The problem is that he craves punishment. Having eliminated the other characters from his theater, he remains the master of his own ceremony of crime and punishment. We learn from the final footnote that the Underground Man didn't follow his own advice.

The drama of free will and its subjugation are stages not only inside the text but also on its borders. The *Notes* have a structure similar to that of the *Notes from the House of the Dead*, only the previous text had a fictional editor, while the *Notes from Underground* are presented as edited by Dostoevsky himself. In the final footnote the author-editor informs us that we are not reading the full text of the confession of the underground. The actual text would last as long as the life of the anonymous hero, the radical expression of his obsessive freer freedom.

The problem of the limit of freedom and imagination is dramatized at the end of the text when the paradoxicalist briefly envisions writing the "bad infinity" that would end only with the end of life itself. This virtual text would have the temporality of Andy Warhol's films with real-time takes, and we leave it to be reconstructed in the reader's boundless imagination. He tells us that he wishes to impose his free will and stop writing. "But enough already. I don't wish to write anymore from the underground." But it takes the radical intervention of the author Feodor Dostoevsky to end the story. He makes an unusual intervention, contradicting his hero: "By the way, this is not the end of the notes of this paradoxicalist. He couldn't restrain himself and continued. But we think that we can stop here." So what makes the *Notes* a literary masterpiece is the fact that it is an interplay between the limitless literary will of the confined Underground Man, spurning his freedom in prison and resentful imagination, and the consciousness of textual limits imposed by the writer Dostoevsky.

The details concerning the writing and publication of *Notes* involve another drama of the freedom of expression. In a letter to his brother Mikhail, Dostoevsky writes that the "cause of the underground was the destruction of faith in the general rules: there is nothing sacred." He complains to his brother that the censors took out of the text the paragraph in which the Underground Man understands the necessity of the Christian faith: "What is it with the censors? Are they in conspiracy against the government? . . . The censors, those swine, approved the places where I mocked everything and sometimes blasphemed for effect but where I deduced the need for faith and Christ from all this—that they prohibited."[55] While the texts indeed were edited by the censor and there is little reason to think that Dostoevsky would gratuitously lie to his brother in a private letter not intended for publication, the history of the Christian passage remains a mystery. Generations of Dostoevsky scholars have been unable to rescue it from the manuscripts. Why would the conservative censor of the tsar eliminate the religious passage? Unlike his later works, like *Crime and Punishment*, in which Dostoevsky explicitly incorporates the Christian solution into its epilogue (which seemed to some scholars to be an artificial addition to the novel), *Notes from Underground* remain open-ended. Only with the aesthetic restraint of the "editor" does Dostoevsky put an end to the bad infinity of the malignant pleasure of his confined paradoxicalist. The writer builds literary walls around the freer freedom of the Underground Man.

Nietzsche, an avid reader of Dostoevsky, did not think that the malignant pleasure of suffering can be cured by a leap of faith that would end the Underground's Man endless conversation with himself. Rather, he wanted a more honest conversation that would engage with the genealogy of slavishness and a critique of resentment, based on assumed humiliation of a person or a nation.

Nietzsche's theory of *ressentiment* / resentment might have been inspired in part by *Notes from Underground*. The word *ressentiment* doesn't translate into Russian, even though the phenomenon is certainly well known, but not necessarily fully reflected upon. Resentment is defined in the contemporary dictionary as "a feeling of displeasure or indignation at a person, an act, or a remark from a sense of injury or insult." The key phrase here is the "sense of" for there is no way to distinguish between actual and imaginary hurt, and sometimes this makes an important different. "Resentment doesn't merely recollect slights, it creates them from is own imaginings, establishing a psychological economy of abjection in which time breeds a quarterly dividend of new shame to swell the capital already deposited in the sufferer's emotional account," writes literary scholar Michael André Bernstein. Resentment literally means feeling again, repeating feeling, but this is a repetition with a significant difference. It ends up equating memory with injury, feeling with feeling insulted, reflecting with revenging if only in one's mind. Feeling again in this sense is a distinctly modern experience because it is haunted by a modern conception of the irreversibility of time. In Nietzsche's conception, the man of resentment experiences a nagging rage at the experience of temporality. He dramatizes "the will's antipathy towards [the] time's 'it was.'" His modernity is constituted at once by his desire for originality and the recognition of his derivativeness. While the man of resentment might stick his tongue out at modern architecture (and sometimes justly so), or occasionally argue for a return to tradition and self-sacrifice (as the narrator of the *Diary of a Writer* does), he is a modern figure, a reinventor of tradition, not a traditionalist. Yet he cannot settle for the Baudelairian *modernité* and worldly cocreation. In this sense resentment is not equivalent to creative nostalgia or melancholia for it tends to sacrifice the affect and wonder of anger and self-laceration. The universe of the man of resentment is a solipsistic space dominated by a free will and will to power that do not translate into action.

Nietzsche, unlike Dostoevsky, questions the sincerity of the man of resentment. For Nietzsche, he is neither upright and naïve, nor honest and straightforward with himself. "His soul *squints*; his spirit loves hiding places, secret paths and back doors, everything covert entices him as *his* world, *his* security, *his* refreshment."[56] The architecture of resentment, with its "hiding places" and secrets, in this case is not the space for adventure or for the unpredictable, but a refuge from worldly checks and balances, from the gaze of the other that can lay bare the fictitiousness of one's remembered injuries. In Nietzsche's polemical vocabulary resentment was a form of slavishness, a symptom of a "squinting soul," and cowardice hiding behind liberational rhetoric.

One of the key psychological and philosophical postulates of the man of resentment is "I suffer: it must be somebody's fault." Nietzsche saw the dynamics of resentment in the erasure of the difference between words and deeds: "[N]atures that are denied the true reaction, that of deeds, and compensate themselves with an imaginary revenge." In the words of Bernstein, "resentment is like an author in search of characters to populate the seedy dramas of its own spite."[57] Resentment provokes dialogue but it is not about the word of the other or the freedom of the other. It is a dialogue with one's own endlessly splitting self that vampirizes the whole world. Resentment might feed imagination, but it is a paranoid imagination, a form of rational delusion that imagines the other only as the other paranoid whose sole raison d'être is to persecute me. I don't like the other, it must be his/her fault. Resentment, like paranoia, doesn't allow for a tragic peripeteia or for a comic joy because it builds too many blind alleys and conspiratorial plots.[58]

The problem with resentment is neither in its endless self-reflexivity nor its engagement in the imaginary; one cannot be a reflective person without it. The problem is in fact the opposite: The man of resentment cannot truly engage either worldliness or the world of imagination because these require wonder, surprise, adventure, loss of self-control. The danger of resentment is worldlessness, the loss of experience, and actual engagement with the world. The man of resentment thinks himself always already a victim and hence cannot recognize the hurt of others. He is always already humiliated and his history is rewritten as a history of humiliation. Similarly, the problem with resentment is not in its actual derivativeness but in the obsession with unoriginality, which precludes a form of cocreation in freedom. The narrator might go traveling but he carries his underground with him like a portable home. The architecture of resentment is an expansive but solipsistic echo chamber with no exit.

Bernstein has observed, "Resentment remains one of the last taboos of contemporary self-consciousness, a motive force for our ideas, values and actions that, unlike sexuality, we are still reluctant to confront." Perhaps we find ourselves as scholars, writers and academics too close to resentment to reflect upon it? My sincere hope is that *Schadenfreude* is not the only kind of joy that the life of the mind can offer.

If Dostoevsky—who called himself "the psychologist in the highest sense"—in the end forgoes a psychological explanation for the sake of a new national religion, Dostoevsky's younger contemporary, Sacher-Masoch, an admirer of Russian literature, pushed the "suprasensual adventure" to the extreme. His Venus in furs is a relative of the Dostoevskian Cleopatra. Sacher-Masoch's *Venus in Furs* (1870) was read as a symptom of the "suprasensual" age and works as a relay between life and fiction. The story was inspired by Leopold's relationship with his lover and playful dominatrix, Fanny Pistor, with whom he signed a contract of deliberate self-enslavement. *Venus in Furs* and its character Wanda von Dunaew in turn inspired many imitatrix. In fact, Leopold gives his future wife the name of his character Wanda and begs her to wear heavy furs and whip him, turning her into a reluctant dominatrix.[59]

Sacher-Masoch's text is sexually more risqué than that of Dostoevsky but it does not advocate masochism as a national religion. It doesn't end in salvation but in a mock sacrifice that reestablishes boundaries between fantasy and reality, literature and politics, men and women. Masoch's suprasensual fantasy has its own imaginary geography that refracts Dostoevsky's. *Venus in Furs* perpetuates the common places of the Westerner's travel accounts to Russia, as a mirror image to Dostoevsky's imaginary travels to the West. For a Western amateur of exoticism, Russia offers a master-slave theater par excellence; to quote the Marquis de Custine, it is the land "drunk with slavery."[60] The "suprasensual" hero of *Venus in Furs*, Count Severin, made his dominatrix lover dress à la Catherine the Great and purchase a whip similar to one that was used "on the Russian serfs." The Slavic masks were adopted not only for the characters in the novella but for Sacher-Masoch himself. Historian Larry Wolff has observed that the reception of the novella in Vienna turned its Galician author into a delinquent Russian. Thus a liberal Viennese newspaper presented Masoch as an agent of nihilism and communism who betrayed the principles of liberty:

> If he, Sacher-Masoch, continues to play the nihilist, I would advise him not only to think in Russian but also to write in Russian, for in Germany there will be as little place for his work as for Russian barbarism in the name of which his Wanda von Dunajew whips her lovers.[61]

There is another uncanny link between Sacher-Masoch and Dostoevsky: both writers witnessed in their youth the flogging of Polish prisoners fighting for independence, Poland having been progressively partitioned among Russia, Prussia, and the Austro-Hungarian empire. Sacher-Masoch's father was a police chief of the city of Lemberg (now L'viv, Ukraine) and Sacher-Masoch witnessed scenes of daily violence in the grim atmosphere of Metternich's empire: "I spent my childhood in the house of the police . . . Military police brought in vagabonds and handcuffed criminals; grim-looking officials; a thin, sneaky censor, spies who dared not look anyone in the eyes; the flogging bench, barred windows through which peeked here laughing, made-up tarts, there pale and melancholy Polish conspirators."[62] For Sacher-Masoch, as for Dostoevsky, those scenes of political violence would be displaced by fictional representations of voluntary and involuntary suffering.

Yet Sacher-Masoch's understanding of the relationship between fiction and life is quite different than that of Dostoevsky. The Underground Man is an existential rebel with boundless ambitions and claustrophobic actions. He plays out his fantasies of domination in his own inner theater. His actual attempts at dominating Lisa are clumsily cruel. Severin, the protagonist of *Venus in Furs*, on the other hand, does not bother to stick his tongue out at the Crystal Palace; he uses his malignant pleasure to feed his artistic rather than political imagination and to playact his fantasies with real-life actors with whom he enters into a paradoxical sensual and consensual relationship.

Severin is a hedonistic Underground Man with more money and a better knowledge of art history. Two terms distinguish Sacher-Masoch's universe from that of Dostoevsky: artistic theater and contract. Both would be forms of evil inauthenticity and hypocrisy in Dostoevsky while for Masoch they help to stage the liberating play of suprasensual desire.

The structure of *Venus in Furs* includes an interrupted dream as well as an interrupted contract between the suprasensual man and his consenting dominatrix. The novella opens with the narrator dozing off while reading Hegel and dreaming of a conversation with the goddess Venus herself, who comes to life from the great Titian painting. The excited dreamer imagines grasping the goddess's marble arm, only to be shaken awaken from his dream by the tawny brown hand of his Cossack servant with a husky alcoholic voice and a strange reverence for great books. (It is the Cossack who proceeds to pick up the fallen volume of Hegel and helps his master along). The uncanny eroticism of *Venus in Furs* does wonders to further the master-slave dialectic beyond the Hegelian system. The novella recreates this dream scenario with many variations. Its main character, Galician count Severin, signs a mock contract and sells himself into temporary slavery to the cruel woman of his choice; in return she has to play out his fantasy for him and before whipping him heavily, puts furs on her delightful naked body just like the Venus in the Titian painting. As dramatis personae he and his cruel lady assume Slavic names: she becomes Wanda von Dunaew and he turns into Gregor and wears Polish livery. Gregor (Grigory), a common name for Russian servants and lackeys (whom Dostoevsky had so much trouble with) will later be immortalized in Franz Kafka's famous story "Metamorphosis." Here we are dealing with a metamorphosis of a different nature.

Severin is at once a playwright, a stage manager and an actor. He proposes to sign a contract just like a theater producer. Curiously, Sacher-Masoch's original contract with Fanny Pistor, with whom he first tried out his script of domination, included a provision that he would have six hours per day for his writing and wouldn't be interrupted for slavery or any other duties. Any writer can appreciate this as a very sensitive arrangement for a suprasensual hero who never neglected his work ethic.[63] The interruption is built into Severin's (and Leopold's) contract. In this case self-enslavement is deliberate and much deliberated. In the vertiginous relationship between Severin and Wanda, cruelty is off-staged by loving tenderness, which is then off-staged by more cruelty. It works as a parabasis, a performance disruption, until the final scene in which the third party appears—the handsome Greek, Wanda's new lover of ambiguous sexuality, who "whips the poetry out" of Severin.

Wanda, however, cast as an authoritarian dominatrix by Severin, is not an author of their shared theater. She is allowed much less free play of imagination than her contractual slave (nobleman in real life) Gregor.[64] Wanda's authorial interventions consist only in wishing to be a lover, not an actress, in overplaying or underplaying, deviating from his stage directions. After all, her pleasure in renouncing a lover and a husband for a whining and demanding servant who wishes to micromanage his own punishment is questionable; no wonder she claims to "detest all playacting and melodrama." The dramatic tension of the story doesn't reside merely in the interruptions of the contract orchestrated by the *maître* of the ceremonies, Severin. Rather, it lays bare the limit of his theater and stage mastery through the actual confrontation with the freedom of the other and with the existing social and political imperatives of the world. The contract is there to be undermined, to be played out more as a law of fiction than as a conventional law.

If in Dostoevsky the ultimate sacrifice and salvation are infinitely delayed, in *Venus in Furs* the scene of sacrifice and cure is rehearsed in cruel, radical, yet playful fashion. Wanda reminds Severin of the story of the tyrant Dionysius (who seems to be an ironic double of the Nietzschean god of tragedy).

> The courtier dreamed up a new torture instrument for the tyrant of Syracuse—an iron bull, in which a condemned man was to be locked and placed over a huge fire. As soon as the iron bull began to glow and the victim screamed, his wailing would sound like the bellowing of a bull.
>
> Dionysius smiled graciously at the inventor and in order to test his work on the spot, he ordered him to be the first to be shut in the iron bull.
>
> —The story is very instructive.
>
> —It was you who inoculated me with selfishness, arrogance and cruelty and you are to be their first victim.[65]

In the original story about Dionysius we have the eternal duo of the tyrant and the artist. The artist hopes to ingratiate himself with the tyrant, to turn tyranny into an artistic masterwork, and instead the tyrant takes over his invention and sacrifices the artist first. This is also an imitation of the traditional sacrifice. The bull is made of iron and it is the human who is sacrificed. The animal in this story is a man-made predator. In this tyrannical practice the difference between political execution and religious sacrifice is blurred, and both are mocked in the tyrannical gesture that is not without a certain degree of poetic justice. This is a corrupted sacrifice par excellence, performed by a tyrant. The artist complicit with tyranny becomes its privileged victim.

In Sacher-Masoch's tale, Wanda reauthors the story to take her artistic revenge. Tired of being cast as an obedient dominatrix in heavy Russian furs, she pushes the story to the limits of her own invention, subjecting Severin to cruel and radical therapy. He is whipped by the Greek Apollo in front of his cruel Venus. Supposedly Apollo teaches Severin that women themselves wish to be slaves and have to be whipped, not worshipped.

In the end, Severin is "cured": he returns to the country to help his aging father and in the process rediscovers the Protestant work ethic and the world of familial obligations. His view of women undergoes a transformation: "Woman as nature has created her and as she is currently reared by man, is his enemy and can only be a slave or a despot, but never his companion. She will be able to become his companion only when she has the same rights as he and when she is his equal in education and work."[66]

Counterintuitive as it may sound, Severin seems to be advocating a political solution to the women's question. In the end he thinks of an alternative to the master-slave dialectic and decides that education and work would ultimately be preferable even if less exciting than mutual whipping. Perhaps this can be dismissed as a moralistic ending attached to a story of passions in order to cheat the censor, only Sacher-Masoch's morality play is more ambivalent than that of Dostoevsky. Its ambiguity is not a mere role reversal but a recognition of corrupted sacrifice that creates an opening for a play of imagination that is a part of cocreation and expansion of freedom.

Sacher-Masoch both pushes and reaffirms the limits of his text. On the one hand, he designs his ideal life scenarios in literature that he wishes to transfer (with a few adjustments) into life. His wife agrees to be cast as Wanda and later exchanges her name for that of the literary character, although she will complain later in her own memoirs of the heavy furs that she had to wear right after bearing her husband's children. On the other hand, Sacher-Masoch is repelled by the politics of corporal punishment that might have inspired his fiction and insists on the difference between private experiments and state practices. Strongly objecting to psychologization and literalization of his artistic fantasies, he was deeply troubled by the fact that his literary creation was treated as a foundation for the neurosis of Richard von Krafft-Ebing and particularly disliked the connections with the Marquis de Sade.[67]

In his study of masochism, Gilles Deleuze examines the dangers and traps of the subtle conflations of political and psychological discourse.[68]

While quoting Dostoevsky in the epigraph to his book, Deleuze never confronts the writer's "malignant pleasure" and the differences between Dostoevsky's and Masoch's conceptions. However, following Georges Bataille, Deleuze lays bare the crucial aspect of the language of masochism in which "the victim speaks the language of the torturer he is to himself, with all the hypocrisy of the torturer."[69] Bram Djikstra described this language as that of the executioner's assistant who usurps the place of the victim. "Masochism is an opiate of the executioner's assistant," he writes, paraphrasing Marx.[70] This way the "executioner's assistant" or the executioner himself appears as always already wounded, always already a victim, who has no responsibility for the infliction of suffering upon others, those involuntary extras of his authorial stagings. The man of malignant pleasure remains a mental double agent who walks a tightrope between the executed and the executioner. We will see that the notion of "double agency" will prove uncannily relevant in the case of Dostoevsky and more suitable than the notion of dialogue.

After all, the artistic male masochist, like Severin, freely chose his theatrical unfreedom. And he flaunts it in the foreground, perpetuating, often unself-consciously, the already existing cultural off-staging of those enslaved against their will. The risk of blurred boundaries between life and literature resides not only in the translation of imaginary scenarios into life, but in neglecting historical and political aspects of power relationships beyond artistic play.[71] Suzanne R. Stewart-Steinberg observes that "masochism establishes a new normativity in the name of anti-normativity and that new normativity has questionable ethical and political effects."[72]

In my view, what is problematic is not the use of political scenarios for individual imaginative and erotic practices, but the eroticization of political domination beyond individual games that in the twentieth century contributed to the phenomenon of fascinating fascism. This happens when masochism stops being an "-ism" of erotic art and becomes an ideology that disavows "suprasensual" individual eroticism for the sake of a collective orgy of violence and suffering. Self-conscious role-playing in this case might present less danger than the radical unmasking of all worldly play and seeing bodily violence as the only site of authenticity and sincerity. Sacher-Masoch only wishes to play an exotic Slav for the sake of suprasensual artifice, while Dostoevsky wishes to be that mythical Russian who transforms his malignant pleasure into the dream of world transformation.

Freud identified such a phenomenon as "moral masochism"; it goes beyond individual psychology and in fact threatens the very conception of individual interiority and human dignity. Whether moral masochism is the correct term for the phenomenon or whether it has little relationship with the art of Sacher-Masoch is another question. In his discussion of civilization and its discontents, Freud proposed to distinguish between the critique of Western civilization from within and the critique that ultimately aims at destroying it. The former focuses on "repression" of the freedom of the individual ego while the latter moves beyond any concern for individual dignity into the area of mass psychosis and domination. Here Freud touches upon a particularly twentieth-century phenomenon of isolated masses susceptible to authoritarian seduction. The anticivilizational critique doesn't operate through the repression hypothesis but rather undermines the foundations of the Western notion of freedom altogether. "The non-psychological form of the new subjectivity had introduced a new form of bondage, one far worse than repression was ever to exact from the body."[73] It is in this realm that "moral masochism" encounters politics.

Already at the end of the twentieth century, Slovenian philosopher Slavoj Zizek was raising the question of loving one's domination in the time-honored Slavic tradition.[74] The charismatic philosopher both lays bare and thrives on the symptoms of the new hypnotic form of moral masochism with the occasional brio of an Underground Man. He describes this as a symptom of the new "postliberal" "postpsychological" subjectivity that is characterized by mass self-effacement rewarded by a surplus of enjoyment. People have become willful consumers of cynical reason. Authoritarian law has been internalized and becomes a "hypnotic agency, that imposes the attitude of yielding to temptation, the injunction functioning like a command: 'Enjoy yourself!' A contemporary type of the male moral masochist is a new "organization man" of the "postliberal public sphere." Like for the Underground Man, this world in such a theoretical fable becomes a "matrix" of sorts, whereas the realm of authenticity resides elsewhere in the mythical brotherhoods of Lenin, or, for some philosophers, of Saint Paul, or both.

Is Zizek's affirmation of loving one's domination a radical or a conservative gesture? Somehow the two become intertwined in the Stockholm syndrome of Western individualism. Only the place of a dominatrix in this "postliberal public sphere" remains vacant and virtually invisible. Madame Media von Dunaew, perhaps? Yet, I wouldn't rush in so quickly with the overdetermined prefix post-, of *postcritical* and *postliberal*, a hypnotic prefix of charismatic postmodern Hegelianism, opting instead for (the less immediately gratifying) alternative route, which off-stages the eros of power, the authority of revolutionary brotherhoods, and the pleasures of mental flogging with the mythical Slavic birch rod.

The Banality of Terrorism between Left and Right

> The revolutionary is a condemned man. He has no interests of his own, no affairs, no feelings, no attachments, no belongings, not even a name. Everything in him is absorbed by a single exclusive interest, a single thought, a single passion—the revolution. . . . He is an implacable enemy of this world, and if he continues to live in it, that is only to destroy it more effectively.
>
> Sergei Nechaev, *The Cathecism of the Revolutionist of the Revolutionary*[75]

> Most likely, I could have never been Nechaev, but a member of the Nechaev circle [*Nechaevets*], perhaps, I can't be sure, possibly, in the days of my youth.
>
> Feodor Dostoevsky, *The Diary of a Writer*[76]

In the novel *The Possessed*, Dostoevsky puts the art of malignant pleasure in the service of radical politics and for the first time in history shows the banality of terror by revealing pettiness and common clichés behind the power of the conspiratorial vision. In the novel, the con-artist / terrorist Peter Verkhovensky, loosely based on Sergei Nechaev, speaks like an Underground Man, only in this case, the underground is not a metaphor but a form of political organization and his words have direct and murderous implications. The title of the novel, *The Possessed* (or more literally, *The Demons*), suggests a kind of phantasmagoria in which literature, religion, and politics are closely intertwined. Dostoevsky called *The Possessed* "a novel pamphlet" because it was written directly in response to the immediate events of the time: the trial of the radical activist and terrorist Nechaev, a disciple of the revolutionary thinker Mikhail Bakunin, on account of the murder of the student Ivan Ivanov, a member of his secret organization. The reading of some aspects of the novel allows us to revisit our key concerns: the relationship between *mania* and *technê* in philosophy and politics, the corrupted sacrifice, the uses of violence and flogging in particular, and a rhetoric of liberation that turns a conversation into a conversion creating a phantasmagoric atmosphere. What is the logic of this novelistic phantasmagoria? Who is the possessor and who is the possessed? Who is the author of the terror plot and who is terrorized by it? Does the petty terrorist-conspirator Peter Verkhovensky "author" the romantic villain and would-be revolutionary messiah Stavrogin, or the other way around?

This is not only a dialogical novel but also a novel about double agents and authorial double agency. The brilliant duplicity of the novel is in the fact that it lays bare and enacts the phantasmagoria of conspiratorial imagination and the rhetoric of liberation.

The genre of the novel is in itself an interesting hybrid, in a way not dissimilar to *Notes from Underground*. *The Possessed* was called a "Russian tragedy" that dwells on the eternal questions and a "novel-pamphlet" that addresses contemporary political issues. In the center of its somewhat rambling edifice are two plots of liberation: first, the revolutionary plot of the radical "atheistic" liberation planned by Peter Verkhovensky; and the second plot is that of Dostoevsky's novel itself, which ultimately promotes liberation from possession by radical demons of terror. The novel is about the power of fiction making that becomes larger than life. The *Possessed* echoes Euripides' *Bacchae*: only instead of the resentful impostor god we have here a modern liberator-conspirator who wreaks havoc and demands from his adepts endless sacrifices for the sake of the "common cause." Like Dionysus, Peter Verkhovensky is intent on the destruction of polis and polite society, but not of the secret police in which he sees his rhetorical and practical ally. The secret police for him are part and parcel of modern orgiastic rites. Between the two liberations there is a sequence of sacrifices of the majority of the novel's characters beginning with the murder of the innocent man with strong Russian ideals, Ivan Shatov, "sacrificed" by the revolutionary sect of conspirators. At the center of my discussion will be Dostoevsky's staging of the relationship between the banal terrorist Verkhovensky and the charismatic and mysterious "phantom-hero" Stavrogin, which in turn echoes the historic relationship between Nechaev and Bakunin.

"Terror in Russia became something of a fashion," writes Walter Lacquer about the situation in the late nineteenth century. In his view, initially, terrorism was the name not of an ideology but of a strategy of radicalism.[77] In fact, those who practiced terror in the nineteenth century often switched from left to right, from internationalism to extreme nationalism. Laqueur comments that contemporary terrorism has given a bad name to the terrorists of nineteenth-century idealism, as they were deeply concerned with social justice and extremely scrupulous about the right to kill. Unlike contemporary terrorists / militants / activists / guerrillas (whichever is the media term of the day), the Russian revolutionaries of the 1860s–1880s were, for the most part, discriminating in their choice of targets and aimed only at the highest military and political elites. Moreover, in some cases, the injury or death of any single innocent bystander was a source of tremendous remorse and self-searching, reflection and change of heart. The indiscriminate terror tactic is a very new phenomenon.[78] The systematic use of terror for the cause of the revolution is developed in the writings of the Russian revolutionaries Nechaev, Tkachev, Nikolai Morozov, and G. Tarnovsky (Romanenko), who actually use the word "terrorism" as a term of self-description. The roots of the Russian radical rebellion lie in the 1860s, at the time of great revolutionary agitation that followed the liberation of the serfs by the proclamation of Alexander II and subsequently Dmitri Karakazov's attempt on the life of the "tsar-liberator" (who turned out to be much less conservative than his sucessors, Alexander III and Nicholas II). This was the time of the flourishing of the revolutionary movements and organizations from Land and Liberation (*Zemlya i volia*) to multiple radical "sects" and secret societies. Due to the nature of the political regime in the Russian empire after the suppression of the Decembrist rebellion, there was very little possibility and subsequently little interest in political transformation of the regime or the development of democratic institutions; instead, the extreme authoritarianism of the tsarist regime was matched by the radicalism of the revolutionary dreamers, who were often rather far removed from the common people on whose behalf they spoke.

Three features characterized the revolutionary movements in nineteenth- and early twentieth-century Russia that, contrary to Lacquer's assertion, establish a direct link between the tactics of terror and the substance of ideology. First, visionary ideas played a central role in the revolutionary movements in Russia and were often more important than practical social concerns and knowledge of the needs of the people. Since the mid-nineteenth century, revolution was described in messianic and utopian terms as the highest spiritual calling or a new religion, almost a liberation for liberation's sake.[79] Second, a vicious circle of codependency developed between the extreme authoritarianism of the state and political radicalism; they perversely thrived on each other. If the secret societies in Russia did not exist, they would have had to be invented by the tsar in order to legitimize new degrees of authoritarianism. Curiously, what both the radicals and the conservative monarchists and nationalists had in common was a hatred for any form of civil society; they used each other to legitimize their own raison d'être. Third, the most conspicuous feature of the revolutionary movements in Russia was a peculiar incestuous relationship between revolutionary secret societies and the tsar's secret police that survived into the twentieth century. Obviously this cannot be used as a generalization for all the revolutionary idealists and believers in social justice in Russia. However, the number of infiltrators and double agents was huge. In some

ways the secret society and the secret police shared the same pact of se-
crecy—as a paradoxical antidote to an open and public social contract. In
fact this unwritten pact may have been one of the reasons for the repeated
failures of a more moderate democratic alternative in Russia.[80]

The case of Sergei Nechaev was striking but also exemplary for the
logic of the later development of terrorism in Russia and elsewhere: it
reveals a combination of bravura and cowardice, of inspirational rhetoric
and everyday pettiness and charlatanism. Nechaev became radicalized as
a student in Saint Petersburg and took part in student revolts. In 1869 he
escaped abroad and traveled to Geneva to see Bakunin, who took an immediate interest in the young rebel. Nechaev looked for legitimization of
his newly established secret society from the celebrated prophet of ecstatic
revolutionary destruction, Bakunin, while Bakunin himself hoped to be a
spiritual guru of the youth movement. They mirror each other's charisma
and admiration, echoing and amplifying them. Nechaev followed some
of Bakunin's radical ideas to the logical extreme, and after his visit to the
legendary revolutionary visionary he composed the *Cathecism of the Revolutionary*, which consolidated his authority over his small sect of student
radicals. Here are some of the key commandments of the *Cathecism*:

1. The revolutionary is a condemned man. He has no interests of his own,
   no affairs, no feelings, no attachments, no belongings, not even a name.
   Everything in him is absorbed by a single exclusive interest, a single
   thought, a single passion—the revolution.
2. In the depth of his being, not only in words but also in deeds, he has
   broken every tie with the civil order and the entire cultured word, with
   all its laws, properties, social conventions and its ethical rules. He is an
   implacable enemy of this world, and if he continues to live in it, that is
   only to destroy it more effectively.[81]

First we observe here that the figure of the revolutionary resembles
Dostoevsky's description of the self-sacrificial personality. His/her main
feature is radical antiworldliness, which demands the severing of all human connections of family, friendships, even revolutionary brotherhood
itself for the sake of such sacrifice. The transgression of human ethics is not
even considered as some sort of "collateral damage" but a necessary rite of
passage. This-worldliness and life itself are barely tolerated: everyday existence is but a springboard for apocalyptic destruction. Thus the cathecism
doesn't merely claim that "everything is permitted" but insists on the need
for transgression. The only thing not permitted is care for humanity.

Apparently during one of the meetings of this tiny student revolutionary sect, People's Revenge, one conscientious student by the name of Ivanov questioned the methods of Nechaev and his right to indiscriminate murder. As an answer, Nechaev proceeded to murder Ivanov himself. (Ivanov happened to be a friend of Dostoevsky's brother-in-law, who spoke highly of his conscientiousness.) Of course, this killing was not presented to the fellow coconspirators as revenge but as a blood sacrifice on the altar of the future revolution, and was intended to bond the members of the organization in defiance of traditional ethics. So Nechaev's radical zeal was not directed at the generals or tsars but at a fellow revolutionary who had the misfortune to publicly disagree with the aspiring great leader. The sacrificed one was the revolutionary dissident, not the class enemy. Once again, Nechaev escapes abroad and from there observes how the members of his secret society are all put on trial. In the words of Albert Camus, Nechaev pioneered violence against his own people, in this case fellow revolutionaries, a practice that would have a wide following in the twentieth century.

There has been much discussion among scholars about who was the true author of the *Cathecism*, Nechaev or Bakunin, or whether it was a coauthorship of sorts. The agreement seems to be that the author is primarily Nechaev, but I would argue that Bakunin was a kind of ghostwriter and a muse behind his writing. Since their first encounter, the relationship between the two men was one of love at first sight, although this mutual infatuation was hardly disinterested. Bakunin needed his man of action, his "dear boy" or courageous *"abrek"* (the merciless rebel from the Caucasus, which is how Bakunin referred to Nechaev). Nechaev needed support from an established charismatic leader of the émigrés. Bakunin's text that most influenced Nechaev was his treatise on true Russian freedom.

> Banditry is one of the most honorable ways of life within the Russian state . . . The nature of Russian banditry is cruel and ruthless; yet no less cruel and ruthless is that governmental might which has brought this kind of bandit cruelty of the people and made it into something necessary and natural . . . Should banditry cease in Russia, it would mean that either final extinction or complete freedom had come to the people.[82]

Bakunin is intoxicated by the Dionysian poetry of destruction, which for him is synonymous with liberation. This is Dionysian *mania à la russe*. He points out that Russian banditry is "no less cruel and ruthless than the government," thus enhancing their mutual codependence at the expense of everything and everybody who may fall in between the tsar and the bandit. The end of banditry is the end of freedom in Bakunin's words, thus freedom is regarded as permanent liberation and destruction.

The list of what is to be destroyed is long: it includes the tsarist regime but also any form of human ethics, political organization, art, and even science. Bakunin's logic suggests that such destructive liberation is both anarchic and in accordance with some higher necessity, thus contorting the law of destruction into a law of history (Bakunin's anarchism did not quite overcome his initial Hegelianism). For Bakunin, the criminal is a revolutionary *avant la lettre* and there is no difference between crime and justice. Or perhaps, that's not phrased in a strong enough fashion: for Bakunin, crime is a form of historic justice. Who is his exemplary criminal? Bakunin does not care much for antiauthoritarian dissenters. His exemplary heroes are Emelian Pugachev and Sten'ka Razin, peasant leaders who declared themselves tsars. The hero is the liberator turned authoritarian imposter who proclaims himself a divinely anointed tsar of Russia appealing to higher laws of history. The author of the treatise identifies with his hero, carving for himself the same coveted space of the *Dionysus Liber / Dionysus Rex* at least in theory, if not in practice. As Herzen observed, there is no space at all for any individual liberties in Bakunin's grand view of history. Bakunin's logic is that of analogy and binary agonism, but he is hardly a systematic thinker of any kind; his writings are peppered with religious imagery and Hegelian metaphors as well as quotes from Alexander Dumas' popular novel *The Three Musketeers*. Perhaps it is pointless to reduce Bakunin's eloquence to logic; it is his charismatic élan that makes him so powerful.

Reading Bakunin, I suspect that, had he been born some eighty years later, he might have been a radical practitioner of the avant-garde or a performance artist and not a political revolutionary. He developed many suggestive terms that could have inspired artistic manifestos, including "amorphism" and "anarchism." Marx, for one, was not amused by Bakunin's lyrical eloquence and failed to appreciate its literary quality. He commented instead on Bakunin's artistic and political unoriginality and his unattributed borrowings from popular literature, from Dumas' *Three Musketeers* to Schiller's *The Robbers*, the favorite play of many Russian revolutionaries and writers, including the young Dostoevsky. In a rare case of agreement between Karl Marx and Isaiah Berlin, the latter also accuses Bakunin of flamboyant banality in spite of his talent, personal charisma, and occasional courage: "Bakunin rebelled against Hegel and professed to hate Christianity, but his language is a conventional amalgam of both."[83] Marx accused Bakunin of a similar double standard and bad conscience: he considered him "the Pope of the revolution," who tries to protect himself in exile by writing a most flattering letter of confesson to the Russian tsar while at the same time in other writings advocating the destruction of all institutions. One thing to be said in Bakunin's favor is that he recognized some of the conflicting features of his own behavior and took pleasure in his own contradictions. In his rather slavish confession to the tsar, Bakunin admits to being an occasional charlatan and con-artist. "I didn't want to be a charlatan, but sometimes I became one." Bakunin's writing reveals a verbal exuberance, bravado, and total disregard for consequences, precision, or human responsibilities. If his historic prophecy had been fictional, it would have been incredibly amusing, but when fiction is presented as history, its entertainment value becomes problematic.

We see in the case of Nechaev and Bakunin a certain continuity between tactics and the ideology of terror. After the murder of Ivanov, Nechaev comes again to see Bakunin but this encounter results in mutual disenchantment, although Bakunin still swears his love for Nechaev, his "darling boy."[84] In the words of Albert Camus, Bakunin, in theory, and his disciple Nechaev, in practice, proved that "politics can be religion and religion can be politics" in a new modern version. What they create together is a radical political religion. Nechaev, according to Camus, "made himself the cruel high priest of a desperate revolution."[85]

Dostoevsky claims that in response to Nechaev's trial, he wanted to write a "tendentious piece" but that in the end his artistic imagination took over. What he captures in the novel is a conspiratorial world view where everyone is guilty and subject to blackmail. The Peter Verkhovensky-Stavrogin duo offers a touch of artistic virtuosity to the conspiracy of liberation. Peter makes his appearance in the novel as if coming from nowhere like a wandering Dionysus; only he is not the joyful Nietzschean fin-de-siècle liberator from repression, but a resentful Euripidean god whose taste in scandal and sacrifice is endlessly voracious. Peter corrupts and destroys everyone. His father, Stepan Verkhovensky, dies with a liberal declaration in French—never a good sign in Dostoevsky; Kirilov commits an atheistic suicide with the words "Liberté, égalité, fraternité ou la morte" (as if the only proof for noble and ethical existence for a nonbeliever is suicide); Maria Lebyadkina the blessed fool and unfortunate wife of Stavrogin, is murdered; Lisa, Stavrogin's one-hour lover, is tortured by a mob; Shatov is murdered; Stavrogin commits suicide after his voluntary exile from Russia; and so on. Not much of a happy ending in sight here.

Like Verkhovensky, Stavrogin is a phantom character—described as a "wise serpent," a "magician," a "beautiful proud young god" "with a halo of sacrifice around his head," in Verkhovensky's admiring words. Verkhovensky and Stavrogin are something of a good-cop, bad-cop pair—the banal demon coupled with the glamorous villain—who feed on each other's dreams and nightmares. Let us examine closely their relationship of secret complicity and mutual blackmail. Predictably, their shared malignant pleasure includes a fantasy of flogging. This dialogue between Peter and Stavrogin takes place on the eve of the decisive meeting of the secret revolutionary sect.

"You've represented me, no doubt, as a member from abroad, an inspector in connection with the *Internationale*?" Stavrogin asked suddenly.

"No, not an inspector: you won't be an inspector; but you are one of the original members from abroad, who knows the most important secrets—that's your role. You are going to speak, of course?"

"What's put that idea into your head?"

"Now you are bound to speak."

Stavrogin positively stood still in the middle of the street in surprise, not far from a street lamp. Pyotr Stepanovich faced his scrutiny calmly and defiantly. Stavrogin cursed [lit., *spit*] and went on.

"Perhaps I will speak there, but afterwards I will give you a flogging and a sound one too, you know."

"By the way I told Karmazinov this morning that you said he ought to be flogged, and not simply as a formality but to hurt, as they flog peasants."

"But I never said such a thing; ha ha!"

"No matter. *Se non è vero.*"

"Well, thanks. I am truly obliged."

"And another thing. Do you know, Karmazinov says that the essence of our creed is the negation of honor, and that by the open advocacy of a right to be dishonorable a Russian can be won over more easily than by anything."

"An excellent thing! Golden words!" cried Stavrogin. . . . "And listen, Verkhovensky, you are not one from [of] the higher police, are you?"

"Anyone who has a question like that in his mind doesn't utter it."

"I understand, but we are by ourselves."

"No, so far I know I am not one of the higher police. Enough, here we are. Compose your features, Stavrogin; I always do mine when I go in. A gloomy expression, that's all, nothing more is wanted! It's a very simple business."[86]

Here we have a phantasmagoric atmosphere complete with the light of a gas lamp, sudden dialogue, and convulsive movements.[87] Flogging, in the center of this bizarre conversation, plays the role of the password of mutual recognition between Verkhovensky and Stavrogin, revealing their ambivalent, quasi-erotic connection. The character to be flogged is the writer Karmazinov, a Westernizer and look-alike of the writer Ivan Turgenev, Dostoevsky's famous nemesis. Peter espouses some of the same ideas that we examined in Dostoevsky's own *Diary of a Writer*, praising flogging, especially when it comes to flogging the Russian Westernizers. Moreover, he shares the rhetorical strategies of the narrator of the *Winter Notes*. Peter's lies notwithstanding, he and Stavrogin bond in their presumed addiction to malignant pleasure. (And we suspect that Dostoevsky himself revels in his own metaphorical flogging of his literary rival.)

What is the nature of their exchange: is it a dialogue or a provocation?

Flogging (actual or potential) plays an important role both in the twists of the plot and in the twists of rhetoric. This is a moment when discussion turns into blackmail.[88] It ushers in a discussion of the "higher police," which calls into question any possibility of sincerity and saying what one means. The one who converses in public about the secret police is always already an agent provocateur. Rather than a dialogue, it is an enactment of the conspiratorial logic of performative contradictions that conjures up ghosts. The dialogue is a "front" for a mock-telepathy, a nonverbal understanding or a deliberate provocation. The time of the dialogue is just as elusive as its space: it is mostly about the past or the future, or of a single compressed moment. The provocation creates its own temporality of threats and reproaches, of rewriting the past in the view of the future, mostly erasing the here and now, as if it were dangerous for the "common cause." There is hardly any dialogic deliberation of reality in the conversation between Peter and Stavrogin; instead, this is a case of conjuring up a fiction in the hope of transferring it into life. The gas lamps with their uncertain light appear like abandoned theatrical props in the middle of nowhere.

For Dostoevsky dialogue has hardly the same virtue that it does for Bakhtin; in *The Possessed* he shows how the dialogic can become "diabolic" and how any agency of free will can become a domain of the agents provocateurs. The "dialogue" between Verkhovensky and Stavrogin seals their conspiratorial pact, which in this case consists in reinforcing the conspiracy theory itself and in keeping the secret that there is no secret.

For Verkhovensky, deliberation is impossible and a dialogue is only a step toward the fulfillment of his vision of revolutionary liberation. The first stage is *"politique du pire,"* or a complete destabilization of reality. Here Peter could use Shigalov's plan of rational liberation: "Every member of society spies on the others, and it's his duty to inform against them. Everyone belongs to all and all to everyone. All are slaves and equal in their slavery . . . Great intellectuals . . . will be banished or put to death. Cicero will have his tongue cut out, Copernicus will have his eyes put out, Shakespeare will be stoned—that's Shigalovism."[89] Dreaming of absolute freedom, Shigalov arrives at absolute despotism.

After this first stage Peter posits the second stage: salvation of the Russian beauty with the help of the fair prince Stavrogin, a "Shigalovism sweetened for the people": "'Russia will be overwhelmed with darkness, the earth will weep for its old gods. . . . Well, then we shall bring forward... whom?' 'Whom.' 'Ivan the Tsarevitch.' 'Who-m?' 'Ivan the Tsarevitch. You! You!' Stavrogin thought a minute. 'A pretender?' he asked suddenly, looking with intense surprise at his frantic companion. 'Ah! so that's your plan at last!'"[90]

The logic of Peter's plot is to blackmail everyone and make sure that nobody is left untouched by and outside his conspiratorial web. The characters who don't speak in conspiratorial tongues, Shatov and Kirilov, the "Russian boys" with "heart[s] open to sacrifice," are not immune to the seduction of liberation turned despotism. Dostoevsky comments on their potential entrapment: "In my novel *The Possessed* I made the attempt to depict the manifold and heterogeneous motives which may prompt even the purest of heart and the most naïve people to take part in the perpetration of so monstrous a villainy. The horror lies precisely in the fact that in our midst the filthiest and most villainous act may be committed by one who is not a villain at all!?" Shatov and Kirilov are caught in the spider web; their idealism and earnest, self-sacrificing natures do not provide an antidote to conspiratorial phantasmagoria. Both die in the novel, one as a collective sacrifice, the other as a self-sacrifice. The only true survivor is the narrator Gorlov, a man of moderate views and an unusual storyteller in Dostoevsky's universe.

The narrative and authorial perspectives of the novel aroused critical controversy. Some of Dostoevsky's contemporaries accused the writer of creating a parody based on the Russian revolutionary movement. In Soviet times, the novel was prohibited as a slander on the revolution. But a closer look at Dostoevsky's artistic form reveals more than the "tendentious" "novel-pamphlet" that he promised in his own notebooks. The writer's notebooks, letters, and the *Diary of a Writer* reveal that his own views defied a clear opposition between radicalism of the left and of the right. In the 1880s Dostoevsky enjoyed a friendship with the reactionary advisor of the tsar Konstantin Pobedonostsev, and yet he also secretly admired the revolutionaries and confessed that in his youth he could have easily been a member of Nechaev's group himself.[91] As late as the 1870s he spoke about his admiration for Karakazov, the regicide, comparing him with one of his favorite characters from *The Possessed*, Kirilov.[92] In the notebooks Dostoevsky gives an answer as to how the novel is to be read: "My view is that these phenomena [the Nechaev case] are not an accident of fate, not isolated instances . . . These phenomena are direct consequences of an age-old divorce of all Russian enlightenment from the native and distinct principles of Russian life."[93] So at the end Dostoevsky blames Western ideas and the Russian Enlightenment: "Our Belinsky and our Granovsky wouldn't believe if they were told that they were Nechaev's fathers."[94] Thus the plot of liberation from demonic possession relies once again on the metaphoric flogging of Russian Westernizers.

Yet analysis of the novel supports neither the opposition between the Enlightenment and Russian ideas, nor a clear opposition between atheism and religion. Both Nechaev and his fictional relative Verkhovensky adhere to the sacrificial concept of individuality that Dostoevsky described as the "Russian personality" and both mobilized Russian national history and the national fairy tale for the version of political religion that they employ for their own plot of liberation. In the phantasmagoric world of impostor believers and imposter revolutionaries, it is becoming harder and harder to distinguish between corrupted and uncorrupted sacrifice. Instead of the opposition between Russia and the West one could trace the opposition between a liberational theology of extreme antiworldliness versus the worldly quest for justice, beauty, freedom, spirituality. The "distinctive features of Russian life" can include all of the above.

The originality of the novel lies also in the portrayal of the nonoriginality of the terrorist instigator Verkhovensky. The literary master in Dostoevsky often works against the ideologue in laying bare the petty everyday contexts and destructive consequences of the politics of enthusiasm. Dostoevsky might have secretly admired Stavrogin's charisma but not Verkhovensky's conventional cunning that nevertheless provokes the desired response of engulfing everyone into the mythical plot. The novel shows the nuts and bolts of terrorist mythmaking: readymade fairy tales, classic blackmail, a charismatic secret (in this case, that there is no secret), and the very realistic enchantment with the secret police. This formula does not fail to mobilize the mechanisms of mass possession and complicity that bond together rationalists and idealists, atheists and religious believers, Russian nationalists and Westernizers through the act of supposed sacrifice. Can or should anybody resist such communal bonding?

Joyce Carol Oates offers an interesting insight into a possible way out of the novel's demonic possession: "The entire account is being given some three or four months later, by the unimaginative but presumably reliable Govorov, an anonymous Everyman, a survivor, a Russian whom the demons were not able to possess. He, and not those brilliant others, is Dostoevsky's future."[95]

This sounds more like a version of an American dream that Dostoevsky certainly didn't choose. Instead, the logic of phantasmagoria engulfs the author himself. The artist Dostoevsky estranges the phantasmagoric plot, but the prophet cannot restrain himself from putting it at his own service. The display of corrupted sacrifice demanded by Russian terrorists does not result in a deliberation on the tragic ambivalence involving the human condition. In the end the writer opts out of the predicament altogether, promising to repair the gaps of estrangement with the creation of a new myth, not that of the fair prince but of a pure-hearted peasant who can become a new redeemer of the people.

Religion of the People and Liberation from Freedoms

> What they were saying about flogging and about Christianity I understood very well. But I was completely mystified by the meaning of the phrase "my colt" or his colt.
>
> Lev Tolstoy, "Kholstomer"

So we return to the genesis of the freer freedom with which we began our exploration. Dostoevsky discovers his own solution to the abyss of free-floating ambiguity that the malignant pleasure offered him. In the 1870s Dostoevsky finds his belated happy ending and catharsis in religious reconciliation. Twenty-six years after his experience in the penal colony, Dostoevsky provides a life-shattering episode missing from *Notes from the House of the Dead*, which he recorded in his *Diary of a Writer*. He remembered what he (and his many alter egos, the prisoners in the house of the dead and the Underground Man) either didn't recall or didn't record: the dream of the peasant Marei and his subsequent religious conversion.

This is how the story is retold in the *Diary of a Writer*: At the beginning of his prison life the prisoner Dostoevsky witnessed a scene of drunk debauchery and brutality perpetrated by the prisoners themselves. (The scene is partially depicted in *Notes from the House of the Dead*.) A few men were left beaten to "half death," as the Russian saying goes, while their fellow prisoners and torturers were singing "disgusting songs" right next to them, playing cards. "The two days of such holiday tormented me. Never could I tolerate the people's debauchery," writes Dostoevsky. Finally, he rushes out of the barracks and runs into a Polish political prisoner arrested for his support for the struggle for Polish independence. "Je haïs ces brigands," said M-kij, the Polish political prisoner, to Dostoevsky in French.[96]

The reaction of the Polish prisoner in fact mirrors Dostoevsky's own feelings at the time. In a letter to his brother Mikhail from 1854 composed right after coming out of prison and before writing *Notes*, Dostoevsky writes that "common people are coarse, irritable, embittered and imbued with hatred towards the gentry."[97] He describes them as "a hundred and fifty enemies" who were intent on persecuting him even as they acknowledge his superiority. When Dostoevsky came to write *Notes from the House of the Dead*, his view of his fellow prisoners undergoes a transformation, and he believes that gentry can and should learn from the people.[98] By 1876 the process of mythologization goes even further. Now Dostoevsky's reaction to M-kij's words is as powerful as to the debauchery itself. Overcome by disgust and guilt Dostoevsky returns to the barrack where he witnesses the vicious cycle of violence. The prisoners take brutal revenge on one of their own, the gigantic "Tatar Hercules," Gazin, known for many violent outbursts.

In a moment of utmost misery, mist envelops the prisoner Dostoevsky, and Marei, a long-forgotten peasant from his childhood, comes to his rescue. The prisoner suddenly remembers how at the age of nine he was overcome by fear of a wolf and had roamed around his father's estate in search for refuge. In the middle of a field he had run into the serf Marei, who comforted him with almost maternal tenderness and understanding: "'There there, cross yourself . . . Christ be with you.' I didn't cross myself . . . then he extended his finger with the black nail with the dirt of the soil and touched my trembling lips." The boy forgot the strange encounter and barely saw Marei afterward, but now as a grown man in a moment of despair he suddenly experiences an acute longing for this human care, for that finger that had touched the soil and calmed his trembling lips. What struck him is that in this encounter, without any witnesses, human kindness had prevailed over social status:

> The meeting was a solitary one, in a vacant field and only God could have seen from above what a profound and enlightened human sentiment, what delicate womanly tenderness may fill the heart of some coarse, bestially ignorant Russian peasant serf who in those days had no foreboding of his liberation. . . . Tell me, isn't this exactly what [Slavophile] Konstantin Aksakov meant when he spoke about the high educational level of our people?[99]

With the experience of that memory (as recollected more than twenty years after the prison experience), Dostoevsky looked at his fellow convicts differently. Now he saw the peasant Marei in their hearts, hidden behind their violent faces. "When I climbed down off the boards of the barrack and looked around I suddenly felt that I could behold these unfortunate men with a wholly different outlook and suddenly, by some miracle, all the hatred and anger completely vanished from my heart. I went along looking attentively at the faces which I encountered. This intoxicated, shaven and branded peasant with marks on his face bawling his hoarse drunken song—why, he may be the very same Marei; for I have no way of peering into his heart. The same evening I ran again into M-kij. Poor man! He couldn't possibly have memories of anyone like Marei and he had no other way of viewing these people differently than "Je haïs ces brigands!" No, the Poles in those days had endured more than we!"[100]

On the one hand, this is a moving and humane story that transcends distinctions of class and social status, bringing together the landowner's son and a peasant serf. It tells of a quiet moment of tenderness, of liberation from fear and anxiety and reconciliation with the world. This memory of human kindness helps the desperate prisoner to find humanity in his fellow convicts and sustains him in the face of irrevocable misery.

On the other hand, Dostoevsky both remembers the peasant Marei and erases his individual particularity, transforming him into a representative of the Russian people. For me this raises an ethical issue: if every convict in the penal colony, independently from the degree of their specific guilt or innocence, is Marei, then Marei has lost his individuality. For Marei had committed no crime. He calmed the scared child, it was his free choice, a spontaneous humane decision. He didn't ask for anything in return. In Dostoevsky's retelling even this minimal degree of individual spontaneity is denied him. Marei's action is regarded as predetermined by his faith and by his background, by his innate enlightenment and connection to the earth. Marei as a person is sacrificed and a new religion of the earth is born in which the bandit and the saintly peasant, the transgressor and the redeemer, are united. Two landscapes, the open field and the claustrophobic prison barrack, contribute to the unworldly architecture of the freer freedom. This might be a moment when a search for new national morality overrides ethical concerns.

Strangely, the story of Marei is framed by the encounter with the Polish political prisoner who mirrors the feelings of the prisoner Dostoevsky. Ultimately the duel is between the Russian and the Polish political prisoner, and the writer expresses an ironic pity and condescension toward the "heartless" Pole, not because he was unjustly imprisoned for political reasons, but because he is incapable of communion with the Russian soil. (Whatever his connections to the Polish common people might have been, they would never match those to the Russian common people.) Thus the parable of inclusion and reconciliation is framed by the story of exclusion of those who by virtue of their background do not accept the religion of the Russian soil.[101] In this retelling, the political background of the Polish prisoners and the memory of M-kij's unjust corporal punishment— that was labeled "un-Christian" by the younger Dostoevsky himself—are erased here. Paradoxically, the very act that was deemed "un-Christian" in *Notes from the House of the Dead* now becomes absolved by the writer's regained Christian vision.

Noting the circumstances of Dostoevsky's recollection of the peasant Marei—the dreamy mystery, heightened emotions, fog of memory— interpreters have been puzzled as to how to interpret Marei's apparition.[102] Is this an account of Augustinian conversion into a Russian religion of the earth, which the writer rediscovers amidst the pain and misery of prison life? A fantastic tale of the double apparition of a saintly Russian peasant and the Russian bandit? Or is it an instance of Dostoevsky's own retrospective self-fashioning as a moral legislator of the people who shares their pain and aims far above and beyond conventional politics?

Dostoevsky's passion for creating his own writerly "total work" and the strange, almost operatic, quality of his settings brings forth a comparison with composer Richard Wagner, only Dostoevsky's national heroes are not virile Valkyries but feminized men. In some way Marei appears as a Russian Parsifal empowered by the holy grail of the Mother Earth herself. In fact, he has never been alienated from her; he carries her "under his skin" and under his nails. Marei combines Russian Christianity and a folk religion of the earth; his gesture of maternal tenderness is a gesture of redemption and salvation, the meaning of which will be realized much later. He puts his finger to the boy's trembling lips, calming him down and giving him voice—not to scream from fear and disgust but to write in a prophetic voice and later to become a Russian messiah who would carry the new truth to Europe. This is a vision of expansionist salvation; in just the way the Russians once stopped the Mongol horde at the edge of Europe, they now must save Europe from itself, to purge it of its enlightened barbarism of legal and political freedoms.

Corporal punishment, the marks of flogging that the government inflicted or threatened to inflict upon the body of the writer, are now transformed into brands of martyrdom and the marks of belonging to the community of people that grants the writer the supreme authority of "the second government" in Russia, to paraphrase Solzhenitsyn's later dictum. The authority of the Russian absolute monarchy that Dostoevsky admired in his later years is transferred from politics into the writer's total work.[103] In other words, the peasant Marei unwittingly becomes Dostoevsky's muse who legitimizes the writer's cultural capital. Dostoevsky rewrites his spiritual autobiography: he is a child of Russia (blessed by Marei, both a paternal and a maternal figure) who as a writer becomes a father for his people, a little father-writer (*batiushka-pisatel'*), not unlike the little father-tsar (*batiushka-tsar*).[104]

The Russian philosopher of the early twentieth century Lev Shestov reflected on the differences in Nietzsche's and Dostoevsky's confrontation with the tragic predicament of humanity.[105] In Shestov's view, Dostoevsky never overcame "the hatred of mankind" that swept over him during his years in prison, yet he was never able to confront that hatred. Shestov observed that in Dostoevsky's view, this world and humanity are only worthy of attention if we believe in the immortal soul, hence the writer subscribed to the model of *pereat mundi*, "let the world perish," for the sake of some higher good. In other words, unlike Nietzsche Dostoevsky shied away from the tragic existential predicament, choosing instead the leap of faith. Moreover, his leap of faith, unlike that of Kierkegaard, was not an individual path towards faith but a road toward national religion. Shestov noted a paradox: Dostoevsky wished to carry the prophecy of the new antipsychological religion to Europe; yet Europeans read him as a "great psychologist." They Europeanized him instead of opening themselves to Russification.

Whether we agree or not with Shestov's strong opinion, we cannot fail to observe the paradoxes of cross-cultural translation when it comes to understanding modernity, liberation, and freedom. The *Diary of a Writer*, in which the dream of the peasant Marei appears, is an unconventional diary; in its literary form it is linked to many West Europeans' works, particularly of the period of the Enlightenment, Diderot and Voltaire included. Yet while using elements of the dialogical forms of Enlightenment literature, it pursues a radically anti-Enlightenment message. Marei is at once "bestially ignorant" and "enlightened"; he is already free, independent from his political status as a serf.

The wealth of literary devices and techniques of seduction and persuasion are used for an extraliterary purpose—to turn readers into converts and to transfer literature into life. Joseph Frank perceptively observes that Dostoevsky's irony is "inverted." In my view, it is not merely inverted but also a conversion device; it is a simulacrum of irony that strives for emotional persuasion and charismatic hypnosis. This rhetorical strategy mimics the dialogical process but in fact transforms conversation into conversion. Arendt's intuition that the world is missing from the dialogues between Dostoevsky's characters is insightful; most of Dostoevsky's heroes are more engaged in the creation of demonic or angelic fairy tale worlds of their own making rather than in inhabiting and understanding the surrounding world. Instead of deliberating on reality they conjure up horrifying or beautiful fictions in the hope of transferring them into life. This kind of liberation is supposed to lead to the "freer freedom," leaping over freedoms in the plural and the traditional realm of political and public discourse. The author of *The Diary of the Writer* speaks in the voice of the victims of the Grand Inquisition of Western civilization, and at the same time wishes to play the roles of Christ and the Grand Inquisitor, who will help to liberate us from the "liberal values" of the West.

Figure 10. Svetlana Boym, chessboard collage with author's photograph of the book of Arendt and Heidegger's correspondence.

FOUR

LOVE AND FREEDOM OF THE OTHER

Totalitarianism for Two, or Adventure in World Making?

Hannah Arendt wrote that a passionate love can result in "totalitarianism for two."[1] In this case, the lovers' crime of passion lies in their obliterating the world around them and forgetting both public and individual freedoms. Indeed, love can obliterate worldliness, but it can also create potential worlds, and this world making sometimes outlasts the lovemaking. The experience of love in itself offers a microcosm of the social world that echoes but never conforms to the power relationships in society, attitudes toward the individual, gender politics, and religious and cultural beliefs. As such, the love relationship becomes a minidemocracy, an enlightened despotism, a theocracy, a tyranny, anarchy.

The relationship between love and freedom reveals an incurable codependency or even a love-hatred. Love can bring upon an individual both bondage and liberation. It can put an end to the individual autonomy of two lovers and shrink their worlds, or on the contrary, carve a new unpredictable "third space" that is never

the sum of the two. Instead, it is measured with the help of the adventurous hyperbolic mathematics of knots, curves, folds, parallel lines, and lives
that can occasionally cross.

Hence, the love experience is an exemplary trial of freedom that tests
its inner and outer boundaries, especially when the lovers happen to be
philosophers. In the case of Søren Kierkegaard and Hannah Arendt, their
conceptions of freedom developed directly from the experience of love,
thus intertwining experiments in living and experiments in thinking, affect
and judgment, not always harmoniously.

"Pleasure disappoints, possibility never," wrote Kierkegaard, suggesting that one's own imagination is the most powerful aphrodisiac.[2] In this
sense, for a philosopher being in love with love (or "being in one's love,"
as Heidegger puts it) can be less disappointing than being in love with another person. However, willy-nilly, the philosopher in love has to encounter the second subject, his or her beloved, who is another unpredictable
individual. If, like Sartre, he imagines that the project of love is to possess
the freedom of the other, which should be freely given, he is doomed to
existential and personal failure however much he plans to "work on the
relationship." The obsession with control can destroy the adventure of
cocreation and openness to the unpredictable. The encounter between
two subjects and two existential projects is among the most complex one
in philosophy. What happens when the philosopher stumbles upon the
freedom of the other, which he/she desires but never conquers? Can the
relationship between two subjects extend beyond master-slave dialectics?
What would the lovescape of the intersection of two freedoms look like,
and what kind of philosophy would it inspire?

Roland Barthes suggested that we no longer know how to speak about
love. In his view, contemporary lovers' discourse is more "obscene" than
the transgressive tale of the "pope sodomizing the turkey" recounted by
Georges Bataille, or any other explicit pornography.[3] It is as if the domain
of affect and attachment is beyond the pale for a serious thinker, more so
than the frank vulgarity or explicit representation of sexuality. A lover's
discourse is made more "obscene" because of its appropriation of popular
culture and psychology. What is the meaning of the obscene in this case?
The word "obscene" has an obscure etymology. It can be related to the
Latin *ob* (on account of) + *cænum* (pollution, dirt, filth, disgust, ill omen).
But there is another, perhaps a popular, etymology that suggests a connection to the stage in Greek and Roman theater—*ob* (tension) + *scaena* (scene,
space of communal ritual enactment, sacred space). In this sense, obscene
doesn't signify anything repulsive, sexually explicit, or dirty, but something

eccentric, off-staged, lateral, unfashionable, or antisocial. It is close to my understanding of the off-modern. Love is "obscene" in the contemporary approach to knowledge in the sense that it is excessive and disruptive of discourses on method or disciplinary practices. (I speak here about love, not the institution of marriage, which might or might not include it.) Love's excess and the asymptote of freedom overlap, but never entirely.

Approaching love from a different perspective, Georg Simmel also commented on the fact that love seems to be off-the-scene of the modern conception of knowledge and that there has been a dearth of a philosophy of love since Plato.[4] At the same time love both informs and transforms the thinking of freedom and unfreedom—from Plato to Mill, Kierkegaard, and Arendt. (Both liberty and libertinage were linked in political thinking and both were considered revolutionary or counterrevolutionary, depending on the historical frame.) Simmel proposes a distinction between Platonic and modern eros that offers a different conception of architecture, a different temporality, and alternative conceptions of beauty and subjectivity. For Plato, love is a daemon that mediates between human and divine, while in the modern understanding, love mediates between two individuals. Plato and Socrates were among the first and last philosophers who considered love to be a driving force of human knowledge and human experience. And yet, Platonic love embodied in the homoerotic relationship between the teacher-lover and his beloved young disciple is inevitably pedagogic; it moves from seduction to sublimation in a vertical line, not occupying itself too much with dramas of human reciprocity. The reciprocity of feeling between the lover and the beloved is irrelevant in the cosmic order of things. Instead, the Platonic eros has its suprasensual instrumentality; it remains an irrational tool in the quest for higher rationality, goodness and beauty which has been incarnated, accidentally, as it were, and always fragmentarily, in the person of the beloved. The time of Platonic love is future in the past, never present, since it is a shadowgraphy of forgotten truths. The issue of freedom is as irrelevant as the actual personality of the beloved.

The Platonic lover cherishes the beauty that is reflected in the individual, while the modern lover loves an individual and finds him or her beautiful: "For us the *beauty* of the individual and the *individuality* of beauty comprise an indivisible unity."[5] By contrast, Platonic eros encompasses beauty and leaves individuality out. For modern reciprocal love, the beautiful beloved is no longer mere human material, the screen for the reflection of the beautiful, or a springboard on the road to the absolute. "The great task of modern man—to comprehend the eternal as something which immediately dwells within the transient," writes Simmel.[6] Hence modern eros doesn't seek to "uplift" and "overstep" the boundary of humanity; rather it dwells in the border zone and on the threshold, in the gap between the past and the future, in the potentialities of human sociability and the playfulness of the present. At best, modern eros can offer us an adventure that pushes us "beyond the threshold of our temporally bounded life."[7] Only, "beyond" in Simmel's conception of modernity is not transcendental. This "beyond" is a pointer, not a destination. It is a horizon behind the visible horizon, a view from the threshold, a dream and a promise of wonder. It directs sideways, toward elsewhere, toward the space of adventure that is both strange and intrinsic to life itself.

Yet in Simmel like in Plato, the relationship between lovers never ends in mystical fusion. Quite the contrary. The architecture of reciprocity includes walls and fences, not happy meadows and the endless steppe. "Modern love," writes Simmel, "is the first to recognize that there is something unattainable in the other; that the absoluteness of the individual self erects a wall between two human beings which even the most passionate willing of both cannot remove and that renders illusory any actual 'possession.'"[8] The unattainable in this case is not the transcendental, but the human; the mystery is the mystery of individuality, not divinity.[9] Simmel's wall of modern eros is not merely an obstacle for lovers, it is also a space of erotic revelation and concealment, the threshold of play. Such horizontal architecture contains as much mystery and potentiality as the vertical of power and transcendence.

However, for Simmel Platonic and modern eros are not merely two antagonists caught in a binary opposition. There is a mysterious and tragic force in both of them.[10] The tragic in modern eros doesn't lie in Fate's plot or in social obstacles to lovers' union, like in a Shakespearean play, but rather in the clash between the blind hopes of lovers and life's transience. In other words, it is the extemporaneous temporality of love and its quixotic battle against necessity that can make it tragic. Thus, the experience of love exemplifies both the potentialities and the boundaries of human freedom: "Out of its own energies [life] has given birth to what is unfaithful to life," writes Simmel.[11] Catharsis here does not lie in the consummation of love, but in the long peripeteias and struggles with the transience of life and chance, with the desire to arrest the moment and to commemorate the fragile lovescape. Modern love experience is about coming to terms with an impossibility to possess the other. Even the possessive pronouns in love like "my" or "yours" do not signify a possession but a creation of an object of love and a landmark within the lovers' secret landscape or cityscape that never before existed: "my" attached to the name is an act of love's baptism, not a property claim.

Simmel's own essay posits a philosophical architecture of love that bridges between and beyond Platonic and modern eros and ends in the "cleavage" of the unpredictable. The lovescape flickers between the promise of the adventure and the advent of inevitable melancholia; love's gaze is the "tentative turning towards something on which the shadow of its own denial already falls."[12]

The language of love vacillates between the banal and the ineffable. We imagine the word itself with the off-centered "O" from a Robert Indiana love image mass-reproduced on postcards and t-shirts of the world. Between the banality and the sublimity of love lies the space of metamorphosis and cocreation. This is the affective architecture of human freedom. Love experiences move between the citadels of inner freedom and official "private properties" built into the public architecture of society, and from there into semiconcealed spaces of secret encounters, balconies, bridges, and side and back alleys, to the hyperbolic planes of amorous imagination. It can become an adventure in agnostic world making, a tender cocreation of potential spaces. The most life-transforming love experiences are queer even when they happen between a man and a woman. It is not by chance that some of the most striking and foundational texts of love were written by non-"straight" thinkers and poets—from Plato to Proust, from Tsvetaeva to Barthes. A love affair can often be an alibi for philosophical experimentation, intimation of mortality, existential boredom, nostalgia, a desire for belonging; but it never remains a mere alibi and always offsets the original premise, occasionally causing paradigm shifts.[13]

Here I will focus on the contradictions of modern erotic architecture, on the encounter of two subjects in love and its historical and political ramifications. We begin with one of the first modern philosophers of love and practitioners of eros, Søren Kierkegaard, who ended up sacrificing love for the sake of inner freedom. Then we move to a pair of passionate thinkers—Hannah Arendt and Martin Heidegger—whose secret lovescape was shaped by major dramas of the twentieth century and that contributed to the development of Arendt's conception of public freedom.

"The Seducer's Diary": An Embrace as an Appeal to Arms

> Melancholia is the most faithful mistress I've known. No wonder, then, that I return the love.[14]

Søren Kierkegaard was a faithful lover. For the sake of his faithfulness, he sacrificed the only woman he loved and lived unhappily thereafter, at least by conventional standards of happiness. His was a voluntary sacrifice, designed and authored by himself, to the point of eccentricity. It was requested neither by society nor by the church. Throughout his short life he endlessly rewrote the story of his love and freedom in different genres and under different pseudonyms and personae ranging from the hedonistic seducer to ascetic hermit. Each repetition brought him further and further away from human reciprocity; each stage in the ascent toward Love with a capital L removed him further from his worldly love experience and the encounter with his beloved. Ultimately he became an architect of his own citadel of inner freedom, in which "shadowgraphy" becomes the main form of communication.

His was a one-man liberation movement and a one-person revolution that challenged the Hegelian system as well as the official church. On his radical road toward self-liberation, he breaks connections with worldly freedoms, becoming like Dostoevsky a modern antimodernist. In this theater Kierkegaard recreates his own love life and replays its many possibilities that defy actualization and challenge the outside world.

The story starts out as a storybook romance. In 1837, the brilliant thirty-year-old Latin teacher Søren Kierkegaard meets Regine Olsen, a beautiful teenage girl with lively "roguish eyes." He spies on her for two years and finally makes her acquaintance. This is hardly a casual encounter since Kierkegaard claims to have "decided upon her" on his father's birthday. Courtship coincides with Kierkegaard's writing his dissertation on Socratic irony, and it seems that the rhythms of the dissertation writing affect the plot of the love story. The young professor carefully plots his way into Regine's house and soon proposes to her. The official engagement and the exchange of rings follow according to the conventional rituals. Yet only after the official engagement does seduction begin for real, and Søren decides to "poeticize" himself into Regine's heart. In spite of his battle with melancholia, his other loyal mistress, Søren fell deeply in love and after months of elaborate seduction managed to win Regine's "total devotion." Yet the closer they are drawn together and the closer the date of the wedding, the more anxious Søren feels. Once his dissertation is completed, he decides to confront what in his mind is the inevitable and sends back the engagement ring to Regine in the mail.[15] Søren is overcome by suffering, but he explains to Regine that his newfound religious calling precludes the possibility of such human happiness. The returned engagement ring will become endlessly poeticized, opening up an erotic and a hermeneutic geometry.

The first retelling of the love story occurs in the part of *Either/Or* known as "The Seducer's Diary," written by Johannes the Seducer. The story is told in a subjunctive mode, not accounting for what had happened but for what could have happened or should not have happened. Johannes is less a Mediterranean adventurer Don Juan and more a reflexive lover. Seduction begins as a pedagogical romance and unhurried indoctrination into the arts of freedoms that have to be taken in slow drafts.

Johannes wants his Cordelia "to develop inwardly, to feel the elasticity of the soul, to be able to evaluate the world." He wants a relationship between "two able minds": "She must owe me nothing, for she must be free. Only in freedom is there love; only in freedom is there diversion and everlasting amusement."[16] Of course, her freedom is not without a design: the seducer wishes his beloved to fall into his arms "as it were by natural necessity." The game of personal pronouns reflects the relationship between one's own freedom and the freedom of the other.

> My Cordelia!
>
> "My"—what does this word designate? Not what belongs to me, but what I belong to, what contains my whole being, which is mine insofar as I belong to it. After all, my God is not the God who belongs to me, but the God to whom I belong, and the same when I say my native land, my home, my calling, my longing, my hope. If there had been no immortality before, then the thought that I am yours would break through nature's usual course.[17]

This is the beginning of the ring cycle. The ring here is still open like a parenthesis. There is an erotic tension and distance between the two lovers, between "my" and "thy." The ring holds a promise, a possibility for lovers of an intimate world of mutuality and freedom. The exchange of pronouns appears like a gift and a surrender of agency, a reversal of cause and effect. You are mine because I am yours. I am active because I am always already passive. Love me any way you want. Only Johannes is a little too eloquent for his own good. The melancholic lover wishes to end his longing with belonging but does not entirely succeed. The experience of love might be one of the few side roads to immortality that escape "nature's accustomed course" and the teleology of finitude. Simmel wrote that personal pronouns preceding the beloved's first name are not markers of love's possession but of love's inventiveness; they create a persona who did not exist and who would cease to exist outside the love game.

In Johannes's later note to his beloved, irony embraces desire, narrowing the gap between the lovers to a tantalizingly shrinking enclosure:

My Cordelia,

"My-Your"—those words, like parentheses, enclose the paltry content of my letters. Have you noticed that the distance between its arms is becoming shorter? Oh, my Cordelia! It is nevertheless beautiful that the emptier the parenthesis becomes the more momentous it is

Your Johannes.[18]

The ring cycle reaches the second stage, the distance between the arms is growing shorter. The eloquent lover coquettishly poses as a self-deprecating writer, willing to sacrifice his deeply felt pleasure in writing love letters for the love itself. The sigh "Oh" before the personal pronoun spells danger.

From a conventional symbol of union, the ring becomes a mysterious hieroglyph that finds its reflection in lovers' syntax (parenthesis) and body language (embrace). The shape of the ring is endlessly repeated, with many ripple effects. Johannes teaches his beloved that the engagement ring is a mere convention; it exposes romantic intimacy to the vulgarization of the public world. Yet he is also aware that his own lover's discourse "defrauds" his beloved of an erotic relationship, transposing it into language that is now imbued with the graphic sensuality of the near-perfect embrace.

In "The Seducer's Diary" it is Cordelia who breaks the engagement even though Kierkegaard believes that he has led her to it:

My Cordelia

You complain about the engagement; you think that our love does not need an external bond, which is only a hindrance. I thereby recognize at once my excellent Cordelia! I truly admire you. Our outward union is still only a separation. There is still a wall that keeps us apart like Pyramus and Thisbe. There is still the disturbance of having others share our secret. Only in opposition is there freedom. Only when no outsider suspects our love, only then does it have meaning; only when all outsiders think that the lovers hate each other, only then is love happy.

Your Johannes.[19]

The reversal is complete—the ring is the opposite of the embrace, liberty resides in opposition. But the embrace is also a "call to arms"—and now the language of love threatens the embrace. Johannes makes Cordelia return the ring out of her free will, as if divesting himself from responsibility for this turn of the plot.

In the legend of Pyramus and Thisbe, the wall that separated the two lovers also became their meeting place. They talked through the wall and even kissed the wall. Yet somehow living by the wall and sharing what separated them was their destiny. The space around the wall was the space of their love in this world. Once they escaped and met near the cave, they were doomed to misunderstanding. He saw her bloodied clothes and rushed to kill himself; she followed him to the grave. Public disclosure threatens the authenticity of their love. The wall is neither merely an obstacle nor a synthesis; it is the space of the lovers' paradox, of the tragedy of the love experience.

The ring in the story of Johannes and Cordelia functions like the wall in the legend of Pyramus and Thisbe. The moment the ring of convention is returned, all the lovers are left with (in Johannes's view) is the embrace. But the embrace can become stifling and turn into the call to arms. Simmel sees in the wall an enabling paradox of the mysterious cohabitation of two individualities that does not end in mutual annihilation. But such a coexistence of the two subjects has no space in Kierkegaard's plot.

And yet, on the eve of the doomed denouement, there is a brief moment of time out of time before the first and last physical consummation of the relationship, when the touching is most erotic, when there is still a breathing space between the lovers and the embrace is not yet stifling. This time is a lovers' gift, a break away from history and nature into a "subjunctive" temporality of hope, imagination, and adventurous possibilities. This is the moment when the erotics of language is in sync with kissing and does not run ahead of itself. The lover, alas, is an impatient writer who dreams of classifying all the memorable and transient kisses that exceed the onomatopoeic approximations of known language. "Sometimes it is a smacking sound, sometimes whistling, sometimes slushy, sometimes explosive, sometimes booming, sometimes full, sometimes hollow, sometimes like calico, etc. etc. . . . The first kiss is qualitatively different from all others."[20] The lover glorifies the unrepeatable and the unredeemable, filled with anticipatory nostalgia. It is as if there is something more at stake in his enchantment with Cordelia: "To love you, is it not to love a world?" Johannes asks in one of his letters.[21] The whisper of kissing enciphers worldliness itself.

The seducer savors the last moment before the denouement, the moment most pregnant with possibilities, before the finality of the resolution. Then comes the long-awaited consummation:

Why cannot such a night last longer? . . . When a girl has given away everything, she is weak, she has lost everything, for in a man innocence is a negative element, but in a woman it is a substance of her being. Now all resistance is impossible, and to love is beautiful only as long as resistance is present; as soon as it ceases, to love is weakness and habit. I do not want to be reminded of my relationship with her; she has lost her fragrance, and the times are past when a girl agonizing over her faithless lover is changed into a heliotrope. . . . If I were a god, I would do for her what Neptune did for a nymph: transform her into a man.[22]

The variety of love experiences, their epiphanic moments and tides of joy and longing, is reduced to the conventional plot of seduction with a beginning, speedy climax, and abrupt denouement. In mock Hegelian fashion Johannes declares that the end of seduction parallels the end of history; from then on the myth begins.

Johannes prepares to rewrite the story as a relationship not between two people but between the artist and his artwork—and not even Pyramus and Thisbe, but instead Pygmalion and Galatea. He might not have created his beloved but he would like to turn her into stone nevertheless. "My Cordelia" becomes a dead Cordelia, a woman turned into a statue, a sunny girl-nymph turned into a drooping sunflower. The lovers' plot is about to erase the beloved from the story of love and freedom. The elasticity of the soul and inwardness of the freedom of the beloved are reformulated in a conventional manner: "As being-for-other, woman is characterized by pure virginity."[23]

The male lover in Kierkegaard plays a multiplicity of roles: feminine, masculine, or hermaphrodite; his soul being a feminine bow to his masculine thoughts. For women Kierkegaard reserves a much more conventional philosophical theater, forgetting the wisdom of Diotima, the teacher of his beloved Socrates. His women are objects, not subjects, of love and philosophy, mere stimulants to the experience. In the end, the fact that Johannes the Seducer wishes to remake Cordelia into a man is his ironic compliment to her; she tempted him with the highest love, with being his worldly soul mate, a poetic hermaphrodite. But the union was not meant to be since it violated the plot of sacrifice.

When personal history is transformed into myth it eliminates the unpredictable encounter with the freedom of the other, blurring the distinction between wishful thinking and action. The imaginary theater of Johannes the Seducer is particularly interesting for the way in which it reverses roles and rewrites the parts of Kierkegaard and Regine Olsen. (Of course, literature shouldn't be read as an endless roman à clef; it plays with possibilities, not with actualities that might threaten the coherence of the myth making and of its single authorship.)

In "real life" (to use an expression that Kierkegaard would no doubt contest), it is doubtful that the relationship between Søren and Regine was consummated at all in such an unconventional manner. Biographers believe that Søren respected the girl's honor. And yet contrary to "The Seducer's Diary," it wasn't Regine-Cordelia but Søren-Johannes who broke the engagement. He returns the ring to her with the following note:

> Above all forget him who writes this, forgive a man who thought he may be capable of something, is not capable of making a girl happy.
>
> To send a silken cord is in the East capital punishment for the receiver; to send a ring is here capital punishment for him who sends it.[24]

The letter is written in the third person, as if the lover is in the process of becoming a literary character, distancing himself from his own actions and responsibilities. It equates the return of the ring with capital punishment. Like in "The Seducer's Diary," the writer wishes to reverse the roles of sender and receiver, of the one who causes and receives the suffering.

According to Kierkegaard's diaries, Regine doesn't accept his disavowal and doesn't play his game:

> What did she do? In her womanly despair, she overstepped the boundary. . . . I suggested giving the appearance that it was she who broke off the engagement, so that she might be spared all offense. That she would not have. She answered: if she could bear the other she could bear this too. And not un-Socratically she said: In her presence no one would let anything be noticed and what people said in her absence remained a matter of indifference. It was a time of terrible suffering; to have to be so cruel and . . . She fought like a tigress. If I had not believed that God had lodged a veto she would have been victorious.[25]

It is ironic that Regine plays Socrates to the Socratean scholar; his poison became her own. The girl whose favorite heroine was Joan of Arc disputes his authorship of their love affair and asks for what is hers: her freedom not to follow his plot. She wants to see their relationship beyond the prescriptive narratives of seduction or conversion.

There is a moment in Kierkegaard's diary when he considers Regine's authorship. He writes that he doesn't wish to make Regine "poetically volatilized": "She has not become a theater princess, so if possible she shall become my wife." That remained a road not taken. When Regine "oversteps the boundary" and trespasses into his private realm, he does not yield to her and does not take back the ring.

So the metamorphosis goes full circle, the gift of love becomes the token of rejection. The lover who scorned convention acts conventionally. The ring of convention turns into the ring of language, which closes the parenthesis excluding the beloved. The circle of the ring, which followed the contours of the embrace, now is the self-referential circle of the philosophical lover which allows him to recoil upon himself. The ring turned out to be a "Trojan horse" of a gift, a sign of reciprocity that became a symbol of the philosopher's inner freedom. The figure of the circle and repetition, a spirited spiral of aesthetic sublimation or faith, will be central in Kierkegaard's philosophy of freedom, only it would no longer include the space of the other subject, that of the beloved girl with the roguish eyes.

Theodor Adorno wrote that Kierkegaard had a dialectic of the spheres and stages of existence.[26] In my view, the hidden figure in the first part of *Either/Or* is that of a long, parenthetical, unfulfilled embrace that doesn't open to include the world but ends in a radical gesture of fencing off the beloved herself as a figure of worldliness. To play further with erotic geometries: the two engagement rings intertwine and overlap, leaving out the ellipsis of the new potential poetic world cocreated by the lovers. Kierkegaard wishes to transform it into a figure of infinity, as two stretched-out ellipses of his own infinite horizon. But there is always a threat that he ends up with less rather than more in a circle of wordless solitude.

At the end of Kierkegaard's personal diary the lover designs his own architecture of loneliness, in which the beloved survives as a souvenir in the castle of the seducer's inner freedom:

> My sorrow is my one castle, which lies like an eagle's nest high up on the mountain's peak among the clouds. No one can take it by storm. From it I swoop down into actuality and snatch my prey, but I do not stay down there. I bring my booty home, and this booty is a picture I weave into the tapestries at my castle.[27]

No longer a nymph with roguish eyes, the beloved becomes a part of the tapestry, the wallpaper of memory. Regine herself once suggested in a moment of ironic desperation that she could live in his cupboard, as a part of his furniture. After breaking up with her, he granted her this wish by building a special shrine for her in his home:

> I had a rosewood pedestal made. It was constructed after my own design, and after the occasion of a word of hers. She said that she would thank me all her life if I would let her stay with me, that she would even live in a little

cupboard. With this in mind it was constructed without shelves. In it every-thing is carefully preserved; everything that reminds me of her, everything that can remind her of me. Here also can be found a copy of each of the pseudonymous works for her; always there were reserved only two vellum copies—one for her and one for me.[28]

Kierkegaard's Interior Design: Shadowgraphy and Architecture

Kierkegaard was a passionate interior designer, in the broad sense of the word. Already in "The Seducer's Diary" Johannes grapples with Cordelia's domestic interiors, which he wishes to transform together with her interior life. At the beginning Cordelia's interiors resemble a Vermeer painting, but Johannes redesigns them beyond the picturesque aesthetics: "Environment and setting still have a great influence upon me. . . . When we sit at a dis-tance from the windows, we gaze directly into the heaven's vast horizon. Cordelia's environment must have no foreground, only the infinite bold-ness of the horizon. She must not be of the earth but ethereal, not walking but flying, not forward and back but everlasting forward."[29]

Unable to transform Cordelia's house or fuse the horizons of the two lovers, Johannes/Kierkegaard turns Cordelia/Regine into the muse of his own inner citadel. Yet this citadel was not quite as ascetic and bare as that of his distant Russian cousin, the Underground Man, who had much less appreciation for the aesthetics or erotics of everyday behavior. And Kierke-gaard excelled in both. Israel Levin, Kierkegaard's assistant and copyist who became the philosopher's main companion in the last years of his life, described in his memoirs Kierkegaard's extravagant house-fortress with many rooms, each of them containing a standing desk, so that the wan-dering writer could jot down his ideas whenever they visited him.[30] Each room of his apartment corresponded to a room in his imagination and had a special persona, overlapping but never coinciding with the name of the author "Søren Kierkegaard." The name of the author is a bridge between public and private, between book and life.

Moreover, the writer usually occupied one floor above the street, which got less sunlight than the upper floors. Levin recalls that Kierke-gaard would not be content until he "closed out the sun and shielded the windows (both outer and inner ones) with white drapes or tapestries." The windows of the house didn't open onto the outside, or if so, only to give some air to breath; they became rather reflective windows/mirrors.

Analogously, in the metaphorical house that Kierkegaard built, the walls are not the dividers and connectors of the modern lovers, the way

Simmel imagines them. They are dematerialized and transformed into mere projection screens for one's inner shadows.

Kierkegaard cherished his nonmetaphoric interior as well, with its many chests of drawers and bookshelves, guardians of life's memorabilia. Walter Benjamin wrote about the creation of such a bourgeois interior in the middle of the nineteenth century as a theater of the individual and a kind of phantasmagoria: "For the private individual the private environment represents the universe. In it he gathers remote places and the past. His drawing room is a box in the world theater."[31] For Kierkegaard the interior is indeed phantasmagoric but in a different way. His is not a "private" space but a "fortress of the soul." For Kierkegaard the category of privacy is in itself problematic. He is both an extremely private individual in a nineteenth-century bourgeois sense, a gourmet and a connoisseur of good furniture and design, and a rebel against the very conception of privacy. Kierkegaard trades bourgeois privacy and intimacy for radical inwardness. His drawing room is a box in the unworldly theater.

Kierkegaard invented a special form of communication for his unworldly theater, his own way of writing on the imaginary wall. He called it "shadowgraphy," a term that combines visuality and writing. Shadowgraphy is a writing of inner reflexive grief:

> When I take a shadowgraph in my hand, it makes no impression upon me, and gives me no clear conception of it. Only when I hold it up opposite the wall and now look not directly at it, but at that which appears on the wall, am I able to see it . . . If I look at a sheet of paper there may seem to be nothing remarkable about it, but when I hold it to the light and look through it, then I discover the delicate inner inscriptions, too ethereal, as it were, to be perceived directly.[32]

Those hieroglyphs of shadowgraphy are woven out of the tenderest moods of the soul. Shadowgraphy becomes the language of inner freedom; the shadows are not cast from the outside, but from inside out, refractions of the inner light, not of the worldly sun.

Every writer knows the temptations and imperatives of shadowgraphy. Without it, one can never cross the threshold of space into the life of the mind. Only, not all shadows must come from inside. Hannah Arendt, an avid reader of Kierkegaard in her youth, proposed instead a conception of luminosity that radiates from human relationships in dark times, and though it might not offer all necessary insight, can at least save us from the worst kind of delusion.

Kierkegaard believed otherwise. He practiced the art of shadowgraphy even when he strolled through the city, avoiding the sun and any source of light other than that of his own mind and soul. Levin observed that Kierkegaard "always walked in the shadows and just like the trolls, could never be induced to step over a sunlit patch." In this Kierkegaard resembles Gogol's copyist with another double name, Akakii Akakievich, in "The Overcoat," who often confused the lines of the street and lines of the text. Since ancient Greece, the art of memory has linked rhetoric and space; in the neo-Platonic theater of memory one is striving for a "total recall" beyond the worldly experience of an individual. Kierkegaard designs his interior as a space where such shadowy recollections of eternal truth can take place. And the better covered the windows on the world, the better the chance one has to become a spectator of one's own inwardness and to open up the infinite horizon of freedom. And yet Kierkegaard's shadowgraphy and the leap into the infinite horizon of freedom remained in subjunctive mode.

It is as if the very instruments that were at his disposal, both linguistic and architectural, drew him in contradictory directions. The author and his multiple alter egos remain mired in language itself and in the uncanny architecture on the threshold between worldliness and its other.

Love/Freedom: Either/Or?

"What a wretched invention human language is; it says one thing and means another."[33] A month before his engagement to Regine, Kierkegaard compared freedom to language, because like language it is partly something "originally given" and partly something that develops freely, something that is cocreated by the individuals themselves.[34] Between silence and gibberish lies the space of freedom.

In *Repetition*, the shape of the ring defines Kierkegaard's theory of love and freedom. He defines three types of freedom, which correspond to the stages of the development of the soul:

A) Freedom first is defined as pleasure or in pleasure. What it immediately fears is repetition, for it is as if repetition possessed a magic power to hold freedom captive . . . But in spite of all the inventiveness of pleasure repetition makes its appearance. Then freedom as or in pleasure falls into despair. In the same instant, freedom makes its appearance in a higher form. B) Freedom defined as shrewdness. Freedom is still in a finite relation to its object and is itself only ambiguously defined aesthetically. Repetition is assumed to exist but it is a task of freedom to see constantly a new side to repetition. Then the shrewdness falls in despair. C) Now freedom breaks forth in its highest form, in which it is defined in relation to itself. Here everything is inverted . . . So what freedom now fears is not repetition but change.[35]

Experience of worldly love is part of the first type of freedom; writing about love is a part of the second type, and ceasing to write about earthly love altogether is the third. The first type of freedom is hedonistic, worldly, and unrepeatable. The second type of freedom turns an erotic infatuation into an aesthetic experience, while the third type of freedom requires a bigger leap of faith and is "heard in the intervals, drowned by the noise of life" and the "chatter of the drawing room."[36]

There is no place for public freedoms in Kierkegaard's typology because the very architecture of the interpersonal public realm is erased from view. Unlike Dostoevsky, Kierkegaard loved traveling and visiting foreign cities and theater shows, yet like his fellow Russian writer Kierkegaard disavows public freedoms as a superficial theater. His worldview is not antitheatrical, as it became for Dostoevsky, but ultimately antiworldly. Kierkegaard frequently ridiculed democratic freedoms as forms of hypocrisy and expressions of mediocrity.[37] Like Tocqueville and Mill, Kierkegaard saw the threat of the "tyranny of the majority" and the rule of mediocrity in democratic society, but unlike them he saw no merit in political rights and liberties that could balance the conformism of bourgeois culture. Renouncing action in love, he also renounced political action in the world, although one might argue that the radical tenor and passionate thinking in his works, especially his critique of the official church, played an important part in public life.

And yet the leap of faith and a new kind of personhood didn't come easily to Kierkegaard. A brilliant writer, he never wished to become an author of a systematic philosophy. He created instead a theater of flickering pseudonyms that echo and contradict one another, inhabiting different rooms of his whimsical castle of self.

In the names of Kierkegaard's alter egos—Johannes the Seducer, Johannes Climachus, Victor Eremita, Constantin Constantinus, Diapsalmata—there is at once constancy and repetition, tautology and difference. Constantin Constantinus cannot be simply "constant"; he needs to be so excessively. The art of possibility, which unlike the art of pleasure is not supposed to be disappointing, is a difficult art. It requires a theater of shadows and generic salto mortale between aesthetics, philosophy, and religion. Johannes Climachus becomes a genius graphomaniac who cannot stop writing. Writing became a particular form of mania for surviving this world and building a bridge into immortality.

The external plurality of masks also reveals the unfinalizable inner plurality of the individual who is forever engaged in many Socratic dialogues. In his philosophical theater Kierkegaard pitches Socrates against Hegel, remaining one of the most ingenuous critics of Hegelian logic.[38] In his "Unscientific Postscript" Kierkegaard finds the ultimate "hero flaw" in the Hegelian edifice. He observes that Hegel would have been the greatest philosopher if he had presented his system in its coherent architecture and then put a footnote at the end saying that the whole thing was a "thought experiment." In other words, if only Hegel had employed some self-irony and allowed a play of pseudonymy, he would have been more honest vis-à-vis his own quest for knowledge and freedom. Had Hegel presented his system as a possibility but not as objective truth, he would have been a genius. Instead, in Kierkegaard's view, Hegel became a destroyer of possibilities and individualities through his rational system, cutting an ultimately "comic figure," unaware of his own theater of thought. In spite of his protest against modernity, Kierkegaard's conception of mysteriously multiple and eccentric individuality is radically modern. Unlike Tolstoy he doesn't wish to remove all masks, for masks are most revealing of the internal architecture of the self. And yet the theater of self, its language and architecture, creates multiple baroque thresholds for the author that make the movement from the second kind of freedom (the reflective and aesthetic) to the third type of freedom (the transcending) particularly difficult.

After liberation from the earthly beloved, Kierkegaard found himself bound to the walls of language and architecture. The author is frequently poised between either and or, caught in the middle of his own self-imposed auto-da-fé.[39] Instead of a philosopher-king he became a heretic shadowgrapher challenging heaven and earth, official Christianity and secular philosophy.

Kierkegaard is trapped in a constant self-translation from one ancient language into another without an escape. Diapsalmata, the Greek translation of Hebrew *selah*, the word that means "refrain" in the Psalms of David, comments: "I feel like a letter printed backward in the line, and yet as uncontrollable as a pasha with three horse tails, as solicitous for myself and for my thoughts as a bank is for its banknotes, indeed, as reflected into myself as any *pronomen reflexivum* [reflexive pronoun]."[40] Exotic mirrors of ancient languages do not allow a breakthrough for the polyglot philosopher. Could he manage to build his own spiral tower of Babel and leap into the sky? What kind of sacrifice would that entail?

Aestheticized Sacrifice

> My Cordelia!
>
> I am in love with myself, people say of me. That does not surprise me, for how would it be possible for them to see that I can love, since I love only you? . . . and thus I love myself because this self of mine belongs to you . . . Therefore, what is an expression of the utmost egotism in the world's profane eyes is in your initiated eyes an expression of the purest sympathy; what is an expression of the most prosaic self-preservation in the world's profane eyes is in your sanctified eyes an expression of most inspired self-annihilation. Your Johannes.[41]

Most likely, Cordelia didn't require this sacrifice; at the end Johannes's voluntary sacrifice of his own love was also an involuntary sacrifice of hers. Self-annihilation can be a mirror of self-love, or of that self that does not build bridges to the other. For Kierkegaard, sacrifice becomes a bridge between personal and divine, but also, strangely enough, between religion, love, and art. Kierkegaard takes up the stories of sacrifice and freedom from Greek, Jewish, and Christian traditions. When it came to Prometheus, Kierkegaard scolds him for granting humans blind hope instead of foreknowledge, but then he plays out the drama of Prometheus for himself, playing all the parts and turning Prometheus into a proto-Christian figure. A passionate reader of the Old Testament, Kierkegaard was obsessed with two stories—Abraham's offer to sacrifice Isaac and the trials of Job. Curiously, Kierkegaard is almost disappointed with the fact that Abraham didn't have to kill Isaac, he was only "tried" by G-d, not forced to commit murder. Kierkegaard/Johannes de Silentio looks for the allegorical reading known to him from the Epistle to the Hebrews in which the sacrifice of Isaac prefigures the sacrifice of Jesus.[42] While discussing some profound distinctions between Christianity and Judaism, Kierkegaard made several insightful observations about the role of worldliness in these two religions that sprang from the same source:

> In the Christian view Isaac is actually sacrificed—but then there is a promise of eternity. In Judaism it is only a test and Abraham keeps Isaac, but then the whole episode will remain essentially in this life.[43]

Actually of all religions, Judaism is explicit optimism; even Greek paganism,
with all its enjoyment of life, was nevertheless ambiguous and above all
lacked the divine authority. But Judaism is divinely sanctioned optimism, sheer promise for this life."[44]

Judaism is godliness that is at home in this world; Christianity is alienation
from this world. In Judaism the reward of godliness is blessing in this
world; Christianity is hate toward this world.[45]

Kierkegaard had extensive discussions with his assistant Levin, an orthodox Jew, who was frequently obliged to stay for elaborate, six-course,
not-very-kosher gourmet dinners with his employer. Levin remembers
that Kierkegaard once said that he envied Levin because for him worldliness was not sinful, but then observed that this choice was not for him.
And yet, the philosopher of acosmism never relinquished his sensual and
aesthetic desires. Kierkegaard's ultimate sacrifice is described through artistic and culinary metaphors:

As a skillful cook says with regard to a dish in which already a great many
ingredients are mingled: "It needs still just a little pinch of cinnamon" . . . so
an artist says with a view to the effect of a color on a whole painting which
is composed of many colors: "there and there, at this little point, there must
be applied a little touch of red . . ."

Oh, the Governance of the world is an immense housekeeping and a grandiose painting. And he, the Master God in Heaven, behaves like the cook and
the artist: "Now there must be introduced a little pinch of spice, a little touch
of red." We do not comprehend why, we are hardly aware of it, since the little
bit is so thoroughly absorbed in the whole. But God knows why.

A little pinch of spice! That is to say: "Here a man must be sacrificed, he
is needed to impart a particular taste to the rest."[46]

In his journals, the governance of the world is presented as an aesthetic
gourmet feast. A touch of whimsy can make an imperfect image into a
work of art. The individual detail is not an accident but can transform the
whole. What in the culinary and artistic realm was added to the work,
in the human world must be sacrificed. Kierkegaard declares himself the
chosen "spice" of the world, the ultimate "touch" of the superior artistic
brush, where red is the color of blood and paint. Paradoxically, the writer
has to sacrifice the taste of the world in order to be transfigured into a
symbol that "imparts taste to the rest." In other words, he must renounce

worldliness to save the world and at the same time must embrace a single divine love. Yet he preserves for himself the authorship of his own act, describes his sacrifice in an aesthetic manner, becoming a demiurge of his own self-annihilation. At the end, the earthly beloved is written out of the story. The modern eros of the love story turns into a Platonic eros, and the ironic and passionate Pygmalion relinquished his Galatea. There is no need for her anymore. The philosophical lover is at once an artist and an artwork, a part and a whole. He sacrifices himself to become a new myth, one that goes by many names.

Arendt and Heidegger: The Banality of Love or Passionate Thinking?

"We must not think of ourselves as soul mates, something no one ever experiences," wrote Professor Heidegger in his first letter to Miss Arendt.[47] For Heidegger, as for Kierkegaard, the love experience is first and foremost "an experience in being in one's love," not a fusion of two. In this rare case, the young beloved shared his desire for distance and later constructed her form of passionate political thinking on the ruins of their romantic lovescape.

It began in Marburg in 1925 as a pedagogical romance between a thirty-six-year-old professor perplexed by the potentialities of being and his nineteen-year-old student whose hero was Søren Kierkegaard. Inspired by Kierkegaard's experimental thinking, Arendt began her studies in Berlin with Professor Romano Guardini, majoring in theology. She then moved to Marburg to explore the new discipline of phenomenology under the guidance of young Professor Martin Heidegger, a former assistant to the founder of the discipline, Edmund Husserl. Heidegger, son of a sexton at Messkirch in Baden, was the most inspiring, unconventional "passionate thinker" she had met up to that point. In the words of Elisabeth Young-Bruehl, "he was a figure of a romance—gifted to the point of genius, poetic, aloof from both professional thinkers and adulatory students, severely handsome, simply dressed in peasant clothes and an avid skier who enjoyed giving skiing lessons."[48] What remained of this romance is not a seducer's diary but letters of the professor to his "beloved girl," her reflective autobiographical fragment "Shadows," and a few letters dating from the years 1928–1929. If we didn't know who the mysterious "wood nymph" of the letters was, we might have never been able to reconstruct the identity of the formidable thinker Hannah Arendt from the descriptions of her lover. We might even have wondered if "she" really existed or was merely an italicized "you" of the philosophical eros.

But for now, we will try to follow the secret romance through its own vocabulary of hints and detours, of escapes from home and homecomings, through enlightenments and shadows. In the first letter Heidegger proposes the figure for their love, not a union, but a shared secret landscape. He discovers her "shy freedom" and "unthreatened hope" and wishes for her "self-liberation," the way he imagines it, that is, through her love for him. "For anything else there are methods, aids, limits and understanding—here alone everything means: to be in one's love, to be forced into one's innermost existence . . ." Love, like freedom, is one modality of human existence that is beyond limits and methods. Love is a shortcut to the "innermost being," not to conventional bourgeois privacy or the institution of marriage. Intimacy in such a philosophical love is not about interiority but about infinity. It moves from the innermost to the infinite, leaping over everything in between.

Heidegger's logic of romantic love follows Kierkegaard's logic of broken engagement that "calls to arms" and strengthens the embrace. Arendt and Heidegger's romance develops in secret; Heidegger's traditional marriage and unwillingness to bring their love into the public light is supposed to strengthen, not diminish, their secret shared lovescape. In Heidegger's thought, however, freedom is never a transgression but always a revelation of the potentialities of being. Love is not a romantic adventure but an advent toward a revelation. Their intimacy is untimely or timeless; it requires a reversal of the conventional relationship between distance and nearness and a cessation of time. For in such love, "Being close is a matter of being at the greatest distance from the other—distance that lets nothing blur—but instead puts the 'thou' into the mere presence—transparent but incomprehensible—of a revelation."[49] In the early letters comes the quote from Saint Augustine, "I love you, I want you to be."[50] Arendt would repeat it throughout her work, from her dissertation on Augustine to an unattributed instance in her unfinished *Life of the Mind*.

If his discourse is all about radiance and revelations, hers is about shadows and distances. At the beginning of their correspondence Arendt sends Heidegger her first self-reflective text, entitled "Shadows" (1925). While using the third person, Arendt does not fashion for herself a stylized persona of a Kierkegaardian shadowgrapher, but discovers a philosopher's distance from her own bewitched adolescent self. She is strikingly unsentimental and almost Flaubertian in the description of her own longing—without belonging and without an object; hers is "a longing that makes up life." She feels "a spellbound sense of being ostracized." Thus her relationship to the world is at once tender and distant, attentive and withdrawn. On the one hand she feels "shy, hesitant tenderness toward the things of the world" and sees something noteworthy even in the most natural and banal things. On the other hand, she is trapped by fear that leads to a "slavishly tyrannical" single-mindedness, to an empty gaze that forgets the multiplicity of the world.

Heidegger takes her text as a gift and offers a lovingly encouraging misreading. He treats her as a fairy tale child-nymph bewitched by the alien world and promises that his kiss will make all her shadows dissipate. It is a reversal of the beauty and the beast; his philosophical beauty will make the beast of her ostracism vanish:

> Shadows were cast by your surroundings, by the age, by the forced maturity of a young life.
>
> I would not love you if I were not convinced that those shadows are not *you* but distortion and illusions produced by an endless self-erosion that penetrated from outside.
>
> There are shadows only when there is sun.[51]

Heidegger's notion of "enlightenment" goes back to the philosophical metaphor of *lumen naturale*, that light that comes from within man; the "enlightened" person is the one who "sheds light" on our being in the world. What matters is existential rather than erotic ecstasy, although in practice the two are hardly mutually exclusive. Shadows in this mystical modernist-antimodernist vision come from the fallen and corrupted modern world. The lovers' freedom is not in their transgressions or liberating emotions. Quite the contrary. Freedom is something mystical, almost passive (although in practice it appears more "passive-aggressive," but now we are looking at theories); it is not about realizing potentialities but about revealing and multiplying them. In Heidegger, lovers' emotions are motions of their souls, far beyond individual psychology.[52] Philosophical love is a moody affair. Tenderness, melancholy, shyness, ardor, expectations, despairs, hopes of anticipation, and belated hopelessness are only crystallizations of the infinite and infinitesimal mood swings that one senses in the letters. Love is an endless hermeneutics of moods. Mood in this case, however, is not merely a transient affect; the moodscape creates a fragile affective topography of human relation toward Being, in Heidegger's understanding, and determines a temporal architecture where intimations of mortality take place together with the anxieties of intimacy and infinity. Yet as I read further into Heidegger's letters of the 1920s I find myself in the mood for melancholy of a distinctly un-Heideggerian hue. In spite of flashes of philosophical and poetic exuberance, the letters shy away from the singularity of that particularly rare human encounter. The love affair becomes an alibi for philosophical or theological revelation.

In fact, there is a striking contradiction between his tender attentiveness for the precariousness of *this* love and the generic romantic setting that "enframes" his beloved. The nature descriptions read like a guide to the predictable sublime one finds on mountain peaks and forest clearings. There is even an unlikely comparison between Hannah and the "saint" who stands revealed in her elevated surroundings: "The flower dream still in your hair—the sweep and line of the mountains on your brow and the trembling of evening cool in your beloved hand. And your great hour—when you become a saint—when you stand completely revealed." Occasionally the saintly girl turns into a Shulamith, the dark Jewish girl beloved of King Somolon, transplanted into a Germanic landscape. More revealing than imagery is the syntax of the letters, which preserves the particular urgency. As in the case of Kierkegaard, the lover's syntax itself becomes erotic. The dashes in the phrases mark the time of eros—both the time of waiting and anticipation, the time of remembrance, the time out of time. They trace secret burrows in the lovers' landscape filled with intimations and silences. She becomes *you*—in italics: "Nothing forced its way into our closeness—nothing merely earthly—blind—wild and lawless. I have only you to thank for that—that it was *you*."[53] But is this an intimate "you" of a lover or the "thou" that unveils the sublime landscape like that portrayed in a work of great art?

Heidegger interprets Arendt's "ostracism" in a romantic manner as a revelation of her (Kierkegaardian) angst, and he gives her a poetic pet name, a "girl from abroad," an intimate stranger. (This is rather unoriginal personal language taken straight from Schiller's poet.) Martin's relationship to Hannah is triangulated via Kierkegaard and the Romantics, for whom angst was the highest manifestation of freedom. In accordance with the reversal of distance and nearness, her home abroad is her true home, which protects her from the "ugly foreignness" of this world. Just as Kierkegaard wished to make Regine his Galatea and an object of furniture, Heidegger tries to make Hannah into his "wood nymph" of the sublime landscape. In Kierkegaard the figure was that of a broken ring, a returned ring, a painful parenthesis, an incomplete embrace. In the case of Heidegger and Arendt it is all about the paths and the frames, the dashes of pregnant silences, the ellipses and hiding places.[54]

But the mood and the circumstances have changed. Once upon a time the philosopher was in the mood for love, but then he found himself in the mood for work. The background, the revelatory landscape of existential

ecstasy, becomes a foreground, while the figure of the particular lover
fades to a shadowy silhouette of memory. In Heidegger's description, the
philosophical labor, "the most magnificent human experience," requires
"the withdrawal from everything human and breaking off all the connections," isolation from the outside and even the sacrifice of his lover.

We know that Arendt and Heidegger exchanged letters until 1933. In
her last letter, which has not survived, she must have confronted him with
the circulating rumors of his increasing sympathy with Nazism, his explicit anti-Semitic remarks, and his exclusion of Jewish students. In his last
letter from this period (winter 1932–1933) he gives her "a clarification of
how he behaves toward Jews," assuring her that none of this can touch
their relationship. The letter is not "moody" in a philosophical sense, but
filled with all-too-human resentment:

> The rumors that are upsetting you are slanders that are perfect matches for
> other experiences I have endured over the last few years. . . . As a clarifica-
> tion of how I behave toward Jews, here are the following facts:
>   I am on sabbatical this winter semester and thus in the summer I an-
> nounced, well in advance, that I wanted to be left alone and would not be
> accepting projects and the like. The man who comes anyway and urgently
> wants to write a dissertation is a Jew. The man who comes to see me every
> month to report on a large work in progress . . . is also a Jew. The man who,
> with my help, got a stipend to go to Rome is a Jew—Whoever wants to call
> that "raging anti-Semitism" is welcome to do so . . . In any case, I have long
> since given up expecting any sort of gratitude or even just decency from
> so-called "disciples." Beyond that I am cheerful at work which is becoming
> increasingly difficult, and wish you all the best, M[55]

One could be sympathetic toward the professor trying to get some work
done on his sabbatical had the date not been 1933 and the place, Nazi Germany. The mood here is that of conspiratorial paranoia, resentment, and
self-pity—of a poor Nazi-sympathizing great philosopher who sees himself
as besieged and emotionally persecuted by his ungrateful Jewish and Aryan
disciples. If there were affects Arendt despised the most, they were resentment and self-pity. Her life after 1933 proved to be—to say the least—more
difficult than his, yet self-pity was a trap she never succumbed to.

After this brief exchange of letters Arendt was arrested by the Gestapo
in 1933 and miraculously escaped, first to Czechoslovakia and then to
France and finally to the United States. Heidegger became rector of the
University of Freiburg, delivered his infamous rector's address expressing

his romantic sympathy for Nazi idealism and its fight against the vulgar "humanism" of the modern world. His direct Nazi collaboration was short-lived, for the Nazi nomenklatura had very little use for the moody philosopher who, despite his admiration for the Germanic forest, kept too close to the ancient Greeks, was suspect for the Orthodox Nazis. Arendt thought that he persisted in his incurable romantic nationalism, blind to its pitfalls and secret burrows.

It seems peculiar that after the renewal of their correspondence almost twenty years later, after many lies, betrayals, war and Holocaust, and her exile, Martin would continue to imagine his Hannah in the same Germanic landscape. In a letter dated September 14, 1950, Heidegger thanks her for a "beautiful evening" and describes the photographs she sent him as if they were works of art. In the first photograph Hannah appears to him as a young Aphrodite: "The way you stand with the coat blowing in the sea breeze speaks to me in language as pure as the birth of Aphrodite . . . It is too bad, though that you evidently had to look into the sun, so your eyes are not as radiant as your figure."[56] In the other photograph of 1950 Hannah appears as the muse in the natural landscape:

Why do I love this one in particular? Because here you are as present as you were in my room in Freiburg. The days are preserved in it—with all your loving mischief. And in the hammock it seems to me that all the exhaustion of the city is still with you, but that it already promises to give way to the waves and the wind and the freedom. The composition of the pictures is singularly beautiful; it frames you so appropriately—especially in the one where you are standing. I am glad to see grass and trees and wind and light around you, instead of the buildings and telephone poles that the frame (*das Gestell*) puts up everywhere in the city. But you would surely overcome this environment, and probably even master it as an element.[57]

In 1950 the philosopher still celebrates his lover's radiance and wishes to dispel her shadows. He tries to liberate her from the "frame of the city," with its buildings and telephone poles—and one might add, diverse urban dwellers, "rootless cosmopolitans," immigrants, and historical memories. What he loves in her is the recognition of his own love for the nymph of the romantic landscape, not that "outside" world that she now inhabits. He reads her photographs as the working of a work of art and "enframes" the girl from abroad, lovingly, but enframes nevertheless. In other words, he passionately excludes anything that constitutes the true mystery of her individuality, her otherness at the core of her new political thinking that she practices at the time of this letter exchange. For Arendt herself, public worldliness and modern urban life became an integral part of her thought and of her own inner plurality. She felt more at home in the modern cosmopolitan city than in the artificial refuge of a glorious landscape in Nazi and postwar Germany.

It is very rare in the history of romantic love that a philosopher's beloved gets her say and develops her theory of freedom, overcoming but never betraying her first love. We will discover that the same lovers' discourse acquires different reverberations throughout their work; the poetic landmarks of their interaction, words like *home, world, shadows, beauty, public light, freedom*, and *judgment*, would be used by both and overlap without coincidence. It is crucial to understand this difference not as mere anxiety of influence but as a radical non-fusion, sometimes a loyalty without faithfulness, and other times, a disagreement without a rupture. Arendt proceeds to redefine "the love for a single one" as "totalitarianism for two" and "enframing" the history of romantic love itself. Her immigrant journey will lead her to embrace *amor socialis* and public worldliness. Gradually she would transform passion into a passionate thinking, moving away from the love for a "single one" towards multiple intimacies with men and women. Being abroad and an outsider will be a foundation for her theory of distance and inner plurality of the human condition. Freedom won't be found in romantic landscapes and beautiful evenings but in worldly performance on the public stage. In her postwar reflection on her trajectory, Arendt would call herself an experimental political thinker, not a professional philosopher carving radically different space for her understanding of the human condition, worldliness, and public freedom. Arendtian political thought would not be rooted in homesickness but in an affectionate embrace of second homes, the ones that we make for ourselves. The old lovers' embrace would be remembered and remain a call to arms, only in the end Arendt would redefine such an either/or dialectic of wounded eros, embracing instead everything in between, worldly curiosity and gratitude for being. And yet, while he claimed to have destroyed her letters in the safety of his Black Forest home, she did preserve his through years of exile, keeping them in the desk drawer in her bedroom, against all odds.

The Life of a Jewess from Love to Worldliness

Arendt finds her way out of personal crisis through writing about others, adulterating the "totalitarian space" of dedication to the single one. She opens up the intimate landscape to the forces of history and mediates her personal story by writing a biography-critique of the original "girl from abroad," Rahel Levin, alias Varnhagen, a writer, friend, and patron of the Romantic poets and writers. This remarkable Jewish German woman is best known for her correspondence and her role as a hostess of one of the first literary salons in Germany that laid the foundation for the literary public sphere. For Arendt, Rahel also embodied the highs and lows of German Jewish assimilation and the double bind of the pariah and the parvenu. Having come into possession of Rahel Levine's letters through Anne Mendelsohn, her best friend from childhood, Arendt decides to write an anatomy of romantic introspection that professes radical liberation but ends up excluding worldliness and limiting public freedom. Rahel was not a representative Romantic poet, but a romantic in life; life was her main "assignment." Rahel experiences life like a storm without an umbrella, she let life "rain on her." She lived out the romantic predicament to the extreme, revealing its worldly contradictions.

One of the best definitions of a romantic life was given by Friedrich Schlegel, who saw it as a "small work of art entirely separate from its surrounding world and as complete in itself as a hedgehog."[58] In his view, "the mood supposedly possesses a power to convert reality back to potentiality and to confer for a moment an appearance of reality to potentialities." Arendt's biography-critique of Rahel Varnhagen is aimed at disrupting "the beautiful evening" of the romantic time out of time. For Arendt, the romantic imagination has great creative powers and reveals many possibilities for personal freedom; at the same time romantic introspection miniaturizes the outside world: "Introspection accomplishes two feats: annihilates an actual existing situation by dissolving it into a mood, and at the same time it lends everything subjective an aura of objectivity."[59] The romantic game of potentialities becomes claustrophobic in spite of its self-professed openness. Ultimately, romantic self-creation takes away from cocreation in the world.

Arendt is fascinated by the dialectic of sincerity and falsehood, truth and lie. Lying is a part of romantic freedom, the freedom of moody creativity that blurs the outlines of actual events. Arendt traces the genealogy of romantic lying back to Rousseau's *Confessions*: "by sentimentalizing memory he obliterated the contours of the remembered event."[60] Such an attitude toward the outside world led to the new cult of intimacy, thus impoverishing an emerging public realm; it also affected philosophical understanding of the mystery of infinity which became an intimate sorrow. What is particularly striking in this anatomy of lying and the particular mendacity of life-creation is that it is couched in the discourse of sincerity and truthfulness, rather than that of theatricality and sociability which is closer to the realm of the political.

Arendt explodes the precious citadel of romantic interiority and focuses on the real adventure in Rahel's life, which she had not predicted. While Rahel was oblivious to history in search of life, to turn Nietzsche's famous dictum on its head, she did become an unwilling actor in the changing historical drama and a witness to her transitional epoch, not unlike the transition from the tolerant 1920s to the Nazi 1930s that Arendt experienced herself. The period of Prussian Enlightenment, during which German Jews enjoyed cultural tolerance, came to an end, giving way to German nationalism, which exposed the historical and political limits of Romantic "beautiful evenings." The social atmosphere of tolerance and diversity that reigned in the artistic salons was taken for granted and made invisible in the fog of romantic sensibility; only when it came to an end, it exposed the fragility of such social trust due to a complete lack of political rights and protections for nonethnic Germans and non-Christians in Germany.

Rahel aged with the Romantic age. Her last dramatic love-friendship with Alexander von Marwitz, a German aristocrat sixteen years her junior with whom she shared a sense of alienation from the world, ended abruptly at the highest pitch in the midst of the sublime romantic landscape. Rahel wrote to Marwitz about her estrangement and her feeling that her life was a ghost story for she never encountered another human being who could make her more "real." Marwitz responded in the best romantic tradition, comparing her to the sublime landscape: "the tempest of fate has raised you up to the high mountains where the view [is] infinite, man far but God near."[61] Rahel's response is striking: "And he also loves me—as one loves the sea, a swirl of clouds, a rocky gorge. That is not enough for me. No longer. The man I love must want to live with me, stay with me." The highest compliment that Marwitz could pay her doomed the very possibility of any relationship.

For Arendt's Rahel these flattering and well-meaning words had an unexpected ring to them: they signaled "the end of human solidarity." They exiled Rahel, once again all alone, to a place where nothing could reach her, where she was cut off from all human things. The high mountains, where "man was far but God near," were only a "metaphorical circumlocution of the abstractness of her existence." (Rahel's insight is not so far from Arendt's own in response to Heidegger's descriptions of romantic landscapes and beautiful evenings, which after twenty years began to acquire a patina of clichés. Perhaps in later years the laughing Thracian maid in the loving Hannah recognized that great thinkers can be dramatically lacking in any sense of self-irony and prone to kitsch, just like the minor Romantics in life from another era.) In the end Rahel marries the man of Enlightenment, a reasonable intellectual and government official, Varnhagen, whom many of her aristocratic and literary friends considered a parvenu.

In Arendt's reading, the landscape of tempests and storms that young Rahel passionately craved made her realize her own estrangement from the clichés of Romantic sublimity. If in the earlier historical epoch she shared her alienation with the Romantics, in an era of growing nationalism she realizes her distance from her former soul mates.

For Arendt, Rahel is a figure of multiple estrangements, a schlemiel who becomes a romantic in life, a woman of introspection who hosts the public salon, a parvenu who mimics and tries to belong to German Christian culture, and finally, a pariah who never loses a "great love for free existence." At the end of her life Rahel embraced her Jewishness and with it, a need for political understanding of the world, as well as a certain sense of self-irony and modern comedy: "Rahel had remained a Jew and a pariah. Only because she clung to both conditions did she find a place in the history of European humanity."[62] The one who is excluded doesn't represent the minority group or the oppressed but the model of (universal) human dignity. "The pariah instinctively discovers human dignity in general long before Reason has made it the foundation of morality." Rahel's motto remained "rights, not origins," and her freedom too was a form of acknowledgment and recognition of political unfreedoms. In other words, it is not the pariah's estrangement and the particularism of the oppressed minority group that Arendt cherishes in Rahel's transformation, but her ability to move beyond it and embrace "rights, not origins." Rahel shared her love "for free existence" with the poet Heinrich Heine, in whom she found intuitive diasporic recognition of "the galley slaves" who "know one another."[63] It was a freedom of liberated slaves who were eager to fight for the equality of rights but who also share a particular sense of the diasporic intimacy and acceptance of the human comedy: "Man is himself only abroad; at home he must represent his past, and in the present that becomes a mask heavy to carry and obscuring the face."[64]

In passing Arendt observes that Rahel didn't disavow love. The passionate and opinionated biographer remarks almost disparagingly that even at the age of fifty-six Rahel continued to believe in the "passion of love" as "the uniquely beautiful, Eden-like phenomenon on earth."[65] Was Arendt too judgmental and, perhaps, hard on Rahel Varnhagen, after all? Arendt's beloved advisor philosopher Karl Jaspers commented that while Arendt's book "contains pages of extraordinary profundity," her portrayal of Rahel Levin was "loveless." Jaspers was equally critical of Arendt's discussion of Rahel's Jewishness: in his view, she focused too exclusively on the Jewish problem and didn't give justice to the German Jewish dialogue during the Enlightenment.[66] Jaspers examines the special friendship between the German writer Gotthold Lessing and the Jewish philosopher Moses Mendelssohn and nearly equates "profound Jewishness" with the general Enlightenment conception of humanity: "Finally and the most important of all, that true profound Jewishness, which is so uniquely historical in its effects without being aware of its historicalness, should be made clearer in Rahel without its being called Jewish for that always has an equivocal effect."[67]

Arendt responds with a certain stubbornness, defending her insistence on Rahel's Jewishness and lashing out against Mendelssohn and quite unjustly calling him "flat and opportunistic" and describing him and Rahel Varnhagen as intellectual parvenus whose primary objective was to "enter society."[68] The amazing part of this description is that Arendt seems to skip the space of her own thought that was more in line with the German Jewish Enlightenment. In fact, her later thinking about the life of the mind and the capacity to judge is very much in line with Mendelssohn's own thinking about human plurality and universalism. Through his discussion of human rights and freedom of conscience, Mendelssohn, who writes an important critique of the dominant form of Christian universalism, is "between" Arendt and Jaspers, informs the thinking of both and points at their limitations. Arendt associated those issues with Lessing and Jaspers, paying little attention to the German Jewish philosophical dialogue that was at its foundation and that informed both Rahel's epistolary philosophy and Arendt's own form of political thinking. As we read through the tortured biography-critique of Rahel Levin Varnhagen, one under many names, we realize that she might have been too close to young Arendt to become a full-fledged character; Rahel appears "loveless" because Arendt knows too much about the traps of love and the banality of the romantic lover's discourse. Arendt's Rahel Varnhagen has not entirely severed the umbilical cord with her loving but brutally unsentimental and self-estranged biographer.

Heidegger the Fox or the Traps of Homecoming

Luckily love's secret landscape allows no paparazzi. The theorist of freedom cannot become a Peeping Tom and expose the darkness of the human heart to all-inquiring minds. Almost twenty years after the cessation of their correspondence in 1933, Arendt and Heidegger met again at the hotel in Freiburg in 1950. No biographer knows for sure what happened between them.

All we know for a fact is that during her visit to Germany on behalf of the Commission for Jewish Cultural Reconstruction, she found herself in

Freiburg and decided in her own spontaneous manner to make contact with "MH." As in the old days, she sent a handwritten note on hotel stationary without a signature. He arrived immediately and they spent a long time together. The accounts of the meeting given by Arendt herself differ. In a letter to her husband, Heinrich Blüher, she writes: "We really spoke to one another, it seemed to me, for the first time in our lives."[69] At the same time in a letter to her close female friend Hilde Frankel, Arendt comments ironically that Heidegger proceeded to recite to her a sort of "tragedy in which I participated in the first two acts." He spoke as if seventeen years hadn't passed and as if they lived in the same space of the present. In the context of post–World War II history, it is unlikely that Arendt and Heidegger inhabited the same world. He persists in the romantic landscape of his childhood as the unworldliness of his path leads him higher, farther away from contemporary history. Heidegger was more distraught about the German defeat than he was about the atrocities perpetrated in the name of Germany.[70] Arendt was concerned with his new philosophical turn, further away from this world and closer to the mystical thought of thirteenth-century theologian Meister Eckhart. In the meantime, she has embraced the notions of worldliness and a cosmopolitan human culture of common history, as well as Jewish causes and American citizenship, and has hopes for the new Germany. The encounter in Freiburg renewed their correspondence and the exchange of literary gifts (some sent, some hidden). He dedicates to her a cycle of beautiful romantic poems,[71] while she writes "Heidegger the Fox," a parable that remained unpublished in her lifetime.

Arendt remarks in the letter that Heidegger has forgotten altogether questions of political science, which in a sense are more specifically philosophical, such as what is politics? Who is a man as a political being? What is freedom? In her correspondence with Jaspers, Arendt shares her deep disappointment with the man once considered Germany's greatest philosopher:

This living in Todtnauberg, grumbling about civilization. . . . is really a kind of mouse hole he has crawled back into because he rightly assumes that the only people he'll have to see there are the pilgrims who come full of admiration for him . . . Nobody is likely to climb 1,200 meters to make a scene. And if somebody did do so, he would lie a blue streak and take for granted that nobody will call him a liar to his face. He probably thought he could buy himself loose from the world this way at the lowest possible price, fast-talk himself out of everything unpleasant, and do nothing but philosophize. And then, of course, this intricate and childish dishonesty has quickly crept into his philosophizing.[72]

The most devastating line here is the last one. Now the former "child nymph" accuses the elder philosopher of being childish. Moreover, this childishness is coupled with dishonesty, and what is even worse still, the sacred separation of life and philosophy is violated. The further he tries to keep from the world, the more "dishonesty" creeps into his philosophizing.

In the notebook that she titled "Denktagebuch" (July 1953), Arendt wrote a parable of Heidegger the Fox, an ambivalent gift of the "girl from abroad" to her homebound philosopher-lover. There the "path" does not lead Heidegger to the revelation of "innermost being" but into a trap. Or maybe the two are connected. The parable begins with the philosopher proudly appropriating the insult that people use against him:

> Heidegger says, quite proudly, "People say Heidegger is a fox." Here is a true story of Heidegger the fox. There once upon a time was a fox so utterly without cunning that he not only constantly fell into traps but could not even distinguish between a trap and a non-trap. This fox had another affliction: something was wrong with his fur [*Felle*], so he was completely lacking in natural protection against the rigors of the fox life. After this fox had spent his entire youth hanging around in other people's traps and not one piece of his fur was, so to speak, left unscathed, he decided to completely withdraw from the fox world and began to build a den [*Bau*]. With hair-raising ignorance of traps and non-traps and his incredible experience with traps, he arrived at an idea entirely new and unheard of among foxes: he built himself a trap as a fox den [*eine Falle als Fuchsbau*], sat down in it, and pretended it was a normal den. . . . Our fox hit upon the idea of decking out his trap as beautiful as possible and sticking clear signs all over it that quite plainly said: Everybody come here, here is a trap, the most beautiful trap in the world . . . If one wanted to visit him in the den where he was at home, one had to go into his trap. Of course, everybody could walk right out of it, except him. It was literally the flesh on his bones. But the fox living in the trap said proudly: "So many fell into my trap, I have become the best of foxes." And there was even something true in that: nobody knows the trap business better than he who has been sitting in a trap all his life.[73]

In the story of Heidegger the Fox, Arendt uses Heideggerian vocabulary but turns it inside out, undermining the foundations of this philosophical architecture. Two key words for the fox's trap and home display their Heideggerian roots. Each is in itself a portmanteau, a double-edged sword: a miniparable places the whole fable in mis-en-abyme. The word *Falle* (trap) is related to *Verfallen*, which suggests the temptations of the "fallen" world of everyday existence that poses as an uncanny synonym for authentic being. In Heidegger's philosophical terms, *Verfallen* refers to "a potentiality of *Dasein* of falling prey to the things of this world and of becoming alienated to its own authentic possibilities, intentions and endeavors."[74] In Arendt's fable, the philosopher who exiled himself to the mountain hut away from the temptations of "the fallen world" (*Verfallen*) might have created a trap for himself that uncannily resembles a real home. In other words, the philosopher's home in the sublime landscape from which he reflects on the traps of inauthentic modernity might have itself been a mere alibi for not making a home in the human world and not assuming responsibility for one's own actions (or inactions) during the "dark times" of Nazism.

The word for the fox dwelling, *bau*, is one of Heidegger's favorites. Its history itself seems to demonstrate the process of modern corruption (*Verfallen*). In his "Building, Dwelling, Thinking," Heidegger writes that "man is insofar as he dwells."[75] Most often modern man merely "builds," that is, turns the world into a picture and forgets the ways of dwelling. Yet the German word for building, *bauen*, preserves the memory of authentic dwelling in the world in its etymology, relating *building* to *being*.

In Arendt's fable, Heidegger's *bau* becomes his home, his residence in the mountain landscape away from the human world. Yet instead of an authentic dwelling it turns into a trap for thinking. The philosopher loses his power of judgment because his *Falle*, his trap, is not merely an exterior construction, not even the *Felle*, the protective fur, but the "flesh on his bones."[76]

It is important that Arendt changes genres; what she writes is not a poem but a humorous parable, a genre in which Heidegger did not excel. It allows for Aesopian doublespeak that is different from the poetic language she had shared with Heidegger. The parable is the genre she shared with Kafka and Benjamin and the Jewish tradition of storytelling, which evades romantic logic and nostalgic ontology. In Arendt's fable, Heidegger the Fox preempts an encounter with the world by setting his own trap, similar to the underground man who finds extreme freedom in his self-imprisonment. The girl from abroad doesn't want to go home; instead, she exposes the dangers of a final homecoming. She is not going to be a "prodigal daughter" who returns to the philosophical dwelling, rather, a thinker at home in her estrangement, not an estrangement *from* the world but *for* the world.

Loving and Judging

Forty years after their romantic love affair and twenty years after the encounter in Freiburg, Arendt and Heidegger exchange letters about the transitive and intransitive use of silence. Arendt asks Heidegger to advise her on the translation of Stephane Mallarmé's "Crise de vers" for her essay on Benjamin. Heidegger sent her two poems by Georg Trakl about transitive silences.

> In Darkness
> The soul silences the blue Spring
> Under damp evening branches
> The brows of lovers sank in showers
> Evening Song
> Spring clouds rise over the dark city
> That silences the monks' nobler times.[77]

"Dear Martin," writes Arendt in response. "Thank you for the letters, thank you for the examples of the transitive use of silence. Very beautiful, I think I understood it immediately, but it doesn't work in Mallarmé, because *tacite* is only an adjective, the verb *taire* can also be transitive, *taire la verite* (to silence truth)."[78]

In these transitive and intransitive uses of silences and multilingual translations, two former lovers shared the whole history of their relationship, speaking albeit very indirectly, about different forms of silencing, both political and poetic, ranging from the adventures of spirit to misadventures of judgment and including invisible and visible arts of freedom. Interpretations of poetry encipher a detective story with many riddles. Heidegger responded to Arendt's question about the transitivity of silence with two poems that perpetuated his poetic philosophy and poetico-philosophical blindness to the world. It was as if he could have sent her those poems forty years before, back in the 1920s, not in the 1970s. In one of the poems, silence goes together with some kind of darkness: "The soul silences the blue Spring" and the "brows of lovers" and in the other the "dark city" silences the "monks' nobler times." As for Mallarmé, he only warns her that Mallarmé is "difficult."

The last period of the Arendt-Heidegger correspondence during the late 1960s–early 1970s, which occurs after a prolonged chill, is tender, affectionate, and literary. Once again, their relationship is triangulated—this time in a public light—through a discussion of Walter Benjamin. It is hard to imagine more improbable circumstances. The aging Martin Heidegger makes his rare appearance at the University of Freiburg to attend Arendt's lecture on Benjamin. While he appears almost incognito, Arendt makes his presence public: "Dear Martin Heidegger, Ladies and Gentlemen"—this is how she begins her lecture and then proceeds to make a polemical declaration that "without realizing it, Benjamin had more in common with Heidegger's remarkable sense for living eyes and living bones that had sea-changed into pearls . . . than he did with the dialectical subtleties of his Marxist friends."[79] To avoid misunderstanding, it is important to note that she specifies that what Heidegger and Benjamin share is poetic thinking, not a relationship to being, history, or politics. But then the question of "public light" will be central to the discussion, and public light is never a realm of complete illumination.

The intellectual journey to this crossroads was unusually tortured. Arendt develops her theory of freedom, transforming some Heideggerian concepts in her monumental work, *The Human Condition*, which she dedicated to Heidegger. Such public dedication received little acknowledgment from the philosopher. Arendt confides her disappointment in a letter to Jaspers:

> Heidegger—yes, it is a most irritating story . . . I sent him one of my books, *The Vita Activa*, for the first time . . . I know that he finds it intolerable that my name appears in public, that I write books. All my life I've pulled the wool over his eyes, so to speak, always acted as if none of that existed, as if I couldn't count to three, unless it was in the interpretation of his own work. Then he was always very pleased that I could count to three and sometimes, even to four. I suddenly felt deception was too boring and so I got a rap on the nose. I was very angry for a moment, but I am not any longer. I feel instead that I somehow deserved what I got—that is, both for having deceived him and for suddenly having put an end to it.[80]

Not only did the man to whom the book was dedicated fail to become its ideal addressee, most likely, he failed to read the book altogether. Arendt believed that the revelation of her public and publishing self, and the unmasking of her private pretense, was what elicited the hostility of the old lover. In his sacrifice of the common world, Heidegger must have sacrificed some key questions of thinking.

In *Life of the Mind* Arendt continues her reflection on thoughtlessness that she began in *Eichmann in Jerusalem*, where it was linked to the "banality of evil." She both pays homage to Heidegger and turns away from the worldlessness of philosophical contemplation. A political thinker, in her view, cannot dwell in nostalgia but must inhabit the gap between the past and the future. Perhaps Heidegger would have sensed in her new work something of a philosophical betrayal, for he famously claimed, "The public light obscures everything."

Nothing is more antithetical to Arendt's conception of politics and freedom. If the world's a theater, the light of the public illuminates our common stage, a space of self-realization, freedom, and cocreation. Arendt does not accept the Heideggerian opposition between inner radiance and revelation versus public obscurity. She develops her own conception of luminosity that characterizes shared worldliness: "It is the realm of *humanitas*, which everyone can come to out of their origins. Those who enter it recognize one another for then they are like sparks brightening to a more luminous glow, dwindling to invisibility, alternating in constant motion. The sparks see one another; and each flames more brightly because it sees others' and hopes to be seen by them." "The warmth of intimacy" cannot substitute for the light and illumination that only the public realm can cast.[81]

Thus the political thinker rehabilitates the shadows of the shy student of philosophy and creates her own luminous poetics of freedom; but now shadows are not only cast onto the private landscape, they overlap and superimpose in the spaces between public and private, just as do those weak lights of human dignity. In the "dark times" of Nazism and Stalinism one expects illuminations not from philosophical concepts but from the "uncertain, flickering and often weak light" that men and women kindle and shed over the lifespan given to them.[82] Once again Arendt takes to heart Heidegger's appeal to "live in the beginning" but radically redesigns it. Beginning for her is not a "sacrifice," as Heidegger called it in his poem to her, but an adventure in human freedom. She develops her theory of political freedom in the 1950s expanding its range of human potentialities; freedom is about infinite unpredictability but it also needs a public stage and a common world for human creativity and self-realization. On a deeper level, Arendt leaves the ground of Heideggerian philosophy and carves a different space for her political thought.

And yet she doesn't merely refute Heidegger's statement about the obscuring nature of the public light, which she calls "most perverse and sarcastic"; rather, she endlessly reframes it throughout her work. In the introduction to *Men in Dark Times*, she observes that this unworldly philosophical declaration that "the light of the public obscures everything" went to "the heart of the matter" and was "the most succinct summing up of existing conditions" of life in Nazi Germany. She recontextualized Heidegger's antipolitical statement by reading it as a comment on the distortion of public life under fascism. Instead of seeing the historical context of Nazism as the "trivial" avatar of corrupted modernity, she regards the philosopher's extreme flight from society in dark times as a symptom of the political era. Is she exculpating while explaining Heidegger? Perhaps through her literary tributes she treats Heidegger the way she treated Brecht, whose concept of "dark times" she has borrowed and whom she respected as a poet but not at all as a political actor. Her essay on Bertolt Brecht begins with an epigraph by W. H. Auden, a poem that would have equally applied to Heidegger: "You hope, yes, / your books will excuse you, / save you from hell: / . . . God may reduce you / on Judgment Day / to tears of shame, / reciting by heart / the poems you would / have written, had / your life been good."[83]

In the essay in *Men in Dark Times* on Walter Benjamin, her reference to Heidegger's line about the public light that obscures everything again acquires a specific historical context; this time it refers to the state of German-Jewish relations (that in some epochs flourished in private salons, but didn't provide foundations for public rights and freedoms). By the early 1930s, the "public light" brought into focus the pariah status of the Jews in Germany. Of course, the political and historical circumstances of Benjamin's and of Heidegger's lives in the dark times are incommensurable: the German Jewish man of letters, twice a refugee, who commits suicide at the French-Spanish border out of fear of forced deportation can hardly be placed alongside the self-marginalized king of German philosophy whose early Nazi idealism ended in a fiasco and who as a man, reveled in self-pity just as much as in his own greatness. Arendt brings them together poetically, offering her essay on Benjamin as a generous gift to Heidegger. As is in the nature of the gift, some creative misreading can be found there.

Arendt's delivery of her lecture on Benjamin occurs in the period of her renewed, tender friendship with Heidegger. In this "autumn of their friendship" they are most frank with each other, the letters are filled with poetic and philosophical discussions, and they no longer keep their friendship in the shadows, but they disagree on interpreting the meaning of silence (in Mallarmé, among other places).

Mallarmé's prose poems, especially "Crise de vers," have a radically modern and ambivalent syntax, which often obscures causality and plays games with chance.[84] Elusive and playful, Mallarmé is not a German Romantic poet; throughout his works he undoes the romantic myth of art and life.[85] Moreover, he doesn't speak about "silencing the truth" (which was a common preoccupation of Arendt and Heidegger) but only about the "silent word." In "Crise de vers," the French poet invokes the myth of the Tower of Babel, which stood simultaneously for the failure of human-divine communion and for the artistic creativity that pours into this asymptotic interval—like the space between the outstretched fingers of God and Adam in Michelangelo's ceiling in the Sistine Chapel. (In fact, in Mallarmé's text, the word for truth, *la verité*, itself reverberates and refracts other words such as *verse, vers* [toward], and *verre* [glass]. Truth is not beyond language; rather, the grains of truth are contained—materially—in the words themselves.)

Modernity, one word notoriously untranslatable into Russian and German, plays a trick here. Mallarmé is not speaking of the crisis of culture in general, even though he shares a decadently ironic attitude toward bourgeois mediocrity; his subject is the crisis of verse. In fact, he is at home in the modern Parisian culture of his day and inhabits urban theatricality just the way that Baudelaire did. Paris, the capital of the nineteenth century, that Benjamin crystallizes in his description, is Mallarmé's native city. Unlike the German romantic poets, Mallarmé is not antimodern. He is a poet of *modernité* in all its modalities—from difficult art to fashion, from the "Crise de vers" to the women's fashion magazine *La derniere mode* (an un-Heideggerian, but very Benjaminian, project). His landscape is not that of Nietzschean or Heideggerian mountain peaks. Like Baudelaire, Mallarmé articulated the artificiality of modern beauty; the flower that fascinates him is that of modern poetry and it is "not to be found in any bouquet."

Moreover, in the syntactical salto mortale of the "Crise de vers" that enacts modernist poetic suicide (and perhaps protects the real-life author from that dreadful temptation), Mallarmé never ceases to smile. His persona is a "mime who bumps against nature with a smile" and the humor is part of his poetic virtuosity.[86] Humor is hardly Heidegger's forte. Jacques Derrida formulated this most succinctly: "There is little room for laughter in Heidegger."[87] To play devil's advocate and to paraphrase Arendt, Benjamin, in my view, was closer to the logic of the French modernist poetry of Mallarmé and Baudelaire than he was to either Heidegger or Marx. Paradoxically, by approximating Heidegger and Benjamin—in her loving and contrarian fashion—Arendt missed in Benjamin's urban texts as well as in those of Mallarmé and Baudelaire the discussions of modernity, which come very close to her own thinking about public freedom as a performance on the modern stage.

"Judgment Is a Difficult Issue"

Romantic landscapes, it seems, had not left Arendt unscarred. In her later texts, Benjamin and Heidegger become uncannily linked through another nature image—that of the storm. Storms are blowing in many of Arendt's works: the rain storm is a metaphor for Rahel's life, the desert storm stands for totalitarian movements that destroy all boundaries and partitions of the public realm. Benjamin's storm is a storm of history understood in an extreme messianic fashion.

In the 1969 radio show dedicated to Heidegger's eightieth birthday, Arendt spoke of storms of philosophical thinking. She explains that for Heidegger thinking is not transitive or goal-oriented. "He never thinks about something, he thinks something." His thinking is "about opening up a dimension, rather than reaching a goal."[88] In such thinking the paths through the woods don't lead to a destination outside the forest but "suddenly end in the unwalked." The philosopher "finds his residence in astonishment," far from human dwelling and "although it can get very stormy in such a place, the storms there are surely even a degree more metaphorical than when we speak of the storms of time; compared with other places in the world, with the places of human affairs, the residence of thinking is a "place of stillness."

Arendt herself speaks from a dual perspective, that of an admiring fellow-philosopher and from the perspective of a laughing "Thracian maid." She recalls Plato's story of a wise man Thales who gazed upward to the stars and fell into a well, and the Thracian peasant girl who laughed that someone "who wanted to know the sky no longer knew what was right at his feet."[89] Since, as Arendt remarks, books are not written by farm girls, the Thracian maid so fond of laughing has even had to hear Hegel tell her that she just has no sense of higher things. Philosophers don't know what to make of laughter or the "gratifying materiality" of daily life.

And philosophers should not play kings in the world of politics because in politics from Plato to Heidegger they have fallen for tyrants and führers due to a certain "deformation professionelle": a tendency toward the tyrannical can be detected in all great thinkers.[90] The outtake from this radio address preserved in Arendt's papers offers a different storm, a different "we," and another quote about silence that reads like a secret coded message to Heidegger: "Let silence commemorate me in your depth."[91] It reads like a message in a bottle to the readers from a different epoch: "May those who come after us, when they recall our century and its people and try to keep faith with them, not forget the devastating sandstorms that swept us up, each in his own way, and in which something like this man and his work were still possible."

These "devastating sandstorms" evoke the image of Walter Benjamin's "Angel of History," the text that Arendt carried with her to her American exile: "The storm is blowing from Paradise and irresistibly propels him into the future to which his back is turned, while the pile of ruins before him grows skyward. What we call progress is this storm."[92] Arendt compares the angel of history to the flaneur whose back is turned to the crowd as he is propelled forward and swept up by it. He too is blown backward toward the future by the storm of progress.[93] Once again, I believe that the original flaneur—not Arendtian, but Baudelairian—doesn't turn his back to the crowd: the crowd is his stage, his space in the ever-fleeting presence, not in the future. The crowd of Parisian urban strollers that the flaneur enjoys is not the same as the lonely totalitarian crowd of the dark times. Baudelairian modernity is more aesthetic and urban and even "cozy" compared to the impersonal global modernity that came after World War II. Benjamin's flaneur is "traumophilic," addicted to the haptic electricity of the Parisian crowd, nostalgic for a more old-fashioned version of urban modernity. Unlike many other German thinkers as diverse as Adorno and Heidegger, Benjamin never totalizes the modern experience and never falls into the antimodern trap. At the end there is another storm blowing *between* Heidegger and Benjamin, separating them. They appear as two sides of the paradox of the critique of modernity; one searched for the stillness of Parmenides, the other for the crystallization of history.

Many readers and scholars of Arendt have wondered whether she ever spoke explicitly and directly about Heidegger's Nazi connection in the 1930s. Did Arendt, the philosopher of judgment, in the end judge Heidegger's Nazi past? Did loyalty to her first love get in the way of her doing so, or did it give her insight into freedom and judgment?

While Arendt disavowed *la grande passion* intellectually, it continued to function in her corpus as a lifelong adventure that decentered, complicated, silenced, and inspired her. Heidegger was by no means her "single one"; her life was rich in love, friendships, and diasporic intimacies with men and women. And yet a dialogue with him lasted for the rest of her life. If at the beginning of the relationship he projected onto her the ideal of a beloved disciple, at the end she internalized him as her (Socratic?) daimon with whom she engaged in a constant soliloquy, one that evolved from disappointment to tenderness, from irritation to admiration, from dedication to humorous friendship, from extreme nearness to a comfortable distance. Passionate thinking works through double estrangement: emotional loyalty undercut intellectual imperatives and the demands of judgment estranged affection. The curve of love and the asymptote of freedom, the unprecedented excess of judging and imagination overlapped but never coincided. For the paths of love and its many metamorphoses are unpredictable and do not offer complete control over chance. The lovers' landscape and its metaphors function as souvenirs and found objects throughout Arendt's philosophy. She became an archeologist of their love who constantly reframed the fragments of their secret landscape, exploring or even exploding their context. "Wisdom is a virtue of old age," wrote Arendt in her essay on Isak Dinesen, and "it seems to come only to those who, when young, were neither wise nor prudent."[94] Love's wisdom (if there is such a thing) is the wisdom of the imprudent who manage to survive passion's intoxicating bondage and liberation and turn its secret landscape into the space of freedom. Sometimes this could take forty years.

In one of his romantic moments, after seeing Arendt in Freiburg in 1950, Heidegger wrote her letters filled with romantic dashes: "No story is as reticent about love, or as powerful in the gentleness of never forgetting it"[95] and two months later: "You—Hannah—the real 'and' in Heidegger and Jaspers is only you. It is beautiful to be an 'and.' But it is the secret of goodness. It happens before all communication. It rings from the deep sound of 'ou' in you."[96]

Arendt did not content herself with being the "and"—albeit a conjunction between two great thinkers. Throughout her writings she expanded lovers' secret space—the wall and the landscape—between and beyond the connections of Jaspers and Heidegger, triangulating and keeping loyalties at home and abroad. For her the most interesting in-between space was the luminous space of worldliness, with its shadowy architecture. The tension of "between" and "beyond" is a foundation of her theory of imagination and judgment, which she never had a chance to develop in full.

Arendt's judging of Heidegger was also a lifelong process that remained unfinished and ended as it began—on a poetic, not political, plane. She asked him fundamental questions that haunted her in the postwar period: one was about judging and the other about "silencing the truth." In their last letter exchange before her death in December 1975 Arendt tells Heidegger that she is working on the book on judging but is not sure if she "will be done with it in October." In the last part of her *Life of the Mind*, Arendt hoped to come to terms with aesthetics—not as a shortcut to being but as a guide to judging through common sense and imagination, a play of the particular and universal. Judging would have provided a tentative bridge between ethics and aesthetics, acting and thinking.[97] Her death left her volume on judging unfinished but for two epigraphs. Judging is a process of negotiation, of sidestepping, weighing and counterweighing, acting, reflecting, posing arguments and emotions in counterpoint. What would have been Arendt's final judgment call? It never came, partially due to her untimely death, but this is only a partial truth. Arendt reveals to us the process and difficulty of judging and balancing between public and private speech, but she never pronounces final judgment. Heidegger's penultimate line to Arendt in his last letter to her is, "Everything else orally, only: judgment is a difficult issue." We don't know what she would have said in response.

Figure 11. Svetlana Boym, chessboard collage combining Victor Shklovsky's knight's move (fig. 2 above) and the anamorphic fragment of the photograph of NKVD employees leaving Lubianka Prison.

DISSENT, ESTRANGEMENT, AND THE RUINS OF UTOPIA

Material existence determines consciousness but conscience remains unsettled.

Victor Shklovsky, 1926

Dissent in the Plural

At the beginning of the twenty-first century we still lived in the shadow of the last fin de siècle and its litany of endings. The "end of art," "the end of history," "the end of the book" overwhelm us, and so do (not entirely imaginary, alas) forebodings of new catastrophes. Unlike our own century, the previous century began with a euphoria of newness that resulted in many social and artistic revolutions. For Arendt, the very idea of freedom is predicated on the ability to begin again, to question the routinization and automatization of modern life; only this beginning comes with a warning sign concerning the zeal of revolutionary destruction that can turn absolute freedom into a new form of absolute despotism, to paraphrase one of Dostoevsky's revolutionaries. In aesthetic theory, Victor Shklovsky's conception of estrangement was a similar theory of a new beginning, in which revolutionary art became an art of dissent and artistic practice was transformed into a dangerous art of living. "Beginning" doesn't mean progress or a new myth of origin, but a possibility of an unpredictable and creative renewal of vision, an unforeseen space of public architecture. The imaginary dialogue between Arendt and Shklovsky brings together their theories of beginning, estrangement, and the public realm and offers us insight into the possibilities of cultural and political renewal in the twenty-first century.

The history of the revolutions in the twentieth century is a garden of forking paths. Some led to authoritarianism on the right and on the left; others to the practices of dissent, civil disobedience, or to the extreme of legal obedience which in some cultural contexts is no less subversive.

Dissent is not the same as destruction. From Socrates to Jesus Christ, dissidents founded philosophical movements and new religions.[1] "Dissident" literally means someone who "sits apart." But how far apart? Being "apart" does not necessarily mean to be outside, on the margin, or in some free autonomous zone. Quite the contrary, it could mean "to be a part of," to be a crucial participant in remaking of public space. The eccentric doesn't escape but reveals the center, or sometimes, as Shklovsky observed, the road to a new beginning follows the lateral move of the knight in the game of chess, the "third route" that Arendt discovered in the unpredictable diagonal of freedom. Dissent and estrangement are forms of adventure that expose the limits of the permissible and uncover the boundaries of the public realm. The Russian dissident writer Andrei Siniavsky (Abram Tertz), who was put on trial for his work in the 1960s and who lived through imprisonment and exile, made an argument in defense of heresies:

> If we are heretics, there should be many heresies. This is how I see the value of dissidence. Dissent shouldn't become an embryo of a new church or a new anti-Soviet state but a pluralistic state, at least on paper.[2]

The etymology of *heretic* comes from "making a choice," and *heresies* refers to the "schools of thought, philosophical sects" without the negative connotations that emerged in the early medieval era often among the members of previously persecuted religions. The heretics themselves were often intolerant toward other heretics. Plurality is the most radical aspect of Siniavsky's conception of dissent. These kinds of heresies, in the plural, are not opposed to religion or to spiritual matters but to any sort of orthodoxy. Heresy estranges orthodoxy to protect the plurality of spiritual aspirations.

While not ignoring cultural differences, it is necessary to map the transnational space of artistic and political dissent and nonconformism. Rather than become a relic of the "era of the cold war," it should instead be brought into the context of the twenty-first century. Of course there is a great diversity in the forms of dissent; even in the former Soviet Union it ranged from monarchism and nationalism to democratic and aesthetic internationalism with many shades in between. Moreover, it is important to draw a distinction between cultures in which plurality is a part of national self-fashioning and those in which national solidarity demands unity and belief, as well as between democracies in which deliberation and a critique of social and economic systems is permitted (if not always encouraged) and those in which differences are censored from the political sphere. The optic of dissidence brings into sharp focus the limits of a particular public architecture but also questions this architectural metaphor for the universal discourse of power—be it a total visibility of the panopticon or the darkness of the hidden dungeon where some can dream of the "freer freedom."

On the one hand, dissent is as common a phenomenon as cultural authority in spite of the difference in its public or semiprivate expression and the degrees of toleration of diversity. While advocating a variety of freedoms, dissidents often threaten communal ties, proposing more reflective forms of civic solidarity. In other words, dissent points at the diversity within each particular culture. Thus it would be a shame to confine the dissidents within the claustrophobic boundaries that they fought to escape. On the other hand, we can't erase cultural and historical differences by translating them into a single bland Western Esperanto. Sometimes what appears as particularism and eccentricity in fact reveals the inner plurality and heterogeneity of the (Western) project of human rights itself. Dissidents lay bare the tensions between civic and national solidarities, between universal and particular, imaginary and practical, individual eccentricity and the freedoms of others. So the reason that I don't wish to encapsulate my stories of dissent and estrangement within a single cultural tradition is because each of the dissidents presented a threat to their own national community and its official patriotism. Not that they were not patriots, but their understanding of *patria* was often more inclusive.

Dissent and artistic estrangement understood in Shklovsky's sense as a renewal of vision enlarge and renew the space of the public and the political (no longer understood as a vertical structure of power but as the space of the *polis*) through artistic and spiritual imagination. It happens when artists engage with public languages albeit through their defamiliarization, politicians engage with moral imagination, private individuals engage with citizenship, or national culture engages with its neighbors and strangers. In my discussion I will distinguish between estrangement *from* the world, which at best encourages the practice of introspection and inner freedom, and estrangement *for* the world, which engages the public life. Dissidence and estrangement *for* the world requires a Socratic syntax, not an authoritarian paradigm. At best, dissent combines a form of permanent revolution with the care for the preservation of worldliness. The ethics of dissent and estrangement consists in "thinking without a banister," not confusing words and deeds, respecting the freedom of the other and engaging in acting and judging to counteract the banality of evil. Once again, dissent is not synonymous with destruction. It was often called "subversive," but the better word might be "versatile." This kind of subversive versatility presupposes a constant interplay between conscience and consciousness, public and private existence, integrity and imagination, cultural mimicry and its occasional disruption. The relationship between art and politics should not be reduced to the predictable politicization of art and the aestheticization of politics, neither appearing to be a good option.[3] It might be more challenging to think this relationship with respect to the architecture of freedom and strategies of dissent.

Yet, are artistic and political forms of dissent often at odds with one another? What kind of monument to liberty and architecture of freedom emerges from the practices of estrangement and dissent in the twentieth century, and what are we to do with the ruins of their abandoned construction sites?

Monuments to Revolutionary Estrangement: Shklovsky and Tatlin

Had Hannah Arendt and Victor Shklovsky crossed paths in Berlin or Marburg in the 1920s they might have discovered that their ideas of estrangement and politics had a lot in common. They were connected not only to the theory and experience of love and totalitarianism but also to the unpredictable conception of liberty. Both Arendt and Shklovsky experimented with the "paper architecture" of freedom that combines political and artistic imagination.

It is little known that Shklovsky, the experimental writer and one of the founding fathers of literary science and the Formal Method, created a verbal monument to the first Soviet Statue of Liberty, a structure that had a short and tempestuous life. It represents the writer's own postrevolutionary anxieties and dreams of dissent, both personal and political. In 1918 in Petrograd, the monument to Tsar Alexander III was covered up by a cardboard stall with all kinds of slogans celebrating liberty, art, and revolution.[4] The *Monument to Liberty* was one of those transient, experimental monuments that exemplified early postrevolutionary visual propaganda before the granite megalomania of the Stalinist period. This is how Shklovsky introduces the story:

> No, not the truth. Not the whole truth. Not even a quarter of the truth. I do not dare to speak and awaken my soul. I put it to sleep and covered it with a book, so that it would not hear anything . . .
>
> There is a tombstone by the Nicholas Station. A clay horse stands with its feet planted apart, supporting the clay backside of a clay boss . . . They are covered by the wooden stall of the "Monument to Liberty," with four tall masts jutting from the corners. Street kids peddle cigarettes, and when militia men with guns come to catch them and take them away to the juvenile detention home, where their souls can be saved, the boys shout "scram!" and whistle professionally, scatter, run toward the "Monument to Liberty."
>
> Then they take shelter and wait in that strange place—in the emptiness beneath the boards between the tsar and the revolution.[5]

In Shklovsky's description, the monument to the tsar is not yet destroyed and the monument to liberty is not entirely completed. A dual political *symbol* turns into a lively and ambivalent urban *site* inhabited by insubordinate Petrograd street kids in an unpredictable manner. (Shklovsky calls them "Petrograd *gavroches*," making an explicit allusion to the French Revolution and its fictional representations.) In this description, the monument acquires an interior; a public site becomes a hiding place. Identifying his viewpoint with the dangerous game of the street kids hiding "between the tsar and the revolution," Shklovsky is looking for the third way, the transitory and playful architecture of freedom.[6] He performs a double estrangement, defamiliarizing both the authority of the tsar and the liberation theology of the revolution. The "third way" here suggests a spatial and a temporal paradox. The monument caught in the moment of historical transformation embodies what Benjamin called the "dialectic at a standstill." The first Soviet statue of liberty is at once a ruin and a construction site; it occupies the gap between the past and the future, in which various versions of Russian history coexist and clash.

Shklovsky's parable about the transformations of the historical monuments functions as a strange alibi for not being able to understand or tell "the whole truth" about the situation in postrevolutionary Russia. The ambivalent tale betrays the precariousness of the writer's own political situation. It is little known that Shklovsky, the founder of Formalist theory, had an adventurous, albeit brief, political career and wrote some of his early texts on the fronts of World War I. His love for poetry and poetics was hardly academic. Severely wounded twice, with seventeen pieces of shrapnel in his body, Shklovsky recited the avante-garde poetry of Velimir Khlebnikov while being operated on in the military hospital, hoping perhaps that this could help estrange, or at least distract, him from the pain. Shklovsky embraced the revolutionary spirit, but as one of his critics would later comment, he "confused the revolutions."

Or perhaps, he got it right? While a supporter of the February Revolution of 1917, he did not initially embrace the events of October 1917 and the storming of the Winter Palace. Like many avant-garde artists and critics Shklovsky belonged to the non-Bolshevik left. In 1918 he joined the Socialist Revolutionary party, which voted against the Bolshevik dispersal of the Constitutional Assembly, the revolutionary parliament. Later he became a member of the anti-Bolshevik underground (together with the writer Maxim Gorky, the future Soviet icon).[7] Shklovsky was an advocate of democratic freedoms (just like Gorky at that time), and in much of his postrevolutionary autobiographical writing the discourse on public freedom is present between the lines of his texts, often through references to the French Revolution and theories of the social contract. This was his own version of "socialism with a human face," if one were to apply an anachronistic definition. Threatened with arrest and possible execution, Shklovsky crossed the frozen Gulf of Finland and eventually found himself in Berlin. His book of sketches, entitled *The Knight's Move*, was written in Berlin as the writer reflected on whether he should return from exile, back to Russia where his wife was being held hostage. The parable about the *Monument to Liberty* becomes an allegory of the revolution and its many lost opportunities.

Shklovsky's *Monument to Liberty* is a testament to his favorite device of estrangement. He coined his famous neologism *ostranenie* in his early essay "Art as Technique" to suggest both distancing (dislocating, *dépaysement*) and making strange.[8] Estrangement brings forth a new beginning and a transformation of vision, echoing Arendt's definition of freedom as a miracle of infinite improbability. In Shklovsky's view, shifting perspective and making things strange can become an antidote to the routinization and automatization of modern life that lead to mass apathy and disenchantment: "Habituation devours things, clothes, furniture, one's wife and the fear of war."[9] Artistic estrangement can make one's wife more lovable and the fear of war more real. It offers the very opposite of anesthesia: a creative awakening. By making things strange, the artist does not simply displace them from an everyday context into an artistic framework; he also helps to return sensation to life itself, to reinvent the world, to experience it anew. Estrangement is what makes art artistic; but, by the same token, it makes life lively or worth living.[10]

It is not by chance that Shklovsky refers to Aristotle's observation that poetic language is always to some degree a foreign language. Foreignness here is of a poetic and productive kind, alluring rather than alienating.[11] In this respect, estrangement is the password for creative immigrants of the world. Unlike Bertolt Brecht's V-effect (possibly influenced by Shklovsky), Shklovsky's original conception is nondidactic; it is based on shared curiosity, not on authorial persuasion. Shklovsky's theory of estrangement was intended to oppose the economic and utilitarian discourse of efficiency and useful expenditure. The device of estrangement places emphasis on the process rather than the product of art, on retardation and deferral of denouement, on cognitive ambivalence and play. From the beginning, *ostranenie* was connected to theatrical experience. Shklovsky recited some of his early theoretical essays in the cabaret "Stray Dog," which offered a livelier context for literary discussions than that of contemporary academia. Shklovsky's conception of estrangement is close to Denis Diderot's "paradox of the actor."[12] Such a paradoxical model of the theater of estrangement is radically different from the Wagnerian conception of drama as the total work of art, which influenced the creation of mass propaganda art in Hitler's Germany and Stalinist Russia alike. In his 1920s review of the theater of Nikolai Evreinov, Shklovsky satirized early Soviet attempts to create a spectacular "total work of art" out of the experience of the October Revolution. Seven years before Sergei Eisenstein's famous film *October*, Evreinov created a mass spectacle in *Storming of the*

Winter Palace, using ten thousand extras, many of whom would later confuse their theatrical memories and their recollections (or lack thereof) of the actual storming of the Winter Palace. Shklovsky called such attempts at a total restaging of history "a vaudeville with a grandiose answer."[13] In his view, estrangement is an exercise of wonder, of thinking of the world as a question, the opposite of the total work. Thus, estrangement lays bare the boundaries between art and life but never pretends to abolish or blur them. It does not allow for a seamless translation of life into art, nor for the wholesale aestheticization of politics. Art is only meaningful when it is *not* entirely in the service of real life or realpolitik, and when its strangeness and distinctiveness are preserved. So the device of estrangement can both *define* and *defy* the autonomy of art.[14]

Shklovsky's understanding of estrangement is different from both Hegelian and Marxist notions of alienation.[15] Artistic estrangement is not to be cured by incorporation, synthesis, or belonging. In contrast to the Marxist notion of freedom that consists in overcoming alienation, Shklovskian estrangement is in itself a form of limited freedom endangered by all kinds of modern teleologies, historical determinism and utopian visions of the future. It is in this sense that postrevolutionary practices of estrangement in life and art begin to shape the practices of dissent.

The aesthetic practice of estrangement does not mean merely a creation of an artistic form or a convincing narrative which was frequently practiced by the state and even the Secret police.[16] To estrange means to question how mythical narratives are made, to lay bare the devices and to offer a new architecture and geometry of understanding. Shklovsky was fascinated by modernist science, from Einstein's theory of relativity to Nikolai Lobachevsky's non-Euclidian geometry. Throughout the 1920s Shklovsky developed his own conception of parallelism. To borrow Nabokov's description: "If the parallel lines do not meet, it is not because meet they cannot, but because they have other things to do."[17] Shklovsky's parallelisms vacillate between irony, analogy, and allegory, all of which are rhetorical figures based on doubleness, double entendre, or speaking otherwise. To describe this device, Shklovsky uses the serpentine diagonal of the knight's move across the gridded space of the chessboard:

> There are many reasons for the strangeness of the knight's move, and the most important reason is the conventionality of art. I write about the conventionality of art. The second reason is that the knight is unfree, he moves sideways because the straight road is banned to him . . .

In Russia everything is so contradictory that we all became witty unwill-
ingly . . . Our torturous road is the road of the brave, but what else can we
do when we have two eyes and see more than honest pawns or dutifully
single-minded kings?[18]

Here the knight exemplifies the paradox of artistic play; the conventional
"unfreedom of art" offers a certain liberation of thinking and judgment.[19]
Shklovsky, who distinguished himself by bravery at the front (and even received a medal for it), defines bravery here in a rather eccentric fashion. The
knight's serpentine road is the road of the brave that allows for the exploration beyond the "honest pawns" and the "dutifully single-minded kings."

One of Shklovsky's beloved architectural monuments was Vladimir
Tatlin's *Monument to the Third International* (1919–1925), known also as the
Monument to the Liberation of Humanity (fig. 12). The monument was never
built, and Shklovsky was the first to recognize the powers of its revolutionary estrangement. In some way the history of the project exemplifies
the unpredictable architecture of freedom that defied the artist's authorial design. Tatlin's goal was to create a radically antimonumental monument. As a manifesto of the architectural revolution, the Tatlin tower
challenged simultaneously the "bourgeois" Eiffel Tower and the Statue
of Liberty. This tower of iron and glass consisted of three rotating glass
volumes: a cube, a pyramid, and a cylinder. The cube was supposed to
house the Soviet of People's Commissars (Sovnarkom) and turn at the
rate of one revolution a year; the pyramid, intended for the executive and
administrative committees of the Third International, would rotate once a
month; and the cylinder, a center for information and propaganda, would
complete one revolution daily. Radio waves would extend the Tower into
the sky, and the printing workshops on the third floor would project the
motto of the day right onto the clouds.

The tower embodied many explicit and implicit meanings of the word
"revolution," a word that came from scientific discourse and whose original meaning was *repetition, rotation*. Only in the seventeenth century did it
begin to signify its opposite: a breakthrough, an unrepeatable event. The
history of the tower reflects upon the ambivalent relationship between
art and science, revolution and repetition. Shaped as a spiral, a favorite
Marxist-Hegelian form, the tower culminated with a radical opening on
top, suggesting unfinalizability, not synthesis. In fact, the tower commemorated the short-lived utopia of the permanent artistic revolution. Tatlin
was one of its leaders. He declared that the Revolution had not begun in

Figure 12. Model for Vladimir Tatlin's tower in the Mosaic Studio of the former Academy of Arts, Petrograd, 1920. Tatlin is the third from the left.

1917 but in 1914 with an artistic transformation; political revolutions followed in the steps of the artistic one, mostly unfaithfully.

A contemporary of Tatlin, the well-known theorist of constructivism Nikolai Punin, described the monument as the anti-ruin par excellence. In his view, Tatlin's revolutionary architecture reduced to ashes the classical and Renaissance tradition, and the "charred ruins of Europe are now being cleared."[20] In his design of the tower Tatlin sabotaged the perfect verticality of the Eiffel Tower by choosing the form of a spiral and leaning it to one side. Yet uncannily Tatlin's monument was not free from the ruin's charm. In its attempt to be the anti–Eiffel Tower, the project started to resemble the leaning Tower of Pisa—or even the Tower of Babel. El Lissitzky praised Tatlin's tower for its synthesis of the technical and the artistic, old and new forms: "Here the Sargon Pyramid at Khosabad was actually recreated in a new material with a new content."[21] The Sargon monument was considered an inspiration for the Tower of Babel, which was in itself an unfinished utopian monument turned mythical ruin. Moreover, in the case of the Tower of Babel, the tale of architectural utopia and its ruination is mirrored by the related parable about language. The Tower of Babel, we recall, was built to ensure perfect communication with God. Its failure ensured the survival of art. Since then, every builder of a tower dreamed of touching the sky, and, of course, the gesture remains forever asymptotic.

Still, every functional modern tower evokes this mythic malfunctioning of the original communication. Roland Barthes's poetic commemoration of the uselessness of the Eiffel Tower could easily apply to its Soviet rival as well.[22] Much of visionary architecture, in Barthes's view, embodies a profound double movement: it is always "a dream and a function, an expression of a utopia and instrument of a convenience." Barthes's Eiffel Tower was an "empty" memorial that contained nothing, but from the top of it you could see the world. It became an optical device for a vision of modernity. Tatlin's tower played a similar role as an observatory for the palimpsest of revolutionary panoramas that included ruins and construction sites alike.

Unlike the Eiffel Tower, Tatlin's was never built. The failure of its realization was not due merely to engineering problems and concerns about feasibility. The tower was both behind and ahead of its time, clashing with the architectural trends of the Soviet regime. Its model was exhibited and used during the parades celebrating the October Revolution, so it existed only as an incomplete theatrical set, a part of official street theater, not gigantic but human in scale, a testimony to revolutionary transience.

Tatlin's tower was "translated" into Western languages in the Babelian fashion: much has been lost in translation. In 1920, articles about the tower appeared in the Munich art magazine *Der Ararat* and caught the attention of the emerging Dadaists. "Art is Dead, declared the Dadaists. Long Live the Machine Art of Tatlin!"[23] Yet to some extent, the Dadaists' celebration of the death of art via Tatlin's spiral guillotine was an act of cultural mistranslation and a common Western misconception about the Russian avant-garde. By no means was Tatlin a proponent of machine-assisted artistic suicide, especially not at the time of the revolution, when the "death of art" was more than a metaphor. Instead, Tatlin argued against the "tyranny of forms born by technology without the participation of artists."[24] Tatlin accomplished his task without having any specific technical knowledge of construction and without proper architectural drawings. Tatlin's own slogans, Art into Life! and Art into Technology! do not suggest putting art in the service of life or technology, nor putting life in the service of political or social revolution. Rather, they propose to revolutionize technology and society by opening horizons of imagination and moving beyond mechanistic clichés. In this case, the two meanings of techné—that of art and that of technical craft—continuously duel with one another: art estranges technology, while new technology provides inspiration for artistic experimentation.

Hence Tatlin's tower is not merely an engineering failure but instead an exemplary case study of constructivist architecture. Architecture was imagined as archi-art, as a framework for a worldview and a carcass for futurist dreams. This made it both more and less than architecture in the sense of a built environment. Revolutionary architecture offered a scenography for future experimentation and embodied allegories of the Revolution. The most interesting examples of experimental architecture were not built monuments but rather dreamed environments or unintentional memorials.[25] Tatlin's tower came into being as a theatrical fragment and an unfinished model of paper architecture, a utopian scaffolding that resembled a future ruin, an avant-garde monument that inspired architecture of dissent.

From the very beginning, the Tatlin tower engendered its double—a discursive monument almost as prominent as its architectural original. Shklovsky was one of the few contemporaries who appreciated the unconventional architecture of the tower. Its temporal vectors pointed toward the past and the future, toward "the iron age of Ovid" and the "age of construction cranes, beautiful like wise Martians."[26] The construction cranes, the wise Martians, and the exiled poet Ovid all collaborated in the making of the tower. Paradoxically, while describing meanings and functions of the tower, Shklovsky speaks of poetry, not of technology: "The word in poetry is not merely a word, it drags with it dozens of associations. This [Tatlin's] work is filled with them like the Petersburg air in the winter whirlwind."[27] Shklovsky ends his essay by laying bare the tower's unconventional materials: "The monument is made of iron and glass and

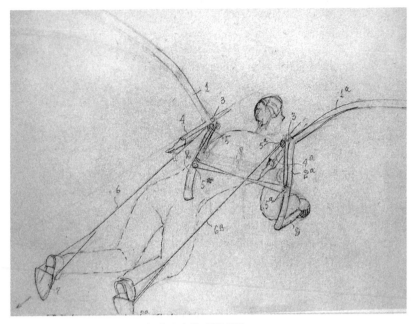

Figure 13. Vladimir Tatlin's drawing for the Letatlin, 1929–1932.

revolution."[28] The air of the Revolution functions as the project's immaterial glue. In the end the *Monument to the Liberation of Humanity* became a monument to the fragile poetic function that defied revolutionary purposefulness. This history highlights an important distinction between *artistic technique*, which lays bare its mode of operation and offers a new vision, fostering a creative consciousness and *special effect* produced with the help of technology, which frequently mystifies its modes of production and the ideology behind it. Tatlin's architectural and technological projects belong to the realm of adventure rather than functionalism.

Even after his tower project, he continued to regard the issue of technique as "third ways between art and technology." Most radically this is demonstrated in his project Letatlin (a neologism that combines the Russian verb "to fly," *letat'*, and the last name of the author) of the late 1920s–early 1930s (fig. 13). If the Tower represented a dream of the perfect collective of the Third International, Letatlin was an individual flying vehicle. A biomorphic structure, it resembled at once a flying bicycle à la Duchamps and the firebird from Russian fairy tales stripped to its bare bones. Tatlin was briefly employed by the Soviet aviation industry, which believed that he could create a perfect spy plane; instead, Tatlin made a vehicle for the belated avant-garde Icarus, which couldn't fly—not in a literal sense, at least.[29]

Letatlin and the Tower belong to a very different history of technology, an enchanted technology, founded on charisma as much as calculus, linked to premodern myths as well as to modern science. Yet they are not so alien to the history of Soviet cosmonautics; in the exploration of the cosmos, science merged with science fiction and ideology occasionally sounded like poetry. The tower resembles the ruin of a mythical space station from which the Letatlins could fly into the sky.

Tatlin's artistic life from the mid-1920s to the mid-1930s is rich in contradictions that refract the era. He designed the coffin of Russia's revolutionary poet Vladimir Mayakovsky, who committed suicide in 1930. In 1934, the Soviet secret police (the OGPU, precursor of the NKVD and later the KGB) invited him, together with other artists and writers, to observe the construction of the Belomor Canal, one of the early sites of Stalin's slave labor. (Victor Shklovsky, whose brother was arrested and imprisoned there, was a part of the delegation as well.) Yet these attempts at collaborating with the regime hardly paid off. At the official "Artists of Russia" exhibit (1933), Tatlin's works were shown in a small hall dedicated to "Formalist excesses" (a successful predecessor to the "Exhibit of Degenerate Art" in Germany). Soviet critics proclaimed that Tatlin's works demonstrated "the natural death of Formal experiments in art" and declared Tatlin to be "no artist whatsoever" (*nikakoi khudozhnik*).

What do artists do when they outlive their cultural relevance? In the Soviet case, we know very little about the output of the later years of the founders of the visual avant-garde, including filmmaker Dziga Vertov and Tatlin, who died in 1954 and 1953, respectively. What may an avant-garde artist produce after his officially declared death?

Tatlin's "postmortem" work consists—literally—of *natures mortes*, and of desolate rural landscapes on backdrops of Socialist Realist theater productions, mostly done in a brown and gray palette (figs. 14–15). In my view, the belated untimeliness of Tatlin's still lifes and landscapes speaks obliquely of their time—the time of purges and war. While figurative, these works hardly reflect the optimistic tone of Socialist Realist art, suggesting instead another existential perspective. *Nature morte* is one of the ancient genres of world painting that has survived historical cataclysms, and artistic and social revolutions. Still lifes are reminders of the nonrevolutionary rhythms of everyday life. They preserve the dream of home, of domesticated nature, and of a long-standing artistic tradition. Tatlin's still

Figure 14. Vladimir Tatlin, *White Jar and Potato*, 1948–1950.

Figure 15. Vladimir Tatlin, color sketch for the set decoration of *Chalice of Joy*, 1949–1950.

lifes look like *memento mori*, foregrounding the fragility of even the most frugal domesticity.[30] There is a subtle tension between the ahistorical still lifes and the dates on the laconic captions: 1937, 1948–1950—the years of the Great Purge before and after World War II. Moreover, the closer we look at Tatlin's still lifes, the more they appear to be exercises in double vision, but not in a conventional sense of political doublespeak. Rather, there is a tension between the figurative flowers and the abstract background. In the foreground are the sparse still lifes, and in the background, the thickly painted planes from which counter-reliefs once sprung. These unspectacular and belated stage sets were abandoned by the biomorphic revolutionary Icaruses. Tatlin's late works resemble desolate "natural settings" in which the projects of the avant-garde had turned into ruins of the revolution.

Never constructed in the actual space of the city, the Tower became a twentieth-century artistic myth and an inspiration for the unofficial art of the postwar era, nostalgic for the boldness of the revolutionary imagination, not for the October Revolution itself (fig. 16).

Rootless Cosmopolitanism and Civic Consciousness

The strange history of Tatlin's tower runs parallel with the history of Shklovsky's revolutionary theory of estrangement. As early as 1923 Shklovsky remarked that after the October Revolution, Russian life had almost turned into a strange art, endangering all aspects of everyday existence.[31] Estrangement itself had been expropriated by the Soviet state, which assumed authorship over a glorious new vision of Soviet reality that radically defamiliarized the everyday perceptions and experiences of ordinary citizens.[32] Therefore, artists had to perform a double estrangement in order to repossess their artistic and existential devices, or to use Lenin's phrase, to "expropriate the expropriated." In a 1926 letter to fellow member of the Formalist circle Roman Jakobson, Shklovsky worries about the survival of both estrangement and freedom in postrevolutionary Russia: "Romka, I am exploring the unfreedom of the writer. I am studying unfreedom as though it were a set of gymnastic equipment."[33] From a device of art, estrangement became an existential art of everyday survival and later a tactic of dissent in Russia and Eastern Europe.

In Western scholarship, Shklovsky's estrangement has often been perceived as estrangement from politics. Thus the Italian intellectual historian Carlo Ginzburg traced the cultural genealogy of estrangement back to the Stoic conception of inner freedom as a form of withdrawal from

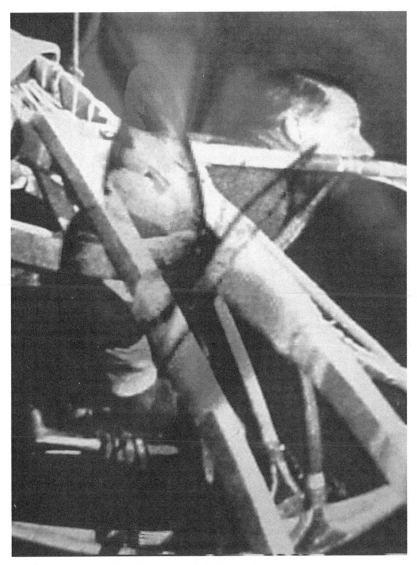

Figure 16. Svetlana Boym, *Hybrid Utopia: Letatlin with Nabokov's Butterfly.*

politics.[34] Regarding the connection between artistic practices and conceptions of freedom, I would argue that Ginzburg's interpretation does not take into consideration the historical contexts of Formalist writings. In fact, Shklovsky's experimental autobiographical texts written in the 1920s–1930s directly and indirectly reflect upon the complex relationship between inner freedom and political freedoms during the early years of Stalinism later illuminated in the works of Hannah Arendt. In Soviet Russia, the theory and practice of estrangement underwent a dramatic transformation, preserving a remarkable political and existential vitality unforeseen in the early conception of the literary device

Shklovsky practices his device of estrangement to confront the violence of the war, unrequited love, and later the growing repression of the Stalinist era. In the 1920s and 1930s Shklovsky wrote three autobiographical texts in which the practice of estrangement lays bare the new poetics of unfreedom through the device of parallelism. The most radical example occurs in *A Sentimental Journey*, an account of the author's many journeys through Iran, Iraq, Turkey, and parts of Central Asia from the fronts of World War I to the Russian Civil War. In this text, Shklovsky uses parallelism to estrange the historical legitimacy of the Bolshevik government itself:

> I'll cite a parallel. I'm not a Socialist—I'm a Freudian.
>
> A man is sleeping and he hears the doorbell ring. He knows that he has to get up, but he doesn't want to. And so he invents a dream and puts into it that sound, motivating it in another way—for example, he may dream of church bells.
>
> Russia invented the Bolsheviks as a motivation for desertion and plunder; the Bolsheviks are not guilty of having been dreamed.
>
> But who was ringing?
>
> Perhaps World Revolution.[35]

A *Sentimental Journey* is an amazing, multigeneric text that recounts Shklovsky's many encounters with local people and records their tales of misfortune. Curiously for the pioneer of estrangement, Shklovsky doesn't frame his travels through Persia and Turkey as a journey to the exotic Orient or to the land of the strange other. Rather unconventionally for a soldier of the Russian Army, he declares, "My orientation was local. There was one feature in the East that reconciled me to them, there was no anti-Semitism here." Shklovsky contrasts that to what he calls a "transsensical anti-Semitism" of the Russian Army, using a literary term to lay bare its irrationality. Shklovsky, like writer Isaac Babel, warned the locals about the pogroms of local Jews as well as other local people targeted by the army, and he once even tried to stage a fake pogrom in order to avoid the real one. (No wonder his fellow soldiers considered him a brave man and a strange man.) The writer attributes this strangeness to his conflicting revolutionary and humanistic imperatives as well as being half-Jewish. "I . . .

am half-Jewish and a role player," writes Shklovsky about himself.[36] The son of a Jewish father and a half-German, half-Russian mother, Shklovsky constantly plays a part in a comedy of errors when it comes to his identity, yet it is this multiple identification and estrangement that allows him to engage with many dislocated and uprooted people that he encounters on his way.

He gets his first experience of the cosmopolitanism in the East through the trials of war. *Sentimental Journey* abounds in descriptions of violence, presented in the most stark and unsentimental fashion. Violence is by no means excused or glorified as a part of the "necessary revolutionary sacrifice" for the sake of some future liberation of humanity. Nor are the numerous descriptions of dismembered bodies presented as examples of modernist aesthetic disfiguration or the "dehumanization of art."[37] In describing pillage, slaughter, pogroms, and the daily cruelty that he witnessed at the front, Shklovsky redirects his estrangement. It no longer "dehumanizes" in Ortega y Gasset's sense but rather makes real the "fear of war"[38] that has become so habitual for soldiers and for the ideologues of violence. Thus, the technique of estrangement lays bare the senseless dehumanization of war. It is as if only through estrangement could the revolutionary writer Shklovsky rediscover that after all he is a humanist. Shklovsky describes the estranged psyche of a friend who, awaiting his sentence, suppressed the will to live, repressed thoughts of his family, and his only fear was that before his death the executioner would make him take off his boots and that he would get tangled up in his shoelaces.[39] Reporting the practices of War Communism—the execution of poet Nikolai Gumilev and the death from starvation of another poet, Alexander Blok—Shklovsky appeals to Soviet citizens:

Citizens!
Citizens, stop killing! Men are no longer afraid of death! There are already customs and techniques for telling a wife about the death of her husband. It changes nothing. It just makes everything harder.[40]

Haunted by the brutal materiality of war, Shklovsky sticks to the "literature of facts" and resists the transformation of violence into metaphor or a mere means to a beautiful end: "I wrote [*A Sentimental Journey*] remembering the corpses that I saw myself."[41] Shklovsky's "sentimental journey" is hardly sentimental in any conventional way, but it is extremely sensitive. It does not try to domesticate the fear of war; it individualizes the dead and the wounded, humanizing them through art.

Shklovsky speaks about dehumanization explicitly in his insightful and generally sympathetic portrait of Maxim Gorky: "Gorky's Bolshevism is ironic and free of any faith in human beings . . . The anarchism of life, its subconscious, the fact that the tree knows better how to grow—these are the things he couldn't understand."[42] Shklovsky never accepts the instrumentalization of human beings (the quote is an unconscious paraphrase of Kant's "crooked timber of humanity" beloved by Isaiah Berlin). Shklovsky's modernist humanism is paradoxical and is not based on the nineteenth-century conceptions reflected in many psychological novels, but rather on anarchic spontaneity, which preserves the "mystery of individuality," to use Simmel's term. This runs parallel to the interest in what Shklovsky calls "local laws" and conventions of art that for him are part of the memory of the world culture. Shklovsky's war memoirs estrange revolutionary teleology and political theology (that of Lenin and conservative thinker Carl Schmitt alike), offering an alternative way to reflect on the modern experience without the sacrifice of human unpredictability—which once again brings Shklovsky closer to the thought of Arendt and Simmel.

In Shklovsky's second attempt at an experimental autobiography written after his escape from postrevolutionary Petrograd to Berlin, estrangement becomes a way of surviving unrequited love in exile. *Zoo; or, Letters Not about Love* is an ironic epistolary romance based on the actual correspondence between Shklovsky and Elsa Triolet, who was the sister of Mayakovsky's muse, Lily Brik, and future wife of writer Louis Aragon. *Letters Not about Love* are, of course, letters about love. Alya, the "new Heloise," declares that she values her freedom most of all, prohibiting her Formalist lover to speak about love and begging him to discuss his literary theory instead. The result is a rare dialogical text about love and freedom. Shklovsky the lover includes (occasionally under erasure) letters by his beloved that completely contradict his own assessment of her. Shklovsky the writer places Alya's texts side by side with his own, which had the effect of launching her literary career. While dialogical, the love remains entirely unrequited. "When you write to me—how, how, how much you love me, on the third 'how' I begin to yawn," writes cruel Alya in one of her last letter. The "new Heloise" is a proper Formalist disciple: she learns some techniques of literary analysis from her teacher, putting the emphasis on the "how" instead of the "what." Contrary to the classical plot of the pedagogical romance, Shklovsky's letters succeed pedagogically but not erotically.[43] Shklovsky's epistolary novel tells the story of the lover's pained recognition of the freedom of the other, in this case, her freedom not to love him in return.

After *Zoo*, Shklovsky returned from exile to Soviet Russia, only to be denounced as "an internal emigré," a practitioner of Formalist criticism as well as a practitioner of the cosmopolitan discipline of comparative literature. By the mid-1920s, the Formalists were under attack on all sides, by Marxists and traditionalists alike, whom Shklovsky called the makers of a "Red Restoration." "Material being conditions consciousness but conscience remains unsettled," wrote Shklovsky in 1926, paraphrasing Karl Marx.[44] His postexilic text *Third Factory* is an autobiography of the "unsettled conscience" that persists in spite of the determinism of "material being." Shklovsky proposes to speak not about estrangement but about the freedom of art and to attempt a theory of unfreedom. The text opens with an anecdote about Mark Twain, who wrote letters in duplicate: the first letter was destined for his addressee and the second one for the writer's private archive; in the second letter, he recorded what he really thought. This is perhaps the earliest formulation of Soviet Aesopian language, which would become a foundational fiction of the Soviet intelligentsia, a technique of reading between the lines and understanding one another with half-words. Between the 1930s and the 1980s, this Aesopian language would bind together the imagined community of the Soviet intelligentsia. *The Third Factory* is one of the first Soviet texts that thinks about censorship as an artistic problem and reflects upon it through literary devices. The text is organized as a collage of the actual text and a draft for a film script that will in the end be shelved. The film script, not coincidentally, deals with sailors right after the French Revolution looking for an island utopia called "Envy Bay" and discussing Rousseau's *The Social Contract*. Yet *Third Factory* itself is an example neither of samizdat nor of dissident writing; rather, it is an attempt to negotiate some kind of contract between the writer and the state according to which the writer gets to preserve the public space and the limited independence and solidarity of the "writers' guild." The pain of the writer's situation is represented through the repetition of the traumatic scene of making flax, in which the writer makes himself the author-product of the state, not merely an author-producer.[45]

Shklovsky wrote that the Soviet writer of the 1920s has two choices: to write for the desk drawer or to write on state demand. "There is no third alternative. Yet that is precisely the one that must be chosen . . . Writers are not streetcars on the same circuit."[46] One of the central parallelisms that Shklovsky explores in *The Third Factory* is the unfreedom of the writer caught in the play of literary convention and the unfreedom of the writer working under the dictates of the state, specifically, an authoritarian power. The two deaths of the author—one a playful self-constraint and the other the acceptance of the state *telos*—are not the same. Inner freedom and the space of the writer's creative exploration are shrinking in the context of public unfreedom. Shklovsky speaks about the secret passages in the walls of Parisian houses that are left for cats, an image that seems to refer to the shrunken literary public sphere in the 1920s. This is a forever shrinking space of freedom.[47]

Thus, Shklovsky's own practices of literary estrangement in his semi-autobiographical texts do not merely point to the tradition of inner freedom and Stoic withdrawal from public life. Rather, Shklovsky's evolution mirrors a different history suggested in the writings of his contemporary, Hannah Arendt. Exploring the genealogy of the Western idea of freedom, Arendt observed that the Stoic conception of inner freedom, as the "inner *polis*" or "inner citadel" of a person estranged from public life, derived from an earlier conception of public freedom of the Athenian *polis*. The connection between inner freedom and public freedom reveals itself at the level of architectural metaphor. It is not by chance that Stoic philosophers such as Epictetus and Marcus Aurelius spoke about the "inner *polis*" of one's self or an "inner citadel," internalizing the concept of freedom, at the time of the disappearance of the public *polis*. The notion of estrangement from worldly concerns and a focus on inner freedom move to the center of philosophical attention at the height of the Roman Empire and a time of growing disappointment with democratic ideals.

Similarly, the evolution of Shklovsky's theory and practice of estrangement has more to do with the vanishing of the postrevolutionary literary public sphere and its transformation into a guarded citadel of inner freedom that could only be revealed to a small network of like-minded friends. The conceptions of private life or even inner life are endangered and redefined. Not surprisingly, Benjamin, who traveled to Moscow in the winter of 1926–1927, commented—with only some exaggeration—that the Bolsheviks "have abolished private life" and also closed the cafés, thus transforming the distinction between public and private into a broader understanding of Soviet collectivism. Estrangement evolved from an aesthetic device, an existential and political practice that lays bare the historical situation of the time rather than allowing any escape from its precarious foundations.

Support for this hypothesis can be found in the testimonies of Shklovsky's contemporaries and friends who considered Shklovsky to be a "free thinker," adventurer, and revolutionary resembling the Decembrists of the nineteenth century.[48] Similarly, in her diary of 1927, Lidiia Ginzburg, the literary critic and younger disciple of the Formalists, observed: "The merry times of laying bare the device have passed (leaving us a real writer— Shklovsky). Now is the time when one has to hide the device as far as one can." The practice of aesthetic estrangement had become politically suspect already by the late 1920s; by 1930, it had turned into an intellectual crime. In 1930, Shklovsky renounced Formalism in a public declaration published in *Literaturnaia Gazeta* under the title "A Monument to a Scientific Error." But what kind of public self-criticism was this, and why did it begin with another tale of building monuments?

The genre of Shklovsky's declaration is a peculiar hybrid of the tamed manifesto and ambiguous apology with foreign novelistic parallelisms. To explain his "scientific error," Shklovsky uses his favorite device of paradoxical parallelisms. He tells the story about a city built by mistake, where the residents decide to erect a monument to scientific error.[49] "I do not wish to be a monument to my own error," writes the seemingly repentant Formalist critic. One is struck by the fact that the monument to a scientific error is a very Shklovskian monument, strategically positioned on the side roads of history. Is it possible that Shklovsky is actually erecting a monument to Formalism in disguise while covering it up with a few politically correct readymades, just like the Soviet *Monument to Liberty* covered up the statue to the tsar?

Shklovsky's fellow Formalists, Yuri Tynianov and Boris Eikhenbaum, did not treat this "monument to scientific error" as treason but as a survival tactic. The textual ambivalences of the declaration did not escape them. Neither did they escape the attention of Shklovsky's Marxist attackers, who correctly observed that Shklovsky confused the revolutions and remained an adept of the "bourgeois" February Revolution with its interest in civic freedoms and artistic independence.[50] One thing remains certain: the practice of estrangement is perceived as having a clear political resonance and, if anything, too connected to the extraliterary realities. Reflecting upon his theory of estrangement sixty-five years later, Shklovsky attempted to dispel historical misconceptions about the Formal method and the relationship between art and the "world":

Ostranenie is a form of world wonder, of an acute and heightened perception of the world. This term presupposes the existence of so-called "content," if we understand by "content" deferred, slowed-down, attentive examination of the world.[51]

Thus, *ostranenie* was never an estrangement from the world, but estrangement for the sake of the world's renewal. In the end, the Formalist critic is not practicing literary science but narrating the end of the literary public sphere. In spite of continuous attacks on his work and the official demands for narrative and ideological coherence, the devices of Shklovsky's texts remained almost unchanged as he continued to speak the Aesopian language of the nearly extinct "Formalist guild." Miraculously surviving various campaigns against him, Shklovsky remained until his death in 1984 a great theorist-storyteller like Walter Benjamin, speaking in elaborate parables, full of self-contradiction, in a unique style of Formalist baroque.

Estrangement *for* the World: Arendt and Kafka

For Arendt, as for Shklovsky, the theory of distance and freedom is linked to the aesthetic experience, to dramas of love and life under a totalitarian regime. Arendt said that she came to political thinking through German philosophy, aesthetics, and poetry. The concepts of estrangement, distance, and remoteness play a crucial role in her early poems and in her self-portrait, "Shadows," that she sent to Martin Heidegger in 1925 at the beginning of their love affair. After the secret relationship, Arendt distances herself from her own romantic introspection and discovers "worldliness." In her thinking on human freedom, she would develop instead the idea of *amor socialis*, love for the neighbor and friend based on respect without intimacy, "a regard for the person from the distance which the space of the world puts between us." This "distance" allows one to reinvent the world, to estrange one's routine, to distance oneself from both self-absorption and ready-made public opinion. Arendt, like Shklovsky, develops a conception of distance that is opposed to both Marxist world alienation and Romantic introspection. Distance becomes "the ground for plurality," a fundamental feature of humanity: "We are all the same, that is, human, in such a way that nobody is ever the same as anyone else who ever lived, lives or will live."[52]

After her double escape, from Nazi Germany and from a French camp for enemy aliens, Arendt reflected upon the other dimension of self-distancing that constitutes the precarious freedom of the outcasts and their unique weapons of independent thinking (*selbstdenken*). In her texts written right after emigration to the United States, "We Refugees" (1943) and "The Jew as Pariah" (1944), she speaks about the hidden tradition of secularized Jews, the tradition of pariahs and parvenus that in a time of catastrophe are grouped together with those, Jews and non-Jews alike, who do not try to pass but rather like Heinrich Heine, Rahel Varnhagen, Charlie Chaplin, Salomon Maimon, and Franz Kafka use their double estrangement from both religious Judaism and modern European culture to preserve disinterested intelligence and humor.[53] In her theater of pariahs she offers several types: Heine's schlemihl, the "lord of dreams" with a liberating humor and irreverent joie de vivre; Charlie Chaplin, the little man perpetually suspect for his potential crimes; Bernard Lazare's conscious pariah; and Kafka's "man of goodwill" who uses independent thinking as his main tool in the struggle against society. Like Shklovsky, Arendt speaks about multiple estrangements of secularized Jews who have conflicting identifications. In the postwar years, Arendt herself exchanged one estranged persona for another: the "maiden from afar" and the philosophical lover becomes a self-conscious pariah and political thinker. However, Arendt herself rarely indulged in explicit self-description and never glamorized her own marginalization. She thought that the intimacy of the pariah and the pariah's contemplative freedom might come at the expense of worldliness, *amor mundi*, and political rights.

A striking connection between Arendt and Shklovsky resides in the way they discuss the experience of totalitarianism (without naming it, in the case of Shklovsky) through artistic and spatial categories. Arendt believes that it is necessary to defamiliarize one's concepts in order to think through the "uncommon newness" of the brutal regimes of Nazi Germany and Stalinist Russia that made "everything possible." The disappearance of the nongovernmental public sphere that Shklovsky observed in the 1920s Soviet Union becomes crucial for Arendt's later theory of totalitarianism. Totalitarianism begins by abolishing the space of public freedom with all its little walls, partitions of civil society, and multiple channels of communication: "To abolish the fences of laws between men—as tyranny does—means to take away man's liberties and destroy freedom as a living political reality."[54] Totalitarian regimes "substitute for the boundaries and channels of communication between individual men a band of iron which holds them so tightly together that it is as though their plurality had disappeared into One Man of gigantic dimension."[55] This results in a peculiar *intimacy with terror*. Sadly, there is a revealing common place in the Soviet culture of the 1930s: the one-on-one conversation with Stalin, which worked its seductive power even on such independent minds as writers Boris Pasternak and Mikhail Bulgakov.

In *The Origins of Totalitarianism*, Arendt distinguishes between loneliness and solitude. In solitude one is not lonely, but in dialogue with oneself. Solitude might be conducive to the practice of critical estrangement and inner freedom that allows one to preserve dignity under the worst circumstances. Unlike solitude, loneliness is a result of the "isolation of the masses" from the political process, a combination of cynicism and gullibility that drives the masses to support an imperialist or a totalitarian regime.[56] Loneliness in this sense is the opposite of estrangement; it is a type of isolation that feeds the extreme forms of modern conformism. The collapse of the public realm results in a combination of extreme scientism and mysticism or conspiratorial thinking. Its outcome is radical antiworldliness with all the possible consequences. Totalitarianism pushes further the maxim of Dostoevsky's deliberate murderer Raskolnikov in *Crime and Punishment* that everything is permitted; in the totalitarian state, everything becomes possible. The strangest and most defamiliarized vision of the world can come true; hence, artistic and critical estrangement becomes a double estrangement that challenges the very logic of the totalitarian remaking of the world.

Public freedom for Arendt is not a dialogue with oneself, but a collective action on the public stage. Freedom, unlike liberation, cannot exist without a public space and democratic institutions, contracts, promises, anchors of common historical memory; yet the experience of freedom is not limited to procedural democracy. Freedom for Arendt is akin to a performance on a public stage that requires a common language but also a degree of incalculability, luck, chance, hope, surprise, and wonder. Similar to Shklovskian estrangement, which focuses on the process rather than on the product, freedom has a value in itself and as an experience that leads to "self-distancing and independent judgment." In other words, Arendt's conception of freedom combines aesthetic, existential, and political dimensions. It is described in language uncannily reminiscent of Shklovsky with its emphasis on performance, wonder, renewal, and "dehabituation" of the routine. Arendt's models are the French resistance and the Hungarian revolt of 1956—and perhaps 1989 Prague would have been another example. Hers is not merely a nostalgic image of the Athenian *polis* or republican freedom, but a radical vision of a participatory democracy of thinking individuals that at this point in time seems, unfortunately, just as utopian as the Marxist model of a classless society in which one herds sheep in the morning, fishes and hunts in the afternoon, and philosophizes in the evening.

In my view, it is possible to distinguish in Arendt's work two kinds of estrangement; I would call them estrangement *from* the world and estrangement *for* the world. Estrangement *from* the world has its origins in the Stoic concept of inner freedom and in the Christian conception of freedom and salvation, as well as in Romantic subjectivity and intro-spection. It suggests a distancing from political and worldly affairs. On the other hand, estrangement *for* the world is an acknowledgment of the integral human plurality that we must recognize within us and within others. This is a way of seeing the world anew, a possibility of a new beginning that is fundamental for aesthetic experience, critical judgment, and political action.

Both Arendt and Shklovsky remained uncanonical, off-modern think-ers who defied a strictly systematic or disciplinary way of thinking. Shk-lovsky never became a systematic literary scientist, and Arendt never even strived to present herself as a systematic philosopher. Neither left a "school of thought," but both developed extraordinary insights. With *The Origins of Totalitarianism*, and specifically in *Eichmann in Jerusalem: A Report on the Banality of Evil* (1963), Arendt begins to connect the experi-ence of freedom to the unconventional practice of the imagination and an ability to think "without banisters." Her conception of the "banality of evil" uses the artistic debate on kitsch and routinization of consciousness to discuss crucial political issues, as will be discussed in chapter 6. We can observe another curious connection between Shklovsky and Arendt: both remained haunted by the specter of Kant, whose work becomes impor-tant again even in those eccentric readings that pay attention to Kant's critique of judgment and his concern with cosmopolitan citizenship or the "crooked timber of humanity" and human dignity. Shklovsky was ac-cused in the 1930s of being a "neo-Kantian" idealist who never embraced Hegelian-Marxist-Leninist dialectics. Indeed, the explicit antiutilitarianism of Shklovskian estrangement and its emphasis on wonder and distance are reminiscent of Kantian aesthetic categories. As for Arendt, she uses the Kantian conception of aesthetic judgment as a foundation for her theory of ethical judgment, which constitutes an experimental creative misread-ing of Kant's theory: "The manifestation of the wind of thought is not (necessarily) knowledge; it is the ability to tell right from wrong, beautiful from ugly. And this, at the rare moments when the stakes are on the table, may indeed prevent catastrophes, at least, for the self."[57]

Thus, in their exploration of estrangement, Shklovsky and Arendt arrived at the same crossroads of consciousness and conscience. In Shk-lovsky's *Third Factory*, conscience was supposed to be determined by ma-terial being and Marxist ideology, but conscience "remained unsettled." For Arendt, too, the life of the critical mind is shaped by the encounter between consciousness and conscience. Conscience, according to Ar-endt, means thinking with oneself and others and reflects "a primordial indebtedness, the tie with the sheer facts of human existence." Conscience is described in dramatic fashion as a dialogue with one's own inner strangers: "Conscience is the anticipation of that fellow who awaits you if and when you come home." This kind of homecoming to conscience remains forever unsettled; it reveals inner plurality and a complex architecture of personal freedom with thresholds, partitions, and openings to the world that is not the same as the Stoic inner citadel. Conscience in such a modern conception is not a matter of religious belief or Kantian morality but care for the world and an ability to think and to judge. Arendtian conscience is neither sovereign, nor autonomous, nor collective; rather, it is interactive. It mediates between the inner plurality of the individual with her many voices and accents and the pluralism of the external world. The practices of dissent originate in this dialogue with oneself and in the tension between consciousness and conscience. Significantly, neither Arendt nor Shklovsky wished to overcome estrangement; both regarded it as constitutive of the modern condition, of worldliness, and of human freedom. In this respect, the two writers are equally opposed to the Hegelian-Marxist philosophy of history as well as to any kind of systematic philosophy that seeks scientific objectivity. At the same time, neither of them flirts with the theological, messianic, or utopian abyss of freedom.

In the moments when Arendt confronts the asymptotic space of freedom in "the gap between the past and the future," and whenever she experiences a philosophical hopelessness, she turns to stories and parables from literature. While she was never a Formalist disciple, her analysis appears strikingly Shklovskian. Arendt's reading of Kafka results in the uncommon geometry of freedom shaped by the invisible diagonal that resembles the knight's move.

In one of her verbal monuments to freedom she commemorates Franz Kafka, a rather unlikely candidate for a freedom fighter and architect of worldliness. Kafka is not an obvious political actor in the public sphere, but in Arendt's reading, through his radical imagination he creates "thought events" that are capable of defamiliarizing our vision and thus of changing the world. In 1937 Arendt presented her first homage to Kafka to a small audience where only three people seemed to know who he was. Among them were Walter Benjamin and Gunther Anders, the latter a writer, disciple of Heidegger, and Arendt's first husband. Whether Kafka wished it or not, posthumously he became a political writer; various communist writers in France and in Germany took part in the campaign "Shall One Burn Kafka?" (1946) and the communist leadership of postwar Czechoslovakia censored Kafka out of his native Prague, to which he returned with a vengeance, and rock star status, even, after 1989, on a par with Elvis and Che Guevara, to judge from images adorning t-shirts.[58]

In the preface to her collection of essays "Between Past and Future," while discussing the lost heritage of twentieth-century freedom in both political life and the life of the mind, Arendt offers her liberating reading of Kafka. She relates the parable that appears in Kafka's diary:

> He has two antagonists: the first presses him from behind, from the origin. The second blocks the road ahead. He gives battle to both . . . But it is only theoretically so. For it is not only the two antagonists who are there, but he himself as well, and who really knows his intentions? His dream, though, is that some time in an unguarded moment—and this would require a night darker than any night has ever been yet—he will jump out of fighting line and be promoted, on account of his experience in fighting, to the position of umpire over his protagonists in their fight with each other.[59]

As is usually the case with Kafka it is hard to say what exactly this is a parable of. Could it be one of liberation? But Kafka wrote that even if his nameless "he" is liberated, he would not know what freedom is. Could it then be a parable about hope? "But Kafka famously said that there is plenty of hope but not for us. Most likely he will 'die of exhaustion,' tired of fighting. Is it then a parable about parables "and who really knows its intentions"?

Kafka is famous for his impersonal constructions and passive voice, alluding to and obscuring the invisible hand that propels him to another plane of existence. In her usual virile fashion, Arendt inserts herself into his syntax and takes upon herself an active role. Through her creative reading she promotes Kafka, but not to the position of umpire. Where then?

Arendt comes up with an ingenious geometry of liberation and even draws a diagram that appears in *The Life of the Mind* where she returns again to the same parable. Arendt claims that Kafka's story, for all its magnificence, lacks the spatial dimension of a thought event. For Arendt the insertion of the man breaks up the continuum and deflects the linear forces from their original direction. "Ideally the action of two forces which form the parallelogram should result in the third force . . . the diagonal . . . whose origin would be the point at which the forces clash . . ." It would be limited at the origin but "infinite with respect to its ending by virtue of having resulted from the concerted action of two forces whose origin is infinity" (fig. 17). This diagonal is a perfect metaphor for the activity of thought: "on this diagonal he would have found the space in time—the

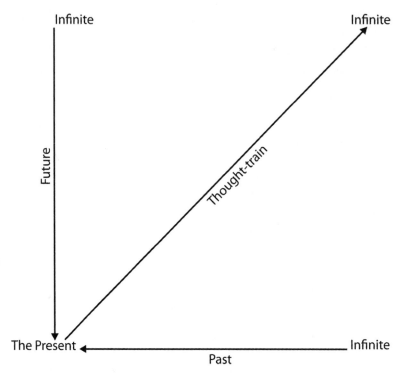

Figure 17. Hannah Arendt's diagram of the diagonal of freedom from Hannah Arendt, *The Life of the Mind* (New York: Harcourt Brace Jovanovich, 1977), 1: 208.

small track of non-time which the activity of thought beats within the time-space of the mortal men."[60] Thus Arendt doesn't offer Kafka an escape but a secret diagonal of human freedom. He is not a political actor, but by sheer force of intelligence and spiritual imagination he created "a breath-taking thought landscape."

In *The Life of the Mind*, Arendt puts Kafka's story together with Nietzsche's tale of Zarathustra's discovery of the "Now" and its Heideggerian interpretation.[61] In Nietzsche's parable, the battlefield of forces doesn't result in that gap but in a *"nunc-stans,"* the eternal "now of thought." Arendt sees in this suprasensual position of umpire the dream of Western metaphysics, from Parmenides to Hegel, of an illusionary lofty liberation from the human condition. By contrast, she chooses the "third way," not dissimilar to the Shklovskian "movement of the knight." Her freedom is neither transcendence nor regression, but a lateral move that explores the potentialities of the human condition.

Arendt doesn't simply try to save Kafka from attacks on the left and on the right for artistic reasons. Her Kafka is not a brilliant pessimist withdrawn from politics into his own castle of imagination. Arendt claims that he offered blueprints for the architecture of the future—neither that of the castle, nor of the Revolution, but the unpredictable architecture of "goodwill" and "human spontaneity": "Kafka envisioned a possible world that human beings would construct in which the action of man depends on nothing but himself and his spontaneity."[62] The hero of *The Trial*, Joseph K., "appears strange" to his fellow unfree citizens, "not because he is deprived of human rights, but because he comes and asks for them."[63] This architecture of the world where one comes and asks for broadly defined human rights can be discovered in Kafka only on the *via negativa*, as if it were a photographic negative of what is usually conceived as the "Kafkaesque."

Kafka's world is radically defamiliarized because it reveals the strangeness of what we conventionally accept as real. His heroes "are not interested in facades but in deep structures." In other words, Kafka's texts function like alternative architectural models that do not reflect the existing buildings but rather offer blueprints for another life.[64] They are examples of the estrangement *for* the world because they offer a reverse mimesis of art that can broaden horizons of life and of contemporary everyday reality "appearing as imitation called to defend itself."[65] It is through her early reading of Kafka that Arendt formulated her conception of worldliness. Ruination is natural in the world; so what human imagination can do is to offer a limited challenge to such laws of nature and even to the Hegelian laws of history.

Something intensely personal is taking place in Arendt's new reading of Kafka after World War II, something that reveals very high stakes. The introduction to "Beyond the Past and the Future" is haunted by an intertextual ghost whose language and images inform the whole book—Walter Benjamin. Kafka's "He" resembles Benjamin's description of Paul Klee's painting *Angelus Novus*, which Benjamin called "the angel of history" and described in his *Theses on the Philosophy of History*, the manuscript Arendt carried with her during her multiple escapes from Europe and that was published after Benjamin's death in 1940. In her creative reading Arendt attempts to save Benjamin and Kafka from themselves, recovering the "forgotten heritage" of freedom in their thought that existed like an *anamorphose*, a hidden figure in their imaginary architecture that neither of them fully illuminated. Kafka and Benjamin were long dead, but Arendt engages them in a posthumous conversation, confronting the invisible daimons of freedom that lurked over their shoulders. Where Benjamin renamed Klee's "new angel" the "Angel of History," Arendt questioned such a messianic and catastrophic idea of history with a capital H: "[W]e may reclaim our human dignity, win it back, as it were, from that pseudo-divinity named History of the modern age, without denying its impor-tance." Benjamin's "Angel of History" turns into Arendt's angel of freedom. There is no humanoid representation of this figure, no embodiment, only a suggestive diagram with many textual folds.

Writers on Trial: Dissent, Legal Obedience, and National Mythology

Let us imagine a different statue of liberty, not Shklovsky's and Tatlin's ludic ruin–construction site but the monument to the great Russian poet Pushkin standing not far from the statue to the Soviet poet Vladimir Mayakovsky on the former Gorky Street.

On Soviet Constitution Day, December 5, 1965, the square around the Pushkin monument became the site of the first voluntary, non-state-sponsored political demonstration since the early days of the Soviet Union. Fifty men and women went to Pushkin Square carrying affirmative ban-ners: "We Respect the Soviet Constitution" and "Open Trial for Andrei Siniavsky and Yulii Daniel." There were about two hundred sympathetic onlookers although the witnesses offer different accounts of who was a participant and who was an onlooker and whether some of the onlookers were scared participants who in the end got cold feet. The event lasted about twenty minutes, after which the KGB officials promptly arrested the participants and destroyed their "provocative" banners.[66] The trial of Andrei Siniavsky (pseud., Abram Tertz) and Yulii Daniel (pseud., Nikolai Arzhak), accused, among other things, of "anti-Soviet propaganda," took place in January 1966 and culminated with their exile and imprisonment. The theory of estrangement, without reference to Shklovsky personally but with an explicit reference to Soviet literary science, was mobilized by the writers' defense to explain the difference between writers and their provocative characters. It didn't help win the trial, yet it carried the day albeit for a small audience and for a brief period of time—because the writ-ers refused to identify with the official language and unofficial practices of compromise and prevented the government from turning their sentenc-ing into a Stalinist-style show trial.

Siniavsky (charged with politically incorrect plagiarism of Kafka, among other things), was a student of modernist literature and revolutionary cul-ture of the 1920s, an avid reader of Mayakovsky and Shklovsky (especially since his own father was, just like Shklovsky, a Socialist-Revolutionary in his youth). Most important, the silencing of the trial was thwarted and the events received more publicity than the Soviet government had expected. The demonstration and the trial seemed to be better known abroad than in Russia and received broad support from many leading writers and intellectuals from Chile to India and from major Western intellectuals including Arendt, Auden, Aragon, and others. Many Russian writers and intellectuals also signed the petitions, for the first time in their lives. For the elderly Shklovsky himself, the trial of Siniavsky and Daniel became an occasion for the first public act of dissent fifty years after the writer's engagement in the anti-Bolshevik underground.[67]

Across the world the 1960s is seen as a decade of dissent, rebellion, and artistic experimentation. Many are still enthralled with unreflected nostalgia for that decade, even those who were born long after it. We still live in the wake of the 1960s and its unresolved failures in cross-cultural communication: the civil rights movement in the United States, student revolts in Paris as well as all over Latin America and Eastern Europe, from Zagreb to Buenos Aires, Soviet tanks in Prague, Soviet stars in Berkeley dorm rooms, and portraits of Mao in Parisian *cinemathèques*, and in Chinese courtrooms where fellow Chinese intellectuals were persecuted. Two events in 1965–1966 in Moscow were crucial for the history of the European and American left: a rare moment of cross-cultural insight and solidarity in the defense of dissent. Yet what was at stake there goes far beyond local circumstances: it forces us to rethink the nature of law and literature, the fate of the public realm and collective memory.

One of the principle organizers of the peaceful protest near the Pushkin monument was Alexander Sergeevich Esenin-Vol'pin, a mathematician and eccentric philosopher who was also the illegitimate son of the translator Nadezhda Vol'pina and the famous "peasant-poet," Sergei Esenin, who committed suicide in 1925, leaving his testament written in blood. The son of the poet and Alexander Sergeevich Pushkin's namesake, Esenin-Vol'pin began as a poet but later moved to the study of sciences and Wittgenstein's philosophy of ordinary language. He describes his interest in mathematics and law as a result of critical suspicion of poetic language, yet confessing in a poem that he remained forever a *frondeur* (a dissenter and anarchist). Let us not forget the staging: Gorky Street with the three poets' monuments decorating it—Gorky, Pushkin, and Mayakovsky. The square near Mayakovsky's monument was the place of many public poetry readings in the early 1960s and Mayakovsky's last home, located next to the Lubianka, the office of the KGB and the infamous prison, is not so far away. Pushkin's monument, where the demonstration took place, was an unwilling hero of performance art in its own right: in the 1930s it went on a fantastic journey around the city to cover up for the destruction of the Strastnoi Monastery during the Stalinist reconstruction of Moscow. Pushkin, in the pre-revolutionary monument at the site where the demonstration took place, is caught in a moment of inner reflection, as if retreating into the space of poetic inner freedom celebrated in his poem "From Pindemonti."

Esenin-Vol'pin and his group differed from the American civil rights activists who practiced civil disobedience in their advocacy of radical civil obedience, legality, and civility. Even his defense for the writers Siniavsky and Daniel too take the shape not of a defense of literature as the famed "second government" of Russian culture, but a defense of *glasnost*, or openness, of the judicial procedure.

The request for transparency of language didn't sit well with Esenin-Vol'pin's KGB interrogators which is clear in their discussion of the banner that read "Respect the Soviet Constitution."

> *Interrogator:* Aleksandr Sergeevich, why did you come to the square?
> *Vol'pin:* In order to express what I was trying to express.
> *I.:* But you were detained with a sign in your hands.
> *V.:* I didn't detain myself; why did others detain me?
> *I.:* No, but still, you were carrying a sign saying "Respect the Soviet Constitution," correct?
> *V.:* Correct.
> *I.:* Why did you make such a sign?
> *V.:* So that people would respect the Soviet Constitution.
> *I.:* What, do you think somebody doesn't respect it?
> *V.:* That was not written [on the sign].
> *I.:* Why [did you choose] this day?
> *V.:* If I had come to the square on May Day with a sign reading Respect the First of May, would that surprise you? Today is Soviet Constitution Day.[68]

This is an example not of theater of the absurd but of secret police interrogation. Transparent language that states what it means is viewed by the interrogator as a provocation that implies subversive intent. Actual events of the day (coming to the demonstration, carrying signs, being arrested) are immediately turned upside down: the interrogator attempts to transform affirmation of the Soviet Constitution into a presumed negation (you affirm because you think other people don't?) and confuses the agency of the persecuted and persecutors (we detained you with the banner, therefore you must be guilty). This is a brilliant example of paranoiac logic that delineates the space of guilt for the arrested in a precise Kafkaesque fashion. "He" is always already guilty unless "he" (no longer Joseph K.) starts to imagine what freedom could look like against all odds and begins to imagine his own lucid diagonal of freedom.

Esenin-Vol'pin carefully resists the interrogator's implications, relying on the "literal" meaning of the Soviet Constitution and sticking to the letter of the law. He even objected to the phrase "respecting the law," preferring "observing the law" instead, to preserve the neutrality of language. The "legal dissident" must avoid emotional language or excessively romantic, nihilistic, or violent practices harking back to the nineteenth-century Russian tradition.

But what was the meaning of such an affirmation in 1965, and was this an act of mimicry or a Dada-like political performance? Why was this affirmation of legality regarded as illegal? One might answer this question with another impossible question (more puzzling to Western observers than to locals): who believed in communism in the Soviet Union and the countries of the former Eastern Bloc? Surprisingly, there were more true believers among the prisoners of the Gulag and dissidents who went through a complex reflection on the nature of utopia and the seduction of ideology, than there were among Soviet bureaucrats and career officers of the KGB. For ordinary people communist ideology was domesticated through a series of "cultural mythologies" that translated Marxism-Leninism (or Leninism-Stalinism) into Russian-Soviet, turning strange aspects of party doctrine into everyday folkways that are no longer questioned. By "cultural mythologies" in this case I understand shared narratives that circulate in a given culture and are not perceived as constructions from above, fabricated with a specific political intent, but as a form of inherited wisdom ("this is just the way it is," with all the required tautologies of "this is just the way it is and always has been").[69] Across cultures, local beliefs (even those that advocate purity) are hybrid and eclectic, combining the wisdom of the past, responses to historical experiences, and political manipulation. What was distinct in the Soviet-Russian case was the fact that those mythologies were cemented by mystery and authority—by fear, the great equalizer, and the ancient Russian superstition of "not throwing the trash out of the hut," that is, not revealing dirty laundry to outsiders and foreigners.

In this case the dialectics of estrangement and domestication are rather complicated. On the one hand, during Leninist and Stalinist times, the new ideology, couched in charismatically incomprehensible language, estranged many everyday experiences of Soviet citizens. During the purges of the 1930s–1950s, this ideology helped to legitimize and make logical bizarre accusations of mass conspiracy and an incredible proliferation of spies, "enemies of the people" and saboteurs within many ordinary families. On the other hand, since the 1930s Soviet ideology had built upon the foundation of common beliefs that were not substantially different from moderate right-wing, national, or imperial ideology. They included pride in the successes of the great Soviet state, the "biggest and most powerful in the world," and the eros of state patriotism is further heightened by the agonistic struggle of "those who are with us and those who are against us," with little gray zone in between. The Soviet Union was surrounded by the hostile outside world of the East (China, primarily) and the "West"—although during the Khrushchev era the myth of the imaginary West took hold among the liberal intelligentsia with its antiheroic heroes, from Hemingway to the Beatles.

What Esenin-Vol'pin does in his practice of reading the Soviet Constitution literally is to lay bare the abyss between the explicitly stated Soviet ideology and the written laws and implicit cultural myths and everyday unwritten laws. Lidiia Ginzburg wrote about the role of tautology and intonation in the preservation of the Soviet way of life: during Stalinist times it was not enough to agree silently; one had to voice agreement with the system, tautologically and publicly, using exactly the right intonation and following the orders and whims of the local apparatchiks, and not merely affirm the general concepts of Marxism-Leninism. Esenin-Vol'pin used tautology and affirmation to sabotage the unwritten Soviet mythologies of everyday behavior. Instead of deviating from the law, Esenin-Vol'pin and his fellow legal dissidents deviated from the unlawful practices of the Soviet regime and the unwritten social contract of the Soviet system, which consisted of the pact between the people and the KGB. The striking mimicry in this case consists not in the dissidents' repetition of the practices of social collaboration but in the disruption of their performance. This was an aesthetic use of mimicry similar to that promoted by Vladimir Nabokov as a strategy of "cryptic disguise," which does not fit into the master narrative about the laws of biological evolution or the laws of history. What distinguishes dissidents of the 1960s from the sophisticated children of the era of Brezhnev stagnation (my generation) was the fact that dissidents dared to question everyday practices of behavior in the public rather than the private sphere, instead of inhabiting and legitimizing them through everyday humor and elaborate guise of "well-recognized necessity" (to quote from memory the Marxist-Leninist definition of freedom as taught in Soviet high schools). The reason that there is such a strong desire today to write dissent out of Soviet history through compromise and innuendo—in the best tradition of "black [i.e., negative] PR"—is the fact that dissident "performance disruption" of the accepted strategies of everyday behavior threatens the domesticated versions of Soviet and Russian history. In other words, Esenin-Vol'pin's "literalism" and legalism were strategies of *estrangement for the world*, just as the appeal to the literariness of language was in the case of Siniavsky. Legal dissidents made us see the law anew while defamiliarizing the conspiratorial language of complicity with the regime.

Arguably the twenty-minute demonstration—five minutes past the fifteen minutes of fame—is an example of the best political performance art to occur in the Soviet Union at that time. The concept of civil disobedience is completely foreign to both the Russian and Soviet tradition, for which the notion of civility is forever suspect and frequently sacrificed for the sake of the national idea and minor disobediences are a part of everyday strategies of survival in a difficult time. Not surprisingly, Esenin-Vol'pin's defense of "civil obedience" was treated by the authorities as disobedience of a higher kind, better dismissed as madness or condemned as treason.

However quixotic and improbably idealistic these tiny groups of dissidents were, their tactic was a recreation of lost Promethean *technê*, not Dionysian *mania*. Andrei Amalrik, a dissident and author of the prophetic book *Will the Soviet Union Survive in 1984?* argued that the difference between Soviet dissidents and the revolutionaries of the nineteenth and early twentieth centuries was their objection to the rhetoric of self-sacrifice.[70] And yet, despite the rhetoric of rationality, Esenin-Vol'pin was a man of many contradictions: anarchist and *frondeur* by temperament and a defender of civil legalism. He was frequently imprisoned and placed in a psychiatric hospital, while being an advocate of lucidity and rationality, not of Russian emotionalism. A poet and the son of a lyrical poet, he was a defender of the literal language of the law. These contradictions appear less incomprehensible, however, if we understand them in the broad context of the performance of estrangement not as nihilistic rebellion or transgression. Estrangement for the world in this case was an attempt to reconquer to a minimal extent a public realm in which language was no longer perverted and domesticated in the Stalinist fashion. Paradoxically, here the language of the law is the language of a different form of behavior and cultural memory connected to another understanding of human dignity and evoking the traditions of Renaissance humanism (which was very popular among the intelligentsia, whose bookshelves were decorated with albums of Renaissance paintings made in Poland or Czechoslovakia) and the theories of an open society.

Theirs was not an economic neoliberalism but a form of socialism with a human face and a functioning legal body, a strange international hybrid that does not translate well into the current version of global culture. Another utopia, perhaps, but at least, not an authoritarian one. Dissident practices might have had little effect on Soviet legal procedures, but they did have an effect on public opinion operating through informal networks and personal contacts.

At first glance, Andrei Siniavsky and Yulii Daniel were arrested for a reason opposite to what brought on Esenin-Vol'pin's arrest. They were incriminated not for a public display of their support of Sovietness but for their secret publication of their works abroad: the problem was not the "letter of the law" but the law of literature. The charge against Siniavsky and Daniel was article 70 of the Soviet Criminal Code: "Agitation and propaganda with the goal of sabotage and the weakening of Soviet power or the committing of particularly dangerous crimes of dissemination with the same goal of slanderous fabrications, or the making and the preservation of such genre of literature with the deprivation of freedom from six months to seven years with exile from two to five years."[71]

Yulii Daniel, a veteran of World War II and a "Jew," according to the "nationality line" of his Soviet passport, was accused of fascism, while Andrei Siniavsky, a literary scholar and a Russian, according to his—but who used the Jewish-sounding pseudonym Abram Tertz—was accused of anti-Sovietism, anti-Semitism, Freudianism, depiction of explicit sexual acts, and the search for God.[72] The lesser charges included plagiarism of Dostoevsky and Kafka (minus Kafka's social critique of "conservative, philistines, and bourgeois") and slander of the Russian people.

What is at stake in the artists' trials is not merely the right to self-expression but also the audience's right to independent thinking and the public architecture that can make it possible. The very architecture of the space of the trial appears to have been very fragile. Mikhail Sholokhov, the general secretary of the Soviet Union of Writers and a Nobel Prize laureate, declared without ambiguity that in the earlier revolutionary Soviet decades, people like Siniavsky and Daniel would simply be executed on the spot without this luxury of democratic theater. Siniavsky's own behavior often defied accepted behavior during the Soviet show trials, as the great writer of the Gulag experience, Varlam Shalamov, suggests, under the influence of drugs and torture. Siniavsky refused to play by the rules of the public show trial and didn't admit his guilt. He insisted that his action was not "illegal" but unofficial, thus naming the in-between gray zone in the binary Soviet system.

However, the openness of the trial was relative. To enter one needed a special invitation, and the majority of the Soviet people learned about Siniavsky and Daniel neither from reading their fiction nor from the records of the trial but from the campaign in the press that preceded it and that anticipated some of its outcome. Here is an example from the famous article "Turncoats" by Dmitri Eremin published in the main periodical *Izvestiia*:

> The enemies of communism are not averse to dirt. In the bourgeois press and radio, information has appeared about the "unsubstantiated arrest" in Moscow of two "writers" who published their anti-Soviet slander abroad. Isn't this a perfect playground for the unclean conscience and the equally unclean imagination of Western propagandists? And here they are painting in broad strokes the mythical "purge in Soviet literary circles" claiming that those circles are "extremely alarmed by the new approach" towards "writers inclined in the anti-communist fashion" and in general against the liberal-minded circles of the intelligentsia.[73]

Later in the article Eremin proceeds to claim that "this [the Western response] was just a false facade. What hid behind it was different: the hatred of our regime, the slanderous blasphemy of everything that is dear to our Motherland and our people."

Let us look closely at how this article develops its argument. Why are there so many words here in quotation marks? Who is this mythical enemy who makes those claims? Mostly these quoted words and passages are used very differently from internationally accepted research practice. They don't come from a particular text and have no accompanying reference. This is a familiar device of Stalinist rhetoric. Two of the severed heads of quotation marks designate slander by the enemy of the people and signal an unspoken complicity between the writer and his readers. This is a way of sharing—not information, but attitude. Curiously, the quoted words and passages present the most adequate description of the situation, an establishing shot, so to speak, of what happened. The rhetoric follows many features we can recognize from Dostoevsky's *The Possessed*, with its phantasmagoric atmosphere of disinformation and the insinuation of mystery and authority. (The other accuser, literary critic Zoya Kedrina, claimed that Siniavsky imitated one of Dostoevsky's most reviled antiheroes—the cook Smerdiakov.)

One aspect of this rhetoric is incrimination through insinuation of a larger conspiracy, not dissimilar to the interrogator's strategy in Esenin-Vol'pin's case. The other is a relentless accusation of duplicity, which we can see in the images of "turncoats" (*perevertyshi*), dissimulators (*dvurushniki*), double agents, traitors, and "internal immigrants," some of the same words that were used in the accusations against Shklovsky and other Formalist critics. Here the insinuation of high treason against the motherland accompanies the accusation of sacrilege against the Russian people. Eremin employs religious imagery, proclaiming that Siniavsky and Daniel used "Judas' pens" to write their texts, as if asking to ban the writers from their community altogether:

> Siniavsky is trying to create an impression that in our country [the Soviet Union] there is anti-Semitism, and the author called "Abram Tertz" supposedly must look to publish abroad if he wishes to write "sincerely" about Soviet life. A miserable provocation, which betrays the literateur (*sochinitel'*) and his bourgeois patrons. Nothing is sacred in our country and its multinational culture.[74]

Why was the pseudonym Tertz like an irritant in the eye of Soviet culture? Was it not supposed to be internationalist and celebrate the diversity and friendship of the Soviet people? Not only did Siniavsky use a Jewish-sounding pseudonym, but he also spoke directly about Stalin's last campaign against "rootless cosmopolitans" (in many cases, Soviet Jews) that took place between 1949 and 1953 and was stopped only by Stalin's death. Many Western intellectuals on the left were puzzled at that time by information about this campaign: the Soviet "internationalist" leader who had defeated Hitler during the war somehow continued in Hitler's footsteps and with the ideas expressed in *Mein Kampf* about cosmopolitanism and rootlessness. However, if one follows the logic of totalitarianism as described by Arendt or the logic of imperial nationalism, the campaign doesn't appear that illogical. Khrushchev criticized Stalin's "mistakes" during his famous speech at the Twentieth Party Congress just ten years later. By the mid-1960s such a critique of Stalinism had not merely subsided, it had become an unspoken taboo in everyday Soviet practice. More significantly, the word "Jew" itself had become an unprintable word, like an insult. Joseph Brodsky writes in his autobiographical essay about his relationship to the word "Jew," which during his childhood was as rare as the word *"mediastinum"* (a membrane in the middle section of the chest cavity). So Siniavsky, a man of Russian Orthodox beliefs, violates the new unofficial code of silence around the issue: not only does he print the name "Abram" but he makes it his own. Once again, while not violating the official ideology of Marxism-Leninism, Siniavsky oversteps the decorum of the new political etiquette and practices of language. By doing so, he exposes a barely visible shift in Soviet policies, not a direct return to Stalinism but a transition to the Brezhnev era when the critique of Stalinism would be domesticated behind a newly found patriotism, the view that reemerges in contemporary Russian history books. Siniavsky's and Daniel's accusers are just as uncomfortable with the language of law as they are with the language of literature.

At the trial Siniavsky's interrogation began with a direct echo of Eremin's article. When asked about the use of the pseudonym "Abram Tertz," Siniavsky answers in an apolitical fashion:

> *Judge*: Why did you choose this particular pseudonym [Abram Tertz]?
> *Siniavsky*: I just liked it. I don't think this can be explained by any national reasons.

While obviously the Jewish-sounding name is not an accident of taste (and throughout his life Siniavsky argued consistently against what he perceived as "chauvinistic prejudice" in the Russian tradition), it is important to remember that the name has another connotation: Tertz relates to the Latin root the "third"—reminding us again of the quest of Shklovsky and others' quest for the third space that is not conquered by the agonistic logic of who is with us and who is against us. It is possible that what appealed to Siniavsky is the polysemic and grotesque quality of the pseudonym evoking simultaneously Babel's gangsters and Dante's *terza rima* and all the nostalgia for world culture accompanying it.

The Siniavsky-Daniel camp mounted a serious public defense, bombarding the court with literary armaments in the tradition of the Formal method. The defenders used quotation marks in a completely opposite manner from the accusers, not referring to presumed prejudices but appealing to scientific precision and demonstrating that all of the quotes used by the prosecutors come from literary characters and not from their authors, thus revealing a lack of comprehension of the elementary laws of literature. In the hostile Soviet court, distinguished scholar and semiotician Viacheslav Ivanov presented the Formalist theory of Shklovsky's literary device (without using the word "Formalist," of course). Appealing to the science of literature and to the scholarly professionalism that was gaining ground in the Soviet Union during the 1960s, Ivanov explained the theory of estrangement and the role of metaphor and narrative perspective in literature.[75] He also observed that all of Siniavsky's statements about Stalin's anti-cosmopolitan campaign were in line with the official Soviet critique of Stalinism, thus confronting the prosecution with their own ideological inconsistencies and lack of professionalism when it came both to the literal interpretation of laws and to literary interpretation in general.

In his concluding speech the accused Siniavsky continues with a discussion of literature in a somewhat uncanny manner, revealing how the actual trial seems to offer an unfortunate literal imitation of his and Daniel's fantastic literature:

> A strange veil is created here [during the trial], a special electrifying atmosphere. This is the atmosphere of the dark anti-Soviet underground which is hidden behind the enlightened face of Siniavsky, the Ph.D. in philology, and the poet and translator Daniel, who create plots, terrorist acts, pogroms, and murders . . . Here, truly it's terrifying and surprising when the artistic device loses its literariness and is taken literally, so that the trial becomes a continuation of the text.[76]

This part of Siniavsky's speech doesn't describe but performs his key literary device, aptly named "free indirect speech" (i.e., the use of the perspective and voice of a character but in the third person). It goes back to the dawn of literature but in the modern era evokes Gustave Flaubert, the nineteenth-century French writer and author of *Madame Bovary*—the exquisite novel of modern romance with romantic love. A century before Siniavsky, Flaubert was accused of promoting obscenity and immoral behavior and his lawyer pioneered a defense of literary devices, especially the "free indirect speech" argument that was also used in Tertz's trial. Siniavsky tells the fantastic story of the evil double agents and traitors Siniavsky-Tertz and Daniel-Arzhak, and spells out in an indirect, literary, yet strikingly precise fashion what was between the lines of the prosecutor's accusation: the change in Soviet policies and a return to the common places of the Russian imperial and Stalinist mythology of state. Siniavsky reveals what is terrifying about literalizing metaphors.

He doesn't share the megalomaniac aspirations of literary geniuses to produce literature that would be a grid for life and create a reverse mimesis. He doesn't wish to create his own "total work" but rather disrupt the total work of the state. In fact, in his politics and literature Siniavsky, like Shklovsky, cautions against losing the distinction between words and deeds—literature and everyday life—that might be dangerous for both. This is for him not only an aesthetic but also an ethical imperative and in this he joins Nabokov, Auden, and others. As an example of political disaster, Siniavsky cites Stalin's literalization of Lenin's metaphors about physically eliminating the enemies of the people (although the process did start in Lenin's time during the period called the "Red Terror").[77]

The accusation of duplicity leveled against Siniavsky is also prefigured in his work. A crucial difference exists between the state and the literary understanding of the concept.[78] The dissident strategies of behavior estrange the unspoken duplicity of both Soviet ideology and the practices of everyday life, which often was Soviet on the surface and state-nationalist in practice. Doublespeak pervaded the discourse of the Komsomol, Communist leaders, and unofficial rock musicians alike (only I would add, with a difference in the relationship to the state power, which is no small thing). By the time of late socialism, this duplicity would be completely naturalized and perceived with nostalgia as a common good of late socialism, but in the 1960s when the memory of Stalinism was still acute and alive, this was not the case.

For Siniavsky "duplicity" is part of the aesthetic play of self-effacement and self-invention, part of an ethical imperative that demands recognition of the inner plurality of individuals and pluralism in public discussion. Such "duplicity" goes to the origins of conscience, harking back to ancient Greece. The story of art and the theater of conscience shared the drama of multiple voices. The Socratic *daimon*—or demon, in this sense—exemplifies simultaneously the dialogue of consciousness and conscience, which is also the foundation of Shklovskian estrangement: "Everyday life determines consciousness but conscience remains unsettled." Many poets and writers spoke of various forms of duplicity, ranging from the use of Aesopian language to hide their message to the Socratic dialogue of conscience and consciousness continuing in the Shklovskian tradition. Thomas Venclova, the Lithuanian poet, dissident, and friend of Joseph Brodsky, wrote eloquently about two inner voices in the conscience of the writer: the voices of the Soviet censor and the devil-jester, which are perpetually dueling with one another, revealing the uncanny nature of the inner life of a thinking person.[79] But it is not merely an operation of cunning self-censorship and accommodation to the regime; it could also be a

game of internal liberation when the writer gives in to the demon-jester
and disrupts the official hide-and-seek.

Such duplicity questioned the unitary model of Soviet and Russian
culture, laying bare its inner plurality. All of Siniavsky's texts take on
topical political, social, and artistic issues—such as the anticosmopolitan
campaigns of the late Stalin era, which were criticized in Khrushchev's
speech at the Twentieth Party Congress, although such critique was soon
silenced or indirectly discouraged; the epidemic of graphomania, a side
effect of the great prestige of literature in Russia and of Soviet literary oppression; sexual and erotic relationships beyond the prudish Soviet norms;
Kafkaesque occurrences, and fantastic creatures who appear and set up
house—without a resident permit—in Soviet communal apartments.

Siniavsky's stories stage the drama of paying humorous homage to
the avant-garde and follow in the interrupted tradition of the literature
of the 1920s, which Siniavsky discussed at the end of his essay "What Is
Socialist Realism?" Sometimes the eccentric off-modern followers of the
experimental tradition end up in the unofficial club of the graphomaniacs,
whose president, self-defined graphomaniac Galkin, one of Tertz' most
successful characters, promotes writerly self-effacement, estrangement,
and parody that question the banality of good promoted by official literature. During the trial of Siniavsky and Daniel, modernist culture is put on
open trial itself for the first time; it never does well in the legal framework,
and certainly not in its fantastic Soviet version. Confusion of the opinions
of the author and his characters, as well as recourse to the language of
moral outrage, wounded patriotism, and implied subversive intent, are
not uniquely Soviet or Russian phenomena and have been used in all trials
against art since the nineteenth century. What is different is the harsh verdict that the writers received ("harsh" by European, not Soviet, standards,
of course).

In the strictly legal sense Siniavsky and Daniel lost their trial: they received a sentence of imprisonment and exile. They were silenced, and
their works were not published in Russia until the end of the Soviet Union.
Thus for the readers of my generation, unfortunately, they remained unknown. However, in their time, the trial and the dissident practice of behavior affected public opinion through informal tactics and strategies of
behavior.[80]

But Siniavsky's trials didn't end with imprisonment and exile. A second trial took place in the emigré press in Paris in 1988 and later in 1989
in Russia. At its center was the scandal around Siniavksy's text "Strolls

with Pushkin" written in the Dubravlag camp and smuggled out in letters to Siniavsky's wife. In 1976 a Parisian emigré critic from the postrevolutionary wave of immigration accused Siniavsky of "boorification" of the Russian language and of "cultural blasphemy." This accusation was echoed by Solzhenitsyn, who claimed that Siniavsky's "aesthetic nihilism" and "duplicity" was a sacrilege against the Russian conception of authority and of "everything that is lofty and pure in Russian culture." Then, after Siniavsky travelled to Russia in 1989 following the death of Yulii Daniel, another more virulent offensive against him unfolded in the Russian magazines. In his article "Russophobia" Igor Shafarevich stated an analogy between Siniavsky's "Strolls with Pushkin" and Salman Rushdie's *Satanic Verses*, turning Pushkin into the Russian prophet and confusing insults against religion with insults against national literature. "Salman Rushdie's famous *Satanic Verses* is apparently something like an Islamic variation on "Strolls [with] Pushkin."[81] "Something like" might be a reference to the author's lack of actual acquaintance with Rushdie's text. Siniavsky was accused of being a "defiler" of Russia's sacred object, Alexander Pushkin. The second trial of Siniavsky thus revealed what was not entirely spelled out in the first trial: the threat of literary freedom to the sacred authority of the nation evoked the notion of blasphemy, which, according to Esenin-Vol'pin, was a tactic more appropriate to the Spanish Inquisition than to Soviet justice.

The second trial echoed the first and revealed what might appear as an unlikely continuity between Soviet, post-Soviet and even immigrant, nationalist mythologies of ultranational patriotism, including opposition to free-spirited literary experimentation, conflation of the opinion of an author and his characters, conspiratorial insinuation, and accusations of the sacrilege and profanation of the "sacred" national poet Pushkin.

Siniavsky commented on the phantasmagoria of his own life, which uncannily imitated his texts and yet escaped his authorial control. Already in exile he found himself a dissident among dissidents, once again revealing the tensions between politics, religion, and literature. Siniavsky commented that some Russian dissidents carried the architecture of the Soviet state in their minds and reassembled it abroad.[82] In exile, even more so than at home, the dissident must remain vigilant to his own latent authoritarianism. Siniavsky speaks explicitly against both what he considers to be Russian fascism and Soviet authoritarianism.

In "Dissent as Personal Experience" Siniavsky reflected on the relationship between political and artistic dissent. The title of the essay is not as transparent as it seems. Like everything else in Siniavsky, it contains an element of ambivalence and paradox. What does it mean for dissidence, which is regarded as a form of action in public, to be personal? How are we to conceive of the personal if it becomes a space of dissent? What does it mean for a writer to be a dissident? Does this diminish the possibilities for artistic play or does it redefine the architecture of dissent? What happens with Pushkinian "other freedom" in dissident rewriting?

First, Siniavsky claims that his disagreement with the Soviet regime as well as with the more conservative circles in exile was of an "aesthetic nature": "Politics and the social organization of society are not my specialty. I can say almost as a joke that my differences with the Soviet power were of an aesthetic nature. Abram Tertz is a dissident for stylistic reasons. But he is an arrogant, unrepenting dissident, inspiring indignation, repulsion in the conservative and conformist society."[83]

Siniavsky creates his own history of dissent, enlisting writers, not politicians, among the early dissidents. He doesn't mention, however, the official Soviet revolutionary writers (not even his beloved Mayakovsky) but instead writes about Pasternak, Mandelshtam and Akhmatova, who cultivated their inner freedom to such a degree that it became a civic virtue.

Here we come full circle, back to the unconventional monument to Pushkin (or the antimonumental Pushkin with whom Tertz is taking a stroll in the Dubravlag labor camp) as a monument to dissident liberty. While the Pushkinian "other freedom" is dear to the writer's heart, this is not the only thing that is affirmed here. The writer becomes a model of eccentric individuality that inspires indignation in any conservative and conformist society.

Here is how Siniavsky defines his idea of liberty and dissent: "It doesn't matter, our vocation is to remain the partisans of liberty, because 'liberty,' like some other 'useless' categories—for example, art, kindness, human thought—are values in themselves and don't depend on historical and political accommodations (*konjuktura*)."

Siniavsky rewrites Pushkinian "other freedom" at once affirming his right as a writer to exist separate from the tsar and the people and yet extending this heretical play into the public realm. In fact, Siniavsky here virtually rewrites the famous definition of freedom given by another exiled writer and political dissident, Alexander Herzen: "Why is liberty valuable? Because it is an end in itself because it is what it is. To bring it as a sacrifice for something else is simply to perform an act of human sacrifice."[84]

While in private a Christian Orthodox believer, Siniavsky insisted on being a public heretic.[85] But the paradoxicalist Siniavsky-Tertz was not supporting heresy for its own sake or for the sake of his personal writerly freedom. Rather, in the tradition of Esenin-Vol'pin he advocated for the freedoms of others, for the separation of church and state and the public protection of heresies in the plural. Heresy estranges orthodoxy in order to protect the plurality of spiritual aspirations and to guarantee a right to imagination that is capable of remaking the world anew. The aesthetic dissidence of Tertz is not about autonomous aesthetics but about estrangement for the world through artistic practice. Siniavsky's writings, trials, and scandals give us an insight into the posthistory of dissent and into ways of rethinking it anew.

My conclusions about the political and artistic afterlife of dissent in the post-Soviet space are hardly cheerful. From a political standpoint, after the death of the distinguished scientist and human rights activist Andrei Sakharov, the role of Soviet-era dissidents and their legacy of a creative rethinking of the public realm have been diminished. It was frequently observed, primarily by Eastern and Central European writers, that in an epoch of dictatorship, the private realm becomes a space of dissent, creating inner circles of publicity, of a quasi–public sphere in the niches of private space. "Private" in this case is often not equated with individual but rather with alternative collectivities, the "kitchen salons," gatherings of friends and informal networks and connections. These are circles within circles that create spirals of gradual change that help to reinvent the future public culture. The danger of such an extension of inner freedom into the public realm, which became manifest after the end of the Soviet Union and the official collapse of communism lies in the fact that it did not translate into the building of new political institutions. The events of August 1991, which drew large public demonstrations in Moscow and Saint Petersburg (arguably) could have been Russia's own colorful democratic revolution that incorporated the lessons of dissent. However, in spite of many debates about the need to build an independent judiciary, legal system, and institutions of public solidarity that are independent of the state and economic elites, history took a different course. The Soviet-era elite structure of the party and security apparatus was preserved virtually intact, and a peculiar version of the free market was taken as a panacea for all the country's problems, as if it were a new utopia, Marxism turned upside down. The creativity of dissent ceded to the introduction of a Russian-style capitalism without any transformation of the political elite or a national revival on a grand scale.

From an artistic standpoint, the effects of estrangement *for* the world are more lasting but often kept in the shadow or willfully airbrushed out of history. It was argued that the avant-garde cannot be transferred into political life and that the avant-garde experiment failed in this sense of the word. However, strategies of estrangement, especially estrangement *for* the world, survived in the playful culture of dissent—against all odds and cultural silencing. The experience of freedom according to Arendt is written out of history and becomes a forgotten heritage. The experience of Soviet dissent of the 1960s (in distinction to Eastern / Central European dissent) is an example of such perpetuated cultural erasure at least on its native soil. For my generation, which grew up during late socialism, dissent might have appeared as a form of quixotic eccentricity, but this does not mean that we have to perpetuate the *ars oblivionalis* imposed upon us in our youth and inhabit a gentrified territory of postcommunist nostalgia.

Artists on Trial: Politics and Religion in the Post-Soviet Frame

In the cult novel of contemporary Russian writer Viktor Pelevin, *Generation "P"* (1999), the postcommunist Statue of Liberty holds a TV set instead of a torch and proclaims the values of demo-cracy. "Democracy" in this case has an alternative etymology, coming not from "demos," the people, but from "demo" short for "commercial demonstration."

To commemorate Shklovsky's favorite device of parallelism, I would like to end the way I began, with the Statue of Liberty. Its fate in Russia has been quite paradoxical. The monument described by Shklovsky was transient and did not survive long, but a more permanent monument to liberty in early Soviet neoclassical style was built in Moscow in the late 1920s—only to be supplanted after World War II by a less "cosmopolitan" monument to the medieval Muscovite prince Iuri Dolgoruky, which was deemed to be a better symbol of the Stalinist state. Iuri Dolgoruky remains the favorite monument of the present-day mayor of Moscow, the prince's namesake, Iuri Luzhkov. It might not be accidental that in 2002 the mayor advocated for the return of another abandoned monument, that of Felix Dzerzhinsky, the head of the Cheka (precursor of the KGB), which was toppled after the Russian "Velvet Revolution" of August 1991.

As if paraphrasing Shklovsky's statement about the advent of the "Red Restoration" in the late 1920s, the hero of *Generation "P"*, Vavilen Tatarsky, a failed poet and a successful "PR technologist," claims that the postcommunist Russia celebrated the definitive "victory of the red over the red," ranging from communist propaganda to Coca-Cola ads with ancient

Egyptian hues in the middle.[86] The new form of alienation reflected in the novel of this hero of post-Soviet youth culture moves toward conspiratorial thinking and unreflective nostalgia.

We can see that estrangement per se is not a guarantee of passionate and responsible thinking; it can function as both a poison and a cure for the political evils of the age. In extreme circumstances, the affirmation of inner freedom might be the most honorable position of an intellectual and serve as an example. This kind of estrangement from the world, however, can easily flip-flop and from a position of dissent become an acquiescence to the tyranny of the existing regime, which might result in an inability to build new political institutions when such an opportunity presents itself. Without the institutionalization of public freedom, critical estrangement *for* the world might end up as estrangement *from* the world and acceptance of the status quo.

If Shklovsky wrote that revolution in Soviet Russia estranged life more than literature, by the 1970s this strange Soviet life had become the norm. Its cruelties and absurdities were domesticated and a slang term had appeared to characterize it, *sovok*—at once a term of deprecation and tenderness, coming from the adjective *sovetskii*, Soviet, but also meaning "scoop," thus combining to mean a dustpan for domestic trash.

By the mid-1990s, the concept of "deideologization" or estrangement from politics came full circle and after 2000, it became the main slogan of the early days of Putin's government. If in the oppositional discourse of the 1970s and the 1980s deideologization meant estrangement or even liberation from Soviet state ideology, in the Putin era "deideologization" came to signify liberation from the critical democratic discourse of the 1980s and early 1990s. It enforced an unspoken taboo on any kind of critique of both the Soviet past and of post-Soviet state capitalism. In fact, since the late 1990s the democratic discourse has acquired the deprecatory name *demshiza*, meaning democratic schizophrenia, a term previously reserved for the supposedly hysterical grandmothers who embraced perestroika a little too vehemently in the 1980s. It was as if political discourse itself had become "aesthetically incorrect" and unfashionable, a good defense mechanism that harkens back to the old Soviet culture of fear. At present public political discourse in Russia has become so "deideologized" and estranged from responsible politics that a double estrangement is once again required.

"There is an anti-Russian plot and everyone is taking part in it," remarks the hero in *Generation "P"*. Of course, if the "plot" involves the

Figure 18. Alexander Kosolapov, *It's the Real Thing*. Courtesy of the artist. The original is in red, not black.

whole population, everyone is guilty and nobody is; hence no one is obliged to take responsibility for the present that leads "to the victory of the red over the red." The novel has a hidden pictorial subtext, the scandalous conceptual painting by Russian-American artist Alexander Kosolapov, *It's the Real Thing* (fig. 18). Made in 1982, it presented a double icon of Lenin and Coca-Cola, the joint venture of Soviet ideology and Western commercialism, both appealing to be the real thing. Made in 1982 when such images appeared shocking and had not yet become a commonplace of global culture, the painting provoked a small scandal. The ambiguity of the work resides in the fact that it remains unclear whether the painting should be read right to left or left to right; in other words, whether Lenin recruited Coca-Cola for the sake of world revolution, or Coca-Cola recruited Lenin to relieve the thirst of the young people. The tension between two mass-reproduced symbols exists precisely because there is no pictorial tension there, no seam, no cut. Rather than a collage, this is more of a surrealist chance encounter, a bizarre and striking juxtaposition that presents itself as a hyper-continuity. The painting was not welcomed, neither in the Soviet Union nor the Unites States. In the Soviet Union, it couldn't be shown until the 1990s for obvious reasons of censorship. The artist, however, was surprised that he couldn't freely exhibit his work in the "land of the free," either, due to the objection of

Coca-Cola Company, which took both overt and covert action to "censor" the painting, claiming that it was abusing its logo. The clash between property rights and freedom of speech became apparent—the border zone of art is not clearly defined and not well protected. Between two kinds of freedom Kosolapov chose the third, legal freedom. He launched a legal battle, hiring the lawyer who successfully defended Andy Warhol in his suit involving his Campbell's soup can painting. (Later in the mid-1990s when the artist wanted to exhibit the painting in the Russian Museum in Saint Petersburg, he encountered another snag: now Coca-Cola was the official sponsor of the exhibit.)

The story of Kosolapov's painting has a new twist. As if quoting himself, as well as changing mass culture in Russia and the West, Kosolapov has recently painted a new version of his *Real Thing* called *This Is My Blood*. In the new work, Jesus Christ (taken from mass-reproduced American Evangelical posters) is juxtaposed to the logo of Coca-Cola with an inscription below, "This is my blood." Once again the artist stages a jarring chance encounter of different ready-mades of contemporary mass culture to comment on the mass reproduction of religious symbols both in American and in the new Russian culture, where the largest cathedral is itself a gilded replica of its former authentic self.

This Is My Blood was vandalized during the exhibit "Caution, Religion" that took place in Moscow's Sakharov Museum in January 2003. Curiously, it was the face of the American Jesus that was splashed with paint, while the Coca-Cola bottle remained intact. Here is a quick outline of the events. The exhibit opened on January 14 at the Sakharov Museum with the participation of artists from Russia, Armenia, Japan, the United States, and Cuba. The name of the exhibit, "Caution, Religion" (*Ostorozhno, Religiia*), is intentionally ambiguous, suggesting both attentive care in dealing with religion and spirituality and an awareness of fanaticism and the new political role of religious institutions. On January 18, six men entered the exhibit and began destroying the paintings and splashing them with slogans (Vermin! Scum! Satan! Sacrilege, You hate the Orthodox Church, you be damned.) The museum guard managed to lock up the room and call the police, and the men were apprehended. However, in a peculiar twist of events, the art destroyers were quickly released, while criminal proceedings were launched against the organizers of the exhibit and the artists, invoking article 282, the promotion of ethnic and religious hatred. Most Russian Orthodox religious organizations, from radical activists from the Social Committee for the Moral Revival of the Fatherland to the Church leadership, supported the actions of the exhibit's attackers, asserting the Church's right to interfere in cultural matters. In February 2003 the Russian Parliament, the Duma, passed a resolution declaring that the purpose of the exhibit was to "incite religious hatred and to insult the feelings of religious believers and the Orthodox Church." A full 265 out of 267 deputies voted in favor of the measure to take legal criminal action against the artists and the museum director. Sergei Yushenkov, one of the two deputies who voted against taking such a drastic measure, went to the podium and declared, "We are witnessing the origins of a totalitarian state led by the Orthodox Church." A few weeks later Yushenkov was murdered in Moscow.[87]

In the few remaining non-state-sponsored publications in Russia, a new hybrid term was coined—"clerical Bolshevism." The scandal around the exhibit is only one of many recent episodes that reveals what can happen when nongovernmental and legal institutions are discredited as a "masquerade of inauthenticity" and as "hypocritical mediators" between the state and the people, which unfortunately is part of a long-standing Russian and Soviet tradition.

The phenomenon of clerical Bolshevism reveals the most important conflict of the post–cold war world: that between political religion and the political culture that insists on the separation of church and state. It shows the persistence of another modern tradition that is antimodern and, often in the case of church rhetoric, anti-Occidentalist. The antimodern is a doppelganger of modernity that points to the uncanny fragility of secularized societies, which antimoderns mimic and sabotage.

The other feature of global culture brought into sharp focus during the debates around the closing of the non-state-sponsored TV stations in Russia from 2000 to 2003 was an ostensible noncoincidence between the development of capitalism and political freedoms. The arguments of "liberalization of the market" were used to curtail the "liberal values" of the non-state-sponsored press and ultimately the "free market" in Russia, turned into state capitalism like in China. For neither in Russia nor in the West is the market ever free from social, legal, and political contexts; in European democracies at best, it relies on civic and legal institutions to create a balance of cultural values. The antipolitical rhetoric of the market is dangerous everywhere: it is not by chance that a hated word of many businessmen and politicians East and West often is "politics." Thus the most interesting art projects engage the political in a diverse and paradoxical way. For even in artistic experimentation one can remain responsible for one's own "unsettled consciousness," as was described by Victor Shklovsky, which in the end is a sine qua non of artistic freedom.

However tempting it is for contemporary novelists to speak about the victory of red over red and imagine a plot of anyone against everyone, one should not read history as a vicious circle and end on the sour note that estrangement, just like nostalgia, is not what it used to be. A new beginning posits an alternative conjectural history that uncovers the genealogy of ideas that for a long time remained on the side roads of the prevailing versions of twentieth-century cultural history. They should be treated as unrealized possibilities, roads not taken, unruined "monuments to scientific errors." Instead of seeing history as something inevitable and predetermined, Arendt projected the idea of freedom into our conception of the past. Looking back at twentieth-century history, Arendt proposed to estrange the immanency of disaster. To do so one has to "look for the unforeseeable and unpredictable," for "the more heavily the scales are weighted in favor of the disaster, the more miraculous will the deed done in freedom appear; for it is disaster, not salvation, that always happens automatically and therefore always must appear to be irresistible."[88]

Figure 19. Svetlana Boym, chessboard collage with the "black square," a fragment from the photograph of an erased (and possibly executed) member of the Communist Party (from David King, *The Commissar Vanishes* [New York: Metropolitan Books, 1997]).

JUDGMENT AND IMAGINATION
IN THE AGE OF TERROR

The Tale of Two Arrests: Arendt and Ginzburg

In 1933 Hannah Arendt and her mother were arrested by Hitler's secret police for providing refuge to German communists and for collecting documentation on German anti-Semitism. Arendt managed to befriend her captor and tell him incredible stories. The Nazi officer, "a charming fellow," confessed that he was new to working with political prisoners and did not know what to do with them. Moreover, she persuaded him to get her cigarettes and better-quality coffee during the few days of her imprisonment. The officer promised to release her promptly after the home search of Arendt's apartment turned up only a few suspicious documents with a hard "code" to crack—which happened to be ancient Greek. This miraculous and entirely untypical encounter with the German secret police soon after the Nazi takeover prompted Arendt to make a major life decision to flee Germany immediately in spite of her deep identification with German culture.[1]

In January 1937, less than four years after Arendt's stranger-than-fiction arrest in Nazi Germany, her Soviet contemporary, Evgeniia Ginzburg, devoted member of the Communist Party and a teacher, was arrested by Stalin's secret police. In fact, Evgeniia was not taken away from her home in the middle of the night, like so many others; instead, she made an incredible decision—to walk on her own volition to the Office of the Secret Police (NKVD), in spite of explicit warnings from and egregious arrests of her party colleagues. Her NKVD officer initially appears equally "charming": he calls Evgeniia on the phone and asks her when would be a good time for her to stop by the office for forty minutes or so. Speaking in a voice "babbling like a spring brook" he suggests that she stop by for a half-hour chat after dinner, in case she needs to go check on her mother. Instead, Evgeniia says that she will come immediately to prove her innocence to her beloved Party. Acting rationally and righteously, with complete personal integrity and in accordance with her moral convictions, Evgeniia came to the NKVD—only to disappear for a decade in Stalin's Gulag like millions of others without having committed any crime and never having been anything less than an ardent supporter of the regime.[2]

In many ways Arendt's good luck is much more exceptional than Ginzburg's "bad luck," if one can even use those concepts in such an instance of modern political tragedy. Even though both women encounter political forces beyond their individual control, their arrest stories are not entirely comparable. In 1933 Nazi secret police officers were much less organized and experienced than were their Soviet counterparts a few years later; moreover, at this point Arendt considers Fascists to be her political enemies while Ginzburg thinks that her interrogators are her Party comrades. Most importantly, this tale of two arrests is not about solving the puzzle of personal predicament and figuring out the single right answer to the dilemma of judging, but about encounters with the unpredictable in unforeseen political circumstances when the very space of free thinking becomes endangered.

How do we make judgments in situations when our worlds appear to collapse? What makes us capable of changing our minds and questioning our worldviews—beyond the prescriptive multiple choice options and group identities? How can one "think without a banister" when our foundations are shaken and the threshold of what is possible moves beyond the boundaries of humanity?

About twenty years after their arrests, Arendt published her *Origins of Totalitarianism* and later *Eichmann in Jerusalem: A Report on the Banality of Evil* and Evgeniia Ginzburg wrote *Journey into the Whirlwind*, her influential account of life in the Gulag in which she reflects on her own judging during dark times and on the blindnesses and blunders that she had come to recognize in herself and her fellow prisoners.

In her memoir Ginzburg tries to reconstruct the events that lead to her arrest, wondering if she could have made different decisions and not played blindly into the system. Two people in her life had advised her at that time to act differently, from two equally eccentric perspectives.

One was her mother-in-law, Avdot'ia Aksenova, "a simple, illiterate peasant woman, born in the days of serfdom," who possessed a "deeply philosophical cast of mind" and who "had a remarkable power of hitting the nail on the head when she talked about problems of life."[3] Avdot'ia calls Evgeniia (Genia) into the room, locks it and whispers:

> "They are setting a trap for you, Genia and you better run while you still can, before they break your neck. Out of sight out of mind, they say. The farther away you are, the better. Why not go to our old village Pokrovskoe . . ."
>
> "But I must prove my innocence to the Party. How can I, a Communist, hide from the Party?"
>
> "Who are you going to prove your innocence to? They used to do the same things in the old days, God and the Tsar are far away. So they still are far away, God and Stalin."
>
> "No, Grandma, don't say that. Even if it kills me, I'll prove it. I'll go to Moscow. I'll fight."
>
> "Oh Genia, Genia, darling. They say, there is none so silly as a clever man" (*uma palata, a gluposti saratovskaia step'*)."[4]

The other advisor that Evgeniia meets on the eve of her arrest is her old friend, a young Doctor Dikhovitsky, who was also branded as politically unreliable for showing signs of "rotten liberalism" and "a lack of vigilance towards the enemies of the people." He offers her a different version of radical escape:

> "Listen, Genia," he said to me, "we're both in for it and we're not likely to do ourselves any good here. We must think of something else. What do you say, for instance, about going off and living with the raggle-taggle Gypsies, O?"
>
> His eyes with their bluish whites flashed as impudently as in the past.
>
> "You can still joke!"
>
> "But I'm dead serious. Listen. I'm a Gypsy by birth and you can easily pass for a Gypsy (*tsiganka Aza*). Why don't we just drop out of circulation for a bit. Not a word to anyone . . . Or there could be a black edged notice in the

newspaper saying P. V. Aksenov announces with sorrow the untimely death
of his beloved companion, and so on . . . You and I would join a Gypsy camp
and wander about for a year or two like tourists until all this blows over.
What do you say?"[5]

Dikhovitsky's advice is as incredible and literary as Avdot'ia's is com-
monsensical and seemingly naive. Dikhovitsky proposes to Evgeniia nothing less than an enactment of the literary plot from Pushkin's romantic
poem "The Gypsies," known to all Russian and Soviet schoolchildren.
In both cases physical escape from the city of Kazan entails also a mental escape from Soviet language of the time, which imprisons reality by
branding individuals as class enemies. In their speech both use quotes that
estrange contemporary Soviet language and appeal to other languages
and frames of reference. Avdot'ia's judgment relies on the folk wisdom
and historic memory of a longer period of time—from prerevolutionary
to Soviet Russia. Dikhovitsky's eccentric plan of escape uses humor, literary plots, and eclectic unorthodox thinking. They don't try to outsmart
the system but to explore its minor errors and loopholes, to mimic the
Gulag's "low tech." Both Dikhovitsky and Avdot'ia possess a perspectivism of imagination and a mental flexibility that enable them to move between different worlds and systems of belief. Clearly the power of judging
does not depend solely on the level of education. In fact, illiterate Avdot'ia
seems a better reader of Russian-Soviet commonplaces than Evgeniia, for
whom there is only one truth and one form of authentic behavior in accordance with her beliefs, that cannot be shaken by her everyday experiences
and the witnessing of incongruities and injustice.

In our historical hindsight we know that there was no single way of
saving oneself from the purges. However, the advice offered by Evgeniia's
mother-in-law and her friend based on the Russian proverb of getting "out
of sight and out of mind" was one plausible strategy that helped many
individuals, including intellectuals and writers such as Mikhail Bakhtin. If
not a road towards salvation, it was at least a reasonable attempt not to be
conspicuously in the way of overzealous Soviet NKVD officers anxiously
filling their quotas of the enemies of the people.[6]

In her memoir Ginzburg offers a bildungsroman of consciousness that
is not about a single conversion but a series of mind-changing and estranging encounters that lead to her recognition of the power of ideology and
its effect on the individual. In one early episode Ginzburg meets a woman
prisoner, Derkovskaia, who is her mirror image: a mother separated from
her son and a devoted political idealist. Only she happened to belong to

a different revolutionary party, the SRs (Socialist Revolutionaries, rivals of the Bolsheviks since 1917). The two women share a crowded cell and strike up a conversation, and Evgeniia feels "devout pity" for the fate of Derkovskaia's son even though Derkovskaia makes no bones about her own feeling toward communists-Bolsheviks. One day Derkovskaia, barely alive after an interrogation, had run out of cigarettes, which were her only respite. Having just received a parcel from her family, Evgeniia eagerly offers a pack to Derkovskaia. What follows is both moving and absurd:

> Derkovskaia blushed and, with a muttered "Thank you," turned away.
>
> "Just a second, I won't be long."
>
> She sat down by the wall and tapped a message. One of the prisoners in the next cell was Mukhina, the secretary of the SR clandestine regional committee. Derkovskaia tapped away, not realizing that I could follow.
>
> "There is a woman Bolshevik-Communist who offered me cigarettes. Should I accept?
>
> Mukhina inquired whether the Bolshevik-Communist belonged to the opposition. Derkovskaia asked me and passed on my reply. Mukhina tapped categorically: "NO."
>
> The cigarettes lay on the table between us. During the night I heard Derkovskaia sigh deeply. Though thin as a rake, she would much sooner have done without bread. As I lay awake on my plank bed, the most unorthodox thoughts passed through my mind—about how thin the line is between high principles and blinkered intolerance, and also how relative are all human systems and ideologies and how absolute the torture which human beings inflict on one another.[7]

Witnessing Derkovskaia, Evgeniia undergoes something of a cathartic revelation that makes her aware of her own intransigence and gives her an insight into the anatomy of intolerance that is often built on the best intentions and idealistic aspirations. The opposition between Bolsheviks and Socialist Revolutionaries seems like a luxury of the free world; in the world of the Gulag zone the method of dividing people into enemy classes becomes the tool of the interrogators, and one needs to shift one's whole frame of thinking in order to be able to understand the unprecedented coexistence of the most optimistic vision of social justice projected by Stalin propaganda and the experience of the Gulag.

Curiously, the two women later bonded through literature, rather than politics. They talked little about ideological differences, preferring to discuss and recite the poetry of Alexander Blok. Russian literature becomes

for Ginzburg an alternative frame of reference; she describes her early in-
tuitions about injustice as "Lermontov's prophetic longing," uses Blok to
speak about her reflective estrangement, and recites Pushkin as a mantra
when in solitary confinement. In the camps, from a reader of literature she
becomes a writer. In the case of Ginzburg, literary dreamlands somehow
brought back other kinds of cultural memory that enabled her to escape,
survive, and come to grips with her stranger-than-fiction, everyday reality
of the camps. In this world of the Gulag, words lost their meaning; literature didn't always return meaning to those imprisoned there but it offered
a virtual zone of imagination where one could play with words again and
inhabit a mental space where human dignity was still possible. Only in this
zone of moral imagination could one locate a minimal space of freedom—
not the "freer freedom" of Dostoevsky's leap of faith, not the radical liberation and paradise on earth in the bright communist future, preached
through Stalin's ideology, but the freedom of individual acts of judging—
more or less adequately—the unprecedented circumstances of existence in
the secret Gulag territory in the midst of the utopian land of justice, freedom, and plenty portrayed in Socialist Realist films of the period.

"I have no wish to soften the saying that to write lyric poetry after Auschwitz is barbaric," wrote Theodor Adorno.[8] This is one of the most-
quoted statements about art after the Holocaust. It is less commonly
known that Adorno continues his reflection in a paradoxical manner.
Literature, he insists, "must resist this verdict. For it is now virtually in
art alone that suffering can still find its own voice without immediately
being betrayed by it." While Adorno doesn't engage the discussion of the
Gulag, Varlam Shalamov, who like Evgeniia Ginzburg is a survivor and a
brilliant and unflinching storyteller of the Kolyma camps, claims a similar
paradoxical imperative for art after the Gulag: "In a new prose—after Hi-
roshima, after Auschwitz and Kolyma, after wars and revolutions—everything didactic should be rejected. Art doesn't have a right to preach. Art
neither ennobles nor improves people. Art is a way of life, not a way of
understanding life (*poznaniia zhizni*). In other words, it's a document . . . a
prose lived through like a document."[9]

But what does it mean for literature to be "lived through like a document"? And what lesson in judging does it offer?

If the experience of Auschwitz profoundly influenced Western political
philosophy of the twentieth century, the experience of the Soviet Gulag
did not. The persistent difficulty in coming to terms with the Gulag, aside
from complex historical and political circumstances, lies in large part in

its dual image: it was represented as paradise and hell, an ideal Socialist construction site and a camp of slave labor.[10] During the Gulag's thirty-year existence, artists, writers, and filmmakers from the Soviet Union and abroad were recruited by Stalin's state to celebrate the utopian land "where men breathe most freely." All the gates and watchtowers of the Gulag zone, where an unknown number of millions of prisoners perished, were decorated with the refrain from a popular song: "Our labor is a matter of honor, a feast of glory and courage." Socialist Realist art mass-reproduced a hypnotic simulacrum of the ideal Soviet territory through Soviet musicals, twins of Broadway and Hollywood, which still enjoy frequent reruns on state television in contemporary Russia. This seductive, euphoric, and entertaining art helped to distract from and domesticate the powerful teleology of revolutionary violence that justified sacrifice for the sake of paradise on earth. Thus not only does the history of the Gulag conjure up a memory of terror, but it also tampers with one of the most powerful utopian dreams of the twentieth century that extended far beyond the Soviet border. Legitimation of the Gulag in Soviet life proved to be a ubiquitous symptom; it estranged the commonsense perceptions and everyday experiences of ordinary citizens. They could only be "rehabilitated" through a double estrangement—of actual Soviet everyday life and of the official state fiction that supplanted it. Like Primo Levi and Hannah Arendt, Soviet witnesses of and writers about the Gulag—Evgeniia Ginzburg, Alexander Solzhenitsyn, Vassili Grossman, Varlam Shalamov, and others—spoke repeatedly about the "changed scales" for understanding the camp experience that apply to all human emotions and relationships—friendship, love, decency, freedom—and require new modes of understanding. It is crucial to incorporate Gulag accounts into a broader twentieth- and twenty-first-century reflection on totalitarianism and terror because they expose both the banality of evil and the banality of good as well as the place of the individual art of judging into focus.

The Banality of Evil and the Art of Judgment

After her arrest and miraculous escape from Germany and later from the displaced persons camp in France, Arendt pondered the issues of luck and individual judgment as well as public rights and the totalitarian "liberation of humanity." Having herself been engaged in many controversial acts of political judging through trial and error, Arendt wanted to write the volume on "judging" as a culmination of her last magisterial work on the life of the mind. At the time of her sudden death, the first page of this effort was in her typewriter, the sheet blank but for two epigraphs. These two strange quotations, which she took from Cato and Goethe, have teased interpreters with their seeming incongruousness.

> The victorious cause pleases the gods but the defeated one pleases Cato.[11]

> Can I all magic from my pathway banish
> Could quite unlearn its spells and bid it vanish
> nature could I face thee, in thy great plan
> Then were it worth the pain to be a man.[12]

We do not know what unpredictable shape Arendt's book might have taken. The space for judging anticipated on this last white page is between the recognition of the defeated and the defiant, a space between human curiosity and the memory of those who lost the historical battles. Or maybe it is the other way around; in spite or even because of the inevitable defeats and pain, the pathways of wonder and imagination cannot be banished.

"Defeat" for Arendt is often a form of dissent against the "divinity of History" and the authority of progress or any other deterministic system of thought. Care for the voices of the "defeated" (not merely those of victims) is a form of historic preservation of human dignity, preservation of particular individual acts and experiences of freedom that would otherwise be erased from history. But mere memory is not enough. The dignity of the defeated resides in their imaginative judgments and rare moments of free thinking often in the conditions of ultimate unfreedom.

In order to make a tentative reconstruction of Arendt's art of judging, one has to remember that she began it while on the subject of the unprecedented and unforeseen, which was the experience of totalitarianism that developed out of imperialism and went beyond it.[13]

Three aspects of Arendtian thought are of primary importance. First, she emphasizes the radical strangeness of the new form of domination, not only by the state but also by totalitarian ideology—that could be stronger than traditional religion and occasionally builds on the sites of the sacred. Such "strange possession" can go against one's self-interest or everyday experience and cannot be fully explained through a conventional social, psychological, or institutional rationalization. In line with Shalamov's notion of radically changed scales of experience, Arendt uses an aesthetic concept of estrangement to think about the power of the "ideology of terror."[14] Its seduction lies in many disguised paradoxes that are rarely exposed. While proposing radical liberation in the future, such a system of beliefs justifies the elimination of freedoms in the present. Similarly, while offering an extremely coherent closed system of thinking, it forces people to distrust the reality of their everyday experiences and their senses. Behind the scientific language and coherent structure, it hides mysticism and antiworldliness. In this sense the logic of the ideology of terror is close to that of the rational delusion of paranoia according to which everything makes sense in the conspiratorial world that is disconnected from daily reality and has a phantasmagoric reality of its own. In short, if the system of thought or belief makes "perfect sense," beware that it might stop being sensible and sensitive; in dismissing worldly imperfection, it can become antiworldly or downright deadly.

Second, Arendt demonstrates how the ideology of terror discredits conventional man-made laws, the contractual sociality and theatricality of public life that are based on the imperfect cultural memory of humanity (and not some moral absolutes) in favor of the suprahuman law of history and truth.[15] Such a noble goal legitimizes any amount of (revolutionary) violence, since the end justifies the means. Arendt questions the basis of the Hegelian-Marxist framework for understanding the laws of history and the relationship between the state and the public sphere. Unlike some twentieth-century thinkers, including Carl Schmitt, Michel Foucault, Giorgio Agamben, and others who are engaged in examining forms of domination and power as the critique of the Enlightenment project without drawing explicit distinction between a democratic understanding of law and a totalitarian understanding of the law of history, Arendt insists on totalitarian difference. Arendt's reflection on manmade laws, always in the plural, as opposed to the suprahuman law in the singular, is linked to her conception of the common world and public realm that has been discredited by many Marxist and post-Marxist thinkers. Moreover, continuing with the key concerns of the Enlightenment, she questions the relationship between violence and politics and develops a conception of laws based on the public memory of the common world.

Third, in spite of Arendt's elaborate analysis of the total control of the state, she looks unflinchingly into the issue of the individual capacity to judge for oneself, and finds there an unusual connection between judgment, imagination, and thinking. Arendt revises Kantian conceptions of "common sense" and imagination in order to develop her original theory of judgment. Imagination for her becomes a form of understanding individual acts of judging and paradigm shifts even in conditions of extremity.

She focuses on a variety of aesthetic practices (from theatrical performance on the public stage to the art of thinking and the life of the mind) that work in counterpoint to the aesthetic "total work" of the state. In a crucial way, such an understanding of practice presents an alternative model of thinking about everyday mythologies without domesticating and naturalizing them, and this allows for a variety of reactions, not limited simply to an enthusiastic embrace or heroic dissent. The task of the interpreter of everyday practices in conditions of extremity is to understand the minimal "zone" of deviation or noncompliance, the minor paradigm shifts, that work in counterpoint to the official documentation of events.

In her controversial account of the trial of Adolf Eichmann, the architect of the Final Solution responsible for the ideological basis of mass extermination, Arendt proposes to judge Eichmann as an individual, not as a devil, nor as a mere cog in the Nazi bureaucratic machine. In other words, she doesn't subsume Eichmann's case into her own theory of state terror. Eichmann appears as the ultimate organization man who speaks in clichés from the beginning to the very end. While in an ordinary context Eichmann's behavior might be considered mere institutional conformism and traditional patriotism, in the context of the Nazi extermination machine this kind of clichéistic conscience leads to "thought and world-defying banality of evil."[16] What does this mean? It does not suggest that evil is banal or that the banality of everydayness is evil. Rather, Arendt draws our attention to the fact that the individual who authorized the worst crimes against humanity was an ordinary civil servant, neither a glamorous Shakespearian villain nor the metaphysical embodiment of a Satan on earth. Arendt claimed emphatically that evil should not be mythologized; it should not be turned into a version of the negative sublime. In fact, Eichmann was described by the Israeli psychiatrist as absolutely normal. It is ironic that while in prison Eichmann was offered Nabokov's novel *Lolita* to read, an offer which he refused as "inappropriate and immoral"; this is perhaps the best defense that Humbert Humbert could have hoped for. Remarkably, in the afterword to *Lolita*, Nabokov claims that true obscenity lies in the "copulation of clichés" and lack of curiosity and imagination, not in erotic subject matter.

Arendt shows that in the case of Eichmann, the automatization of his mind, his clichéistic consciousness and "failure of imagination" (understood broadly as moral imagination) led to the "colossal error in judgment" for which he carries individual responsibility. Arendt doesn't subscribe to the concept of collective guilt that might blame everybody and hence nobody; for her, guilt is individual and particular.

While Eichmann's case can be explained sociologically, politically, and historically, it cannot be excused. To analyze the newness of his existential position, Arendt uses aesthetic concepts: the failure of imagination and banality. Arendt's conception of banality is reminiscent of Nabokov's critique of *kitsch* and *poshlost'* and those of Hermann Broch, Theodor Adorno, and Clement Greenberg.[17] In her last, unfinished project, *The Life of the Mind*, Arendt connects the question of ethics and responsibility directly to the issue of thoughtlessness on an unprecedented scale, reflecting in particular on "thoughtless" collaboration with a regime.[18]

Individual capacity to engage in judging depends on the ability to mediate between the universal and the particular, between a system of beliefs and lived experience, between consciousness and conscience. Judging requires a double movement—defamiliarizing experience through the practice of thought and defamiliarizing habits of thought in response to changing experience. The possibility of judgment is not determined by strict adherence to a moral code but by moral imagination. Even the most antisentimental witness of the camps, Primo Levi, a scientist and an agnostic, wrote about the role of curiosity and culture in Auschwitz.[19] First, like Shalamov, he disavowed any romantic or redemptive quality of aesthetic experience, but then he proceeded to explore a link with another cultural memory and issues of curiosity and imagination. Imagination and judgment are part of the architecture of freedom, which relies not on banisters and superficial props but on deep foundations that support thresholds and doors. Imagination bridges not only spatial but also temporal discontinuities. It pushes the boundaries of the camp, opens up the space *between* the cracks and *beyond* the structures of the dominant language.

Of course, "failure of imagination" is hardly the sole explanation for the banality of evil. For Arendt the key lies in the destruction of the public realm and the public world, and the resulting corruption of communication and the intimacy with terror that conditions the dependence of citizens on a regime and the proliferation of vicious circles of victimization. Hence the irreducible political dimension of the totalitarian regime that cannot be domesticated. Yet the moral imagination might provide a form of necessary "perspectivism," an opening of other horizons.[20] Imagination can engage in existential play that thinks of freedom by means of freedom; as long as it doesn't "liberate" itself entirely from care for the world, entertains potentialities and conjectural histories, and moves through lapses and ellipses engaging other forms of communication. Imagination can be defined as what is in-human in humans in the sense that it is a capacity for self-distancing and discovering inner plurality, for moving beyond individual psychology into the experience of the common world. The activities of judging and imagining depend on cultural commonplaces but are not entirely bound by them.

I believe that an understanding of the camp experience requires a form of passionate thinking that is at once interdisciplinary and rigorous. Arendt was familiar with some of the Gulag literature and with Ginzburg's memoir but most likely not with the work of Shalamov, which appeared in translation only around the time of her death. Yet his stories speak directly to the relationship between judging and imagination in totalitarian circumstances: in the *Kolyma Tales* he explores the boundaries of the Gulag zone inside and outside of the human psyche. Shalamov wished to "deaestheticize evil"[21] through the tactics of intonation, uses of blemish, human error, mimicry, and minor gift exchanges that mark unofficial solidarities and elective affinities.

The Ethics of Intonation and Human Error in *Kolyma Tales*

Shalamov's biography and the story of his arrests and miraculous survival offer an interesting coda on Russian history and goes against the grain of some of the commonplaces of Russian national mythology. Shalamov wrote that his name is related to two words—*shalost'* (whim, frivolity, play) and *shaman;* whether etymologically correct or not, this was his own poetic reinvention of his origins. A son of an Orthodox priest from Vologda in the Russian north, Shalamov rebelled against his father and, disappointed from an early age in all forms of institutional religion, he chose literature instead. Shalamov commented that he was born too late to take part in the "storm of the sky," referring to the February and October revolutions of 1917, but he was an active participant in the revolutionary culture of the 1920s, frequenting the LEF gatherings of Osip Brik and Sergei Tretiakov, discussing the experimental art of Kazimir Malevich, Marc Chagall, and Wassily Kandinsky and the new political and legal theories. Like many fellow artists and writers on the left, he was not a party-line Bolshevik. In November 1927, for the tenth anniversary of the October Revolution and right after the expulsion of Trotsky from the Soviet Union, he took part in the demonstrations of the opposition led by Kamenev and Zinoviev, which demanded transparency in party politics. He was arrested in February 1929 at the underground printing press that printed the full text of the Lenin's *Testament*, which contained criticism of Joseph Stalin. Shalamov was sentenced on article 58; he received a five-year sentence for "KRTD," which was the abbreviation for "counter-revolutionary Trotskyist activity." Later Shalamov would say that the T in this abbreviation stood for both *Trotsky* and *tribunal*. He was rearrested repeatedly in 1937, 1938, and then again in 1943. One of the reasons for Shalamov's other arrest was his having affirmed that an émigré writer, Ivan Bunin, had received a Nobel Prize for Literature. Once again, as in the case of Lenin's testament, Shalamov is accused of "anti-Soviet propaganda" merely for uttering factual or documentary truth. He was rehabilitated from his two later arrests in the Soviet times, but for his initial "KRTD" only in 2000. After his miraculous "tricking of fate" and surviving in the Gulag for seventeen years, Shalamov dedicated the next twenty years of his life to writing his stories and poetry, which, unlike the work of Alexander Solzhenitsyn, remained unpublished and largely unknown in his native country until Perestroika, in 1988–1989. Shalamov refused Solzhenitsyn's offer to collaborate on a history of the Gulag and considered Solzhenitsyn's writing to be a "lacquering of the camp experience" and a literary celebration of slave labor and enforced human suffering. In the last act of the tragedy, Shalamov died in 1982, after being forcibly transported secretly and in bitter cold weather, from a retirement home to a hospital for the mentally ill. The nurses reported that he screamed and resisted until the last moment. The cause of Shalamov's death was the pneumonia he caught during this transport, as if the cold of Kolyma and the Soviet state had finally caught up with him.

There is something radically unassimilable in Shalamov's prose: it describes the experience of extremity but doesn't offer redemption through labor, suffering, religion, or national belonging. Varlam Shalamov's Kolyma stories, like Ginzburg's memoir, confront the reader with the inhumanity of experience and yet Shalamov claimed that "there is nothing in *Kolyma Tales* that wasn't the overcoming of evil and triumph of the good—if we understand it in the plane of art."[22] How are we to understand this affirmation of humanism *via negativa* and "in the plane of art?" Was this for Shalamov the only way to avoid the banality of the good?

In one of Shalamov's few letters to the prominent Soviet literary scholar Iuri Lotman, he writes that his real desire is to work on poetic intonation.[23] At first there seems to be a degree of incommensurability between Shalamov's witnessing of the Gulag and his concern for "purity of tone." Yet intonation acquired great importance in the time of terror. The writer, scholar, and student of the Formal method, Lidiia Ginzburg, recorded in her diary that people's degree of collaboration with and affirmation of Stalinism often didn't reside in the obvious pronouncements: "In the years of Stalin's terror the 'untruth' resided not in the general ideological worldview, but often in the intonation, in the public display of one's agreement with the regime."[24] The practice of speaking in ideological clichés (in public and in private, including in personal diaries) persisted through the Soviet regime and beyond as a necessary incantatory practice; as with medieval icon painting, its interpretation depended on minor iconographic / intonational variations.[25] These minor variations revealed the degree of collaboration with the regime or, in Arendtian terms, of complicity with banal evil.

Shalamov's documentary prose exposes the breaking points of cultural myths that open possibilities for paradigm shifts. The narrators of the *Kolyma Tales*, even more than Ginzburg in her autobiographical account, often resort to the apparent mimicry of Soviet discourse and the technologies of the Gulag, but only to challenge any coherent conception of "Soviet subjectivity," either enthusiastic or defiant. Instead of performing ideology, they lay it bare.

There is an important difference in Shalamov's and Evgeniia Ginzburg's approach to the Gulag experience regarding judging and imagination. Ginzburg's memoir is constructed chronologically and documents multiple historical moments: 1937, 1956, the Khrushchev thaw and the subsequent disappointments. At each stage of her journey she offers a double perspective—of her own younger self, the prisoner of the camps, and of the writer who reflects on the experience. In a way hers is a pedagogical narrative: she confronts her surroundings with curiosity, anger, and amazement and describes how she came to the new understanding of the Stalinist experience, which brought her views closer to the East and Central European "socialism with a human face" and liberal humanism. Ginzburg's memoir is a multilayered buildungsroman—of the woman prisoner and of the evolution of a Soviet citizen together with changing cultural frameworks.[26]

Shalamov's stories are always in the present. The narrator speaks as Pluto, the permanent resident of the underworld, not as Orpheus, an overly excited one-time visitor. The readers are forced to inhabit the uninhabitable world of Kolyma and acquire a horrifyingly intimate perspective. They are put in the position of fellow convicts, newcomers but not outsiders. Usually the stories begin and end in medias res, as if familiarizing the inhuman world of Kolyma with its shifted scales of existence. However, "as if" here is crucial and is at the core of Shalamov's double estrangement. His stories are modern parables written in a documentary style reminiscent of the "literature of fact" of the 1920s and the Formalist poetics through which Shalamov learned his literary skills.[27] Creating this kind of visceral prose, which is not a description of experience but an experience in its own right, was for Shalamov an exhausting physical process akin to exorcism. He "screamed out every word of the story, screamed, threatened, cried, drying up tears only when the story was over."[28] Each story is a creative document that stands in counterpoint to official historical documentation.

In his *Kolyma Tales* Shalamov seeks uncompromising "purity of tone," which is linked to what Arendt called "the dignity of the defeated"—something that remains between the lines but shapes them like the prisoners' tracks in the Kolyma snow. Yet intonation is not the "sincere tone" and light touch of the political thaw but a particular authorial tool that threatens the practices of Soviet mimicry.[29] Repetitions in Shalamov don't perform ideology but open up the dimension of difference and space for independent judging and imagination.

Intonation complicates the readability of the stories but also gives insight into the complexity of the Gulag system of communication that is reflected in many documents. Purity of tone doesn't mean monologism or authorial omniscience, but an aesthetic and ethical dissent in the face of what Shalamov calls the "banalization" (*oposhlenie*) of the camp experience. To make the reader understand what it is like to "return from the hell" of Kolyma, Shalamov fights against the clichés of the "so-called Russian humanist tradition" that teach acceptance of suffering and authoritarian morality: "Russian humanist writers of the second half of the nineteenth century carry a great sin in their soul, for the human blood shed in their name in the twentieth century. All terrorists were Tolstoyan and vegetarian, all fanatics were the students of Russian humanists."[30]

Harsh as this verdict might appear, it is important to understand that Shalamov's reading is not so much of Tolstoy's literary works but of his "cultural text," shaped largely by his prophetic late writing, the Soviet canon of Socialist Realism, and Solzhenitsyn's appropriation of Tolstoy.[31] In Shalamov's view, moralistic and religious clichés and the discourse on the historic necessity of violence betray the "corpses of Kolyma." This issue comes up directly in the striking dialogue between Shalamov and Solzhenitsyn, recorded in Shalamov's notebooks—a dialogue worthy of Dostoevsky's pen. The two writers touched upon issues of faith, integrity, Russia and the West, Thomas Jefferson, Voltaire, and the U.S. book market, but it is the issue of the "banalization" of experience that becomes crucial in Shalamov's final break with Solzhenitsyn. Shalamov accused Solzhenitsyn of "lacquering reality" and couldn't forgive the epic author of the *Gulag Archipelago* an "impurity of tone."[32]

Shalamov's own prose focuses on the cracks in the process of lacquering reality. Intonation for Shalamov is a trace of oral speech in the poetic form of the story that affects the stories' narrative voice and syntax, linking his unique artistic form to collective experience. Shalamov wanted to avoid what he considered to be a conventional psychologism, dubbed dismissively "the surface peel (*shelukha*) of halftones in the representation of psychology."[33] This kind of psychologism domesticates and erases the modern specificity of the camp experience. Intonation in Shalamov's texts creates a special balance between an insider's voice and the estranging viewpoint.

But what is "literary" about Shalamov's documentary prose? Aesthetic and antiaesthetic moments coincide in Shalamov. Like the OPOYAZ members in the 1920s, he attacks conventional literary form in order to explore the foundation of estrangement and the radical practice of judgment and imagination. Shalamov's approach to storytelling consists in aesthetic and ethical "sculpting" (removal of everything unnecessary) and at the same time, the preservation of traces of the singularity of experience and witnessing, including the author's misprints, repetitions, and blemishes, everything deemed irrelevant in the Hegelian-Marxist-Leninist understanding of the "laws of history." To the great irritation of his helpful editors, Shalamov insisted on leaving misprints and repetitions in his texts.[34] For him they form another nonlinear "hypertextual" (in contemporary language) network that links the stories among themselves. Shalamov shared this peculiar poetics of misprint with other modernist writers who also addressed issues of totalitarianism—in particular, Nabokov and Milan Kundera. Nabokov uses mistakes, misrecognition, and misprints, as in *Pale Fire* ("Life everlasting based on a misprint?") to create an ironic epiphany, a revelation with difference that incorporates human error and "the crooked timber of humanity" into the text. For Kundera, the totalitarian system of removing traces of communist *personae non grata* from every photograph was never complete, leaving blemishes that open up spaces for another history.[35] I call it the "poetics of blemish," a crucial weapon of the weak and of the watched. In Shalamov, the author's misprints similarly compose a theme with variations, a variation on the singularities and human errors that could represent a deviation from collective teleology. Their preservation is the author's right, which he sometimes equates with a human right par excellence. In my view, these misprints and missteps should not be interpreted as unconscious "Freudian slips" that empower us readers to catch the author unawares. Rather, they could make us complicit in the alternative tactic of camp communication, if we are willing to be tactful readers.

Misprints, according to Shalamov, do not betray the author but encompass his signature. In his *Kolyma Tales*, the "human errors" become triggers of secret narratives that tell stories of trickery and minimal liberation from the clichés of the banality of evil that permeate language and everyday practices of the Stalin era. A close reading of Shalamov's stories doesn't merely reveal "how a literary work is made," it also shows how ideology is made and what forms of communication can corrode or elude it.

Rationing Clichés, Documenting Terror

Shalamov's "Dry Rations" opens almost like a fairy tale, with four convicts embarking on a mythical journey to explore a limbo region of the Gulag and build a road through the snow. The story begins with them crossing beneath the gates of the camp with their familiar inscription: "Our labor is a matter of honor, courage, and glory." Overwhelmed with joy at their momentous luck, they don't dare break the silence, as if afraid to discover that their short escape was somebody's error, a joke or a misprint in some bureaucratic circular.

The official clichés of camp life frame the story like the barbed wire of the zone. In fact, the Russian title of the story should be translated as "By Dry Rations" (*sukhim paikom*). This elliptical adverbial construction indicates a mode of existence. The syntax of the title pushes us directly into the "rations" of camp language. "Dry rations" function as an "advance of short-lived liberation" that determine the time and space of the prisoner's journey outside the zone. The rationing of food, labor, freedom, pain, punishment, and cruelty is central to camp life. Rationing was a form of the rationalization of terror.

The story proceeds by disrupting various clichés as well as official and unofficial rationalizations of the camp existence. The four unlikely fellow travelers represent a cross-section of the camp society. Yet they are not representative men in any shape or form, but singular individuals with uniquely (but not exceptionally) unlucky fates. Ivan Ivanovich, slightly older than his companions and described as "the most decent" prisoner, used to be "an excellent worker," "almost a hero of camp labor." The reasons for his arrest are of the everyday order (*bytovye*) and are not explained in detail. The youngest of the prisoners, Fedya Shapov, is a teenager from Altai with a not very strong "half-grown body." His crime was "slaughtering a sheep" on his own farm in order to feed his mother and himself. Accused of sabotaging collectivization, he was punished by ten years in the camps. The third prisoner is a Moscow student named Saveliev. Once a loyal member of the Young Communist League, he was accused of conspiring to create a counterrevolutionary cell that consisted of two members—himself and his fiancée. His romantic letter to his bride was used as evidence of anti-Soviet propaganda and "agitation," for which he was given ten years of hard labor in Kolyma. The fourth convict is our narrator, a political prisoner from Moscow and a veteran observer of camp tactics, the prisoner without a biography.

Just as the convicts leave the gates of the zone with its uplifting slogan, "Our labor is a matter of honor, feast of courage and glory," they begin to ration their own efforts and debate the value and meaning of work in the camp. The narrator wonders if "honest" work could still exist in the Gulag context, and Saveliev advances his own theory of surplus labor. First he speaks about the surplus of language that covers up the conditions of slave labor: "The only ones who call for honest work are the bastards who beat and maim us, eat our food and force us living skeletons to work to our very death. It is profitable to them but they believe in honest work even less than we do."[36]

The concept of "loafing" (*filonit'*) is crucial in Shalamov's camp world. His storytellers are not heroes of labor but "artists of the spade" and masters of dissimulation. One of the camp slang words for "loafing" is "Kant," a slang word for "light labor" and the "artistry of the spade," that is, a minimally creative and survivalist approach to camp labor. The irony that the philosopher's name coincides with a reprieve from camp duties and artistry instead of effort is not lost on Shalamov.[37] Love for "Kant" exemplifies the prisoner's parodistically anti-Marxist theory of surplus value; it is the surplus value of "loafing," of (relative) idleness and evasion that constitutes the prisoner's personal "capital" of disobedience.

Saveliev teaches little Fedya the ways of camp survival through the tactics of language and labor. He tells him a story about one dissenting loafer who refused to work. "They made a report. Said that he was 'dressed appropriately for the season.'" "What does that mean, 'dressed appropriately for the season'?" asks Fedya. Saveliev explains that this phrase was used when a prisoner couldn't fulfill the labor norm or died, but instead of listing all the missing items of his clothing, boots and mittens and so on, the bureaucrats simply affirmed in his report that the prisoner was "dressed for the season," as a supposedly logical justification for inhuman labor:

"Well, they can't list every piece of summer or winter clothing you have on. If it's in the winter they can't write that you were sent to work without a coat or mittens. How often did you stay in the camp because there were no mittens?"

"Never," said Fedya timidly. "The boss made us stamp down the snow on the road. Or else they would have had to write that we stayed behind because we didn't have anything to wear."

"There you have it."[38]

Behind a seemingly innocuous bureaucratic cliché, "dressed appropriately for the season" was a shortcut to cover up the naked truth that hardly anyone was ever dressed appropriately for labor conditions of the camp.

Such conversations bond prisoners together through an unofficial code of minimal camp decency that is never entirely deciphered. None of the prisoners "transgress" certain ethical taboos of directly collaborating with the authorities and informing on other prisoners or becoming a "foreman" and giving orders to the other prisoners. Somehow, in spite of the fact that they live at a time when everything is permitted and everything is possible, all four exercise inner restraint. They are most happy in the brief moments of loafing and storytelling—"storymaking-daydreaming" (*vranie-mechtanie*), half-lies, half-dreams. Fedya particularly enjoys tales of the urban miracles, such as the Moscow metro. They let their imagination "go visiting" to escape the frost of Kolyma.

Yet there is a time bomb at the very heart of the story. The gasp of excessive freedom (relatively speaking, of course) for a convict of the zone is like a surplus of bread for one who is starving. It can kill. As they are finishing their dry rations, the foreman from the camp arrives and immediately figures out their loafing and rationing tactics and orders them back to the camp. They have only one night left to daydream outside the camp. Ivan Ivanovich is the only one who continues working until the twilight with the same tragic diligence.

The next morning Saveliev finds Ivan Ivanovich hanged from a tree "without even a rope." The best worker among the four companions, the "decent man" Ivan Ivanovich chooses his own way out. The foreman panics, tries to distract the convicts from the sight of the corpse. Saveliev, who, unlike the veterans of the Gulag had not yet turned the spectacle of death into a daily routine, picks up an axe and brings it down on his own four fingers—only to be promptly arrested for self-mutilation, or rather, for the mutilation of a worker—since the body of the able Gulag prisoner was considered state property. Andrei Siniavsky wrote about the prisoners of the first Soviet labor camp, the Solovki, who put their mutilated body parts into the logs of wood processed for foreign export. These were their messages to Western buyers about the nature of the labor and product. Saveliev's fingers sent a message that nobody might have received, yet it was his only, horrific opportunity for self-expression.[39] Fedya and the narrator take Ivan Ivanovich's clean clothes and return to the zone, to the same berths in the same barracks.

Late at night the protagonist wakes up and finds Fedya in a state of stupor, composing a letter to his mother. The narrator reads it, eavesdropping "across Fedya's shoulder." And here we arrive at the end of the story: "Mama,—Fedya was writing—Mama, I live well. Mama, I am dressed according to the season."[40]

The ending with the central cliché of the camp dissimulation—"dressed appropriately for the season"—stuns us into silence. We the readers, just like the convicts at the beginning of the story, are afraid to break into speech and rush to interpretation. Something in the narrator's intonation forces us to pause and rethink our assumptions.

Is Fedya knowingly telling half-truths to assuage his mother's fears? Or is he so shocked that even he can only repeat the official clichés, even in his most personal letter? Is this exploration of the limbo zone an initiation into the banality of evil or a lesson in dissent? Is Fedya's letter then an act of explicit conformity or of covert disobedience?[41]

This is an instance of Shalamov's signature intonation. The word "Mama" is repeated three times, and this makes all the difference.[42] The "document" is interrupted. The intonation bursts open the official clichés of the letter. In one line we have two types of repetition: repetition as mimicry of the camp clichés and repetition as lament. The invisible author is eavesdropping over Fedya's shoulder, making minor notations that turn the bureaucratese of the letter into a lament: Mama, Mama, Mama, like Chekhov's broken string in the background. There is a desperation of the address here that expresses the sheer phatic function of language; this is not even a desire to communicate but just to test the fragile communication. Such nuance makes the story a great work of fiction and "hurts" moral imagination.

The catharsis of the story is neither the death of Ivan nor Saveliev's self-mutilation, but instead his stunning ambivalence of Fedya's epistolary document that breaks the frame of the story and unhinges our frame of reference. Shalamov is not interested in ecstatic Dostoevskian scenes of suffering or Eisensteinian eccentric pathos. His stories deny the reader the instant gratification of empathy and communal purification, which might explain why many interpreted Shalamov as a "cruel," unemotional, nihilistic, or covertly religious writer even against his frequent protestations to the contrary. More than instantaneous catharsis, he is engaged in the torturous peripeteias of camp luck.

The tragic predicament plays a very important role in Shalamov, but his understanding of tragedy is modernist. It has much in common with the notion of tragic catharsis that was developed by the psychologist Lev Vygotsky, who was also close to the critics from OPOYAZ and was interested in the psychology of art. According to Vygotsky, "a work of art always contains an intimate conflict between its content and its form, and the artist achieves his effect by means of the form, which is capable of destroying the content."[43] In this understanding of the psychology of art, catharsis resides in the clash of ambivalence. Form "murders" the content or, rather, transports it into the domain of imagination, immortalizing the experience and disrupting the chain of victimization.

How does Shalamov give us a lesson in camp literacy and understanding of the documents of the Gulag? Let us for a moment imagine the hypothetical historian of the future in some distant provincial archive getting this letter to Fedya's mother. He or she spent a lot of effort after going through many official documents, finally rejoicing at finding the personal one. The expression "dressed according to the season" might jar the historian a little, but then verifying the words in the dictionary, he/she concludes that the peasant prisoner might have been *gramotnyi*, that is, well educated in the new Soviet school built in his village in the Altai mountains. Fedya's "Soviet subjectivity" as expressed in his own words tells our imaginary historian that some (not all) "lived well" in the camp, especially those who knew how to work hard. Were Fedya's letter to reach its addressee, it would most likely be misread.

Shalamov's story is about the clash of two texts: Fedya's "document" of camp life and the story of making such a document. The aesthetic ambiguity turns into the ethics of judgment and understanding. In fact, the whole story is about the deviousness of language that has lost its meaning.

The story works through constant disruptions and subversion: that of the prisoners' fears and expectations, of the reader's conventional framework, of the clichés of "humanist" redemption, and of Soviet reeducation.[44] The minimal "freedom" of the author and the reader is that they now share the other way of reading "over the shoulder" (*cherez plecho*) of the stupefied camp novice who learned the hard way the temptation of nonconformity. Judging, in this literary form, is the ability to discriminate in reading, to acquire tact, to preserve multiple perspectives and multiple human fates, and to respect the choices. Judging is not about being judgmental but about giving imaginary space to the defeated, to their impossible human choices, leaving space and acknowledging the dreams of exit in a no-exit situation and according to the tactics of the Gulag. The secret of Gulag communication is in the intonation, in the singular irreducibility to any master plot, in the "small successes" of the condemned. The story is also about tactics of minimal singularity. Each prisoner reacts to the gasp of freedom by choosing a different tactic: suicide, self-mutilation, the resilient survival of Gulag veteran and writer-witness, and Fedya's ambivalent lesson of pushing the boundaries of the zone. Each reaction is an unpredictable form of judging for oneself, a personal choice that doesn't agree with the official objectification and subjugation of the "human material." Thus "By Dry Rations" is not about "a *liberal* subjectivity" some historians love to hate, but *liminal* subjectivity that bends the barbed wire ever so slightly and yet significantly. Shalamov works through the Russian and Soviet clichés as one works through trauma, grieving over every word, every turn of phrase.

Mimicry, Misprint, and Technologies of the Gulag

If the first part of Shalamov's *Kolyma Tales* deals with the early stages of the prisoner's Gulag sentence and is about the difficult initiation into camp life and the survival of unfreedom, the second part of the book deals with the difficulty of liberation and self-liberation after years in the zone. The hero of the story "Lida," Krist, is a veteran survivor of the Kolyma camps who is approaching the end of his sentence but cannot see the end of the conspiratorial frames of the Gulag system of well-wishers and informants, the "human chain" of the enthusiastic perpetrators of the banality of evil. He is afraid that due to his political status, the end of his sentence won't bring him liberation but rather another term of imprisonment, another round in the vicious circles of Gulag labor. Like Shalamov himself, rearrested many times, Krist is "branded" by a special letter "T" in the abbreviation "KRTD" in his file, a term that applied to the most dangerous political prisoners. T stood for Trotskyism and therefore, for the "death tribunal," giving his boss and anyone else who might discover this information from his secret file a "poetic license" for endless persecution or even license to kill. Krist anticipated the many eager little Eichmanns forming the "human staircase" of informants that was the foundation of the "low-tech" Gulag system, which did not rely on technology like the Nazis did but rather on "relentless manpower."[45]

The perpetual question "What is to be done?" occupies Krist. His name notwithstanding, he is hardly a suffering hero or a charismatic redeemer. A survivor of the "bookish Russia," Krist does not believe in a personal savior but thinks that in the world "there are many truths" and one must discover—cocreate—one's own. In the world of the camp, where all scales have shifted, he has to rediscover what liberation means. For him survival is more than just a personal matter, it is a personal vendetta against the regime.

After months of torturous meditation, Krist comes up with a "poetic license" of his own. Once during a particularly intense night of thinking he experiences an intense "illumination" that comes to him "just like the best lines of a poem." The name of the solution is "Lida." Krist recalls an incident that happened several years before, when he worked as doctor's assistant in the camp hospital. One night the doctor on duty from the political prisoners had asked him for a small favor. It concerned a young secretary from among the nonpolitical convicts whose husband had died in the camps and whose boss, the lieutenant, was threatening her after she refused to "live with him" (i.e., to be raped by him). The young woman hoped to hide in the hospital until the lieutenant was moved to another station. Krist asked to see her. "A not very tall, blond young woman appeared in front of Krist and bravely looked him in the eyes. Many people passed by Krist, many thousands of eyes were understood and figured out. It was very rare that Krist made mistakes. 'OK,' said Krist, 'put her in the hospital.'"

It is important that neither the doctor nor Krist knows the woman. They understand each other with half-words and gestures, following some kind of unwritten code of honor among the noncollaborators. This wasn't a major act of disobedience, but a minor dissent, mimicry of the bureaucratic hierarchies that could cost them much or nothing, for the sake of a stranger. Lida managed to escape her pursuer, too small a fish in the Gulag pond. The chief doctor of the hospital treated the lieutenant with bureaucratic disrespect. Krist and Lida never talked about the incident again but occasionally exchanged knowing glances. Now Lida once again worked as a secretary and typed passport forms and prisoners' files. Krist thinks to ask her for a different kind of professional favor.

After his night of poetic revelation, Krist approaches Lida and tells her casually that she will soon type his documents of liberation.

> "Congratulations," said Lida, and brushed off the invisible dust from Krist's fel'dsher's robe.
>
> "You will type old convictions, there is such a line there, right?"
> "Yes, there is."

"In the word 'KRTD,' drop the letter T."

"Understood," said Lida.

"If the boss notices when he signs it, just smile, say you made a mistake. Spoiled the form."

"I know what to say myself."[46]

Two weeks later, Krist is called to the office to receive his new passport. In the nefarious abbreviation "KRTD" the letter T had disappeared.

Was it a misprint, a human error? Krist's friends try to decipher his luck but none suspect that Krist cocreated his liberation with his own hands.[47] Once again, catharsis occurs in the ellipsis, in what remains unsaid. Like a Greek tragedy, the story is about the confrontation of different laws, and the improbable law of Krist's poetic art gains a temporary victory.

The minimalism of communication is the reaction against the banalization of speech in the camp and "impurity of tone": "The camp didn't like sentimentality, didn't like long and unnecessary preambles, and various 'approaches.'"[48] Krist and Lida were "veterans of Kolyma" and understood each other with half-words.

Lida's final action is not merely returning a favor. It does not function within the economy of *blat* (the Soviet informal network of barter, which existed among the privileged and not so privileged in the circumstances of scarcity). Instead, it belongs to the improbable circulation of minor gifts and acts of kindness among strangers who survived against all odds in the space of the Gulag.

The absence of explicit moral or ethical discussion is compensated only by the description of the night of Krist's feat of imagination. The impersonality of the Gulag machine and the chain of informants that voluntarily perpetuate the banality of evil are not counteracted by a Tolstoyan- or Solzhenitsyn-style morality tale that might turn into the banality of good but by minimal human solidarity and exercise in extreme imagination. The epiphany of solution is described in aesthetic terms as a radical act of poetic composition, not religious conversion.[49] The inhuman effort that Krist expends to come up with the solution is the price of the "inhumanity of imagination" that is capable of counterbalancing the inhumanity of the system.

In each of Krist's moments of judging, ethics and aesthetics become closely intertwined even when it is a matter of life and death. Krist's first brief encounter with Lida is an "ethical encounter," in a sense that Emmanuel Levinas understood it: it is about a face-to-face meeting that calls for an "anarchic responsibility" toward another particular human being.[50]

But the story is not only about empathy but also about judging and cocreating in the Gulag "philosophy of composition." This is not about the individual's romantic battle against the totalitarian system but about matching the "living chain" of denouncers with the chain of decent human beings who exchange gratuitous gifts. What breaks the vicious circle is an ingenious mimicry of the "low-tech" Gulag system. One could distinguish different forms of behavioral mimicry in the totalitarian circumstances as a form of collaboration, survival, or belonging, and the nuanced distinctions are of crucial importance. In this case, however, mimicry is neither obedience nor the imitation of power, neither tautology nor a parody.

The best understanding of this kind of mimicry comes from the writer and lepidopterist Vladimir Nabokov. Mimicry in the Nabokovian definition is a "cryptic disguise" and a "nonutilitarian delight" that defies the Darwinian evolution of the fittest and the Hegelian laws of history:

> The mysteries of mimicry had a special attraction for me. Its phenomena showed an artistic perfection usually associated with man-wrought things. . . . When a butterfly has to look like a leaf, not only are all the details of a leaf beautifully rendered but markings mimicking grub-bored holes are generously thrown in. "Natural selection" . . . could not explain the miraculous coincidence of imitative aspect . . . , nor could one appeal to the theory of "the struggle for life" when a protective device was carried to a point of mimetic subtlety, exuberance, and luxury far in excess of a predator's power of appreciation. I discovered in nature the nonutilitarian delights that I sought in art.[51]

Such mimicry that "exceeds the predator's power of appreciation" persists as a form of trickery and as a homeopathic antidote to the Gulag bureaucracy. Mimicry, in the words of Homi Bhabha, is at once "resemblance and menace":[52] in this particular case, it foregrounds clichéistic conscience, a survivalist collaboration with the regime and its different forms of daily "camouflage," revealing practices of creative "cheating" and judgment. Such mimicry works as an example of Arendtian "enlargement of mentality" that estranges the ethos of making everything permitted and possible, of domesticating terror through new and old master narratives.

The "human error" and the authorial signature of the prisoner's illicit creativity coincide in Shalamov's texts. Blemish and poetic license work like the prisoner's ephemeral individual traces in the virginal snow of Kolyma. The most striking expressive gesture of this stripped-down story is Lida's brushing off the invisible dust from Krist's medical uniform at the moment when he asks her to make a typo. This gesture is irreducible to any single moral symbol: it is at once a sign of gratitude, of wistful mutual understanding, of care, of the "shamanism and mischief" that Shalamov believed to have been ciphered in his old Russian family name. In fact, the story performs a shamanic act of transforming the deficient official passport into an artistic document: "Poetic intonation is a literary passport, that personal 'brand,' that provides the poet's place in history. We don't have a patent bureau and intellectual property rights for the poetic intonation."[53] The writer's intonation functions like a fingerprint of his unofficial identity. Here Shalamov echoes Nabokov, another author obsessed with visas and watermarks. "Art is the writer's only passport," wrote Nabokov, the author of many tales of passportless spies.[54]

Poetic reflection for Shalamov is not a domain of autonomous literature but a practice of judging, of devising other horizons and reimagining a different system of coordinates for human existence. "In the visceral depth of any physical phenomenon we can find a poem and then switch this perception into real life."[55] Moreover, Shalamov's authorial ambiguity goes beyond the Aesopian language practiced by the intelligentsia of the thaw and afterward; he breaks open the nature of Soviet fabulization with his inassimilable stories. His is the radical elaboration of Victor Shklovsky's conception of art as a technique, in this case a technique of surprising survival through intense artistic and existential estrangement. Shalamov is one of Russia's great modern writers who follows their own modern track beyond the official Soviet modernization or the route that goes from the grave of the avant-garde to the Socialist Realist necropolis. His is not the modernism of self-expression, invention of personal language, and Stoic inner freedom. Rather it is a public modernism, which engages the political in a non-party-line manner, in the line of Primo Levi, W. H Auden, Albert Camus, and others.

Shalamov shares Arendt's view that clichés that produce a banal evil as well as a banal good not only package the experience but collaborate in the perpetuation of totalitarian horror. While opposing the clichés of both authoritarian humanism of the nineteenth century and the even more authoritarian antihumanism of the twentieth century's teleologies of universal happiness, Shalamov proposes a new form of imaginative documentary prose that doesn't describe but cocreates the experience. Shalamov and Arendt share one particular literary interest: the American writer William Faulkner. His statement that "[t]he past is not dead, it is not even past," especially beloved by Arendt, reflects Shalamov's relationship to memory. Shalamov claimed Faulkner to be one of his favorite writers who practiced "fractured, exploded prose." For Shalamov, as for Faulkner, past and present have equal urgency; the past explodes the present while the present actualizes the past. Memories for Shalamov are as real as bodily aches and pains. "Memory gnaws at you like a frostbitten hand at the first cold wind." Memory is a phantom limb, numb and undead.[56] This kind of memory, which is part of the "dignity of the defeated," works against the Hegelian teleology of the law of history and the justification of historical violence.[57]

Diamonds in the Sky and the Gulag Effect

When asked about her experiences in the Gulag, my grandmother, who spent six years in the camps during the anticosmopolitan campaign and was released only after Stalin's death, would look up to the sky and recite a few lines from a monologue in Anton Chekhov's *Uncle Vanya*: "Oh, one day we will see the diamonds in the sky. . . ." She would say that while in the zone she had met very distinguished actresses, and they would rehearse in whispers their favorite plays. Considered "tall tales" during my childhood, my grandmother's accounts proved mostly to be a reality that was stranger than fiction. Her first memory would always be of an unofficial and unsanctioned theatrical performance in the barracks; in spite of everything she had witnessed and experienced, she would speak mostly about escapes from terror, and those escapes were also conduits to forbidden experiences of camp freedom.

Art played an ambivalent role in the context of the Gulag. If we were to imagine an exhibition of Soviet art from the Gulag era, we would be astonished—not by what we would see, but by the glaring absences. We would see joyful photomontages of construction sites, solemn portraits of the great leaders exhibiting their tough love towards their people, and Stalin's favorite genre: a musical comedy, featuring flights into the stratosphere and resembling in style the Hollywood comedies of Busby Berkeley. Many prisoners took part in the cheerful, official Gulag performances that served as a means of distraction and often offered a few modest privileges. Much of real Gulag art is not preserved and resides in the half-forgotten practices of alternative imagination. Albert Camus tells the story of a German prisoner in the Gulag who made himself a tiny wooden piano and practiced music every day—mutely. This mute piano playing (in contrast to the official loud musical performances) could be seen as an accompaniment for Gulag art. Some of the most moving "artifacts" of the Gulag are what can be called trickster objects: portraits carved on wooden logs at the NKVD construction site, cigarette lighters made out of cartridges, locks with "secrets" made out of bolts and wire. It was the practice itself and not direct representation that often mattered. Poetry writing, loafing, daydreaming, making gifts: these activities should not cancel the radical inhumanity of the camp experience, but should come as surprises, exceptions to the rule, survival in "the stolen air," to paraphrase Osip Mandelshtam.

There is a striking difference in the historical remembrance of the regimes of Hitler and Stalin. Though the revelation of the Nazi camps and the Holocaust had a profound influence on Western thought and has been powerfully represented in works of visual art, the Gulag experience did not have the same type of representation.[58] Even the nonconformist artists of the 1970s and 1980s rarely made Gulag history the central theme of their work, in spite of the fact that camp survivors lived among them and the Gulag experience was still a living memory.[59] The reasons for this are complex. For better or for worse, political speech of any kind was regarded in the late Soviet period as compromised, almost aesthetically incorrect.

Often the artists focused on modes of manipulation and the charisma of utopian mythology and their personal detours from it. When I curated one of the first exhibits that dealt with the Gulag and contemporary art, "Territories of Terror," I had to confront a dilemma: how to represent what had not been spoken about, how to stage the unfinished business of memory in uncovering the secret territory of terror that existed side by side with the joyful utopia now remembered with so much nostalgia. One of the projects that addressed the paradox of utopia and terror, of aspirations and fears, was Leonid Sokov's sculpture *Flying Cage* (fig. 20). Sokov works with the icons of the international avant-garde as well as with folk art, prison art, military architecture and even the tools of the slave labor used in the Belomor Canal construction site. *Flying Cage* reproduces the wings of Vladimir Tatlin's famous biomorphic flying vehicle Letatlin (1931–1932; see chap. 5). After these experiments Tatlin was declared to be "no artist at all" and was unable to exhibit his works during his lifetime. The *Flying Cage* is a juxtaposition of extremes: liberation of cosmic proportions and an evocation of the claustrophobia of a prison cell. We are reminded of the words of Dostoevsky's character Shigalev, who says in *The Possessed*: "Beginning with a premise of unlimited freedom I arrive at unlimited despotism."[60] The dream of radical liberation—a cosmic leap into the kingdom of freedom—often goes hand in hand with authoritarianism.

Figure 20. Leonid Sokov, *The Flying Cage*, from the exhibit "Territories of Terror" (2006–2007), curated by Svetlana Boym.

But Sokov's *Flying Cage* is not merely a didactic vehicle; like Tatlin's Letatlin, this is a dysfunctional poetic machine that evokes Russian fairy tales. And the best fairy tales, in the artist's view, are those that, unlike political fantasies, should remain dreams and never come true.

Sokov made many drawings of the wings of Tatlin's Letatlin, whose metal vertebrae were supposedly discarded in the Leningrad yard after the artist's death in 1953. The contemporary artist sees in them the mementos of the posthistorical life of the experimental art made at the time of Stalin's purges in the 1930s and the phantom limbs of alternative cultural imagination in which the unfulfilled projects of the avant-garde and the forgotten art of the Gulag continue their virtual life.

Examining the Gulag effect and thinking of the art of judging today demand a different urgency. It means confronting internal domestic oppression and the uncomfortable history of one's own country, which cannot be blamed on foreign invaders and colonizers. In this sense its significance expands beyond the Russian border to involve all of world history. Contrary to the opinion that one encounters in countries with authoritarian regimes, confrontation with the oppression in the national past does not blemish national prestige on the world stage, quite the contrary. Such acknowledgment of one's own history is the only way to gain international recognition and rebuild a freer common world. In the present moment there is no widespread "Gulag denial"; in fact, the brief opening of the archives and the activity of many Russian and international historians and researchers of the memorial made a lot of information publicly available. Yet in the new political climate, the increasing amount of information is in inverse proportion to the public interest in understanding the past. There is an uncanny persistence of authoritarian eros in post-Soviet culture and the Gulag legacy, which in this case means the legacy of unconfronted memories, of critical history turning into a protected domain of national heritage. When history becomes heritage and the past is a realm of state-sponsored national nostalgia there is little space for critical questioning. Shalamov's work reveals how the "Gulag effect" is made and how easy it is to domesticate terror and erase minor courageous acts as mere "misprints" in the official plot of history, acts that could transform the imperative to remember into an imperative to judge and preserve the minimal play of freedom by means of freedom, which in Shalamov's understanding occurs by means of the imagination.

Yet once again, the art of judging is not only the art of memory but also the art of freedom. The writer Italo Calvino tells of the different ways of inhabiting the invisible cities of the inferno but not entirely succumbing to them and resisting collaboration:

> There are two ways to escape suffering [the inferno]. The first one is easy for many: accept the inferno and become such a part of it that one can no longer see it. The second is risky and demands constant vigilance and apprehension: seek and learn to recognize who and what, in the midst of the inferno, are not inferno, then let them endure, give them space.[61]

This space of the noninferno within the inferno preserves the blueprints of the architecture of freedom.

FREEDOM AND ITS DISCONTENTS

Freedom by Numbers?

"All good words have faded, words like 'spring,' 'love' should be forbidden," writes Victor Shklovsky, only to speak again about spring and love from a new, unexpected perspective. Sometimes it seems that the word "freedom," too, should be forbidden, or at least temporarily suspended so that we can really think through what it means to lose it. Artistic scandals today illuminate the limits of freedom, the larger issues that face its architecture: the relationship between religious and secular space, between fundamentalisms and toleration, between corporate privatization of space and the public domain.

At the end of the cold war, Russian American artists Vitaly Komar and Alexander Melamid decided to engage, or possibly even reconcile in a paradoxical manner, Soviet and American mythologies, pledging to use a scientific method and to fulfill the promise of both Socialist Realist art and capitalist advertising. They decided to conduct an experiment: abandoning artistic freedom

Figure 21. Vitaly Komar and Alexander Melamid, "USA's Most Wanted Painting" from the "People's Choice" project, 1996–1998. Courtesy of the artists.

in the narrow sense of the word, they would instead satisfy "popular demand" and make art by numbers, following the polls and the expression of the "people's choice." They diligently conducted scientific polls of artistic tastes from Kenya to China (with the United States and Russia in between), using local teams of sociologists and statisticians who interviewed a representative population sample on all aspects of art. The questions ranged from favorite colors and shapes to the figures to be depicted on a painting. For instance, people all over the world were asked whether they prefer a "realistic" painting or a "different-looking" one, whether the painting should be the size of a dishwasher or a refrigerator and whether it should have "ordinary or famous people" depicted in it or no people at all. The global poll produced a shocking discovery. The "most wanted" painting, regardless of race, class, and gender (with just a few exceptions), turned out to be a landscape, with a predominance of blue, the world's favorite color. The painting had to present a few "ordinary and famous people" in the foreground ("fully clothed" was the preference in the United States and "partially nude" in France. When the choice was proposed between "realistic" or "different-looking," the world population overwhelmingly rejected things "different-looking." Even in the lands of diversity, like the United States and Western Europe, "different-looking" is often a euphemism for rejection. One of the artists,

Figure 22. Vitaly Komar and Alexander Melamid, "Russia's Most Wanted Painting" from the "People's Choice" project, 1996–1998. Courtesy of the artists.

Komar, commented about the American poll: "In a society famous for freedom of expression, freedom of the individual, our poll revealed the sameness of majority. Having destroyed communism's utopian illusion, we collided with democracy's virtual reality."[1] It seems that in meticulously measuring national diversity, the artists revealed the uniform homogeneity of international calendar art instead of a multiculturalism of taste.

Wondering whether polls are now a substitute for democratic politics and have become a new institution, Komar and Melamid made polling the main aesthetic attraction of the exhibit. The exhibit was dominated by the ubiquitous presence of the colorful scientific graphs that resembled abstract paintings, which were just as prominently featured and on display as the "most wanted" paintings, as if exhibiting the narcissism of polling and proceduralism for its own sake (fig. 23). In their project the artists took the polls at face value, exposing this peculiar combination of highly sophisticated technology and literal-mindedness, bringing it to the edge of absurdity. They then painted many national blue landscapes with George

Figure 23. Vitaly Komar and Alexander Melamid, polling graphs from the "People's Choice" project, 1996–1998. Courtesy of the artists.

Washington and children at play for the Americans (fig. 21, p. 286), and Jesus Christ and children at work (on popular demand) for the Russians (fig. 22, p. 287), with a Kenyan rhinoceros and Russian bears.

If we look more closely at the "most wanted painting," we notice that there is trouble in Komar and Melamids's pictorial paradise in blue. The eyes of the wandering George Washington never meet the gaze of the contemporary vacationers. In Russia's "most wanted," the Jesus Christ look-alike seems to turn his gaze away from the laboring youth. They inhabit the same painting but seem to exist on different planes. The smooth surface of the painting is deceptive. There is a sense of excess in it: like Total cereal, it has an extra helping of everything the people want without any relationship between the ingredients. The poll-driven painting appears haunted by the specter of crypto-surrealism. The seamless surface of the art-by-numbers is in fact a collage and a disjunction. Something is deliberately out of joint here. Can it be that the "most wanted paintings" are the ones that nobody wants?

Those who are "most wanted," after all, are usually fugitives. Ultimately the chase for the elusive "people's choice" and the universal language of art, and the very documenting of the project, ended up being more inspiring and surprising than its end result and the actual "most wanted" paintings. Sometimes the artists appear as homicide detectives who are investigating the murder of a painting.[2]

In the process of collecting information, the artists conducted a number of town meetings and focus groups creating overall a phantom public sphere, mobilizing democratic traditions and institutions and the market culture, often pitting one against the other; thus polls can be pitted against politics, the tyranny of the majority against minority rights, conformity against eccentricity. Often individual remarks at the town meetings went beyond any kind of polling and were much more interesting. For instance, the focus groups and town meetings produced very different results than the polls; minoritarian democracy threw a punch at the tyranny of the majority's taste. Individual wishes expressed in the footnotes to the books included "painting an octopus driving a Ferrari, a dying republican," or "painting something we had never seen before." At the end Komar confessed his hope that "people who come to see our Most Wanted will become so horrified that their tastes will gradually change."[3]

The project reveals ample contradictions: global versus local, democratic versus elitist, technological versus traditional, actually conspire together to create a mediocre end result that everybody "should" want but nobody actually does. The project also confronts different logics of polls and polity, of quantitative and qualitative analysis, of democratic and artistic freedom, and offers us a phantasmagoria of the "people's choice."

A carefully measured multiculturalism of taste calculated by multicultural statistical teams exposed international uniformity. Cultural pluralism calculated "by numbers" ends up suppressing the inner plurality of cultures and tastes. The use of the most advanced statistical and technological analysis results in the most unoriginal neotraditional painting. A celebration of the freedom of consumer choices produced an installation of artistic unfreedom. A supposed antielitism in art suppressed the eccentric and creative opinions of minoritarian democracy, making it an art of caution endorsed by management teams, which doesn't wish to offend the advertisers and tries to pass for the "people's choice." In a way Komar and Melamid's project preempted an attempt to make a risk-free art as a new global "derivate" product.

The People's Choice project itself remains artistic in its phantasmagoric theatricality, which preserves the ghosts of the nonconformist artistic happening. What is artistic in their project is what is political in a broad sense and not an explicit ideology, often a flaunting of all chic radical positions or as a scandal value that serves the masters on both the left and the right. Dissatisfied with the results of "what is," the artists crack open the agnostic space of the art of "what if." What if the People's Choice project is a perverse defense of the arts of freedom—a *via negativa*?

After all, in speaking of freedom, the *via negativa* is very appropriate. The quest for another freedom is always a search for freedom's inherent otherness; it explores contradictions and contact zones of different kinds of freedom: individual, public, civil, artistic. The story of another freedom is always a tale of freedom and its discontents. In parallel to Freud's classic *Civilization and Its Discontents*, the critique of freedom can be divided between the one that leads to the expansion of freedom and the one that threatens its existence. In other words, critiques themselves can be agnostic or agonistic. The twentieth-century reading of Freud focused on the liberation from repression and the other flaws of the civilizing process; the twenty-first-century reading might focus on the flaws of the un-civilizing process and the protection of at least one aspect of the much maligned civilization, the responsible acknowledgment of the aggression and paranoia that have expanded everywhere in the "second life" and in the "first life," in virtual and nonvirtual reality.

In my book I have been searching for a "third way" of thinking the space of freedom through close analysis of texts and political and artistic practices. My understanding of the term "third way" goes back to Shklovsky's theory and does not signify either a collaboration or a compromise, but a double estrangement of two extremes balanced by a "third term of comparison," a *tertius comparationis*, the care for the common world that requires an unconventional exercise in radical moderation. Politics of worldliness is new and must differentiate itself from triumphant globalism and the charismatic seduction of agonistic political theology. Sometimes I felt quixotic and exhausted in my quest for another freedom in the public imaginary but giving it up seemed worse.

In some way, Komar and Melamid's project foreshadowed the late twentieth-century syndrome: the euphoric expansion of polling and living "by numbers" at the expense of the expansion of freedom and the belief in calculable risks—in politics and arts—that would conquer the uncertainty. The project dates back to the time when O. J. Simpson trial and the Ken Starr wars wasted national energy and the narratives of the end of politics and the end of history and the mushrooming of dot.coms and dot.cons distracted from the deeply historical and non-virtual events in the world—from the war in the former Yugoslavia to the strengthening of the neofundamentalist ideology.

The first decade of the twenty-first century ended abruptly the speculations about the ends of history, politics and culture. The tragic dates

9/11/2001 in New York, 7/7/2005 in London, 3/11/2004 in Madrid and 11/26/2008 in Mumbai and what followed revealed that ideology of terror and the "politics of the the worse, the better"—*politique du pire*—are alive and powerful. We also learned that there is no single evil empire but multiple authoritarian agendas that operate with their own paranoid and pragmatic efficiency. The financial crisis of 2008 led many to reconsider the philosophical foundations of the "free market." The question with which I began the book—what should or could we be certain of to be able to live with a measure of uncertainty—must be revisited again in this context. At the core of the economic debate in the first part of the twentieth century was the distinction between "risk" (randomness that can be calculated with the help of advanced mathematical formulae) and "uncertainty" (randomness that is a part of the human existence in the world and is beyond such calculations). This distinction is at the foundation of the whole economic edifice and is more basic than the discussion of the role of the state versus laissez-faire capitalism, or public versus private investment. John Maynard Keynes thought that there was a residue of genuine uncertainty that defines our existence in the world and that made disaster of any kind an ever-present possibility.[4] It might seem counterintuitive that the acknowledgment of such radical uncertainty made Keynes more interested in cultural conventions and public foundations of social existence. Thus in a rather unconventional manner he continued the ideas of the founding father of the free market, Adam Smith, who proposed a broad theory of moral sentiments where self-love and self-interest went together with prudence and public spirit. However, late twentieth-century free-market theorists have tried to encourage the blurring of the distinction between uncertainty and risk, believing in the progressive rationalization or domestication of radical uncertainty and the expansion of mathematical formulae for the creation of the new financial products that promise endless growth and short-term profits. Today, thinking with uncertainty seems wiser and more contemporary; it helps us rebuild the architecture of freedom with the connections between existential, financial, and social dimensions of life and learn to coexist with the unpredictable.

Here I have searched for these connections through stories and debates on freedom. In the end, each of my stories of freedom yielded a surprise. The public space of freedom was connected to tragedy, but not in a sense of becoming "tragic," that is, unrealizable, fatally flawed, but on the contrary, it came into existence with political and artistic theater in which religious sacrifice opened up deliberation about the polis and human responsibility, *mania* and *technê*, inner and public freedom.

Pushkin's parable of another freedom showed that the quest for inner freedom was not independent from public architecture. The desire to "feel free" is not the same as living and acting in freedom. Thus Pushkin, looking for an escape "away from the tsar and the people" into the natural and artistic delights of another freedom, sided with the moderate imperial censorship. Poetic practice of inner freedom did not contradict the poet's qualified support for the absolute monarchy. Yet, his experience inspired poets a century later to develop their own version of another freedom, framing the art of political censorship through the use of Aesopian language. We know that antidemocratic regimes frequently murdered their poets, but they didn't find an antidote to the unofficial cult of the artist as an arbiter in the matters of freedom. As for the most inspired writings of classical (nonmarket) liberalism from Tocqueville to Berlin, they owed more to literature and philosophy than to polls and policies. Thus Berlin defined his liberal freedom as a *via negativa* after his journey to the Soviet Union and poetic night with Anna Akhmatova.

Interestingly, in her recent study of the idea of human rights, historian Lynn Hunt reveals the connections between law, politics, and literature. She demonstrates how the development of the novel in the eighteenth century and with it the new conception of self and of "moral sentiments" contributed greatly to the idea that human rights have become "self-evident."[5] Yet my stories on the cultural border zones demonstrate that the discussion of moral sentiments and artistic experiments, while enriching the self, do not always guarantee the expansion of public freedoms. Dostoevsky's journeys east and west and the "dialogues" with Karl Marx and Sacher-Masoch revealed that the quest for radical liberation and freer freedom requires all kinds of sacrifices—from the acceptance of flogging to the abolition of human rights for the sake of mythical national unity. Dostoevsky lays bare the anatomy of resentment that is not entirely explicable in terms of social contexts and external circumstances but driven by the internal logic of malicious pleasure and paranoid exclusion of the other. He sheds light on the beginnings of modern antimodernism on the borders of Europe. At the same time, in his own inner dialogue with his demons, Dostoevsky offers a striking portrayal of a terrorist as a petty and cruel conman, not a Shakespearian villain (but not a little Eichmann, either) and gives us rare insight into conspiratorial belonging and the manic destruction that this can cause. We see how the revolutionary strategy of the *politique du pire*, "politics of the worse, the better," developed in nineteenth-century Europe and Russia, promotes destruction for its own sake as a means of destabilization and fear.

Recently I was struck once again by Dostoevsky's prophetic description of the banality of the terrorist while reading excerpts from the diary of a contemporary self-prophesied terrorist, a British citizen implicated in planning a bomb attack in London. His diary reveals signs of urban alienation expressed in the international language of youth culture and the desire to embrace radical ideology as a form of gaining status and belonging to a community rather than out of religious or political convictions.[6] The diary, written in the East London slang shared with many of his compatriots and including many references to popular culture and contemporary technological gadgets, also contained racial slurs against members of the Pakistani community, among other things. I think the contemporary retelling of *The Possessed* waits to be written.

We see that the reflection on freedom is not an exercise in armchair radicalism but a lifelong practice in the world with many paradigm shifts. The experiences of political and personal violence and love influence philosophies of freedom in an unpredictable manner but do not extinguish the characters' tragic flaws. Kierkegaard breaks the engagement to the woman he loved and renounces worldly love for the sake of the ultimate leap of faith and a higher freedom even as he remained a most sensuous connoisseur of the arts of living. Hannah Arendt, for her part, abandoned the love for the single one and went on to discover the space of public worldliness, becoming a political theorist who practices passionate thinking.

Continuing my distinction between estrangement *from* the world and estrangement *for* the world that came from the study of Arendt, I discovered a deep connection between artistic estrangement and political dissent. Shklovsky, best known as a literary theorist and a writer, offered an ingenuous parable of the third-way thinking through diagonals and zigzags as he describes the strategies of estrangement that would be used by dissidents forty years later. Similarly Franz Kafka, an unlikely political actor, becomes in Arendt's interpretation a thinker of freedom who designed (unbeknownst to himself) a diagonal where freedom can take place through his radical thinking. Dissent might be local and embedded in local cultural practices but it goes against the grain of state nationalism and patriotism and remains a dangerous but necessary heresy for building an alternative future.

No understanding of twenty-first-century history is possible without reconsideration of the totalitarian ideology and totalitarian experience. My focus was on the lesser-studied experience of the Gulag and on the problem of judging, ethics, and paradigm shifts under the circumstances of extreme unfreedom. I began by listening to the accounts of the survivors to see how they articulate the issues of freedom. Surprisingly, the survivors spoke not only about extreme suffering, trauma, inhuman conditions, and the "biopolitics" of the camp existence, but also offered rare insight into the seduction of the ideology of mass terror and ways of cheating its implacable logic. Such ideology offers a vision of a paradise on earth and the ultimate fulfillment of the laws of history and social justice. It also works through the logic of who is not with us is against us and the "mass chain" of collaborators and informers. Shalamov, Ginzburg, and Arendt show various tactics for interrupting the logic of the banality of evil and historic determinism through the "ethics of intonation," imagination and unofficial human solidarities that survive against all odds.

Ultimately I have tried to suggest a new conceptual vocabulary and a new mode of thinking, but I am aware that my exemplary stories are a part of the future *Decameron* of freedom tales rather than a typology. I would have liked to write a second volume of *Another Freedom* that would deal with contemporary art and politics from around the world offering positive solutions and a clear vision of what is to be done. But I am well aware of what happened to Russian writers who made such promises. Nikolai Gogol promised to write a second volume of *Dead Souls* that would present positive characters and employed less laughter through tears, but he ended up burning the draft. All we are left with is the masterpiece of human comedy without single-minded answers.

Is Freedom Lost in Translation? Cultural Critique of Freedom

As I conclude, I look back at the time when I got my first insights into the paradoxes of freedom. I owe them to an encounter with complete strangers in the Moscow restaurant Petrovich during the bygone summer of 1999. My neighbor Gosha, a "liberal financier," politely inquired:

"Why would a nice girl like you live in America?"
  "Why not?" I asked
  "There is no freedom there!"
  ?!
  "You see prohibitions everywhere: No Trespassing, No Smoking, No Loitering. What if I want to smoke under the No Smoking sign? Or loiter? You can't do good business in such an environment. It's just too boring."
  "But here in Moscow there are fences everywhere, doors with no signs, and 'face control' when you try to enter cafés and clubs."

"Well, you got to hang out with the right people. With us all the doors are open to you. We know Americans who prefer to do business in Russia."[7]

It might surprise Americans that a friendly Russian economist who had spent time in the United States thought that it lacked freedom. My Russian acquaintance Gosha perceived contractual practices and public lawfulness as a form of hypocrisy and social conformity. He was not surprised by the No Smoking sign but by the fact that nobody actually smoked next to it. What was "boring" for Gosha was not so much the existence of prohibitions but their transparency and visibility. In Russian cultural mythologies, freedom was not to be sought in the political or even economic realm but in antipolitics, or at best, in literature and alternative spirituality, from Pushkin's "other freedom" to Dostoevsky's "freer freedom" imagined in the penal colony.

My conversation about freedom took place in that murky and euphoric moment of the extreme fin de siècle when so many historical possibilities still seemed open, when the American press was debating the stain on the dress of a White House intern and Russian feminist artists marched in support of then president Clinton. During a friendly dinner at the restaurant Petrovich, decorated in a gentle version of Soviet kitsch (still an unofficial retro, not the official state style), Gosha told me that he supported a democratic candidate for prime minister who subsequently lost his post to Vladimir Putin and his politics were by no means nationalist.[8]

In hindsight, rethinking the experience of the Russian financial markets, we see that expansion of global free trade didn't promote the expansion of freedom in the sense that Amartya Sen understands it. Quite the contrary, the defense of the supposed free-market and business objectives were frequently used to trump public freedoms and the freedom of press and non-state-sponsored media. Therefore Karl Marx was turned upside down once again (just like in another Komar and Melamid project) and authoritarian capitalism followed socialism and happily cohabited with nationalism and rebirth of religion. Moreover, the pyramid schemes and other financial bubbles that burst in the "wild East" in the 1990s were not so culturally unique. Uncannily, they have prefigured the bursting of the financial bubbles in the wild West of Wall Street only a decade later.

So *is* there really No Trespassing of cultural differences, or does the defense of cultural difference become an alibi to justify local forms of authoritarianism and to eliminate internal dissent? It is time to abandon the cold war paradigm and move to the examination of the contemporary multipolar world, but only if we learn a more paradoxical lesson from the romances of the cold war and the asynchronic dreams of freedom that they produced.

The cold war was not merely an explicit confrontation of communism and capitalism but also a secret codependency and even a romance between enemies. A larger number of Soviet citizens admired America during the cold war than Russians do now. (Their "Amerika" was embodied in Jack London, Ernest Hemingway, Frank Zappa, Janis Joplin, and the Beatles [well, not quite American, but never mind] more than by Disney and Coca-Cola—in other words, American/Western "counterculture," high culture, and a way of life that won their hearts.) East Europeans knew their Beatles just as well as did their Western counterparts, only they didn't wish to be "Back in the U.S.S.R.," but just to the bar before the last beat: "Back to the US—." "Freedom's just another word for nothing left to lose," the refrain from "Me and Bobby McGee" was sung by Janis Joplin, too, but slightly off key. For East Europeans, the song was something of an exotic dream and a cultural luxury: a celebration of negative freedom and social liberation in the late 1960s–early 1970s when feeling good and feeling free was, or at least seemed, easy. Easterners in those days tended to be the most passionate defenders of individual liberty (with an emphasis on liberality, not on liberalism) without understanding capitalist economy. Many of their Western counterparts harbored visions of collective justice and social utopias without authoritarian repercussions, without Gulags, and with a more or less comfortable private existence. Once the borders opened, the dissenting intellectuals didn't recognize their own dreams in those of others and in fact discovered that they had tampered with each other's fantasies. Their worlds existed in counterpoints offering parallel versions of modernity and freedom. The slogan of May 1968 in Prague was "Liberty"—in the broadest possible sense as a new social art that permeated all spheres of existence, while the slogan in Paris 1968 was "Revolution," since liberty was a bourgeois cliché in the way that revolution was the official communist cliché for their Czech brothers and sisters.[9]

Now these encounters continue between East and West with a similar degree of misrecognition of the global nature of the other and deep-seated local allegiances of oneself. If we imagine a counterfactual (but not entirely implausible) scenario that the change in Eastern Europe happened in 1968 rather than in 1989, perhaps priority will be given to the experiments in social democracy. Similarly, if the United States did not support authoritarian regimes in Latin America, we might have witnessed more plural democratic experiments that would have expanded the space of freedom. Today, however, Western dissenters often don't recognize the dissenters and the prodemocracy movement activists from the Muslim world and Asia because their language, based on real political experience, often sounds outmoded to the Western ear or like an amplified version of the familiar. The discourse on rights and liberty offered with a surplus of passion and a foreign accent is often met with displeasure since it embarrasses the boundaries of right and left, Western self and Eastern other, and tampers with established worldviews. I remember meeting Iranian writer Azar Nafisi on a panel at which we had to speak about loss and memory somehow representing our respective collective identities. Instead of conforming to our roles as representative spokeswomen of communities imagined by others, we concurred in our nostalgia for our urban cosmopolitan dreams with a distinct local color, hers in Teheran and mine in Leningrad as well as love for the same writers, Nabokov and Arendt, who offered at least an attempt at understanding authoritarianism beyond national borders.

Still, is such cross-cultural imagination only wishful thinking? Can freedom easily circulate across borders and become a common world currency? Should there be a politically and bureaucratically correct "freedom passport" that includes a "nationality line"?

Orlando Patterson, a sociologist and historian of freedom in the Western world, stated that in non-Western civilizations a certain integral conception of freedom that fuses together public, civic, and individual freedoms was not particularly valorized and was often "stillborn."[10] One seemingly universal feature, however, is what Patterson polemically identifies as "absolute freedom," that of a king / emperor / tyrant or authoritarian leader for whom almost everything is permitted. This ancient debate about the cultural values of freedom came to the political forefront in 1993 at the Human Rights Conference in Vienna, at which many Western and non-Western nations were looking forward to signing the Universal Declaration of Human Rights as the new Esperanto after the end of the cold war but were confronted instead with the Bangkok Declaration of Asian values that curiously echoed some (non-Asian) arguments presented by Dostoevsky and Marx a century and a half earlier, now with a new cultural twist. The declaration claimed that freedom was never a universal concept, that it has no root in the Asian societies that have always valued national sovereignty, and that economic development should be considered an equal human right (a paraphrase of Marx, only this time, not in defense of socialism but of a particular brand of capitalism).

But many historians and philosophers have argued that there were indeed many local sources for the discourses and practices of freedom that receive much less attention than the official version of history that equates cultural tradition with the views of the current government. Amartya Sen argued that "Asian" is not a unified category and that there is in fact a classical philosophical, literary, and political tradition of thinking issues of universalism and toleration that runs parallel to the Western tradition and does not support the claim that freedom is a feature of Western exceptionalism.[11] In India there was Emperor Ashoka (c. third century BCE), who championed universal toleration, and Kautilya, who developed a more particularist practical philosophy comparable to that of Aristotle. At the dawn of the European Middle Ages, the poets Rumi and Omar Hayyam in Persia wrote exceptional poetry that possesses many features later associated with the European Renaissance but dates from three centuries or so earlier. In China alone there is a rich variety of native discourses on freedom that run parallel to the Western debates even if we do not witness the same fusion of political, civic, and individual freedoms.[12]

The Bangkok Declaration categorized internal diversity of opinion and any form of dissent as a non-Asian value in spite of historical evidence that reveals the inner plurality of Asian cultures. Moreover the substance of the conception of "Asian values" derives from the Western Marxist critique of civil society and the emphasis on economic rather than legal developments. Usually governments are perfectly happy about the flow of capital but not about the flow of rights and ideas, even when they contribute rather than take away from economic development.

Paradoxically, Western entrepreneurs frequently wish to see a more centralized, or even authoritarian, "Eastern" other because it is presumably easier to do business under such conditions. While appearing like an acknowledgment of the "multipolar world" and pluralism, this could be another form of Western narcissism and justification of contemporary expansion of capitalism without expansion of freedom.

Thus the specter of a fascinating unfreedom is haunting global culture. It remixes many aspects of a legitimate critique of the experience of freedom into a new pop-cultural myth. Like Susan Sontag's conception of fascinating fascism, it aestheticizes power (and defrauds aesthetics). The followers of fascinating unfreedom embrace the eros of power and worship the absolute freedom of VIPs of any kind and nationality. They can also be attracted to the newest variations of the oldest political theologies that promise malignant pleasures and mystical certitude.

Intellectually they are always looking for the latest "post-" and often find a barely forgotten "pre-": trying to understand postcommunism, they embrace imperial nationalism; looking for postenlightenment, they discover neomedievalism; and aspiring for the radiant future, they dwell in a restorative nostalgia, combining the zeal of neophytes and fashionistas with the professional packaging of corporate managers.

Indeed, there might be something outmoded about cultivating a space of freedom that requires what Nietzsche called "unfashionable observations." The space of freedom does not coincide with any national border. The land of Freedonia, as we remember, where the corrupt banks had to be bailed out by the state, was successfully ruled by the Marx Brothers in 1933—another prophetic fiction that reflected and anticipated history. The space of freedom is preserved and reinvented through cocreation. It does not grow automatically. But we know that neither capitalism alone nor technological advances will take care of freedom by itself, glorious promises aside. While openness and interconnectedness of cyberspace is of extreme importance, it too is not entirely transparent. Recently the "invisible hand" of technology became visible in the growing number of political scandals that explode the compromised relationship between the new technology and cultural and political controversies. I refer to the scandals involving Yahoo, Google, and Microsoft, which, while advocating "universal access" and promoting the free flow of speech, have collaborated extensively with foreign governments in both suppressing critical sites but also in providing confidential information that has harmed courageous bloggers. It revealed that the cyberspace shares in the same political architecture as their nonvirtual brothers and sisters. Politics, not technology, was driving their action. It took journalists without borders to question the compromised borders of internet censorship.

Moreover, the most contemporary practices in blogosphere and internet technologies are not opposed to reflective nostalgia. The "slow blogging" that takes time and produces new creative content becomes more fashionable than "tweeting" the soundbites or "friending" hundreds of virtual strangers producing relationships that hardly survive the duration of such sound bites. And the newest versions of Photoshop don't merely allow us to brush out the chancy errors and undesirable records but instead reveal the layers of manipulation of the digital files making us aware once again of the acts of touching and framing—literal and figurative. Once again, the specter of history haunts the ruinscape of the internet.

Technology and freedom are frequently in a double bind and often in contradiction to one another. This relationship depends largely on whether technology is understood as a medium (which can then be mediating the experience of freedom) or whether technology is conceived as an artificial limb without which we are powerless, all-too-human humans. For the lack of freedom cannot be cured with new software.

Freedom is not scientifically verifiable. It operates through "fuzzy logic" that might be more honest for confronting the unforeseen in human life. The logic of passionate thinking, however, is not unrigorous. Only this might be the rigor of a dance, not a diagram.

Is it possible that freedom itself was such an instance of the unforeseen in the process of human evolution? Vladimir Nabokov believed poetically that similar "aberrations" gave us mimicry, play, creativity and imagination (and to his list we can add freedom), that in some extreme situations offered humans the strategies of survival. Rather than as an aberration, I have attempted to think of freedom as an adventure that is both eccentric and central to the human condition, a foreign body that reveals what is uniquely human. The future work of freedom might be that missing painting proposed during the deliberations of the People's Choice project, the painting "that we have never seen before."

Introduction

1. In the view of the political philosopher Michael Sandel there is a particular urgency for this today, when the "fundamentalists rush in where liberals fear to tread." Michael Sandel, *Public Philosophy: Essays on Morality in Politics* (Cambridge, MA: Harvard University Press, 2005), chapter 2 ("Beyond Individualism") and chapter 28 ("Political Liberalism"). This is exactly the space where the quest for the meaning of human life can occur and where tales of freedom have to be told.

2. Michael Kammen, *Spheres of Liberty: Changing Perceptions of Liberty in American Culture* (Madison: University of Wisconsin Press, 1986). Her other attributes are equally contradictory—the scepter, a symbol of self-control, and the cat, a symbol of a lack of restraint. In the eighteenth century, Liberty takes on the eclectic features of classical goddesses, Minerva, Eos, or Artemis, the Virgin Mary (in the French emblem, Marianne), or Mary Magdalene, as well as African and Native American queens. Throughout the book I follow Kammen's view and use the words "freedom" and "liberty" interchangeably in the contemporary context.

3. The first Soviet statue of Liberty built in the early Stalin era was quickly replaced by a more heroic monument to the medieval prince Iuri Dolgoruki, the legendary founder of Moscow. More on the avant-garde statues of liberty in chapter 5.

4. Hannah Arendt, "What Is Freedom?" in *Between Past and Future* (London: Penguin, 1979), 170.

5. Georg Simmel, "The Adventurer," *On Individuality and Social Forms*, ed. Donald Levine (Chicago: University of Chicago Press, 1971), 187–198. Simmel himself fit neither into the German academic establishment of his time nor into contemporary disciplinary systems of thought. Adventure was not only his topic but also an intellectual and existential modus operandi.

6. Simmel, "Adventurer," 193.

7. "It is a foreign body in our existence which is yet somehow connected with the center; the outside, if only by a long and unfamiliar detour, is formally an aspect of the inside." Ibid., 188.

8. Simmel's theory of adventure was at once a critique of the capitalist commodification of daily life but also an alternative to the Marxist conception of the public realm and civil society, and to Weber's and Lukacs's understanding of modernity as disenchantment and transcendental homelessness. In response to the Weberian disenchantment of the modern world enforced by the bureaucratic world of states and corporations, adventure promises reenchantment in a minor existential key.

9. Albert Camus, *The Rebel: An Essay on Man in Revolt* (New York: Vintage International, 1960), 295, emphasis in the original.

10. Arendt, "What Is Freedom?" 143–173.

11. Is it possible that in light of the early twenty-first-century terrorist attacks, wars, destruction, and disasters, we might ask, have we ever been postmodern? Or was that "post-" after all premature just like the proclamation of the "end of history"?

12. Amartya Kumar Sen, *Development as Freedom* (Oxford: Oxford University Press, 1999).

13. Arendt, *The Human Condition* (Chicago: University of Chicago Press, 1957), 53. I discuss the differences between the Heideggerian and Arendtian conceptions of the "world" in chapter 4.

14. Ibid.

15. Arendt made the distinction in one of her public conversations: "People who believe that the world is mortal and they themselves are immortal are very dangerous characters because we want the stability and good order of *this* world." *Hannah Arendt and the Recovery of the Public World*, ed. Melvyn Hill (New York: St. Martin's Press, 1979), 311. See also Kenneth Frampton, "The Status of Man and the Status of His Objects: A Reading of *The Human Condition*," in *Labor, Work, and Architecture: Collected Essays on Architecture and Design* (London: Phaidon, 2002).

16. Aristotle compared philosophical reflection and judging with building. In his view, not all things can be determined by law, which does not mean that they don't use their own measures: "Where a thing is indefinite, the rule by which it is measured is also indefinite as the leaden rule used in Lesbian construction work. Just as this rule is not rigid but shifts with the contour of the stone, so a decree is adapted to a given situation." Aristotle, *Nichomachean Ethics* (Englewood Cliffs: Prentice Hall, 1962), 142. The molding on buildings on the island of Lesbos had a famous "undulating curve" accommodating beautiful irregularities of the stone. Lesbian construction work mastered the art of matching irregularities, and Aristotle reminds us that this was "a kind of equity" and justice, not a deviation from it.

17. Orlando Patterson, *Freedom in the Making of Western Culture*, vol. 1 (New York: Basic Books, 1991), 37.

18. On the original conception of "corrupted sacrifice," see Froma I. Zeitlin, "The Motif of the Corrupted Sacrifice in Aeschylus' Oresteia," in *Transactions and Proceedings of the American Philological Association* 96 (1965): 463–508.

19. For the creative interpretation of *leudhe* / liberty, see Jean-Luc Nancy, *The Experience of Freedom* (Stanford: Stanford University Press, 1993). It is common among historians to distinguish between the Roman and later European tradition of liberty, which was a republican ideal, and the Anglo-American notion of freedom, which was perceived as noncoercion and noninterference resulting in a later liberal conception of individual freedom as a space outside politics.

20. Greek *nomos*—law—historically concerned drawing boundaries and respecting agreements, building a manmade space. Law can be seen as a response to violence or as a form of repression and prohibition, but it is also a part of collective existential topography. Similarly, economic and libertarian understandings of freedom also come from specific cultural and historical contexts. Adam Smith, the philosopher of the free market, believed in the connections between the wealth of nations, the invisible hand of the marketplace, and "moral sentiments," as did Friedrich Hayek, whose theory of the free market came into being in reaction to the bureaucratic autocracy of the Austro-Hungarian Empire. The public architecture of common memory is crucial in understanding conceptions and practices of freedom. More specific debates on the nature of the public realm and civil society, on private individuals and citizens, on state and the public sphere, are connected to cultural common places.

21. Cosmopolitanism is frequently reproached from a class position as elitist and as indifferent to one's specific surroundings. This accusation goes back to the Marxist critique of the internationalist aspirations of the bourgeoisie. In other words, as the accusation goes, the cosmopolitan citizen is a citizen of no country. Yet cosmopolitan citizenship is not the same as global corporation: it is not about "off-shoring" affection but rather about grounding it in the common world, in a particular place and language, not in a carefully guarded national territory.

22. For a cultural critic, the "world" might appear as an outmoded universalizing concept that does not take into account cultural pluralism. In fact, thinking worldliness does not exclude thinking about plurality within a common aspiration. On contemporary understanding of cosmopolitanism see Anthony Kwame Appiah, *Cosmopolitanism: Ethics in a World of Strangers* (New York: W. W. Norton, 2006); and Homi K. Bhabha, *A Measure of Dwelling: Reflections on Vernacular Cosmopolitanism* (Cambridge, MA: Harvard University Press, 2008).

23. In recent political theory there has been an attempt to offer a more complex understanding of agonism, redefining it as agonistic pluralism in opposition to a simple antagonism that presents the public realm as a battleground of powers, of friends and foes, of those who are with us and those who are against us. The agonistic understanding of the public realm was developed in the twentieth century by the German political thinker (and after Hitler's rise to power, the president of the Union of National Socialist Jurists) Carl Schmitt and by his recent followers, who propose a more subtle discussion of radical democracy and of differences between agonistic and antagonistic public realm and who apply Schmittian conservative political theology to the political philosophy on the left. See Carl Schmitt, *The Concept of the Political*, trans. George D. Schwab (1927, 1932; Chicago: University of Chicago Press, 1996; expanded ed. with an introduction by Tracy B. Strong, 2006). Among the most interesting recent work in this area that elaborates a more nuanced distinction between agonistic and antagonistic public realm (or treats "pluralistic agonism"), see Ernesto Laclau and Chantal Mouffe, in *The Challenge of Carl Schmitt*, ed. Chantal Mouffe (London: Verso, 1999). See also Chantal Mouffe, *Deliberative Democracy or Agonistic Pluralism*, Political Science Series, 72 (Vienna: Institute for the Advanced Studies, 2000). Bonnie Honig develops the agonistic conception, placing it in dialogue with feminism and

multiculturalism in Bonnie Honig, *Democracy and the Foreigner* (Princeton: Princeton University Press, 2001). Proponents of agonistic thinking insist on the perpetuity of conflicts in society and deep divisions that cannot be happily resolved through mere consensus building, rational argument, and institutional practices. Taking conflict seriously, I will contest and deliberate throughout conceptions of the public realm and the space of freedom. Yet such cross-cultural examination also prompts me to reconsider some of the foundations of contemporary agonistic thought. While acutely aware of the need for pluralism, many agonistic thinkers are still deeply indebted to the uncomfortable marriage of the two Carls—Carl Schmitt and Karl Marx—whose respective conceptions of "political theology" and the "leap into the kingdom of freedom" often veered into antiworldliness, *politique du pire*, regarding modern public realm as a masquerade or phantasmagoria, a deceptive spectacle of inauthenticity (chap. 3). I would propose a different genealogy of politics and political action oriented towards freedom and not only liberation

Hannah Arendt is an interesting example of an unconventional thinker who is inspired by the Nietzschean conception of agonism and creativity but not at all by Schmittian "political theology." Rather, in her work she advances the understanding of political action as artistic performance and combines some elements of Greek, Roman, and Enlightenment thought together with modern philosophy and aesthetics. See Dana R. Villa, *Arendt and Heidegger: The Fate of the Political* (Princeton: Princeton University Press, 1996); and Seyla Benhabib, *The Reluctant Modernism of Hannah Arendt* (Landham, MD: Rowman & Littlefield, 2003). I focus on the intertwining of the political and the aesthetic in Arendt's thought in chapters 4–6. I try to follow an alternative, non-Schmittian geneaology of understanding the public realm, worldliness, and violence (chaps. 1, 3, and 6).

24. Johan H. Huizinga, *Homo Ludens: A Study of the Play-Element in Culture* (Boston: Beacon Press, 1955), 3; and Friedrich Schiller, *On the Aesthetic Education of Man*, trans. Reginald Snell (New York: Frederick Ungar, 1965).

25. Yet the political and the aesthetic are never harmoniously reconciled. While the "science" of aesthetics was based on *"sensus communis,"* a shared human ability to self-distance and go beyond individual psyche into the realm of imagination, aesthetic and democratic understandings of the common sense and common good, of the end of life and freedom, have always been accompanied by conflict (chaps. 2, 6).

26. Walter Benjamin, "Short Shadows," in *Selected Writings, Volume 2 (1927–1934)*, trans. Rodney Livingston, ed. Michael W. Jennings, Howard Eiland, and Gary Smith (Cambridge, MA: Harvard University Press, 1999).

27. Hannah Arendt, *Men in Dark Times* (New York: Harcourt Brace Hovanovich, 1968), preface, ix–x, and "Karl Jaspers: Laudatio," 80.

28. Thomas Hobbes, *Leviathan* (London: Harmondsworth, 1980), 3.

29. One of the most famous examples of anamorphism is Hans Holbein's painting of the ambassadors where a skull becomes visible from a certain perspective creating a counterpoint, a memento mori to the celebration of earthly riches.

30. Howard Caygill, *The Art of Judgment* (London: Basic Blackwell, 1989), 20–21. Hobbes was close to the Mersenne circle, which was preoccupied with physical and metaphysical implications of optics, perspective, and illusion making. Catoptics focused on what appeared to be distortions of perspective but were in fact exploring creative possibilities of double vision. This was an early example of phenomenological exploration of "interactive optics."

31. Optics for Hobbes is more important than imagination, which he first defines as "decayed sense" because it engages fancy and reason. In his later work Hobbes celebrates poetry and writes an autobiographical poem to tell the story of his life.

32. Denis Diderot, "Paradox of an Actor," *Selected Writings on Art and Literature*, trans. and with an intro. and notes by Geoffrey Bremner (London: Penguin Books, 1994). This is similar to Jonathan Lear's conception of irony. See Jonathan Lear, *Therapeutic Action: An Earnest Plea for Irony* (Other Press, 2003).

33. Ibid.

34. It is a kind of reverse mimesis: life is like a theater, a gentle epiphany of a "natural actor" who is on the verge of recognizing his own artifice. Diderot offers us a paradoxical and chiasmic encounter: while the man of estrangement and the self-possessed actor becomes overcome with sensibility, or when a "natural man" begins to praise nature for being picturesque and looking like a beautiful landscape. The ironic limits of the dialogue are those moments of "excess" when opposites meet but only through the twisted parabolic peripeteia, creating complex optics and not breaking the glass in a violent fashion. Diderot's dialogues are not merely pedagogical; they offer amusing slices of prerevolutionary life. At one moment Diderot's paradoxicalists-critics decide to go to the theater and become spectators (instead of talkers) but there are no seats left in the theater, so they remain in the theater of life. They talk to each other, talk with themselves, daydream, keep silence, indulge in moments of empathy and feeling and then disavow emotions with humor. Echoing Locke and Hobbes, Diderot makes a direct analogy between the society and the theater: "It is the same with a play as with a well-ordered society, where everyone sacrifices some of his original rights for the good of the whole. Who will best appreciate the extent of this sacrifice? Will it be the enthusiast, the fanatic? Indeed not. In society, it will be the just man, in the theater, the actor who has a cool head." Diderot, "Paradox of an Actor," 114. See Eyal Peretz, "Identification with the Phantom"; book in progress.

35. Tom Gunning, "Illusions Past and Future: The Phantasmagoria and Its Specters," http://www.MediaArtHistory.org, a text for the First International Conference on the Histories of Art, Science and Technology, 2004.

36. Karl Marx, "The Eighteenth Brumaire of Louis Bonaparte" (1852), in Karl Marx and Frederick Engels, *Collected Works*, vol. 11 (New York: International Publishers, 1978), 99–197.

37. Theodor Adorno to Walter Benjamin, letter dated November 10, 1938, in Walter Benjamin, *Selected Writings* (Cambridge, MA: Harvard University Press, 1997), 4: 100–101.

38. Hannah Arendt, *The Life of the Mind*, vol. 1, *Thinking* (New York and London: Harcourt Brace Jovanovich, 1977), 153. "Professional thinkers, whether philosophers or scientists, have not been pleased with freedom and its ineluctable randomness." See the chapter "The Abyss of Freedom and the *novus ordo seclorum*," in *The Life of the Mind*, vol. 2, *Willing*, ed. Mary McCarthy (New York: Harcourt Brace Jovanovich, 1978), and "Willing," 2: 198–199. These concepts are developed throughout Arendt's work; see "Thinking," 1: 5–7.

39. Quoted by Arendt, *Life of the Mind*, 1: 185.

40. Joseph Brodsky, "On the Condition We Call Exile," in *On Grief and Reason: Essays* (New York: Farrar, Straus and Giroux, 1995), 34.

41. Unbeknownst to him, in his tale of transformation of a "freed man" into a "free man," Brodsky recounts the metamorphosis of Greek *eleutheria*.

42. Hannah Arendt, *Lectures on Kant's Political Philosophy*, ed. Ronald Beiner (Chicago: University of Chicago Press, 1982), 79–85. For a discussion of Arendt's theory of judgment, see Ronald Beiner, "Hannah Arendt on Judgment: Interpretative Essay," in *Lectures on Kant's Political Philosophy* (Chicago: University of Chicago Press, 1982), 89–156. For a reference to the "inhuman," see Hannah Arendt, "On Humanity in Dark Times:

Thoughts about Lessing," in *Men in Dark Times* (New York: Harcourt Brace Jovanovich, 1968), 24. Arendt's reading of Kant does not focus on moral imagination and categorical imperative but rather on his *Critique of Judgement* and on the connection between practical and theoretical reason in Kant. Her theory of freedom and judging is linked to Kant's work on the reflective and aesthetic judgment as developed in this volume.

43. Arendt discusses those issues in *The Life of the Mind*, vol. 1, *Thinking*, 98–109. In philosophy the theory of imagination plays an important role in the philosophy of Hume, Kant, Schiller and Shelling and then in the Romantic poetics of Coleridge, Wordsworth and Shelley. See Mary Warnock, *Imagination* (Berkeley and Los Angeles: University of California Press, 1976). I don't follow strictly the distinction between imagination and fancy or between primary and secondary imagination.

44. For a discussion of the banister, see an exchange between Hannah Arendt and Hans Jonas in Melvyn Hill, ed., *Hannah Arendt and the Recovery of the Public World* (New York: St. Martin's Press, 1979), 311–315; and Arendt, "Basic Moral Propositions," in *Lectures 1966*, University of Chicago, Hannah Arendt's Papers, the Manuscript Division, Library of Congress, Washington, DC, container 46, p. 024608. Kant gave at once the most lucid and the most labyrinthine definition of reflective judgment, one that is crucial for Arendt's revisionary theory: "Judgment orients itself according to something both within and without it, something which is neither nature nor freedom, in which the theoretical and practical are bound together in a way that is common but unfamiliar."

45. For the discussion of freedom as social art, see Jean Starobinski, *The Invention of Liberty* (New York: Rizzoli, 1987).

Chapter One

1. Aeschylus, *Prometheus Bound*, in *Aeschylus, 2*, ed. David R. Slavitt and Smith Palmer Bovie (Philadelphia: University of Pennsylvania Press), 166.

2. "The tragic poets make use of this legal vocabulary, deliberately exploiting its ambiguities, its fluctuations and its incompleteness." Jean-Pierre Vernant and Pierre Vidal-Naquet, "The Historical Moment of Tragedy in Greece," in *Myth and Tragedy in Ancient Greece*, ed. Jean-Pierre Vernant and Pierre Vidal-Naquet (New York: Zone Books, 1990), 25. The tragic action "is a kind of wager on the future, on fate and on oneself." Jean-Pierre Vernant and Pierre Vidal-Naquet, "Tensions and Ambiguities in Greek Tragedy," in *Myth and Tragedy in Ancient Greece*, 44, also idem, "The Myth of Prometheus in Hesiod," in *Myth and Society in Ancient Greece* (New York: Zone Books, 1990).

3. While my tentative distinction of two models of freedom is exemplified by two immortal males, in fact the mortal female heroines are the exemplary freedom fighters, so to speak, who challenge and impersonate principles both Promethean and Dionysian. As has been shown in many studies, Antigone, Electra, and Clytemnestra take this stance, while the Bacchae and Pentheus's mother, Agave, will enact the Dionysian liberation and its consequences. *Women in the Ancient World: The Arethusa Papers*, ed. John Peradotto and J. P. Sullivan (Albany: State University of New York Press, 1984); Judith Butler, *Antigone's Claim: Kinship between Life and Death* (New York: Columbia University Press, 2000); George Steiner, *Antigones: The Antigone Myth in Western Literature, Art and Thought* (Oxford: Clarendon Press, 1986); Eva Cantarella, *Pandora's Daughters: The Role and Status of Women in Greek and Roman Antiquity* (Baltimore: Johns Hopkins University Press, 1987).

4. "At the opening of the play we see Prometheus hanging on the verge of the abyss, atop the rock with nothing more to lose but his chains. Dionysus, too, trades on the verges

and borders; he is an itinerant god of no place and of every place." Jean-Pierre Vernant, *The Universe, the Gods and Men: Ancient Greek Myths* (New York: HarperCollins, 2001), 135.

5. F. E. Peters, *Greek Philosophical Terms: A Historical Lexicon* (New York: New York University Press, 1967).

6. Aeschylus, *Prometheus Bound*, 173.

7. Fire is overwrought with cultural symbolism, from immortality, to domestic hearth, to explosive sexuality. There are interesting ambiguities in the symbolism of the Zeusian thunderbolt. See Gregory Nagy, *Greek Mythology and Poetics* (Ithaca: Cornell University Press, 1990), and idem, *Poetry as Performance: Homer and Beyond* (Cambridge: Cambridge University Press, 1996).

8. Zeus will "match" Prometheus's gift to the humans, offering them a beautifully clad and perfumed female creature, Pandora, who would marry Prometheus's brother Epimetheus and who carries with her a "Pandora's box" of ills and vices that would be spread around the world, with only hope remaining in the bottomless box.

9. Émile Durkheim examined the ambiguity of the idea of the sacred. In various religious beliefs around the world, the pure and impure are not diametrically opposed to one another, but rather exist on a continuum that are equally embedded in communal practices. Émile Durkheim, *The Elementary Forms of the Religious Life* (New York: Free Press, 1965).

10. "The Prometheus of Aeschylus is a Dionysian mask," 72, in Friedrich Nietzsche, *The Birth of Tragedy*, in *The Birth of Tragedy and The Case of Wagner*, trans. Walter Kaufman (New York: Vintage: 1967), 15–147.

11. Vernant and Vidal-Naquet, "Tensions and Ambiguities in Greek Tragedy," 44. The word "drama" comes from the Doric *dran*, which corresponds to the Attic *prattein*, "to act."

12. Euripides, *Bacchae*, trans. William Arrowsmith, in *Euripides V*, ed. David Grene and Richmond Lattimore, Complete Greek Tragedies (Chicago: University of Chicago Press, 1968).

13. Peter Euben, "Membership and 'Dismembership' in the *Bacchae*," in *The Tragedy of Political Theory: The Road Not Taken* (Princeton: Princeton University Press, 1990), 131. Euben quotes from Charles Balestri, "The Bacchae," in *Homer to Brecht: The European Epic and Dramatic Tradition*, ed. Michael Seidel and Edward Mendelson (New Haven: Yale University Press, 1977), 211. For the most comprehensive and insightful analysis of the tragedy, see Charles Segal, *Dionysiac Poetics and Euripides' Bacchae* (Princeton: Princeton University Press, 1997). See also Martha Nussbaum, *The Fragility of Goodness: Luck and Ethics in Greek Tragedy and Philosophy* (New York: Cambridge University Press, 1986).

14. Semele, the mortal mother of Dionysus, was Europa's niece, daughter of the foreigner Cadmus. Cadmus in turn was the brother of the itinerant Asian maiden Europa, who came to Greece from the Middle East. Having married divine Harmonia, Cadmus, the founder of Thebes, tried to reconcile the native "warriors of the soil," the *Spartoi*, with the foreigners, the humans, and the divines, but harmony did not reign in the city of Thebes. Yet we see that Thebes, like most great cities, was founded by foreigners and populated by immigrants who intermixed with the natives.

15. Dionysian trance is not achieved through asceticism and solitude; monastic mysticism is quite different from the sylvan orgy of the *thiasos*. Jean-Pierre Vernant warned against a Christianized interpretation of the Dionysian mystical liberation, stressing the this-worldliness of his mysteries: "The undeniable desire to be free, to escape into elsewhere, is expressed not as a hope for another happier life after death but within the present life, through the experience of extra dimension, an expansion of the human condition,

which thereby accedes to the blessed otherness." Vernant, "The Masked Dionysus of
Euripides' *Bacchae*," in *Myth and Tragedy in Ancient Greece*, 388. "Otherness" refers to the
culture of the polis.

16. In "Masked Dionysus of Euripides' *Bacchae*," 381–412, Vernant demonstrates how
Mania and *Sophia* interplay in tragedy and how there is more mania in Pentheus's supposed "common sense" than meets the eye.

17. Segal, *Dionysiac Poetics and Euripides' Bacchae*, 50.

18. Euripides, *Bacchae*, 168.

19. Vernant and Vidal-Naquet, "Tensions and Ambiguities in Greek Tragedy," 37.

20. Aristotle, *De arte poetica liber*, ed. Rudolf Kassel (Oxford: Clarendon, 1965). For
the *Nicomachean Ethics*, see the Oxford translation by W. D. Rose ([S.I.]: Oxford Univer-
sity Press, 1925). A good bibliography and commentary is given in Aristotle, *Poetics; of
Aristotle*, introduction, commentary and appendixes by D. W. Lucas (Oxford: Claren-
don, 1968). An intellectual history of the conception of catharsis can be found in Teddy
Brunius, *Inspiration and Katharsis: The Interpretation of Aristotle's "The Poetics" VI, 1449 b 26*
(Uppsala: Almqvist & Wiksell, 1966). For the interpretation of M. D. Petrusevski, see *Ziva
Antika = Antiquité Vivante* [Skopje] 4, no. 2 (1954). A detailed summary is given in French.
Petrusevski's arguments are partly derived from Heinrich Otte, *Kennt Aristoteles die soge-
nannte tragische Katharsis?* (Berlin: Weidmann, 1912).

21. David Hume, "Of Tragedy," in *Four Dissertations* (1757), discussed in Teddy Brunius,
Dictionary of the History of Ideas: Studies of Selected Pivotal Ideas, 5 vols., gen. ed. Philip P. Wie-
ner (New York: [n.p.], 1973–1974), in idem, *Inspiration and Katharsis*; and in Lev Vygotsky,
"Art as Catharsis," in *The Psychology of Art* (Cambridge, MA: MIT Press, 1971), 215.

22. Vygotsky, "Art as Catharsis," 215.

23. The argument for the thesis is rather detailed. First of all, there are different readings of the manuscripts. Instead of *pathematon* there is an alternative reading of *math-
ematon*, which is nonsensical. Second, there is the ambiguous wording in the definition
of tragedy, which is against Aristotle's rules of definition. Third, there is a switch from
objective to subjective qualifications, which is also against Aristotle's rules of definition.
Fourth, there is a commentary in the *Poetics* on the different parts of the definition, but
catharsis is not included. Petrusevski has identified these words as *pragmaton systasin*, and
the meaning is then that tragedy involves pity and fear in the actions that are brought
together. These words are commented on by Aristotle in the later chapters of the *Poetics*.
The explanation of a misreading is that Aristotle's writings were damaged and then edited
by copyists who made the emendation because they had read in the *Politics* that Aristotle
intended to explain catharsis in the *Poetics*. But in the definition he did not use the word
"catharsis." In fact, according to Petrusevski, there is no tragic catharsis, only a musical
one. For an interesting contemporary attempt to rethink the relationship between catharsis and deliberation, see Alan Singer, *Aesthetic Reason: Artworks and the Deliberative Ethos*
(University Park: Pennsylvania State University Press, 2003).

24. Aby M. Warburg, *Images from the Region of the Pueblo Indians of North America*, trans.
with an interpretive essay by Michael P. Steinberg (Ithaca: Cornell University Press, 1996),
107. I am grateful to Michael Steinberg for introducing me to this text by Warburg. See
also Philippe-Alain Michaud, *Aby Warburg et l'image en mouvement* (Paris: Macula, 1998), in
English, *Aby Warburg and the Image in Motion*, trans. by Sophie Hawkes, preface by Georges
Didi-Huberman (Cambridge, MA: MIT Press), 332. See also Georges Didi-Huberman,
L'Image survivante: Histoire de l'art et temps des fantômes selon Aby Warburg (Paris: Éditions de
minuit, 2002).

25. Warburg, *Images from the Region of the Pueblo Indians of North America*. The lecture, entitled "Images from the Region of Pueblo Indians of North America," was delivered brilliantly and received most enthusiastically, only to disappear among his papers until 1988.

26. Georges Didi-Huberman and Michael Steinberg spoke about Warburg's fascination for Nietzsche and, specifically, his work on tragedy. Instead of Apollonian and Dionysian, I propose to look at Warburg through Promethean and Dionysian, which avoids the either/or approach: either the discussion of beauty (and what Warburg called "aestheticizing art history") or the discussion of symptomatic violence of representation to the "third space," what Warburg called "the interval," to trace creative self-liberation, violence, and chaos. On a different approach to the iconology of the interval, see Giorgio Agamben, *Potentialities: Collected Essays in Philosophy*, trans. Daniel Heller-Roazen (Stanford: Stanford University Press, 1999).

27. Warburg, *Images from the Region of the Pueblo Indians of North America*, quotations on 38.

28. Jacques Derrida, *Dissemination*, trans. Barbara E. Johnson (Chicago: University of Chicago Press, 1983).

29. Warburg, *Images from the Region of the Pueblo Indians of North America*, 17.

30. Aby Warburg, *The Renewal of Pagan Antiquity: Contributions to the Cultural History of the European Renaissance*, intro. by Kurt W. Forster, trans. David Britt (Los Angeles: Getty Research Institute for the History of Art and Humanities, 1999), 41.

31. Steinberg, "Interpretative Essay," 108–109.

32. Warburg, *Images from the Region of the Pueblo Indians of North America*, 54.

33. Didi-Huberman also talks about "pathic thinking" but without the reference to Hannah Arendt's "passionate thinking." In his insightful description, pathic thinking includes prehension and comprehension. *L'Image survivante*.

34. While we see many parallelisms between Warburg's search for the "iconology of the interval" and Walter Benjamin's "dialectic at a standstill," there is also a significant difference. Benjamin looked for crystallizations of the ambivalence and occasionally for the tragic cleavage; Warburg tries to delineate the fragile modern space where ambivalences can be preserved. My reading is informed by Giorgio Agamben's essay but ultimately I arrive at a different conclusion: Warburg is not about messianic abyss and radical cleavage but about a fragile space where Goethe and Nietzsche can sympathetically cohabit. There is no space for such humanistic ambiguity in Agamben's world.

35. Franz Kafka, in *The Complete Stories*, trans. Willa and Edwin Muir, ed. Nahum N. Glatzer (New York: Schocken Books, 1971), 432. I modified the translation to better reflect Kafka's original. The English translation of the two German words has been adjusted to better preserve Kafka's linguistic networks; thus *grund* is rendered as "substratum" instead of "ground," which loses connection with the "groundless affair" and *erklaren* is translated as "to explain," which doesn't keep association with light and enlightenment. Kafka's other parable in Arendt's interpretation will be discussed in chapter 5.

36. One of the Stalinist marches—"We were born to make fairy tales come true"—was rewritten several decades later by an anonymous Soviet writer in a humorous fashion: "We were born to make Kafka come true."

37. Osip Mandelstam: *50 Poems*, trans. Bernard Meares and with an intro. by Joseph Brodsky (New York: Persea Books, 1977).

38. One expression in Russian, "emu chto ni kazn'—to malina," has puzzled translators because the word "malina," literally, raspberries, is "blatnoi" or criminal slang.

39. Nadezhda Mandelshtam, *Hope Against Hope*, trans. Max Hayward (New York, 1970), 203.

40. One may remember that the building of the Hotel Moscow had different, asymmetrical windows because Stalin signed two versions of the project, and nobody dared to ask him a second time which one he meant.

41. Hannah Arendt, *The Origins of Totalitarianism* (1958; New York: Harcourt, Brace Jovanovich: 1969), 466. Similarly, in his essay "Moscow" (1927), Walter Benjamin made a striking observation about the collapse of the distinction between the public and private sphere in Soviet Russia. He noted that Bolsheviks had abolished private life and closed the cafes where pre-revolutionary artistic life had flourished. Walter Benjamin, "Moscow," in *Reflections* (New York: Schocken Books, 1986), 124–136.

42. Arendt, *Origins of Totalitarianism*, 465–466.

43. Sadly, there is a revealing topos in Soviet culture of the 1930s: the conversation with Stalin, which worked its seductive power even on such independent minds as Boris Pasternak and Mikhail Bulgakov. Intimacy with terror became the central paradigm of Russian-Soviet culture.

44. J. M Coetzee, "Osip Mandelstam and the Stalin Ode," *Representations* 35 (Summer 1991): 72–83.

45. N. Mandelstam, *Hope Against Hope*, 200.

46. Vladimir Nabokov, *Speak, Memory* (New York: Vintage, 1978).

47. Mandelstam, *50 Poems*, 90. I have slightly modified the translation to bring it closer to Mandelshtam's original.

Chapter Two

1. Mikhail Bakhtin, "Problema soderzhaniia, materiala i formy v slovesnom khudo-zhestvennom tvorchestve," in *Estetika slovesnogo tvorchestva* (Moscow: Iskusstvo, 1979), 25. The English translation is by Caryl Emerson and Gary Saul Morson in *Mikhail Bakhtin: Creation of a Prosaics* (Stanford: Stanford University Press, 1990), 51. In their work on Bakhtin, Emerson and Morson offer a passionate defense for the potentials of such unfinalizable cultural dialogues: "For any culture contains meanings that it itself doesn't know, that it itself has not realized; they are there as potential . . . the process of dialogue may itself create new potentials, realizable only through future activity and dialogue" (55).

2. Alexis de Tocqueville, *Democracy in America* (New York: Alfred Knopf, 1994), 434. *Democracy in America* was translated into Russian in 1861 in Kiev. See S. F. Starr, *Decentralization and Self-Government in Russia, 1830–1870* (Princeton: Princeton University Press, 1972), 71–90.

3. A closer linguistic examination reveals that *svoboda* and *volia* are uncanny doubles of one another. According to the Vasmer *Etymological Dictionary*, *svoboda* is a derivative from *sloboda*, referring originally to a town/neighborhood of escaped serfs. In this sense it is quite similar to the history of the Western concept of liberty. In the later nationalist version of the etymology of *svoboda* supported by some contemporary Russian philosophers, *svoboda* goes back to Sanskrit and Indo-European roots and is defined as "our" [i.e., Russian] community, in opposition to the Western polis of "liberal values." Max Vasmer, *Etimologicheskii slovar' russkogo iazyka* (Moscow: Progress, 1971), 3: 582–583 (in the original, *Russisches etymologisches Wörterbuch* [Heidelberg, 1950–1958]). *Volia* is connected to the common Indo-European roots of *will* (English) and *volonté* (French) and refers both to a feeling of joyful, ecstatic and transgressive liberation, but also to a specific political practice of granting freedom to serfs in the Russian empire (Vasmer, *Etimologicheskii slovar' russkogo*

iazyka, 1: 347–348). Russian proverbs—the resource of the insightfully realistic and definitively unromantic voice of the Russian people—are silent about *svoboda* but are eloquently ambivalent about freewheeling *volia*, which brings bitter fate ("vol'naia volia, gor'kaia dolia"). For the proverbs, see *Poslovitsy i pogovorki Russkogo naroda* (Moscow: Siuita, 1996).

4. George Fedotov, *Rossiia i svoboda: Sbornik statei* (New York: Chalidze, 1981), 174.

5. Fedotov, *Rossiia i svoboda: Sbornik statei*, 183. In his other work, Fedotov also examines the Russian religious mind and the dimensions of spiritual freedom. A historical investigation into the Russian conception of freedom must confront cultural mythologies, legal / political / historical documents and actual social practices.

6. Fedotov, *Rossiia i svoboda*, 174.

7. Moreover, according to Fedotov, there was more space for freedom in Russia under Mongol occupation than during the subsequent reign of Muscovy, which consolidated the centralization of Russian lands under Ivan the Terrible.

8. Here great literature flourished under the conditions of despotism, countering the remark of Tocqueville's admirer, John Stuart Mill, that only democracy produces geniuses.

9. Pushkin was killed in a duel with the Frenchman Baron George D'Antes, who supposedly courted the poet's wife.

10. Alexander Pushkin, "From Pindemonte," translated by Walter Arndt in *Pushkin Threefold; Narrative, Lyric, Polemic, and Ribald Verse* (New York: Dutton, 1972), 256–257. I have slightly modified the translation to bring it closer to the original.

> Не дорого ценю я громкие права,
> От коих не одна кружится голова.
> Я не ропщу о том, что отказали боги
> Мне в сладкой участи оспоривать налоги
> Или мешать царям друг с другом воевать;
> И мало горя мне, свободно ли печать
> Морочит олухов, иль чуткая цензура
> В журнальных замыслах стесняет балагура.
> Всё это, видите ль, *слова, слова, слова.**
> Иные, лучшие мне дороги права;
> Иная, лучшая потребна мне свобода:
> Зависеть от царя, зависеть от народа —
> Не всё ли нам равно? Бог с ними.
>   Никому
> Отчета не давать, себе лишь самому
> Служить и угождать; для власти, для ливреи
> Не гнуть ни совести, ни помыслов, ни шеи;
> По прихоти своей скитаться здесь и там,
> Дивясь божественным природы красотам,
> И пред созданьями искусств и вдохновенья
> Трепеща радостно в восторгах умиленья.
> — Вот счастье! вот права . . .
>   [* Hamlet—*Прим. Пушкина*].

11. The initial version of the poem included explicit references to the French Revolution: "With the sonorous words Equality and Freedom, as if possessed and drunk, revel the people" (the word *besnovat'sia* is connected to demonic possession or mania). I cite the text according to Pushkin, *Polnoe sobranie sochinenii* (Moscow: Akademiia Nauk SSSR,

1937–1959), 3: 1029. Further references to this edition will be given in abbreviated form, with roman numerals indicating volume number and Arabic numerals, page number. For a discussion of attitudes toward the French Revolution and the philosophy of the Enlightenment in Pushkin's poetry, see Efim Etkind, *Bozhestvennyi glagol: Pushkin, prochitannyi v Rossii i vo Frantsii* (Moscow: Iazyki russkoi kul'tury, 1999), 347–420. See also L. I. Vol'pert, *Pushkin v roli Pushkina* (Moscow: Iazyki russkoi kul'tury, 1998).

12. If in the first part Pushkin uses the rhetoric of persuasion and addresses implied readers in the second-person plural (*vidite*), which then becomes first-person plural (*ni vse li nam ravno*), the second part starts with the emphatic *"nikomu"* (no one) and affirms the license of the poetic self (*sebe lish' samomu*) beyond the conventions of the lyrical first person.

13. The better freedom is designated as "other." In Russian there are two words for "other" (*drugoi* and *inoi*), just as there are two words for "truth." In Pushkin's time, the two words were considered synonymous, yet with slight semantic differences. *Drugoi*, the word used in the translation of Western philosophical texts and the one favored by Mikhail Bakhtin, is related to *drug*, "friend," and originally denotes some form of proximity to the other, either spatial adjacency or temporal sequence. Thus *drugoi* could mean "the next" or "the second," someone close to, rather than different from, oneself. In Russian philosophical thought (apart from Bakhtin, of course), consideration for "the freedom of the other" (J. S. Mill), where the "other" is another individual, is hardly prominent at all. Pushkin uses the word with a stronger connotation of difference and even foreignness. The *Dictionary of Pushkin's Language* lists *inoi* and *drugoi* as synonyms (*Slovar' iazyka Pushkina*, ed. V. V. Vinogradov, 2nd ed. [Moscow: Azbukovnik, 2000]; for *drugoi*, see 1: 735–739; for *inoi*, see. 2: 244–245). However, Dal's dictionary lists different examples and connotations for the two words; see Vladimir Dal', *Tolkovyi slovar' zhivogo velikorusskogo iazyka*, 7th ed. (Moscow: Russkii iazyk, 1978–1980); for *drugoi*, see 1: 1232; for *inoi*, see 2: 103.

14. Alexander Zholkovsky explored the role of infinitive constructions in Russian poetry. See Alexander Zholkovsky, "Schast'e i prava sub specie infinitivi ('Iz Pindemonti' Pushkina')," *Pushkin i ego sovremenniki* 4, no. 43 (2005): 451–473. I am grateful for Alexander Zholkovsky's comments on my lecture at the University of Southern California in April 2003.

15. For the works that set the poem in its literary context, see E. A. Toddes, "K voprosu o kamennoostrovskom tsikle," in *Problemy pushkinovedeniia: Sbornik nauchnykh trudov* (Riga: Latviiskii gos. Universitet im. P. Stuchki, 1983); and Sergei Davydov, "Pushkin's Easter Triptych," in *Pushkin Today*, ed. David Bethea (Bloomington: Indiana University Press, 1993). On the relationship between Pushkin and Alfred Musset, see Boris Tomashevskii, *Pushkin i Frantsiia* (Leningrad: Sovietskii pisatel', 1960). Oleg Proskurin examines the poem by focusing on its intertextual connection to Baratynsky's poem "Hamlet" (Oleg Proskurin, *Poeziia Pushkina ili podvizhnyi palimpsest* [Moscow: NLO, 1999], 262–275). My interpretation of Pushkin's "other freedom" is closer to that of Davydov and Toddes. In my view, attempts to see continuity between Christian preoccupations in "Iz Pindemonti" and Pushkin's "Polkovodets" are suggestive but somewhat forced. A more Christian interpretation of Pushkin's aesthetic quest seems to be in the spirit of Pushkin interpretations of the late 1990s and does not entirely do justice to the contradictions of the poem.

16. Alexander Pushkin, "Elleferiia, pred toboiu" (1821) in Pushkin, *Polnoe sobranie sochinenii*, 2: 176. Since the tsar did not allow Pushkin to travel to the West, he traveled east and south in search of liberty, to the border with Asia—to the gypsies of Moldavia, to the Kalmyks and Cossacks of the Urals, to the Circassians and Georgians of the Caucasus. In *A Journey to Arzrum* (1829), Pushkin encounters a Turkish pasha who greets him as a

"master of the universe": "[T]he poet is the brother of the dervish (*poet brat dervishu*), he has neither motherland nor earthly goods . . . he is equal to the master of the universe." Pushkin, *Polnoe sobranie sochinenii*, 8: 475. It seems that the image of the free poet anticipates the discourse on the "other freedom" in Pushkin. The poet no longer held such a status in the West, but it still survived east of the Russian border.

17. Alexander Pushkin to P. Ia. Chaadaev, letter dated January 19, 1836, in *Pis'ma poslednikh let: 1834–1837*, ed. N. V. Izmailov (Leningrad: Nauka, 1969). See also Natan Eidelman, "Pushkin i Chaadaev (poslednee pis'mo)," *Rossija/Russia* 6 (1988): 3–23, quotation on 12. Around the same time, Chaadaev wrote to a friend that Tocqueville had plagiarized him: "U Tokvilia est' glubokaia mysl', kotoruiu on ukral u menia, chto tochka otpravleniia narodov opredeliaet ikh sud'by." P. Ia Chaadaev, *Sochineniia*, annotated by Vera Proskurina (Moscow: Pravda, 1989), 388. Pushkin scholar Alexander Dolinin presents an insightful discussion of one possible source for Pushkin's "From Pindemonte": a poem by Robert Southey, "Inscription for a Monument at Old Sarum," Alexander Dolinin, "Ob odnom istochnike stikhotvoreniia Pushkina 'Iz Pindemonti,'" *Lotmanovskii sbornik*, no. 3 (Moscow: OGI, 2004), 252–260.

18. "S izumleniem uvideli demokratiiu vo ee otvratitel'nom tsinizme, v ee zhestokikh predrassudkakh, v ee nesterpimom tiranstve . . . Takova kartina Amerikanskikh shtatov, nedavno vystavlennaia pered nami," Pushkin, *Polnoe sobranie sochinenii*, 12: 104 ("Dzhon Tenner"). At the end of this essay, after recounting the adventures of John Tanner, Pushkin meditates on the permeable boundaries between civilization and barbarism and pokes fun at his perfect "Yankee" John Tanner, who lives in a slave-owning society and who may join the ranks of the Prohibitionists. (In Pushkin's usage, "Yankee" is a synonym for "American" and does not denote an inhabitant of the U.S. North.) Pushkin appears to suggest that democracy in America itself is a form of barbarism masquerading as civilization. This, of course, is a common topos of early Enlightenment self-critique, known in the French philosophical tradition from Diderot to the Marquis de Sade.

19. This is in the tradition of bucolic poetry of the eighteenth century (Pindemonte being one of its lesser-known examples), Stoic writings, and German and French Romantic poetry from Schiller to Alphonse de Lamartine. Schiller's *On the Aesthetic Education of Man* offers a model of freedom as play and mediation between political, artistic and social life. I see some implicit similarities between this notion and the one proposed by Pushkin.

20. Pushkin both suffered from and was inspired by censorship; in his two "epistles to the censor" (the first one written in the same poetic form as the poem "From Pindemonte") he claims that he is not on principle opposed to censorship: "Chto nuzhno Londonu, to rano dlia Moskvy" (What is needed in London is too early for Moscow), referring explicitly to political rights. Pushkin, "Poslanie tsenzoru" (1822), in *Polnoe sobranie sochinenii*, 2: 237.

21. Pushkin, "Puteshestvie iz Moskvy v Peterburg," in Pushkin, *Polnoe sobranie sochinenii*, 11: 238. Earlier in this passage Pushkin formulates his notion of writers as an "aristocracy of talent" (11: 236) more influential than aristocrats, whose power depends on wealth or family.

22. The younger Pushkin offered a critique of serfdom in his poem "The Village" ("Derevnia") 1819, which did not, however, get him into trouble with the emperor, and he spoke in radical fashion about its place in Russian history. However, by the 1830s his position had shifted and was much closer to a more conservative historian Karamzin than to Radishchev. In the estates that he inherited from his father, the practice was that of a

more "progressive" quitrent (*obrok*), not the more brutal form of serfdom, *barshchina*. I am grateful to Professor William Mills Todd III for his insights on this matter.

23. Jean Charles Leonard de Sismondi, *Historical View of the Literature of the South of Europe*, trans. Thomas Roscoe (London: Henry G. Bohn, 1853), 2: 70.

24. The poem is quoted in Italian in Sismondi, *Historical View of the Literature*, 71. See also Ippolito Pindemonte, *Le prose e poesie Campestri del Cavaliere Pindemonte* (Verona: Mainardi, 1817).

25. I am grateful to Professor Lino Pertile for his observations on Pindemonte and Antonio Gramsci in his presentation at the roundtable "Literature and Fascism" at the Minda de Gunzburg Center for European Studies, Harvard University, March 3, 2005.

26. Michael Holquist, "Corrupt Originals: The Paradox of Censorship," *PMLA* 109, no. 1 (1994): 14–25.

27. The political theorist George Armstrong Kelly coined an interesting term, "Parnassian liberalism," or the liberalism of disgust, in reference to Flaubert. Perhaps we can find some of this, if not in Pushkin, then in the later practitioners of Hamletian poetics. See George Armstrong Kelly, *The Humane Comedy: Constant, Tocqueville, and French Liberalism* (Cambridge: Cambridge University Press, 1992).

28. Tocqueville believed that the Southern states with their tradition of slavery had little in common with the Northern states, and while an advocate of the Northern political institutions, he was indifferent to the cause of the American Union. See Larry Siedentop, *Tocqueville* (Oxford: Oxford University Press, 1994); Alan Ryan, introduction to Alexis de Tocqueville, *Democracy in America* (New York: Alfred Knopf, 1994); Alan Ryan, ed., *The Idea of Freedom: Essays in Honour of Isaiah Berlin* (Oxford: Oxford University Press, 1979); and Irena Gruzniska Gross, *The Scar of Revolution: Custine, Tocqueville, and the Romantic Imagination* (Berkeley: University of California Press, 1991).

29. Tocqueville, *Democracy in America*, 1: 7.

30. Tocqueville himself practiced the art of freedom in his writing but also considered his texts to be political acts, not merely forms of self-expression of an individual genius. The text preserves the author's irony but never displays a blasé cynicism; it also reflects the ambivalences of the "new political science" that mediates between hopes and fears, ideals and actual daily reality, the political and the social realm, law and religion. Tocqueville, like Pushkin, wrote poetry in his youth (obviously much less distinguished than the Russian poet's), and his writing and thinking remained poetic, infused with imagination, irony, and wonder.

31. Isaiah Berlin, *Russian Thinkers* (London: Penguin, 1978), 88.

32. Tocqueville, *Democracy in America*, 1: 334.

33. I am grateful to Alexander Dolinin for bringing this to my attention.

34. Tocqueville, *Democracy in America*, 2: 98.

35. Tocqueville, *Democracy in America*, 1: ch. 15, 263.

36. Tocqueville, *Democracy in America*, 2: ch. 1, 5.

37. Tocqueville, *Democracy in America*, 2: ch. 1, 7.

38. Tocqueville writes that were Americans to lose liberty, they would miss it more as a custom, as the daily business of democracy, and less as an ideal. For Americans, then, freedom is perceived not as a distant ideal, a goddess, or a hope for the future. It exists in the present, in the eternal present of the American democracy.

39. I am grateful to Caryl Emerson for her comments on my Christian Gauss Lecture, March 3, 2003.

40. Moreover, unpublished for ten years, Akhmatova was able to reappear in the So-
viet press in the 1930s as a translator of Pushkin . . . not from the mythical Italian but from
French into Russian. For detailed accounts of the encounter, see Isaiah Berlin, "Conversa-
tions with Akhmatova and Pasternak (1980)," in *The Proper Study of Mankind* (New York:
Farrar, Straus and Giroux, 1997), 525–553; György Dalos, *The Guest from the Future: Anna
Akhmatova and Isaiah Berlin* (New York: Farrar, Strauss and Giroux, 1996); and Michael
Ignatieff, *Isaiah Berlin: A Life* (New York: Henry Holt, 1998). Most recent research in
Russia contests some aspects of Berlin's account of the encounter and shows that both
he and Akhmatova were under NKVD surveillance, which in the end they managed to
evade. See L. Kopyleva, T. Pozdniakova, and N. Popova, *I eto bylo tak (And Thus It Was):
Akhmatova and Berlin* (St. Petersburg: Akhmatova Museum, 2009). I am grateful to Olga
Voronina for sharing this with me.

41. Anna Akhmatova, *Stikhotvoreniia i poemy* (Leningrad, Sovetskii pisatel', 1976), 354.

42. Andrei Zhdanov, "Doklad na sobranii partiinogo aktiva i na sobranii pisatelei v
Leningrade" *Pravda*, no. 225, September 21, 1946.

43. Osip Mandelshtam, "O sobesednike," in *Sobranie sochinenii v chetyrekh tomakh*
(Moscow: Art-Business Center, 1993), 1: 182–188. See also Svetlana Boym, "Dialogue as
'Lyrical Hermaphroditism': Mandelstam's Challenge to Bakhtin," *Slavic Review* 50, no. 1
(1991): 118–126.

44. There is an entire tradition in Russian letters of the negative love affair, from
Alexander Pushkin's poem "No, it's not you that I love so passionately" (Net, ne tebia tak
pylko ia liubliu) to Marina Tsvetaeva's "I like it that you aren't love-sick with me" (Mne
nravitsia, chto vy bol'ny ne mnoi) to Evgenii Evtushenko, "Here is what happens to me,
not the right woman comes to me" (So mnoiu vot chto proiskhodit, sovsem ne ta ko mne
prikhodit).

45. Joseph Brodsky, "Isaiah Berlin at Eighty," in *New York Review of Books*, 17 August
1989, 44–45.

46. Ignatieff, *Isaiah Berlin: A Life*, 161.

47. Both agree on Tolstoy's moralism and authoritarianism. Twentieth-century
authors like Kafka, who offer the most creative descriptions of the radical dehumanization
of the individual, do not interest Berlin, who instead sees twentieth-century politics and
art as a continuation of nineteenth-century trends.

48. Akhmatova, "Est' v blizosti liudei" (1915), "There is in the intimacy of two people"
(Est' v blizosti liudej zavetnaia cherta, ee ne perejti vliublennosti i strasti," Akhmatova,
Stikhotvoreniia i poemy, 91.

49. Berlin, *Russian Thinkers*. In his review of John Stuart Mill, Herzen echoes Pushkin's
reading of Tocqueville and reacts passionately against both the tyranny of majority in
the present and the shining ideal of radical liberation in the future for which the present
ought to be sacrificed.

50. At the same time, he does not go so far as to speak of the incompatibility of democracy and genius, as Tocqueville did.

51. "Isaiah Berlin in Conversation with Steven Lukes," in *Salmagundi* 120 (Fall 1998):
52–135, quotation on 93.

52. "No zhivogo i naiavu / Slyshish' ty, kak tebia zovu / I tu dver', chto ty
priotkryl / Mne zaxlopnut' ne xvatit sil." Akhmatova, *Stikhotvoreniia i poemy*, 236.

53. Alekhander Etkind, preface to Isaiah Berlin, *Istoriia svobody: Rossiia* (Moscow:
NLO, 2001).

54. Isaiah Berlin, "Two Concepts of Liberty," 130n, in *Four Essays on Liberty* (Oxford: Oxford University Press, 1969).

55. Isaiah Berlin, "Vissarion Belinsky," in *Russian Thinkers* (London: Penguin, 1978), 159–160. Inspired by Etkind's work, I do not concur with Etkind's observation that Berlin's concept of negative freedom is connected to Pushkin's inner freedom (Aleksander Etkind, *Tolkovanie puteshestvii / Rossiia i Amerika v travelogakh i intertekstakh* [Moscow: Novoe Literaturnoe Obozrenie, 2001], 47). Indeed, both were interested in Benjamin Constant, but Berlin took certain political rights for granted and did not always feel the need to spell them out, while Pushkin in his later years began to disavow the political dimension of liberty altogether. Moreover, for Berlin, the Stoic conception of inner freedom is a part of "positive freedom."

56. Berlin, "Two Concepts of Liberty," 135.

57. Berlin, "Political Ideas in the Twentieth Century," in *Four Essays on Liberty*, 40.

Chapter Three

1. Friedrich Engels, "Progress of Social Reform on the Continent," first published in *New Moral World*, vol. 19, 4 November 1843, in Karl Marx and Frederick Engels, *Collected Works*, vol. 3 (New York: International Publishers, 1975), 392–408, quotation on 393.

2. Fyodor Dostoevsky, *Winter Notes on Summer Impressions*, trans. David Patterson (Evanston, IL: Northwestern University Press, 1988), 48–49. The comparison between Dostoevsky and Marx is discussed in Andrzej Walicki, *The Slavophile Controversy* (Notre Dame, IN: University of Notre Dame Press, 1989), 548–549. For an interesting comparison of Dostoevsky and Marx, see his *Marxism and the Leap to the Kingdom of Freedom: The Rise and Fall of the Communist Utopia* (Stanford: Stanford University Press, 1995).

3. Mikhail Bakhtin, *Problemy poetiki Dostoevskogo* (Problems in Dostoevsky's Poetics) (Moscow: Sovetskaia Rossiia, 1979), 294.

4. Mikhail Bakhtin, *Toward a Philosophy of the Act*, trans. by Michael Holquist and Vadim Liapunov, University of Texas Press Slavic, 10 (Austin: University of Texas Press, 1993), 139. "*Architechtonics*—as a focused and indispensable, non-arbitrary distribution and linkage of concrete, singular parts and aspects into a finished whole—is possible only around a given person as a hero." Discussed in *Rethinking Bakhtin: Extensions and Challenges*, ed. Gary Saul Morson and Caryl Emerson (Evanston, IL: Northwestern University Press, 1989), 22.

5. Hannah Arendt, "Lecture Notes on *The Possessed*," in *Essays on Art and Culture*, ed. Susannah Young-Ah Gottlieb (Stanford: Stanford University Press, 2007), 280.

6. Mikhail Bakhtin, *Problemy poetiki Dostoevskogo*, 6. "Like Goethe's Prometheus he [Dostoevsky] creates free people, not voiceless slaves, capable of standing next to their creator and not agreeing with him."

7. Fyodor Dostoevsky, *Memoirs from the House of the Dead*, trans. Jessie Coulson (Oxford and New York: Oxford University Press, 1983), 80, 359; referred to in text by a more literal translation of the title, *Notes from the House of the Dead*. Translation is slightly modified to be closer to the Russian original.

8. Dostoevsky, *Memoirs from the House of the Dead*, 8.

9. Ibid., 21.

10. Ibid., 16.

11. Ibid., 13.

12. Ibid., 328.

13. Ibid., 237.

14. Leonid Grossman, *Dostoevsky: A Biography* (New York: Bobbs-Merrill Company, Inc., 1975); Nancy Ruttenburg, *Dostoevsky's Democracy* (Princeton: Princeton University Press, 2008), and idem, "Dostoevsky's Estrangement," *Poetics Today* 26, no. 4 (2005): 719–751.

15. Dostoevsky, *Memoirs from the House of the Dead*, 80. In this text, Dostoevsky makes a rare reference to the Marquis de Sade, "the gentleman of the old days," whose enjoyment of flogging his victims was both "sweet and painful." Dostoevksy offers a deep insight into the despotic nature of corporal punishment and the insidious connection between the executioner and his victim.

16. Arguably the prisoner's melancholia here is not only a Freudian neurosis but also a utopian affliction in the classical conception of melancholia offered by the seventeenth-century philosopher Robert Burton in his *Anatomy of Melancholy*. It is a part of longing for a better world but also an intoxication with one's own suffering.

17. Dostoevsky, *Memoirs from the House of the Dead*, 359.

18. Dostoevsky, *Winter Notes on Summer Impressions*, 15.

19. The writer tells us that he was bored on the train to Europe and his mind wandered into superfluous detours. When the mind wanders, it stumbles inevitably upon its obsessions: for him the malignant pleasure of pain and the relationship between Russia and the West. The writer promises to inflict his boredom and his obsessions upon his reader, offering a "superfluous" chapter with a discussion of Russian Europeanism.

20. Gary Saul Morson makes an insightful analysis of the "radically inconsistent and heterogeneous" nature of the diary, in which "irony alternates with contempt for irony, humorless polemics with satires on humorless polemicists, dogmatic ideology with metaliterary play." Gary Saul Morson, *The Boundaries of Genre: Dostoevsky's "Diary of a Writer" and the Traditions of Literary Utopia* (Austin: University of Texas Press, 1981), 6. Morson is right on the mark when he speaks about the silencing of certain more radical tendencies of Dostoevsky's nationalist utopianism, which calls for the ultimate decline of the West and Russia's salvation and redemption of mankind. Morson observes that the way in which Dostoevsky is regarded in contemporary Western criticism as a master psychologist and humanist is a kind of "negative apologetics." At the same time in his analysis of the first chapter of *Winter Notes* he regards Dostoevsky's statements as "a parody of xenophobia in a later chapter," and a form of "metaparody" in the tradition of *Tristam Shandy* (25–26). I think this is a simulacra of parody, which I call later in my chapter "converting irony" that is not open-ended and ambivalent, but on the contrary, seduces and hypnotizes the reader into Dostoevsky's "truth." In other words, this is a technique of persuasion not a technique of reflection, or a quest for understanding. Joseph Frank, introduction to *The Diary of a Writer*, trans. Boris Brasol (Santa Barbara, CA: Peregrine Smith, 1979); and Gary Saul Morson, introduction to *A Writer's Diary*, trans. and annotated by Kenneth Lantz (Evanston, IL: Northwestern University Press, 1993).

21. Dostoevsky recalls a conversation with his contemporary whom he tries to persuade to embrace Russian folk justice.

"Yes, the third gentleman said to me . . . I shall show up somewhere and suddenly at one of their meetings, they'll hand out a communal sentence for me to be flogged. What then?"

"And even if they did," I suddenly wanted to say but didn't because I was afraid to . . . Even if they did, I thought to myself, even if they flogged you, so what? Among professors of aesthetics such turns of affairs. Is that really reason enough to live isolated from the community?

Dostoyevsky, *Winter Notes on Summer Impressions*, 14, translation is slightly modified. Dostoevsky's sarcastic response to his contemporaries' preoccupation with legal reform is to subject themselves instead to the people's justice, even if it involves a good beating.

22. Dostoevsky, *Winter Notes on Summer Impressions*, 20.

23. The writer provides a utopian epilogue to the captain's marriage, in which his aged and no longer–pretty wife sits by his bedside, taking good care of her beloved husband, resigned to his occasional beatings that make her feel loved.

24. Dostoevsky, *Winter Notes on Summer Impressions*, 21.

25. "One day this autumn I picked up one of the most progressive newspapers . . . Headline: 'Remnants of Barbarism Remain.'. . . The story relates that a cab was seen one morning this autumn in Moscow; in the cab sat a drunken matchmaker dressed in ribbons and singing a song. The coachman was also covered with bows, also drunk, also humming some tune! Even the horse was in bows. Only I do not know whether it was drunk too; probably drunk. In her hands the matchmaker paraded a small parcel which she had brought from some newlyweds who had apparently spent a happy night. The parcel, of course, contained a certain undergarment which, among the common people, is usually shown to the parents of the bride the next day. Looking at the matchmaker, the people laughed: a lighthearted item." Ibid., 22–23. In the English translation *rabskaia* is translated as "servile."

26. Michel Foucault, *Discipline and Punish*, quoted from *The Foucault Reader*, ed. Paul Rabinow (New York and London: Pantheon Books, 1984), 172.

27. Ibid., 177.

28. Dostoevsky, *Winter Notes on Summer Impressions*, 68–69.

29. Ibid., 49.

30. For the discussion of these literary predecessors, see Svetlana Boym, *Common Places* (Cambridge, MA: Harvard University Press, 1994).

31. Dostoevsky, *Winter Notes on Summer Impressions*, 61.

32. Dostoevsky, *Winter Notes on Summer Impressions*, 48–49.

33. Dostoevsky stresses that he doesn't seek depersonalization but personality in the highest sense, which only exists in Russia. His is not a traditional Orthodox Christian conception of sacrifice but his own more modern version of the "religion of the people." Incidentally, Russian legal historians since the nineteenth century have noted that there is no word for "individual" in the old Russian codexes of laws and the word "person," *litso*, is used in the instances of the denial of personal dignity and a kind of personal slavery. The notion of theatricality also addresses the question of cultural difference. The other culture often appears more theatrical than one's own. For a discussion of cultural conceptions of self, see Boym, *Common Places*, 80.

34. Baudelaire was influenced by Pierre-Joseph Proudhon, on the left, and de Maistre, on the right, and like Dostoevsky, who became a convert to an unorthodox version of Orthodox Christianity, in his later years Baudelaire was more and more interested in Roman Catholic philosophy and belief. Another similarity: both depict subversive financial transactions. In Dostoevsky's novel, Raskol'nikov kills for money but then gives it away to the suffering prostitute. In Baudelaire's poem "Assommons les pauvres!" (Let's Knock out the Poor!) the urban wanderer gives a fake coin to the homeless man not merely to insult him but to provoke a different form of bondage that threatens the social economy of capitalism.

35. *Selected Letters of Charles Baudelaire: The Conquest of Solitude* (Chicago: University of Chicago Press, 1986), 45.

36. Charles Baudelaire, "The Painter of the Modern Life," in *Selected Writings on Art and Literature*, trans. P. E. Charvet (London: Penguin: 1993), 402.

37. Walter Benjamin, "On Some Motifs in Baudelaire," in *Illuminations*, ed. Hannah Arendt, trans. Harry Zohn (New York: Schocken Books, 1968), 169.

38. Baudelaire is one of the first to find in the experience of the city the different kind of sociability that will be described by Simmel as a peculiar kind of creative lightness that salvages human relations and relations with the material world from bureaucratic or institutional reification and obsolescence.

39. Baudelaire, "The Painter of the Modern Life," 400.

40. Even that most self-reflective and open-minded Russian thinker, Alexander Herzen, saw the model of the democratic individual not in the figure of an urban wanderer but in the middle-class, small-minded family man who thinks only of how to get some soup for his son. This becomes a topos among Russian travelers to the West: laments over a Western lack of spirituality based on first impressions that ignore the inner diversity of other cultures. In his *Winter Notes on Summer Impressions* Dostoevsky follows in the footsteps of Herzen in his accounts of the petit bourgeois paradise.

41. Anna Dostoevskaia, *Vospominaniia* (Moscow: Pravda, 1987), 417.

42. Karl Marx, "The Eighteenth Brumaire of Louis Bonaparte" (1852), in Karl Marx and Frederick Engels, *Collected Works*, vol. 11 (New York: International Publishers, 1978), 99–197, quotation on 103. Marx's phantastmagoria evokes a "world-historical necromancy" conjuring up the ghosts of the dead (106).

43. Ibid., 107–108.

44. Ibid., 105.

45. See also Tom Gunning, "Phantasmagoria and the Manufacturing of Illusions and Wonder: Towards a Cultural Optics of the Cinematic Apparatus," in *Le cinématographe, nouvelle technologie du XXe siècle / The Cinema, a New Technology of the 20th Century*, ed. André Gaudreault, Catherine Russell, and Pierre Véronneau ([Lausanne]: Éditions Payot Lausanne, 2004), 31–44.

46. Walter Benjamin, "Paris, the Capital of the Nineteenth Century," in *Charles Baudelaire: A Lyric Poet in the Era of High Capitalism* (London: Verso, 1989), 170. Comparative readings of Marx and Baudelaire rarely take into account that the very figure of the Baudelairian wanderer and critic of modernity would be extinct in the Marxist ideal kingdom of freedom. However much Benjamin tried to rescue the Baudelairian flaneur from the orthodox Marxist critique of his own time, comparing him at once to the gambler and the worker, he was unable to convince his critics. The flaneur is an in-between figure who does not fit into any specific class, the so-called "fellow travelers" are sometimes more dangerous in Marxist thinking than explicit enemies because they veil and challenge the dual structure of revolutionary combat and the clear friend-enemy distinction.

47. Walter Benjamin, "Some Motifs in Baudelaire," in *Charles Baudelaire*, 122. The breadth of Marx's critique goes beyond the specific regime of Louis Bonaparte. He equates authoritarian bourgeois politics, the corrupt government of France, with the whole project of political liberties and human rights in general. The rule of law and political liberties do not offer a corrective to industrial capitalism but merely dissimulate it.

48. In Marx's observation, bohemians "dress [themselves] in galloned coats with the same caricature of dignity as the high dignitaries of Soulouque." (Similarly, the intelligentsia, to which to some extent all writers and political philosophers themselves belong, is a mere caricature of class.) Marx, "The Eighteenth Brumaire of Louis Bonaparte," 196.

49. Hannah Arendt, *On Revolution* (New York: Viking, 1963), 64.

50. Fyodor Dostoevsky, *Notes from Underground*, trans. Mirra Ginzburg (New York: Bantham, 1974), 6–7.

51. Ibid., 26–27.

52. Curiously, the Underground Man's critique of utilitarianism parallels that of John Stuart Mill, the former utilitarian who himself in "On Liberty" advocates for a liberty that includes individual eccentricity. Temperamentally, of course, the two men could not have been more different. Moreover, the conceptions of the "freedom of the other" and public action is profoundly alien to the Underground Man.

53. Dostoevsky, *Notes from Underground*, 147.

54. Ibid., 151.

55. Discussed in Donald Fanger's introduction to *Notes from Underground*, xxv.

56. Friedrich Nietzsche, *Genealogy of Morals and Ecce Homo*, trans. Walter Kaufmann and R. J. Hollingdale (New York and London: Vintage, 1989), 38, emphasis in the original.

57. Michael-André Bernstein, "The Poetics of Ressentiment, " in *Rethinking Bakhtin: Extensions and Challenges*, ed. Gary Saul Morson and Caryl Emerson (Evanston, IL: Northwestern University Press, 1989), 197–223, quotation on 206. See also *His Bitter Carnival: Ressentiment and the Abject Hero* (Princeton: Princeton University Press, 1992).

58. Bernstein connects the Nietzschean conception of resentment to Freud's discussion of hysteria. In my view, the principle formulated by Nietzsche, "I suffer: it must be somebody's fault," and the need for enemies is more similar to the paranoiac projection discussed by Freud in the case of Schreber. Freud, "The Case of Schreber," *The Standard Edition of the Complete Psychological Works of Sigmund Freud*, ed. James Strachey (London: Hogarth Press, 1968), 14. Paranoia is a form of rational delusion based on the transposition, "I hate them therefore they persecute me." Not all resentment results in such paranoia but the man of resentment has a predisposition for assuring his victim status. Hope and forgiveness, two ways of insuring the preservation of worldliness in Arendt's view, are alien to him. He doesn't forgive anyone and at the same he forgets, and more often than not, forgets his own forgetting. Resentment, *ressentiment*, repeated feeling is also a fear of radical unoriginality and derivativeness, a distinctly modern phenomenon that relies on expectations of newness at all costs. Freedom for the man of resentment is exclusively defined in terms of free will and sovereignty. The first brilliant practitioner of literary and philosophical resentment, Jean-Jacques Rousseau, ended up with the radical free will of the ever-confessing and self-pitying modern individual, on the one hand, and the general will of the premodern community, on the other hand, with little in between. Arendt believed that the equation of freedom with willpower was a philosophical dead end that blinded philosophers to the architecture and experience of freedom. The experience of freedom for Arendt is never sovereign but porous and intersubjective; it takes place on the worldly stage where one can make an appearance and act, judge. In Dostoevsky the space of free will is the underground.

59. *The Confessions of Wanda von Sacher-Masoch* (San Francisco: Re/Search Publications, 1990).

60. Custine cited in Leopold von Sacher-Masoch, *Venus in Furs*, trans. Joachim Neugroschel with an introduction by Larry Wolff (New York: Penguin, 2000), xvi.

61. Larry Wolff, introduction to Sacher-Masoch, *Venus in Furs*, xi.

62. Sacher-Masoch, quoted in Suzanne R. Stewart-Steinberg, *Sublime Surrender: Male Masochism at the Fin-de-siècle* (Ithaca: Cornell University Press), 174. Sacher-Masoch, *Das schwartze Kabinett und, Soziale Schattenbilder: Aud den Memoiren eines österreichischen Polizeibeamten* (Berlin: Verlag das neue Berlin, 235). Sacher-Masoch's personal fantasies included many scenarios of Slavic folklore: he enjoyed playing at being a bear or a bandit

and at the same time their victim, pursued, tied up, and punished. Sacher-Masoch writes that such fantasies of domination are not his personal perversions but common forms of behavior well known among Russians and Germans.

63. Severin's contract with Wanda is much more severe and so is Sacher-Masoch's later contract with his wife, who is clearly more attracted to him as a writer than as a slavish lover.

64. It is significant that the novella's protagonist is a nobleman, in other words, a person of the highest social status who chooses to play a slave to a woman who has fewer political and social rights than he does.

65. Sacher-Masoch, *Venus in Furs*, 114.

66. Sacher-Masoch, *Venus in Furs*, 117.

67. Gilles Deleuze had argued for the separation of masochistic and sadistic symptoms. One could say that masochism is contractual while sadism is institutional. No wonder Sade was interested in the instituting practices of radical libertinage as a right after the French Revolution; masochism dwells in imagination, aesthetics, and drama. It is ultimately about costumes and pretenses, about the drama of inflicting pain in which the "victim" is in fact the author of his own imaginary scenario.

68. Gilles Deleuze, *Masochism: Coldness and Cruelty; Venus in Furs* (New York: Zone Books, 1991).

69. Deleuze follows George Bataille's argument for dissociating Nazi political violence from the Sadian type of violence. In Bataille's view, Sade's discourse of violence is paradoxical because it is essentially that of a victim. "As a general rule, the torturer doesn't use the language of violence exerted by him in the name of the established authority; he uses the language of authority. .The violent man is willing to keep quiet and connives at cheating." "Ought we to conclude," continues Deleuze, "that the language of Masochism [is] equally paradoxical in this instance because the victim speaks the language of the torturer he is to himself, with all the hypocrisy of the torturer?" (17).

70. Bram Dijkstra, *Idols of Perversity: Fantasies of Feminine Evil in Fin-de-Siècle Culture* (New York: Oxford University Press, 1986).

71. Suzanne R. Stewart noted the fragility of Sacher-Masoch's contractual fantasies: "[W]here these limitations are overstepped the consequences are catastrophic. One such transgression is marked by a too literal reading of role playing; another when history enters the picture in the form of real relationship of power." Stewart-Steinberg, *Sublime Surrender*, 200.

72. Ibid., 13.

73. Stewart-Steinberg, *Sublime Surrender*, 193. Freud, "Moses and Monotheism," *The Standard Edition of the Complete Psychological Works of Sigmund Freud*, ed. James Strachey (London: Hogarth Press, 1968), 23: 54.

74. The issue of domination is discussed throughout Zizek's oeuvre. See, for example, Slavoj Zizek, *Looking Awry* (Cambridge: MIT Press, 1991). For a historical contextualization and critique of Zizek's work, see Dominick LaCapra, *History in Transition* (Ithaca: Cornell University Press, 2004).

75. Sergei Nechaev, "Cathecism of the Revolutionary," in *Voices of Terror*, edited by Walter Laqueur (New York: Reed Press, 2005), 71. Translation of the title is slightly modified to correspond to the Russian original.

76. Fyodor Dostoevsky, "One of Contemporary Falsehoods," in *The Diary of a Writer* quoted and discussed in V. A. Tunimanov, "Bezumie i 'vechania velikaia mysl'," in Fyodor Dostoevsky, *Besy* (Leningrad: Lenizdat, 1990), 627.

77. The earliest examples of terror as a strategy of radicalism can be found in the religious sects that professed millennialism and courted death and martyrdom, like the Assassins who appeared in Persia and Syria and were suppressed by the Mongols, and theories of tyranny and tyrannicide go back to ancient Greece and Rome. It is after the French Revolution in Europe and in Russia, in particular, that tactics of terrorism became widespread. In the early nineteenth century the words "freedom" and liberation" are often connected with radical practices, as in the title of the German *Freiheit*, in which Karl Heinzen published his advocacy of the use of individual murder as a revolutionary tactic: "The spirit of freedom will have to familiarize itself with daggers and poison and the good cause will have to study the mysteries of powder and fulminating silver." Laqueur, *Voices of Terror*, 64.

78. Laqueur, *Voices of Terror*, 2. For more on Russian revolutionary movements, see Anna Geifman, *Thou Shalt Kill: Revolutionary Terror in Russia, 1894–1917* (Princeton: Princeton University Press, 1993).

79. Terrorist and other radical practices could not be explained solely by sociological background, social concerns, political needs, or psychological characteristics of particular individuals. In the end they were often more driven by the logic of revolutionary ideology and the survival of the secret revolutionary conspiracy itself, almost a liberation for liberation's sake. They were focused on liberation rather than building a society based on freedoms; individual freedoms and rights were not their principle focus.

80. In imperial Russia many secret societies were infiltrated or even originated by the secret police. Rachkovsky, responsible for the coauthorship of the *Protocols of the Elders of Zion*, began as an informer in the revolutionary organization "People's Liberation" *Narodnaia Volia* (*volia* can be translated as both "Will" and "Liberation"). Informing on or serving in the secret police was not regarded as a stain on a revolutionary's curriculum vitae. The practice continued into the Soviet and post-Soviet period.

81. Laqueur, *Voices of Terror*, 71.

82. Bakunin in Laqueur, *Voices of Terror*, 72.

83. Isaiah Berlin, *Russian Thinkers*, 108.

84. The older comrade explains to his "darling boy" that he had been too infatuated with Jesuitic and Macchiavelian methods, which had led him to erase the distinction between his friends (including Bakunin himself) and enemies. Nechaev's writings, like those of Bakunin, are more about destruction of the present than about a vision of the future.

85. Albert Camus, *The Rebel: Essay on the Man in Revolt* (New York and London: Vintage, 1985). For further discussion of the historical background of Dostoevsky's novel, see Nadine Natov, "Philosophical Subtext in the Novel *The Possessed*," *Actualité de Dostoevskij* (Genoa: Quercia Edizioni, 1982), 21–33, and idem, "The Theme of '*Chantage*' (Blackmail) in *The Possessed*: Art and Reality," in *Dostoevsky Studies* 6 (1985). See also Michel Confino, "Bakunin et Nečaev: Les débuts de la Rupture. Introduction à Deux Lettres Inédites de Michel Bakunin—2 et 9 Juin 1870," *Cahiers du Monde Russe et Soviétique* 7, no. 4 (Oct.–Dec. 1966): 624–696. In Russia, Nechaev and his fellow members from the Russian Revenge society claimed that Ivanov was a traitor to their cause, although absolutely no evidence of Ivanov's connection to the secret police was ever found. His only crime was dissent. Yet no other member of Nechaev's group rebelled against the authoritarian group leader and supported the dissident. It was more like a paranoiac projection: we killed him, therefore he must have been guilty. However, while Nechaev enjoyed wide popularity among revolutionaries for the most part, some more conscientious members of the social-democratic movement like Vera Figner criticized his methods and questioned his influence on the revolutionary movement as such.

86. Fyodor Dostoevsky, *The Possessed*, trans. Constance Garnett (New York: Heinemann, 1956), 351–352 (translation slightly modified for accuracy). I cannot do justice here to this complex novel and will focus on the relationship between Stavrogin and Peter.

87. This scene is a phantasmagoria in quotation marks—since it is a direct allusion to Gogol, both to the play *The Inspector General* and the *Petersburg Tales*, in which many fantastic happenings take place under the uncertain light of a gas lamp. Here, Dostoevsky's sarcasm and conspiratorial imagination sets a very different tone from the focus on the absurd in Gogol.

88. This is complicity through antagonism and negation; Verkhovensky and Stavrogin come into "their own" through their shared dislike of the "other," the Westernizer Karmazinov.

89. Dostoevsky, *The Possessed*, 379.

90. Dostoevsky, *The Possessed*, 382–383.

91. New documents reveal that Dostoevsky might have been or dreamed of being a member of the secret militant core of the otherwise rather restrained Petrushevsky circle. Joseph Frank, *Dostoevsky: The Years of Ordeal, 1850–1859* (Princeton: Princeton University Press, 1983).

92. "Kirilov embodies the idea which belongs to the people: to sacrifice oneself for the truth. In his view, even Karakozov did at the time believe in his truth. To sacrifice oneself, to sacrifice everything for the truth—that is the national trait of the generation. For the problem amounts to no more than the question as to what ought to be considered truth. That is why this novel was written." Quoted in Joseph Frank, *Dostoevsky: The Mantle of the Prophet*, 59.

93. Frank, *Dostoevsky: The Mantle of the Prophet*, 58.

94. Ibid.

95. Joyce Carol Oates, "The Tragic Rites in Dostoevsky's *The Possessed*," in *Contraries: Essays* (New York: Oxford, 1981).

96. This is the same person who was described in *Notes from the House of the Dead* under his actual name, Mirecki.

97. Fyodor Dostoevsky to Mikhail Dostoevsky, letter dated 1854, quoted in the introduction to *Notes from the House of the Dead*, xviii.

98. Yet in the *Notes from the House of the Dead*, the narrator treats such an attitude with some understanding. He claims that Russians in prison never mistreated the Poles, and he also describes that the Poles were friendlier with Isaiah Fomish (the fictional Jewish character in the book) as well as with the Circassians and the Tartars.

99. Fyodor Dostoevsky, *The Diary of a Writer*, trans. Boris Brasol (Salt Lake City: Peregrine Books, 1985), 210, translation slightly modified.

100. Fyodor Dostoevsky, *The Diary of a Writer*, 211

101. The prisoner Mirecki from *Notes from the House of the Dead* was the one who witnessed the flogging of the elderly Ziolkowski who had dared to speak up to the authorities and defined himself as a political prisoner. Witnessing corporal punishment apparently scarred Mirecki for life.

102. Dostoyevsky's letters testify that the conversion was not quite Augustinian, but rather a tortured and prolonged process, yet many Western scholars of Dostoevsky take at face value the writer's later assertion and rewriting of his experiences. It is what makes Dostoevsky more Russian but also what allows the critics to sidestep the writer's extreme political views. For a more in-depth discussion, see Nancy Ruttenburg, *Dostoevsky's Democracy* (Princeton: Princeton University Press, 2008).

103. Many recent scholars, while admiring Bakhtin's theory of dialogical imagination, challenged its applicability to Dostoevsky. See, for example, Harriet Murav's discussion of authority and authoritarianism in Dostoevsky in *Russia's Legal Fictions* (Ann Arbor: University of Michigan Press, 1998).

104. How are we to read the parable of Marei? Nietzsche asks the same question about the Wagnerian Parsifal. "That poor devil and nature boy Parsifal, whom he [Wagner] finally made into a Catholic by such captious means—what? Was this Parsifal meant seriously? For one might be tempted to suppose the reverse, even to desire it—that the Wagnerian Parsifal was intended as a joke, as a kind of epilogue and satyr play with which the tragedian Wagner wanted to take leave of us. . . . Is Wagner's Parsifal his secret laughter of superiority at himself, the triumph of his ultimate artist's freedom and artist's transcendence?" Stewart-Steinberg, *Sublime Surrender*, 92.

105. Lev Shestov, *Dostoevskii i Nitshe (filosofiia tragedii)* (St. Petersburg: Tip. M. M. Stasiulevicha, 1903), translation, *Dostoevsky, Tolstoy, and Nietzsche* ([Athens]: Ohio University Press, 1969).

Chapter Four

1. Hannah Arendt, *The Human Condition* (Chicago: University of Chicago Press, 1958), 242.

2. Søren Kierkegaard, "Diapsalmata," *Either/Or*, part 1, ed. and trans. Howard V. Hong and Edna H. Hong (Princeton: Princeton University Press, 1987), 17–44, quotation on 41 (translation slightly modified).

3. Roland Barthes, *A Lover's Discourse: Fragments*, trans. Richard Howard (New York: Farrar, Straus and Giroux, 1978), 177–178. See Svetlana Boym, "Obscenity of Theory," *Yale Journal of Criticism* 4, no. 2 (1991): 105–128: "Whatever is anachronistic is obscene. As a (modern) divinity, History is repressive, History forbids us to be out of time. Of the past we tolerate only the ruin, the monument, kitsch, what is amusing; we reduce this past to no more than its signature. The lover's sentiment is old-fashioned, but this antiquation cannot even be recuperated as a spectacle."

4. Georg Simmel, "Eros Platonic and Modern," in *On Individuality and Social Forms*, ed. Donald N. Levine (Chicago: University of Chicago Press, 1971), 235–248.

5. Ibid., 242.

6. Ibid.

7. Ibid., 247.

8. Ibid., 246.

9. Individuality for Simmel is neither completely autonomous nor sovereign, but it remains noninstrumentalizable and nontotalizable.

10. Simmel's essay itself has a chiasmic structure—knowledge and love become intertwined and at the end instead of resolution we are left in the interstices. The life experience lies neither in the Platonic nor in the modern conception but can only be experienced "in its own depth," in between and beyond but never transcending them.

11. Georg Simmel, "On Love" in *On Women, Sexuality and Love*, trans. Guy Oaks (New Haven: Yale University Press, 1984), 172.

12. Simmel, *On Women, Sexuality and Love*, 151.

13. When I began thinking about love and freedom, I planned to work on utopian communities in which explicit prohibitions on sexuality and social hierarchies were proclaimed to have been abolished. I started from the Marquis de Sade's order to copulate with strangers from all sides in front of multiple statues of liberties but never to indulge

in love, which is the real prohibition. From there I moved to study Russian radical communities in the United States in the late nineteenth century, where sex was regarded as an important activity to be rationed and discussed during regular public confessions and "self-critiques." But then between the lines of the entire memoirs of Grigory Machtet, who spent time working in the Russian American community in Kansas in the 1880s, I discovered that the most transgressive and imperfect thing he did was visit a Russian neighbor on the prairie and drink some coffee there and possibly engage in unscripted "adultery" with the community leader's wife. This tale of imperfections persuaded me that the experience of two subjects and their many philosophical and existential "adulterations" proved to be, strangely, more controversial and more related to cocreation and adventure of freedom than an experiment in communal living.

14. Kierkegaard, "Diapsalmata," 20, translation occasionally modified.

15. In the philosophical realm the love affair unfolds between three philosophical relationships—to Hegel, Socrates and Schelling (whose lectures Kierkegaard goes to listen to when he breaks the engagement with Regine).

16. Søren Kierkegaard, "The Seducer's Diary," Either/Or, part 1, ed. and trans. Howard V. Hong and Edna H. Hong (Princeton: Princeton University Press, 1987), 301–446, quotation on 360.

17. Ibid., 406.

18. Ibid., 419.

19. Ibid., 425.

20. Ibid., 417.

21. Ibid., 399.

22. Ibid., 445.

23. Ibid., 430.

24. Discussed in Josiah Thompson, Kierkegaard (New York: Alfred A. Knopf, 1973), 114.

25. Søren Kierkegaard, "Journals," August 24, 1849, in A Kierkegaard Anthology, ed. Robert Bretall (Princeton: Princeton University Press, 1962), 17. In her letters Cordelia threw back at him his personal pronouns; no longer as lover's pleas but as curses. Moreover, she rejects his proposal "In a Socratic fashion." In spite of her subordinate social position, youth, and lack of classical education, Irony, a negative freedom, is hers as much as his; or rather it is on the side of the unpredictable that even the most poetic ironist cannot control or repeat. Repetition and reflection battle against reciprocity and the irreversibility of time.

26. Theodor W. Adorno, Kierkegaard: Construction of the Aesthetics, trans. Robert Hullot-Kentor (Minneapolis: University of Minnesota Press, 1989).

27. Kierkegaard, "Diapsalmata," 42.

28. Thompson, Kierkegaard, 113.

29. Adorno discusses the archaic and modern elements of Kierkegaard's interior in Kierkegaard: Construction of the Aesthetics, 43. The image of the theater is central in Kierkegaard and is in opposition to the antitheatrical asceticism and frugal authenticity of his brother's brand of Lutheranism.

30. Thompson, Kierkegaard, 123.

31. Walter Benjamin, "Paris, the Capital of the Nineteenth Century," in Reflections: Essays, Aphorisms, Autobiographical Writings (New York: Harcourt Brace Jovanovich, 1978), 154–155.

32. Søren Kierkegaard, "Silhouettes," in Either/Or, 173, translation modified. The word in Danish is skyggerids, literally "shadow outline." I prefer the term "shadowgraphy" used in other Kierkegaard translations.

33. Søren Kierkegaard, "Journals" (July 18, 1840), in *A Kierkegaard Anthology*, ed. Robert Bretall (Princeton: Princeton University Press, 1946), 12.

34. Ibid., 12.

35. Quoted and discussed in Walter Lowrie, "Editor's Introduction," to Søren Kierkegaard, *Repetition: An Essay in Experimental Psychology* (New York and London: Harper and Row, 1964), 11–12.

36. Peter Fenves, *"Chatter": Language and History in Kierkegaard* (Stanford: Stanford University Press, 1993).

37. His negative view of the press might in part be explained by his own unfortunate experience in the literary public sphere. He was ridiculed on the pages of the satirical journal *Corsair*, and this caricatured view of him as a local eccentric translated directly into his everyday life. Cartoons played on Kierkegaard's physical appearance and idiosyncrasies, his literary practices of pseudonyms and constant self-refashioning. Copenhagen was a relatively small city, and the ridicule on the pages of the magazine translated into ridicule on the city streets.

38. For a discussion of pseudonomy in Kierkegaard, see Stephen Crites, "Pseudony-mous Authorship as Art and as Act," in *Kierkegaard: A Collection of Critical Essays*, ed. Josiah Thompson (Garden City, NY: Anchor Books, 1972).

39. While thinking about the title "either / or," Kierkegaard toyed with the Latin *aut / aut*, which suggests an identical repetition even though he proclaims the need for radical difference, choice, and renunciation.

40. Kierkegaard, "Diapsalmata," 22.

41. Kierkegaard, "The Seducer's Diary," 404.

42. Louis Mackey, "The View from Pisgah: A Reading of *Fear and Trembling*," in *Kierkegaard: A Collection of Critical Essays*, 422.

43. *Søren Kierkegaard's Journals and Papers*, entry 2223, 1853, ed. Howard V. Hong and Edna H. Hong (Bloomington: Indiana University Press, 1970), 2: 508–509.

44. *Søren Kierkegaard's Journals and Papers*, entry 2224 (1854), 2: 509.

45. *Søren Kierkegaard's Journals and Papers*, entry 2221, 2: 506.

46. Kierkegaard, "Journals," quoted in *A Kierkegaard Anthology*, xxvi.

47. Martin Heidegger to Hannah Arendt, letter dated February 10, 1925, in *Hannah Arendt and Martin Heidegger: Letters, 1925–1975*, ed. Ursula Ludz, trans. Andrew Shields (New York: Harcourt Inc., 2004), 4.

48. Elisabeth Young-Bruehl, *Hannah Arendt, for Love of the World* (New Haven: Yale University Press, 1982), 49. For an in-depth discussion of the philosophical relationship between Arendt and Heidegger, see Dana R. Villa, *Arendt and Heidegger: The Fate of the Political* (Princeton: Princeton University Press, 1996).

49. Heidegger to Arendt, letter dated February 10, 1925, in *Hannah Arendt and Martin Heidegger: Letters*, 4.

50. For the discussion of Saint Augustine, see Heidegger to Arendt, letter dated May 29, 1925, in *Hannah Arendt and Martin Heidegger: Letters*, 23. Researchers have been unable to find its exact location. No wonder, it requires a different kind of thesaurus—that of the discourse of secret lovers. But what does "I love you: I want you to be" mean in the lovers' context? Does it mean I want you to be the way I love you, or "I want you just the way you are," à la the pop song? What kind of landscape do the lovers cohabit?

51. Heidegger to Arendt, letter dated April 24, 1925, in *Hannah Arendt and Martin Heidegger: Letters*, 17. Most of the letters were preserved thanks to Arendt, who kept Heidegger's letters and his poems to her in the desk drawer in her bedroom. He did not

preserve her letters, supposedly, according to his son, because of their agreement to destroy them.

52. For Heidegger the metaphor for their relationship is "the flash of light": "In the rare abruptness, Being's flash of light / We peer, protect—turn towards the sight." Quoted in the foreword to *Hannah Arendt and Martin Heidegger: Letters*, viii. My focus is primarily on Arendt's poetic and philosophical transformation of their common lovers' language.

53. Heidegger to Arendt, from letter dated May 13, 1925, in *Hannah Arendt and Martin Heidegger: Letters*, 21.

54. Heidegger's masterpiece, *Being and Time*, which was inspired—by his own admission—by his love for Arendt, does not develop any theory of love, but it reflects on the care for being and develops a theory of mood.

55. Heidegger to Arendt, letter from winter 1932–1933, in *Hannah Arendt and Martin Heidegger: Letters*, 52–53.

56. Heidegger to Arendt, letter dated May 21, 1925, in *Hannah Arendt and Martin Heidegger: Letters*, 9.

57. Heidegger to Arendt, letter dated September 14, 1950 in *Hannah Arendt and Martin Heidegger: Letters*, 93–94.

58. Hannah Arendt, *Rahel Varnhagen: The Life of a Jewess* (New York: Harcourt, Brace Jovanovich, 1974), 21. A newer edition with an excellent introduction by Liliane Weissberg is Hannah Arendt, *Rahel Varnhagen: The Life of a Jewess*, ed. Liliane Weissberg, trans. Richard and Clara Winston (Baltimore: John Hopkins University Press, 1997).

59. Arendt, *Rahel Varnhagen: The Life of a Jewess*.

60. Ibid., 11.

61. Ibid., 173.

62. Ibid., 227

63. Ibid., 227.

64. Ibid., 229.

65. Ibid., 212.

66. Karl Jaspers to Arendt, letter dated August 23, 1952, in *Hannah Arendt / Karl Jaspers Correspondence, 1926–1969*, ed. Lotte Kohler and Hans Saner, trans. Robert and Rita Kimber (New York: Harcourt Brace Jovanovich, 1992), 192–193. In the 1950s, Karl Jaspers, Hannah Arendt's former dissertation advisor and close friend, personified for her a new postwar Germany. She thought of him as a keeper of German and European dignity. Jaspers who had miraculously survived in Germany during the war with his Jewish wife Gerthrud (at one point they contemplated joint suicide if she was arrested), cut connections with Heidegger over his Nazi collaboration and especially over Heidegger's refusal to communicate with Jaspers during the war and his postwar silence. Jaspers also didn't like Arendt's discussion of anti-Semitism and believes that Arendt would have treated Rahel differently "after Heinrich [Blüher, her husband] [had] come into her life." But the issue of anti-Semitism occupies an important part in Arendt's reflection on modernity, and it cannot be reduced to personal circumstances. See also Hannah Arendt, "Karl Jaspers: Citizen of the World?" in *Men in Dark Times* (New York: Harcourt Brace and World, 1968), 81–95.

67. Jaspers to Arendt, letter dated August 23, 1952, in *Hannah Arendt / Karl Jaspers Correspondence, 1926–1969*, 193.

68. Arendt to Jaspers, letter dated September 7, 1952, in *Hannah Arendt / Karl Jaspers Correspondence, 1926–1969*, 197. Reading Arendt's response, one understands Jaspers's touching, almost parental, worry about her and his warning that she might be misunderstood in the light of the public and that her strong opinions, combined with personal

fragility, will be misjudged—as if foreseeing the Eichmann controversy ten years later. This stubbornness might betray her unconventional "Zionism by grace of Goethe."

69. Young-Bruehl, *Hannah Arendt, for Love of the World*, 246.

70. Anson Rabinbach discusses the opportunistic circumstances in the publication of Heidegger's "Letter on Humanism" (1946), which enraged Jaspers. Heidegger, who previously had despised Marxism, now included praise for Marxism in order to appeal to the French left, which had indeed embraced Heidegger's philosophy. This was largely due to its philosophical insight and the bridge that it offered from existentialism to the philosophy of language that became prominent after the war. However, the particular circumstances of its publication also reveal that elements of fashionable antihumanism, anti-Americanism, and an opportunistic invocation of Marx—whom Heidegger otherwise loved to hate—also contributed to Heidegger's new acceptance in the academic world and the silencing of his political past. Anson Rabinbach, *In the Shadow of Catastrophe: German Intellectuals between Apocalypse and Enlightenment* (Berkeley: University of California Press, 2001).

71. The new poem entitled "The Girl from Abroad" employs the images from their correspondence from sixteen years earlier, as if they still existed in the lovers' time out of time:

> The stranger even to yourself she is:
> a mountain of joy, sea of sorrow.
> Desert of desire. Dawn of arrival.
> Stranger: home of the one gaze where world begins.
> Beginning is sacrifice.
> Sacrifice is loyalty's hearth
> still outglowing all the fires ashes and igniting: embers of charity.
> Shine of silence. Stranger from abroad, you—may live in beginning.

Heidegger to Arendt, poems undated probably from 1950, in *Hannah Arendt and Martin Heidegger: Letters*, 63.

72. Arendt to Jaspers, letter dated September 29, 1949, in *Hannah Arendt / Karl Jaspers Correspondence, 1926–1969*, 142.

73. *Denktagebuch* entry by Hannah Arendt (handwritten), July 1953 from Hannah Arendt, *Denktagenbuch, 1950 bis 1973*, ed. Ursula Ludz and Ingeborg Nordmann, in cooperation with Hannah Arendt Institute, Dresden, 2 vols. (Munich and Zurich: Piper, 2002). For an English translation, see *Hannah Arendt and Martin Heidegger: Letters*, 304–305.

74. Alfred Denker, *Historical Dictionary of Heidegger's Philosophy* (Lanham, MD: Scarecrow Press, 2000), 28.

75. Martin Heidegger, "Building, Dwelling, Thinking," in *Poetry, Language, Thought*, trans. Albert Hofstader (New York: Harper & Row, 1971), 147.

76. The parable of Heidegger the Fox bears an uncanny resemblance to Kafka's parable of the law in its structure:

> Before the Law stands a doorkeeper. To this doorkeeper there comes a man from the country and prays for admittance to the Law. But the doorkeeper says that he cannot grant admittance at the moment. The man thinks it over and then asks if he will be allowed in later. "It is possible," says the doorkeeper, "but not at the moment." Since the gate stands open, as usual, and the doorkeeper steps to one side, the man stoops to peer through the gateway into the interior. Observing that, the doorkeeper laughs and says: "If you are so drawn to it, just try to go in despite my veto. But take note: I am powerful. And I am only the least of the doorkeepers.

Kafka, "Before the Law." The strange thing here is that "the man from the country" is naïve, while Heidegger is a smart fox yet one that lacks cunning. See also Benjamin's essays "Franz Kafka" and "Some Reflections on Kafka," in *Illuminations*; and Arendt's own essay on Kafka and discussion of Kafka's parables in *Between Past and Future*, discussed in chapters 1 and 5.

There is, of course, a crucial difference. Heidegger the Fox is not merely a powerless little man from the country, he also thinks himself as the guardian of the law with his long Tatar beard, and as a philosophical priest who can explain all the parables. He sets a unique trap / home for himself alone. Like the man from the country, Heidegger doesn't know whether darkness comes from the outside world or from inside himself, and he tends to blame the outside world. In Kafka's and in Arendt's parables, the open architecture is transformed into a closure, into a self-imposed underground or prohibition. The man from the country stoops to peer through the gateway of the law, no longer free in his own world. It is unclear if he is deceived or is deceiving himself.

77. Arendt to Heidegger, letter dated February, 27, 1967, in *Hannah Arendt and Martin Heidegger: Letters*, 135. In response to her demand, he offered her two poems.

78. Ibid., 135.

79. Here between the lines Arendt argues against Adorno's appropriation of Benjamin. Indeed, personal relationships sometimes clouded poetic analysis even among the most antibiographical readers. For Benjamin's essays on modernity, see "Paris, the Capital of the Nineteenth Century," and "Some Motifs in Baudelaire," discussed above.

80. *Hannah Arendt / Karl Jaspers Correspondence, 1926–1969*, 457.

81. Hannah Arendt, "Karl Jaspers: Laudatio," in *Men in Dark Times*, 80.

82. Arendt, *Men in Dark Times*, preface, ix–x.

83. Arendt, "Bertolt Brecht: 1898–1956," in *Men in Dark Times*, 207.

84. Arendt refers to the following fragment from Mallarmé's prose poem and poetic manifesto, "Crise de vers": "Languages are imperfect in that although there are many, the supreme one is lacking: to think is to write without accessories, or whispering, but since the immortal word is still tacit, the diversity of tongues on the earth keeps everyone from uttering the word(s) which would otherwise, in one unique (strike), render truth itself in its materiality . . . Only, we must realize, poetry would not exist; philosophically, verse makes up for what languages lack, completely superior as it is." In French, see Stéphane Mallarmé, "Crise de vers," in *Oeuvres completes* (Paris: Gallimard, 1945), 363–364.

85. What they all share is the belief that "philosophically, the verse makes up for what languages lack," that poetry is superior to ordinary language and reverses the relationship between nearness and distance. The more difficult the verse's syntax, the more multiple and evocative its vocabulary, the closer it might come to poetic truth and to poetic freedom. Ultimately, in Mallarmé, freedom expresses itself through aesthetic reason and play. Such freedom is not crippled by the lack of access to the single mystical truth but rather enabled and made alive by such inaccessibility. "Crise de vers" is Mallarmé's poetic manifesto in which he abdicates the Romantic myth of the poet and a creation of life as a work of art. This text was resurrected by the French poststructuralists and treated as the theoretical declaration of the "death of the author." What matters is not the biographical self but the "pure work" that in Mallarmé's words implies "the disappearance of the poet as speaker, yielding his initiative to words," which light up with "reciprocal reflections." Reciprocal reflections of words produce luminous effects and echoes. For a discussion of Mallarmé's poetic revolution and modern mythology, see Svetlana Boym, *Death in Quotation Marks: Cultural Myths of the Modern Poet* (Cambridge, MA: Harvard University Press, 1991).

86. Stéphane Mallarmé, "Crise de vers," 364.

87. Jacques Derrida, *The Politics of Friendship*, trans. George Collins (London and New York: Verso, 2005), 57.

88. Hannah Arendt "Heidegger at Eighty," in *Hannah Arendt and Martin Heidegger: Letters*, 152. The text of the radio address was recorded in New York on September 25, 1969. There are slight differences between the spoken and printed versions. This quotation is from the version that Arendt sent to Heidegger in the letter dated September 26, 1969.

89. Ibid., 159.

90. Yet, "it is finally a matter of indifference where the storms of their centuries may blow them. For the storm that runs through Heidegger's thought—like the one that after millennia, still blows toward us out of Plato's work—does not come from the century. It comes from the ancient, and what it leaves behind is something consummate that like anything consummate, reverts to the ancient." Arendt, "Martin Heidegger at Eighty," 162. See Dana R. Villa, *Politics, Philosophy, Terror: Essays on the Thought of Hannah Arendt* (Princeton: Princeton University Press, 1999). In her address, Arendt values the act of thinking more than what is thought. Such a conception of thinking would occupy her in *The Life of the Mind*.

91. Arendt, "Heidegger at Eighty," 162.

92. Benjamin, "Theses on the Philosophy of History," in *Illuminations*, trans. Harry Zohn (New York: Schocken Books: 1969), 257–258.

93. Arendt, "Heidegger at Eighty," 152. This is a storm of history with apocalyptic connotations; only Benjamin's angel remained a modern painting, not the ancient Greek temple used as an exemplary art work by Heidegger.

94. Arendt, "Isak Dinesen," in *Men in Dark Times*, 109.

95. Heidegger to Arendt, letter dated March 1950, in *Hannah Arendt and Martin Heidegger: Letters*, 67.

96. Heidegger to Arendt, letter dated May 16, 1950, in *Hannah Arendt and Martin Heidegger: Letters*, 89.

97. Unlike Benjamin, Arendt is not concerned with the messianic "final judgment" but rather with the ability to judge and the process of judging. In his "Interpretative Essay" in Hannah Arendt, *Lectures on Kant*, Ronald Beiner connects Benjamin's flaneur to Arendt's conception of passionate thinking. These issues will be further discussed in chapter 6 below.

Chapter Five

1. The original conception of individuality doesn't come from ideas of autonomy but from the idea of a right to dissent. It is not by chance that one of the central philosophical texts, John Stuart Mill's "On Liberty," offers a defense of eccentricity against the tyranny of the majority; yet such eccentricity is never a transgression of the freedom of the other. The notions of the political defense of minorities and of eccentricity of behavior and beliefs alike are more central to the thinking of individuality than free trade and economy.

2. Andrei Siniavsky, "Dissidentstvo kak lichnyi opyt" (Dissidence as Personal Experience), *Sintaksis* 15 (1986): 131–147, quotation on 141.

3. The formulation is from Walter Benjamin, "The Work of Art in the Age of Its Technological Reproducibility" (1939), in *Selected Writings*, vol. 4, 1938–1940 (Cambridge, MA: Harvard University Press, 2003), 251–284. Benjamin spoke about the fascist "aesthetization of politics." He had in mind this model of a grand "total work" of art that destroys

the sphere of political action by turning it into state-sponsored spectacle. What is more problematic is his notion of the "politicization of art" in the Soviet context, which he seems to celebrate here. However, in "The Author as a Producer" Benjamin shows how such conception would ban the estrangement and flaneurie that he embraces. I would argue that Benjamin's essay "Moscow" may offer a more complex perspective on those two alternatives, neither of which really appealed to Benjamin himself.

4. The statue of Alexander III was erected by the sculptor Paolo Trubetskoi in 1909 on Znamensky Square near the Nicholas Station, now Vosstaniia Square.

5. Victor Shklovsky, *Khod Konia* (The Knight's Move) (Moscow and Berlin: Gelikon, 1923), 196–197; see Jurif Striedter, *Structure, Evolution and Value: Russian Formalism and Czech Structuralism* (Cambridge, MA: Harvard University Press, 1989). Later "Formalist" became a form of insult and Shklovsky was forced to denounce the errors of Formalism. See Svetlana Boym, "Politics and Poetics of Estrangement: Victor Shklovsky and Hannah Arendt," in *Poetics Today* 26, no. 4 (Winter 2005): 581–613. Volumes 26–27 of *Poetics Today*, which I co-edited with Meir Sternberg, are dedicated to the revision of the conception of estrangement.

6. This ludic architecture can be compared to the baroque figure of anamorphosis which I use in my collage at the introduction to the chapter. As in Hans Holbein's famous painting *The Ambassadors* (1533), it reveals the skulls and "skeletons" in the closet of the revolution, which are represented here by the dangerous games of street kids trying to escape from revolutionary reeducation.

7. Richard Sheldon, "Victor Shklovsky and the Device of Ostensible Surrender," in Victor Shklovsky, *Third Factory*, ed. and trans. Richard Sheldon (1926; Ann Arbor: Ardis, 1977), vii; and A. P. Chudakov, "Dva pervykh desiatiletiia," in Victor Shklovsky, *Gamburgskii schet. Stat'i, vospominaniia, esse, 1914–1933*, ed. Aleksandr Galushkin and Aleksandr Chudakov (Moscow: Sovetskii pisatel', 1990), 17.

8. *Stran-* is the root of the Russian word for country, *strana*, and the word for strange, *strannyi*, its Latin and Slavic roots superimposing upon one another, creating a wealth of poetic associations and false etymologies.

9. Victor Shklovsky, "Art as Technique," *Four Formalist Essays*, ed. and trans. Lee T. Lemon and Marion J. Reis (1917; Lincoln: University of Nebraska Press, 1965), 3–24.

10. To some extent, the theory of estrangement depends on the demonization of *byt*, which is perceived in Russian culture as the monster of everyday routine, opposed to the poetic and spiritual *bytie*; for a discussion of *byt*, see Svetlana Boym, *Common Places: Mythologies of Everyday Life in Russia* (Cambridge, MA: Harvard University Press, 1994).

11. From the very beginning, Shklovsky's *ostranenie* is defined differently than "alienation," the latter usually translated by the Russian term *otchuzhdenie*.

12. In "Art as Technique" Shklovsky examines Tolstoy's descriptions of theater as examples of estrangement; in his later work he speaks of the importance of the trope of "parabasis" that was frequently employed in German Romantic theater to lay bare and play with theatrical illusions.

13. See Shklovsky, *Gamburgskii schet*, 118–119.

14. The technique of estrangement differs from scientific distance and objectification; estrangement does not seek to provide the "Archimedean point" from which to observe humanity. Kafka suggested in one of his parables that humanity found the Archimedean point but used it for its own destruction. In the *Life of the Mind* Arendt identified this search for the position outside the human world as a major philosophical problem with many forms of scientific knowledge.

15. In his essays on the phenomenology of art, Hegel also speaks about freedom and alienation as well as art's particular role in mediating between different realms of existence. In a discussion of Dutch paintings, he calls art a "mockery" of reality, a form of irony. These ideas are close to those of the Formalists, yet Shklovsky by no means embraces the larger frame of the Hegelian system. In his later work, Shklovsky engages directly with Hegelian theories of literature. Speaking of Don Quixote, for example, Shklovsky (in *O teorii prozy* [1925; Moscow: Sovetskii pisatel', 1983], 370) observes that Hegel was not interested in "Don Quixote but in Don Quixotism," disregarding the particular strangeness of art. "In the words of Hegel there is no movement. Hegel had an impression that he sees everything from the hindsight of eternity, including the imperial police." The Brechtian V-effect can be read as a creative reinterpretation of Hegel.

16. See Cristina Vatulescu, *Police Aesthetics: Literature, Film and Secret Police in Soviet Time* (Stanford: Stanford University Press, 2010). In his first revolutionary exercise in literary criticism, "The Resurrection of the Word" (1914) Shklovsky describes the ornamental and nonfunctional arches of the nearby historicist eclectic building on Nevsky Prospect. Shklovsky's own imagined architecture of freedom came to be represented not by the functionalism of the international style, but rather by the poetic function shaped by the knight's move and Lobachevskian parallelisms.

17. See Vladimir Nabokov, *Lectures on Russian Literature* (New York: Harcourt Brace Jovanovich, 1981), 58.

18. See Shklovsky, *Khod Konia*, 9–10. Nabokov used the figure of the knight for his first English-language novel, *The Real Life of Sebastian Knight*. In his *Speak, Memory* (New York: Putnam, 1966), Nabokov tells the story of leaving Russia on a ship called *Hope*; not suspecting the finality of this departure, young Vladimir played chess with his father, moving the knight across the board as the ship zigzagged out of the harbor. Shklovsky shares with Nabokov and Saussure an affection for chess.

19. The genre of Shklovsky's writing in the early 1920s is also exemplarily modernist. The Formalists and the members of LEF (Levy Front Isskustva [Left Front for the Arts]) advocated the denovelization of prose, estrangement of plot and the exploration of new everyday genres of the literary public sphere: the newspaper feuilleton, the sketch (*ocherk*), the anecdote, and the document in order to produce "the literature of facts." See Victor Shklovsky, "K tekhnike vne-siuzhetnoi prozy," in *Literatura Fakta*, ed. Nikolai Chuzhak (Moscow: Federatsiia, 1929), 222–227. Yet Shklovsky's own practice of *ocherk* and *literatura fakta* harks back to Charles Baudelaire's conception of the sketch of the "painter of modern life" who represents the present (discussed in chap. 3 above). Another curious parallelism: when Walter Benjamin traveled to Moscow in the winter of 1926–1927, he refused to offer any "theory" about the Soviet experience, claiming enigmatically in a letter to Martin Buber that in Moscow "all factuality is already theory" and that the role of the critic is to collect those "facts" of the fleeting present in the land of the future (Benjamin's letters to Martin Buber and Jula Radl published in *Moscow Diary*, ed. Gary Smith, trans. Richard Sieburth [Cambridge, MA: Harvard University Press, 1986]). "Fact" does not refer to a positivistic notion of fact, but rather to *literatura fakta*, close to the German tradition of the new objectivity (*die neue Sachlichkeit*). While capturing the materiality of daily existence, those "facts" in the writings of both Shklovsky and Benjamin always hover on the brink of allegory; the closer to material existence they are, the more "auratic" and aphoristic they become, thus defamiliarizing both the notion of the document and the discourse of ideology. The unity of such denovelized prose is held together by the storyteller, not by the subject matter.

20. Nikolai Punin, *Pamiatnik Tret'emu Internatsionalu* (Petrograd: Otdel IZO Narkomprossa, 1921), 2. For a detailed discussion of Tatlin's tower, see Svetlana Boym, *Architecture of the Off-Modern* (New York: Princeton Architectural Press, 2008).

21. El Lissitzky, "Basic Premises, Interrelationships between the Arts, the New City, and Ideological Superstructure," in *Bolshevik Visions*, ed. William G. Rosenberg (Ann Arbor: University of Michigan Press, 1990), 2: 188. The project in Khosabad was actually a ziggurat, a pyramidal structure with a flat top that most likely corresponded to the mythical shape of the Tower of Babel, which was itself modeled on the ziggurat at Babylon, called Etemenenanki. See John Elderfield, "The Line of Free Men: Tatlin's "Towers" and the Age of Invention," *Studio International* 178, no. 916 (Nov. 1969): 165. Elderfield also compares the form of the spiral to the "figura serpentina" in baroque architecture. See Julia Vaingurt, "Wonderlands of the Russian Avant-Garde: Art and Technology in the 1920s," Ph.D. diss., Harvard University, 2005.

22. Roland Barthes, "The Eiffel Tower," in *The Eiffel Tower and Other Mythologies* (New York: Noonday Press, 1979), 3–18. Barthes wrote that while Eiffel himself saw his tower "in the form of a serious object, rational, useful, men return it to him in the form of a great baroque dream which quite naturally touches on the borders of the irrational."

23. Cited in Anatolii Strigalev and Jürgen Harten, eds., *Vladimir Tatlin, Retrospektive* (Cologne: DuMont Buchverlag, 1993), 37.

24. "The house of the foundation of heaven and earth, and its symbolism that of the holy mountain, and the spiral stair the path to its summit" (Elderfield, "The Line of Free Men," 226). I am interested not in symbolic forms of conscience but in the existence of forms in the world and in human creativity.

25. Two centuries ago, Friedrich Schlegel commented on the pace of the transformation of modern ruins: "Many of the works of the Ancients have become fragments. Many of the Moderns are fragments the moment they come into being." Friedrich Schlegel, quoted in *Irresistible Decay: Ruins Reclaimed*, ed. Michael S. Roth with Claire Lyons and Charles Merewether (Los Angeles: Getty Research Institute for the History of Art and the Humanities, 1997), 72.

26. Victor Shklovsky, "Pamiatnik tret'emu internatsionalu," in *Khod konia* (Moscow and Berlin: Gelikon, 1923), 108–111; in English, *The Knight's Move*, trans. Richard Sheldon (Normal: Dalkey Archive Press, 2005).

27. Shklovsky, "Pamiatnik tret'emu internatsionalu," 110.

28. Shklovsky, "Pamiatnik tret'emu internatsionalu," 111.

29. Svetlana Boym, "Kosmos: Remembrances of the Future," in Adam Bartos, *Kosmos: A Portrait of the Russian Space Age* (New York: Princeton Architectural Press, 2001).

30. Contemporary artist Leonid Sokov recalls that during the first Tatlin exhibit after the artist's death, in the 1970s, various elderly women who worked in the mosaic factory or in the local theaters brought with them small pictures of Tatlin's forgotten still lifes, which the artist apparently had given them in exchange for money and food.

31. Victor Shklovsky, "Sentimental'noe puteshestvie," in *Eshche nichego ne konchilos'* . . . (1923; Moscow: Propaganda, 2002), 260; for an English translation, see Victor Shklovsky, *A Sentimental Journey: Memoirs, 1917–1922*, ed. and trans. Richard Sheldon (Ithaca: Cornell University Press, 1984), 271.

32. This concept is based on Hannah Arendt's notion of "totalitarian fiction," a form of ideological fiction created by a totalitarian (or "authoritarian," in my preferred usage) state. This concept was recently elaborated by Dariusz Tolczyk, *See No Evil: Literary Cover-ups and Discoveries of the Soviet Camp Experience* (New Haven: Yale University Press, 1999).

33. See Victor Shklovsky, *Third Factory*, 36, translation slightly modified. For the original, see Victor Shklovsky, *Tret'ia fabrika* (Moscow: Krug, 1926), 67.

34. Carlo Ginzburg focuses in particular in the work of Marcus Aurelius, one of Tolstoy's beloved writers, and criticizes Shklovsky for ignoring his own philosophical heritage and focusing mostly on Russian examples.

35. Shklovsky, "Sentimental'noe puteshestvie," 76, idem, *Sentimental Journey*, 60.

36. Shklovsky, "Sentimental'noe puteshestvie," 195, idem *Sentimental Journey*, 195.

37. The term "dehumanization of art" was coined by the Spanish philosopher José Ortega-y-Gasset, who argued that in contrast to Renaissance art and the nineteenth-century novel, man is no longer at the center of modern art; the new art does not "imitate reality" but operates through inversion, by bringing to life a reality of its own and realizing poetic metaphors: "[T]he weapon of poetry turns against the natural things and wounds or murders them." José Ortega-y-Gasset, *The Dehumanization of Art*, trans. Helen Weyl (1925; Princeton: Princeton University Press, 1968), 35.

38. Victor Shklovsky, "Art as Technique" (1917), in *Four Formalist Essays*, ed. and trans. Lee T. Lemon and Marion J. Reis (1917; Lincoln: University of Nebraska Press, 1965), 3–24, quotation on 12.

39. Shklovsky, "Sentimental'noe puteshestvie," 232, idem, *Sentimental Journey*, 238.

40. Shklovsky, "Sentimental'noe puteshestvie," 232, idem, *Sentimental Journey*, 238.

41. Shklovsky, "Sentimental'noe puteshestvie," 76, idem, *Sentimental Journey*, 60.

42. Shklovsky, "Sentimental'noe puteshestvie," 195–196.

43. Later Elsa Triolet would choose a different aesthetics, persuading her future husband Louis Aragon to move from Surrealism to Socialist Realism.

44. This translation has been slightly modified; the original is: "Bytie opredeliaet soznanie, no sovest' ostaetsia neustroennoi," Shklovsky, *Tret'ia fabrika*, 7. The slogan "material being conditions consciousness" has been attributed in the Soviet sources to German philosopher Ludwig Feuerbach, Hegel, Marx, and Lenin. It is significant that in Shklovsky's context, this slogan opened a 1924 declaration of the Literature Section of Constructivists (LTsK), a radical constructivist group, that declared that the writer must serve the demands of the social and industrial revolution. "Tekhnicheskii Kodeks," quoted in Goriaeva, *Politicheskaia Tsenzura v SSSR* (Moscow: Rosspen, 2002), 123.

45. This is at once a polemic with the constructivists and with Tolstoy, in which Shklovsky explicitly distances himself from Tolstoy's didactic conception of art. To describe the current situation of the Formalist "second factory," Shklovsky tells a story about the "Flax Factory" in the chapter "On the Freedom of Art":

FLAX. This is no advertisement, I'm not employed at the Flax Center these days. At the moment, I'm more interested in pitch. In tapping trees to death. That is how turpentine is obtained.

From the tree's point of view, it is ritual murder.

The same with flax.

Flax, if it had a voice, would shriek as it's being processed. It is taken by the head and jerked from the ground. By the root. It is sown thickly—oppressed, so that it will be not vigorous but puny.

Flax requires oppression . . .

I want freedom.

But if I get it, I'll go look for unfreedom at the hands of a woman and a publisher.

Shklovsky, *Third Factory*, 45. The flax factory offers an interesting allegory; the author tries to persuade himself that freedom and unfreedom are only a matter of a point of view, yet we observe his "shrieks and jerks" in the process of social production and the adaptation to "oppression." On estrangement and Aesopian language, see Anne Wexler Katsnelson, "My Leader, Myself: Pictorial Estrangement and Aesopian Language in the Late Work of Kazimir Malevich," *Poetics Today* 27, no. 1 (Spring 2006): 67–97.

46. Shklovsky, *Third Factory*, 47–49.

47. The number three in the title of Shklovsky's last experimental autobiographical text is not accidental: using the Soviet productionist metaphor, Shklovsky speaks about his school as the "first factory," his training in the Formalist circle OPOYAZ as the beloved "second factory," and his place of employment, the Third Factory of Cinema, as the factory of Soviet life. Shklovsky promises to surrender to it in the end, yet he asks it to preserve the rights of the writers' guild and their need to breathe the air of a free city. Notably, Shklovsky's three autobiographical texts end in "ostensible surrenders" to the Soviet "factory of life"; these are insightfully discussed by Richard Sheldon in his introduction to *The Third Factory*. One should keep in mind both the historical and personal circumstances of these surrenders: Shklovsky's exile after the unfolding of the "Affair of the Socialist Revolutionaries," during which many of them were executed, as well as his wife being taken hostage. Also, each surrender is written as a cruel and ambivalent parable at the end of the text, in which the author asks the Soviet authorities not to repeat "the Arzerum story." In this fable of tragic miscommunication during the Persian campaign of World War I supposedly told to Shklovsky by Il'ia Zdanevich that the Asker people were found murdered, wounded in the head and in the right arm, "because when the Askers surrender they raise their right arm." Victor Shklovsky, *Zoo, ili Pis'ma ne o liubvi* [1923] in *Sentimental'noe puteshestvie; Zoo ili Pis'ma ne o liubvi* [A Sentimental Journey; Zoo, or Letters not about Love] (Moscow: Novosti, 1990), 347. In the first Soviet publication of *Zoo*, the story was simply eliminated by the censor. Shklovsky survived the Stalin era, remaining friends with many family members of arrested friends, including Nadezhda Mandelshtam. In the 1930s, Shklovsky tried to write the new Soviet prose and even contributed to a collective volume by Soviet writers praising the Stalinist construction site, and a site of forced labor, the Belomor Canal; Shklovsky went there to visit his arrested brother. After the political activism of his youth, he did not engage in any form of public dissent (of which very little survived). In 1966 he signed the letter in support of Andrei Siniavsky and Yulii Daniel, who were put on trial for their writings. Shklovsky's writings, however, were continuously criticized for their "estranged manner," regardless of the subject matter. He was accused, for example, of writing "in the same style about Dostoevsky, about a movie and about the military campaigns of the Red Army, so we don't see Dostoevsky and we don't see the Red Army. The only thing we see is Shklovsky." See A. P. Chudakov, "Dva pervykh desiatiletiia," in Shklovsky, *Gamburgskii schet*, 25.

48. Boris Eikhenbaum, *Moi Vremennik* (Leningrad: Izdatel'stvo pisatelei, 1929), 132. "Shklovsky is not merely a writer, but a special type of writer. In this respect, his role and position are exceptional. In another epoch, he would have been a Saint Petersburg freethinker, a Decembrist revolutionary, would have wandered around the South with Pushkin and fought duels."

49. Lidiia Ginzburg, *Chelovek za pis'mennym stolom* (Leningrad: Sovetskii pisatel', 1989), 59.

50. Victor Shklovsky, "Pamiatnik nauchnoi oshibke" [A monument to a scientific error], *Literaturnai Gazeta* 4, no. 41 (1930): 1. After a tactical display of quotes from Engels, he

presents the Formalists not as ideological enemies of the Soviet Marxists but as absent-minded scientists who built their theory of nontendentious literary science in error like that imaginary novelistic city. Shklovsky, a veteran of World War I, manipulates the military metaphors frequently used in Soviet public discourse, only instead of pursuing an ideological civil war between those who are with us and those who are against us, Shklovsky speaks about the "neutralized areas of the front," which he equates with "nontendentious art" (*nenapravlennoe iskusstvo*)—the new name for the "third way" or the "knight's move." Instead of practicing the Marxist sociological method, he follows Iuri Tynianov's theory of cultural evolution and his own practice of Lobachevskian parallelisms. In his *Art and Revolution* (1924) Lev Trotsky criticized "the Formal school" for its anti-Marxist bourgeois tendencies, calling it an "aborted fetus" of idealism. Parodying Shklovsky's method of parallelism, Gelfand tells the story of King Midas, likening the "reformed" Shklovsky to disguised Midas with Formalist ears. At the end Gelfand raises the stakes by asking, "What happened to Victor Shklovsky?": "One cannot renounce false and reactionary methods. One can either eliminate them or remain enslaved by them. Shklovsky failed to understand this truth. Nothing happened to Victor Shklovsky. His declaration demonstrates that Marxist literary science has to face the most acute and urgent necessity to eliminate the school of the 'neutralizers,' the school of militant literary reactionaries." See M. Gelfand, "Deklaratsiia tsaria Midasa, ili chto sluchilos' s Victorom Shklovskim?" *Pechat' i revoliutsiia* 2 (1930): 15, emphasis in the original. If the year of Gelfand's critique had been 1937 and not 1930, this kind of threat of elimination would have been taken literally, threatening the writer's life, not only his critical practices. M. Gelfand published a harsh critique of Shklovsky's supposed apology in his essay "The Declaration of King Midas, or What Happened to Victor Shklovsky" (1930). In spite of the ominous undertones of Gelfand's critical rage, his observations are quite perspicacious: he accuses Shklovsky of "Kantianism" and a lack of Hegelian-Marxist dialectics. Moreover, Gelfand attacks Shklovsky's "neutralized area of the front," claiming that Shklovsky confused the revolutions and remained an adept of the "bourgeois" February Revolution with its interest in civic freedoms and artistic independence. (One can hardly disagree with this statement; indeed, the February Revolution and its constitutional program must have remained for Shklovsky a lateral possibility, the road not taken by Russian history.) See Boym, "Politics and Poetics of Estrangement."

51. "There is an old term, *ostranenie*, that was often written with one n even though the word comes from *strannyi*. *Ostranenie* entered life in such a spelling in 1917. When discussed orally it is often confused with *otstranenie*, which means 'distancing of the world.'" Victor Shklovsky, *Izbrannoe v dvukh tomakh* (Moscow: Khudozhestvennaia literatura, 1983), 2: 188.

52. Arendt's plurality is not particularism, identity politics, nor even the politics of the other. It thrives in distinctiveness and multiplicity, not in the agonistic marriage of the self and the other. Only in interaction with other people and self-distancing do we reveal not what but who we are." Hannah Arendt, *The Life of the Mind* (New York: Harcourt Brace Jovanovich, 1977), 179–193. This represents an explicit reversal of the Rousseauean conception of authenticity; one is in fact "authentically" human and free only on the stage of the world theater. Hannah Arendt, *The Origins of Totalitarianism* (1958; New York: Meridian Books, 1969), 466.

53. Hannah Arendt, "The Jew as Pariah: A Hidden Tradition," in *The Jew as Pariah: Jewish Identity and Politics in the Modern Age*, ed. Ron H. Feldman (New York: Grove Press, 1978 [1944]), 90.

54. Arendt, *Origins of Totalitarianism*, 465–466. Similarly, in his essay "Moscow" (1927), Walter Benjamin made a striking observation about the collapse of the distinction

between the public and private sphere in Soviet Russia. He noted that Bolsheviks had abolished private life and closed the cafes where prerevolutionary artistic life had flourished. See Walter Benjamin, *Reflections* (New York: Schocken Books, 1986), 124–136.

55. Arendt, *Origins of Totalitarianism*, 185.

56. Ibid., 191.

57. Arendt, *Life of the Mind*, 149–177.

58. On Kafka's cult status in postcommunist Prague, see Svetlana Boym, *The Future of Nostalgia* (New York: Basic Books), 235–238. The campaign was called "Faut-it Bruler Kafka?"

59. Hannah Arendt, "The Gap between Past and Future," in *Between Past and Future* (New York: Viking, 1968), 7. I quote the parable in Hannah Arendt's rendition. She followed English translation except in a few places introducing a more literal translation. She references "HE" from "Notes from 1920," in *The Great Wall of China*, trans. Willa and Edwin Muir (New York: Viking, 1946). For an expanded reflection, see "The Gap between the Past and the Future," in *The Life of the Mind*, 202–213. Arendt's diagram with the diagonal of freedom is on p. 208. Arendt sends Kafka's parable to Heidegger in her private correspondence, and he makes an insightful comment after reading her interpretation: "The Kafka text is very revealing. I agree with your interpretation. Only as far as what unsettled me under the heading 'Clearing' is concerned it is not merely what is outside space and time but what gives space and time to time-space as such; that is, it is precisely not the extratemporal and extraspatial. The escapist distinction between time and eternity is too feeble. It may be enough for theology, but for thinking it will always be too coarse." *Hannah Arendt and Martin Heidegger, Letters, 1925–1975*, ed. Ursula Ludz, trans. Andrew Shields (New York: Harcourt Inc., 2004), 134.

60. Arendt, "The Gap between Past and Future," in *Between Past and Future*, 10–11.

61. Arendt, *Life of the Mind*, 204.

62. Hannah Arendt, "Franz Kafka, Appreciated Anew," in Hannah Arendt, *Essays on Art and Culture*, ed. Susannah Young-Ah Gottlieb (Stanford: Stanford University Press, 2007), 100.

63. Ibid., 100.

64. Ibid., 107.

65. Ibid., 106.

66. Benjamin Nathans, "The Dictatorship of Reason: Aleksandr Vol'pin and the Idea of Rights under 'Developed Socialism,'" *Slavic Review* 66, no. 4 (Winter 2007). The essay provides a comprehensive account of Vol'pin's biography and view of dissent. I am indebted to Ben Nathans for his profound insights into the history of dissent in the Soviet Union and for advice on bibliography. For comprehensive accounts and memoirs, see Andrei Sakharov, *Memoirs* (New York: Alfred A. Knopf, 1990), 273, 314; and Valery Chalidze, *To Defend These Rights: Human Rights and the Soviet Union* (New York: Random House, 1974), 56; Liudmila Alekseeva, *Soviet Dissent: Contemporary Movements for National, Religious, and Human Rights* (Middletown: Wesleyan University Press, 1985), 275, idem, *The Thaw Generation* (Pittsburgh: University of Pittsburgh Press, 1990); Aleksandr Sergeevich Esenin-Vol'pin, *Filosofiia. Logika. Poeziia. Zashchita prav cheloveka: Izbrannoe*, comp. by A. Iu. Daniel' et al. (Moscow: Rossiiskii gosudarstvennyi gumanitarnyi universitet, 1999), 243–245. For an insightful history of conscience in Russia, see Philip Bobbyear, *Conscience, Dissent and Reform in Soviet Russia* (London: Routledge, 2005). The dissenters in the late Soviet era were divided roughly between those who dreamed of the return of national religion (with monarchy or theocracy of the writer-tsar in power, in the case of Alexander

Solzhenitsyn). The others dreamed of socialism with a human face or some kind of Western democracy (with little conception of capitalist economy, which occupied almost no space in the thought of early dissidents in the 1960s).

67. For the text of the letter, see "Pis'mo 62 pisatelei" (most likely written, according to Nathans, in March 1966), among whose signatories were Bella Akhmadulina, Kornei Chukovskii, Lidiia Chukovskaia, Il'ia Ehrenburg, Veniamin Kaverin, Lev Kopelev, Bulat Okudzhava, Raisa Orlova, David Samoilov, Victor Shklovsky, and Vladimir Voinovich; reproduced in *Tsena Metaphory; ili, Prestuplenie i nakazanie Siniavskogo i Danielia*, ed. L. S. Eremina (Moscow: "Iunona," 1989), 499–500.

68. A. Iu. Daniel' and A. B. Roginskii, eds., *Piatoe dekabria 1965 goda v vospominaniiakh uchastnikov sobytii, materialakh Samizdata, dokumentakh partiinykh i komsomol'skikh organizatsii i v zapiskakh Komiteta gosudarstvennoi bezopasnosti v TsK KPSS* (Moscow: "Memorial," 1995), 40–41. Quoted and discussed in Benjamin Nathans, "Dictatorship of Reason."

69. On the concept of "cultural mythology" in the Russian and Soviet context, see Boym, *Common Places*. An example of such mythology can be found in one of most popular songs of the time, "Our Country Is the Land of Beauty," in which the country is loved "like a bride" and patriotism explicitly eroticized.

70. Andrei Amal'rik, *Zapiski dissidenta* (Ann Arbor: Ardis, 1982).

71. Alexander Ginzburg, ed., *Belaia kniga. Sbornik dokumentov po delu A. Siniavskogo i Iu. Danielia* (Frankfurt am Main: [n.p.], 1967), 167. For insightful analysis of the trial of Siniavsky and Daniel, see Catherine Theimer Nepomnyashchy, *Abram Tertz and the Poetics of Crime* (New Haven: Yale University Press, 1995); and Harriet Murav, *Russia's Legal Fictions* (Ann Arbor: University of Michigan Press, 1998), chap. 6. For insightful discussion of Siniasky and Solzhenitsyn, see Donald Fanger, "Conflicting Imperatives in the Model of the Russian Writer: The Case of Siniavsky / Tertz," in *Literature and History*, ed. Gary Saul Morson (Stanford: Stanford University Press, 1986), 111–124.

72. Discussed by Murav, *Russia's Legal Fictions*, 204; and Nepomnyashchy, *Abram Tertz*.

73. Dmitri Eremin, "Perevertyshi," in *Tsena Metaphory*, 21–23.

74. Eremin, "Perevertyshi," in *Tsena Metaphory*, 23.

75. In particular, the use of stylized "skaz narration," in which the narrator is another character, not the biographical author, was a device brilliantly employed by Nikolai Gogol.

76. *Tsena metaphory*, 474. I allowed myself the poetic license to translate *uslovnost'* as "literariness."

77. Ibid., 117; Nepomnyashchy, *Abram Tertz*, 36. Siniavsky is not exactly amused by the fact that the interrogation itself and the trial seem to imitate his text. The "dead" author, to use Roland Barthes's term, becomes a prophetic Cassandra-like storyteller who anticipates and defines the terms of his own interrogation, trial and exile.

78. For the prosecution, "duplicity" was synonymous with treason and betrayal of motherland. On the surface it presumes a certain coherent and moral unified subjectivity and transparency as professed by the codex of the young Soviet communist. However, on another level the outrage in the official letters against Siniavsky and Daniel is directed toward something else: the unauthorized behavior, the literal use of Soviet ideology, such as the critique of the cult of Stalinism, which always occupied an ambivalent place within the official discourse.

79. Thomas Venclova, "The Game of the Soviet Censor," in *Forms of Hope* (Riverdale on Hudson: Sheep Meadow Press, 1999), 186–191. Discussed in Philip Boobbyer, *Conscience, Dissent and Reform in Soviet Russia* (London: Sage, 2005), 161.

80. Boobbyer, *Conscience, Dissent and Reform in Soviet Russia*, 150–168.

81. Shafarevich claimed that Russian culture is threatened because "all members of the liberal intelligentsia—and particularly émigrés—are Russophobes, and all Russophobes either are Jews or are under the control of Jews." Nepomnyashchy, *Abram Tertz*, 30–31.

82. Siniavsky claims that many political dissidents were in their past model Soviet citizens with high convictions, principles, and revolutionary ideals. It is their idealism that made them initially question and estrange themselves from everyday Soviet practices, but this idealism alone might not protect them from reconstructing the authoritarian edifice on a different foundation.

83. Siniavsky, "Dissidentstvo kak lichnyi opyt," 133.

84. Berlin, "Herzen and Bakunin on Liberty" in *Russian Thinkers*.

85. Siniavsky explained that he had been an Orthodox Christian since the 1960s but never considered that his private spiritual beliefs should be confused with his public practices; he always upheld the separation of church and state, public and private spheres, and insisted on inner plurality and public pluralism. Siniavsky represents the liberal tradition within Russian Orthodox Christianity. George Fedotov, sociologist and theorist of freedom, was another interesting intellectual advocate of it. There were also the Orthodox priest Alexander Men' and various dissident priests who criticized the position of the church leadership during Stalinism. On spiritual dissent, see Boobbyer, *Conscience, Dissent and Reform in Soviet Russia*.

86. Victor Pelevin, *Generation "P"* (Moscow: Vagrius, 1999), 110. For a more detailed reading of the novel, see Svetlana Boym, *Obshchie mesta* (Moscow: NLO, 2003); this Russian-language edition contains an extra chapter. For the conception of *stiob* and "pretense recognition" in the last Socialist generation, see Alexei Yurchak, *Everything Was Forever Until It Was No More: The Last Soviet Generation* (Princeton: Princeton University Press, 2003); and Boym, *Future of Nostalgia*, 154–157.

87. For a detailed discussion, see Konstantin Akinsha, "The Orthodox Bulldozer," *Art News* (April 2004). Article 282, the law against inciting religious hatred and anti-Semitism, was never used against neo-Nazis or other explicitly xenophobic nationalist movements. It was first used against the artist Ter Oganyan. The rhetoric on both sides of the debate around the closing of "Caution, Religion" mobilized many tropes of Soviet cold war discourse. Prominent Russian writers and artists and scientists including Il'ia Glazunov, Nikita Mikhalkov, and Igor' Shafarevich signed the statement supporting the destruction of the exhibit, accusing it of "conscious Satanism" claiming that "Russians and the Russian Orthodox live on the reservations in Russia," thus rather preposterously comparing the situation of Orthodox Russians in Russia to that of native Americans in the United States living on reservations, a common cliché of the Soviet cold war discourse. The liberal press called the exhibit the "Orthodox Bulldozer," referring to the "bulldozer exhibit" of 1974. Similar artistic scandals in the United States, Japan, England, and Sweden resulted in the interference of legal and civic organizations that mediated between artists and the state or religious authorities. In contemporary Russia the courts proved to be dependent on the state and the Church religious orders. The conception of "freedom of conscience"—and freedom of belief—was turned upside down according to a paranoiac formula (we, the vandals, hate the artists, therefore they persecute us). For an insightful analysis of the event, see also Mikhail Ryklin in *Zurück aus der Zukunft: Osteuropäische Kulturen im Zeitalter des Postkommunismus*, ed. Boris Groys and Anna von der Heiden (Frankfurt am Main: Suhrkamp, 2005).

88. Arendt, "What Is Freedom?" in *Between Past and Future*, 170.

Chapter Six

1. Young-Bruehl, *Hannah Arendt*, 106–107.The officer recommended that Arendt not hire a lawyer and save her money, because in his words, "Jews don't have money now."

2. Evgeniia Ginzburg, *Journey into the Whirlwind*, trans. Paul Stevenson and Max Hayward (New York: Harcourt, Brace and Co., 1995). In his introduction to the book Ginzburg's son, writer Vassili Aksenov, says that his mother often wished that she had resisted Stalinism in the name of true socialism, so that at least there would have been a more "legitimate" reason for her imprisonment. Ginzburg's memoir uses a double perspective: that of an idealistic communist believer puzzled by the new period in party politics and that of the Gulag survivor writing after the Twentieth Party Congress. She uses a "free indirect discourse" that recreates as much as possible her perspective from the 1930s–1940s and moderates it with her conclusions from the 1950s.

3. Ginzburg, *Journey into the Whirlwind*, 20.

4. Ginzburg, *Journey into the Whirlwind*, 21–22.

5. Ginzburg, *Journey into the Whirlwind*, 22–23.

6. At the time of writing her memoirs, Ginzburg believed that the strategy of escaping arrest by getting out of sight and out of mind was often a way of cheating the implacable system. "Yes, people looked for every possible way out. And those in whom common sense, shrewdness and independence of mind outweighed the effect of a dogmatic Soviet education and the mystic spell of Party slogans, did in fact sometimes escape." Ginzburg, *Journey into the Whirlwind*, 24. In 1936, Evgeniia does the opposite by going to Moscow and attracting attention to her case.

7. Ginzburg, *Journey into the Whirlwind*, 112–113.

8. Theodor Adorno, "Commitment," in *Aesthetics and Politics* (London: Verso, 1980), 188–189.

9. Varlam T. Shalamov, "O novoi proze" (On the New Prose), in *Sobranie sochinenii v shesti tomakh* (Moscow: Terra-Knizhnyi Klub, 2005), 5: 157. The translation of the quotes from Shalamov's essays is mine. The early version of my discussion of Shalamov and Arendt appeared as 'Banality of Evil,' Mimicry, and the Soviet Subject: Varlam Shalamov and Hannah Arendt" in *Slavic Review* 67, no. 2 (Spring 2008). I am grateful to the anonymous reviewers of the *Slavic Review* and editor Mark Steinberg for their comments and insights.

10. Dariusz Tolczyk explores the history of the dual image of the Gulag in *See No Evil: Literary Cover-ups and Discoveries of the Soviet Camp Experience* (New Haven: Yale University Press, 1999). For documentary account of the history of the Gulag, see N. Vert, S. V. Mironenko, and I. A. Zuzina, eds., *Istoriia Stalinskogo Gulaga: Konets 20-kh –pervaia polovina 50-kh godov; Dokumenty v 7-i tomakh* (Moscow: ROSSPEN, 2004); Anne Appelbaum, *Gulag: A History* (New York: Doubleday, 2003). For the most insightful recent accounts, see Lynne Viola, *The Unknown Gulag: The Lost World of Stalin's Special Settlements* (New York: Oxford University Press, 2007); Golfo Alexopoulos, *Stalin's Outcasts: Aliens, Citizens, and the Soviet State, 1926–1936* (Ithaca: Cornell University Press, 2003); and Irina Paperno, *Stories of the Soviet Experience: Memoirs, Diaries, Dreams* (Ithaca: Cornell University Press, 2009). For a discussion of diaries from the time of the Great Terror, see Véronique Garros, Natalia Korenevskaia, and Thomas Lahusen, eds., *Intimacy and Terror: Soviet Diaries of the 1930s*, trans. Carol A. Flath (New York: New Press, 1995); as well as writing on diaries: Jochen Hellbeck, *Revolution on My Mind: Writing a Diary under Stalin* (Cambridge, MA: Harvard University Press, 2006); and Igal Halfin, *Terror in My Soul: Communist Autobiographies on Trial* (Cambridge, MA: Harvard University Press, 2003). For debate

on "Soviet subjectivity" and approaches to Stalinist cultural research, see the journal *Ab Imperio* 3 (2002); and for a critique Foucault applied to the Russian context, see Laura Engelstein, "Combined Underdevelopment: Discipline and Law in Imperial and Soviet Russia," in *Foucault and the Writing of History*, ed. Jan Goldstein (Cambridge: Blackwell, 1994); and Jan Plamper, "Foucault's Gulag," in *Kritika* 3, no. 2 (2002). For an insightful literary discussion of the "poetics of documentary prose," see Leona Toker, "Towards a Poetics of Documentary Prose—from the Perspective of Gulag Testimonies," *Poetics Today* 18, no. 2 (1997): 201–207, idem, *Return from the Archipelago: Narratives of Gulag Survivors* (Bloomington: Indiana University Press, 2000); and Leona Toker, ed., "Documentary Prose and the Role of the Reader: Some Stories of Varlam Shalamov," in *Commitment in Reflection: Essays in Literature and Moral Philosophy* (New York: Garland, 1994), 169–193. I have benefited greatly from the discussion at the conference "History and Legacy of the Gulag," organized by Stephen Barnes at the Davis Center at Harvard University, November 2006.

11. Cato, discussed in Ronald Beiner, "Hannah Arendt on Judgment: Interpretative Essay," in *Lectures on Kant's Political Philosophy* (Chicago: University of Chicago Press, 1982), 131; and in Young-Bruehl, *Hannah Arendt*, 533.

12. Goethe, *Faust 2* (act 5), trans. George Madison Priest (New York: Knopf, 1941).

13. After the fall of the Soviet Union, Arendt's concept of totalitarianism was called into question and discarded a number of times as a relic of the cold war. More often than not, it was turned into a straw man of a concept, understood literally as total state control, and into a straw man of total domination over all dimensions of life. The broader existential, philosophical, and aesthetic aspects of Arendt's conception of freedom and of totalitarian experience, of responsibility and judgment, received much less critical attention.

14. In Arendt's view, totalitarian ideology tends to be quite successful due to the "common-sense disinclination to believe the monstrous": "The reason why totalitarian regimes can get so far in realizing a fictitious topsy-turvy world is that the outside nontotalitarian world, which always comprises a great part of the population of the totalitarian country itself, indulges also in wishful thinking and shirks reality in the face of real insanity." Arendt, *Origins of Totalitarianism*, 437.

15. Arendt argues that the totalitarian state cannot be understood within a traditional opposition between the constitutional state (that enforces laws more or less successfully) and the tyranny that is lawless and arbitrary. Rather, totalitarian ideology "pretends to have found a way to establish the rule of justice on earth—something which the legality of positive law admittedly could never attain." Arendt, *The Origins of Totalitarianism*, 462.

16. Arendt, *Eichmann in Jerusalem*, 252, and idem, *The Life of the Mind*.

17. Vladimir Nabokov, "On Philistines and Philistinism," in *Lectures on Russian Literature* (New York: Harcourt Brace Jovanovich, 1981). For a detailed discussion of cliché, *poshlost'*, and kitsch, see Boym, *Common Places*, 11–20. For a discussion of the banality of evil and radical evil, see Richard Bernstein, *Radical Evil: A Philosophical Interrogation* (Cambridge: Polity Press, 2002).

18. There is a form of thoughtlessness, as exhibited by Eichmann, which is not mere shallowness or stupidity but an ethical problem and a key to understanding war crimes from the point of view of the perpetrators. "Might the problem of good and evil, our faculty for telling right from wrong, be connected to our faculty of thought?" Arendt asks. Arendt, *The Life of the Mind*, 5. Dana R. Villa, *Politics, Philosophy, Terror: Essays on the Thought of Hannah Arendt* (Princeton, NJ: Princeton University Press, 2001). Arendt explores the foundations of thoughtlessness as the ground for nonjudgment through the practice of estrangement *for* the world as discussed in chapter 5.

19. Primo Levi, *The Drowned and the Saved* (New York: Summit Books, 1988), 138–139.

20. Hannah Arendt, "Understanding and Politics," *Partisan Review* 20 (1953): 392. For a more detailed discussion of imagination, see Hannah Arendt, *Lectures on Kant's Political Philosophy*, ed. Ronald Beiner (Chicago: University of Chicago Press, 1982), 79–85; Ronald Beiner, "Hannah Arendt on Judgment: Interpretative Essay," in *Lectures on Kant's Political Philosophy*, 89–156; and Howard Caygill, *Art of Judgment* (Oxford: B. Blackwell, 1989), 366–380. Arendt's reading of Kant with a focus on aesthetic judgment is rather eccentric to the tradition, yet crucial for her discussion of public freedom.

21. Shalamov wrote that the "celebration of Stalinism is the aestheticization of evil (*estetizatsiia zla*)," in *Vospominaniia, Zapisnye Knizhki, Perepiska, Sledstvennye Dela* (Moscow: Eksmo, 2004), 309.

22. Varlam Shalamov, "O proze" (On Prose), in *Sobranie sochinenii v shesti tomakh*, 6: 148.

23. Intonation, according to Shalamov is a "completely underdeveloped topic in our literary studies." Varlam Shalamov to Iu. M. Lotman, in *Vospominaniia, Zapisnye Knizhki, Perepiska, Sledstvennye Dela*, 933. Shalamov's short texts on intonation include "Poeticheskaia intonatsia" (Poetic Intonation), 21–30, and "Vo vlasti chuzhoi intonatsii" (Under the Control of Foreign Intonation), in Shalamov, *Sobranie sochinenii v shesti tomakh*, 5: 31–38. The study of intonation belongs to the interdisciplinary field of social linguistics, rhetoric, and social anthropology. I have discovered the work of the founder of Soviet musicology, Boris Asaf'ev (1884–1949), who developed an interdisciplinary conception of intonation as a form of social communication and aesthetic innovation.

24. Lidiia Ginzburg, *Chelovek za pis'mennym stolom* (Leningrad: Sovetskij pisatel', Len. otd-nie., 1989), 310, translation mine. This is further discussed in Svetlana Boym, *Common Places: Mythologies of Everyday Life in Russia* (Cambridge, MA: Harvard University Press, 1994), 93.

25. By the late Brezhnev era, irony and doublespeak that relied on clichés were superseded by the *stiob* discourse that used ersatz irony and relied on the "pretense recognition" practiced by everyone, including the KGB agents. On the rhetoric of *stiob* and the legacy of the culture of stagnation, see Svetlana Boym, *The Future of Nostalgia* (New York, 2001), 154–156.

26. Ginzburg planned to publish her memoir in the Soviet Union so the text has a certain degree of inner censorship that in itself is a feature of the time. It doesn't have many explicit descriptions of brutality; sensationalism of this kind is simply not Ginzburg's point and often she is protecting the dignity of her fellow prisoners. (This is not merely the issue of censorship, but of cultural difference as well.) The text incorporates hesitations, judgments, political decisions, and writing practices of different times.

27. In fact, Shalamov's discussion of documentary prose is not dissimilar from the 1920s discussions of the "end of the novel" and the new "prose of the document" (*proza dokumenta*), which is not accidental given Shalamov's studies and friendship with the members of the Formalist circle. Shalamov avoids ostentatious literary devices of narrative framing, multivoicedness, or explicit decorative tropes.

28. Shklovsky, *Varlam Shalamov*, 54.

29. Right after Stalin's death, at the dawn of the Khrushchev era, Soviet "thick magazines" were engaged in a passionate debate—not about the experience of the Gulag or justice for the victims—but about "sincerity" in tone. The term "thaw," introduced by the writer Il'ia Ehrenburg, was connected to this discussion. In cultural politics Khrushchev's thaw was ushered in by a gentle revolution that didn't turn upside down the structure of society or Soviet discourse but affected only its syntax and intonation. The unofficial (but never antiofficial) thaw culture of poets and bards depended on the new intonation that

functioned like a password for an alternative network of Soviet friendships. The revolution in intonation—a rebellion in a minor key—was the first step in the Soviet unwritten "contract" with the state. Tone, like gesture, represented an invisible notation, unreadable to multiple "well-wishers" and informants, that nevertheless could serve as "white ink," invisible glue to seal the imperfect informal networks of the Soviet era.

30. Shalamov, "O novoi proze," in *Sobranie sochinenii v shesti tomakh*, 5: 160.

31. Shalamov, *Vospominaniia, zapisnye knizhki, perepiska, sledstvennye dela*, 53–56.

32. In his notebooks Shalamov recounts several conversations with Solzhenitsyn, often not identifying him by his full name but giving the first initial S. Shalamov called Solzhenitsyn a "graphomaniac," dealer (*delets*) of the Gulag, and a "polisher of reality" (*lakirovshchik deistvitel'nosti*). Consider for example the following account of "S" teaching a less successful Shalamov the way to publish his work abroad—an account that comes from Shalamov's notebooks:

> For America—said my new acquaintance quickly and instructively—the hero must be religious. They even have a law about this, so that no American publisher will take a story in translation where the hero is an atheist or simply a skeptic or a man of doubts.
> —And what about Jefferson, the author of the Declaration of Independence?
> —Well, but this was a long time ago . . . Now I look through your stories and haven't found a story where the hero was a man of faith. So, the voice was shushuring, don't send it to America.
> The small fingers of my new friend quickly leaf through the typed pages.
> —I am even surprised, how can you not believe in God?
> —I don't have a need in such a hypothesis, just like Voltaire.
> —But after Voltaire came World War II.
> —That's precisely why. . . .
> Kolyma was Stalin's extermination camp. I experienced all its particularities. I could never imagine that in the twentieth century there could be a writer who would use his memoirs for personal reasons.

Shalamov, *Vospominaniia, zapisnye knizhki*, 372–373. In the next entries Shalamov observes, "The cheaper the 'device,' the more success it had. This is the tragedy of my life" (373).

It is not for us to resolve the profound dispute between Solzhenitsyn and Shalamov, worthy of a Dostoevsky novel. What is curious is that the encounter is framed by Shalamov with a discussion of banality: the issue for him is not even faith, or America, or possibilities of publication. The issue is the "cheapening" of devices and selling the least sellable experiences.

33. Shalamov, "O proze," 6: 152.

34. Ibid., 155–156.

35. Milan Kundera, *The Book of Laughter and Forgetting*, trans. Michael Heim (New York: Penguin, 1986), 65–68. For a discussion of the "poetics of blemish," see Boym, *Common Places*, 242.

36. Shalamov, "Sukhim paikom" (Dry Rations), in *Sobranie sochinenii*, 1:73. Saveliev explains that even if they survive the camp they will remain sick men, suffering from endless bodily aches and memory swoons. Yet among their many sick days there will be a few good ones, a few almost happy days, equal in number to those that the prisoners managed to spend "loafing" in the camp.

37. "Kant is a widely popular camp term. It refers to something like a temporary rest, not a full rest. . . . but just a kind of work that doesn't make one work to the limit of his

possibilities, choosing instead easier temporary work [*pri kotoroi chelovek ne vybivaetsia iz sil, legkuiu vremennuiu rabotu*]." Shalamov, "Kant," in *Sobranie sochinenii,* 1: 73.

38. Shalamov, "Sukhim paikom," 83. Translation mine.

39. Andrei Siniavsky, "Srez materiala," in *Shalamovskii sbornik,* pt. 1 (Vologda: Izd-vo Instituta povysheniia kvalifakatsii i perepodgotovki pedagogicheskikh kadrov, 1994), 224–228.

40. Shalamov, "Sukhim paikom," 87.

41. To complicate matters further, Fedya is telling the literal truth, since he took the clothes of Ivan Ivanovich and now finds himself "dressed for the season." And like the nameless convict in Saveliev's story, he too has "loafed" appropriately for the circumstances.

42. I am grateful to Leona Toker for drawing my attention to the repetition during the Gulag Symposium at Harvard, November 5, 2006.

43. Lev Vygotsky, "Art as Catharsis," in *The Psychology of Art* (Cambridge, MA: MIT Press, 1971), 215. For another interesting discussion of the "aesthetic phenomenon of Shalamov," see E. B Volkova, "Esteticheskii fenomen Varlama Shalamova," *in Mezhdunarodnye Shalamovskie chteniia* (1997): 7–22, and idem, "Paradoksy katarsisa Varlama Shalamova," in *Voprosy filosofii* 11 (1996): 43–57.

44. The title "By Dry Rations" has a syntactic similarity with another saying that uses a similar adverbial expression that might be invoked here: "Not by bread alone is man alive."

45. Shalamov, "Lida" in *Sobranie sochinenii,* 1:320–321.

46. Shalamov, "Lida," 1: 326–327.

47. The reasons for Krist's luck proposed by the fellow are interesting in themselves. One sees there an accident of fate, the other believes it is a sign of the thaw, of the change in political climate, and the doctor sees there the "will of god."

48. Ibid., 1: 326. Krist is afraid to speak in the moment of liberation, just like the convicts at the beginning of "Dry Rations," incredulous over their transient luck. The most important things are not to be "profaned" through impurity of tone.

49. "Revelation (*ozarenie*) arrived suddenly as usual. Suddenly but after an enormous effort—not only intellectual, not only of the heart, but of his whole being. It arrived the way poems or the best lines of a story came to him. One thinks of them day and night without a response and then revelation comes as the joy of the exact word, as the joy of a solution. Not the joy of hope—for Krist had encountered already too many disappointments, errors and backstabbings. The revelation came. Lida" (1: 324). Both metaphors and materiality of writing play an important role in Shalamov's story. The physical document in the center of the story, the hand-stamped passport of the liberated prisoner, if it were ever to be found in some imaginary archive—would require a "thick description" and multiple layers of reading.

50. Emmanuel Levinas, "Ethics as First Philosophy," in *Levinas Reader,* ed. Sean Hand (Oxford: Blackwell, 1997), 84.

51. Brian Boyd and Robert Pyle, eds., *Nabokov's Butterflies* (New York: Beacon Press, 2000), 85–86. On the conception of "mimicry," see Boym, *The Future of Nostalgia,* 265–266.

52. Homi Bhabha, "Of Mimicry and Man: The Ambivalence of Colonial Discourse," in *The Location of Culture* (London: Routledge, 1995), 85–92. Bhabha offers important insights into the hybridity and subversion of mimicry, but his discussion is focused on the postcolonial and colonial contexts and has to be recontextualized when applied to the Stalinist context.

53. Varlam Shalamov, "In the power of the alien intonation" ("*Vo vlasti chuzhoi intonatsii*") in *Sobranie sochinenii*, 5:31.

54. Vladimir Nabokov, *Strong Opinions* (New York and London: Vintage International, 1990), 63. See also Boym, *The Future of Nostalgia*, 266–274.

55. Shalamov, "Poetry Is a Universal Language," *Sobranie sochinenii v shesti tomakh*, 6: 52–53.

56. Shalamov, "O proze," in *Sobranie sochinenii v shesti tomakh*, 6: 148.

57. Paraphrasing Marx, Shalamov writes: "History that first appeared as tragedy, reappears a second time as farce. But there is also the third embodiment of the plot: as absurd horror." Shalamov, *Vospominaniia, zapisnye knizhki, perepiska, sledstvennye dela*, 309. Marx's original aphorism from "The Eighteenth Brumaire" paraphrases Hegel, who claimed that history repeats itself. Besides the striking insight that this observation offers, it is curious that Shalamov uses Formalist literary vocabulary and speaks of historical "plots."

58. Neither were the experiences of cultural revolution in China, Cambodia, or Cuba. Contemporary art from Spain, South Africa, and Latin America—particularly Chile, Argentina, and Colombia—offers many interesting examples of dealing with *desaparecidos* and historical erasure. In the case of patriotic public relations (a shorthand of propaganda and public relations that curiously merged in post-Soviet Russia), the continuity of the power structures in Russia and elsewhere ensured that in spite of striking fictional and nonfictional accounts by Shalamov, Ginzburg, Solzhenitsyn, Dombrowski, Grossman, and the work of the memorial, no consistent and serious work of memory and self-critical reflection and public recognition of the history of domestic oppression has occurred.

59. There are a few exceptions. One of the best examples is the well-known painting by Leonid Lamm, *To Freedom with a Clear Consciousness*, which represents the space of the Soviet prison with photorealistic precision and uses an official slogan as its title.

60. Dostoevsky, *Besy (The Possessed)* (Leningrad: Lenizdat, 1990), 352.

61. Italo Calvino, *Invisible Cities* (New York and London: Harcourt Brace Jovanovich, 1978), 165.

Conclusion

1. *Painting by Numbers: Komar and Melamid's Scientific Guide to Art*, ed. JoAnn Wypijewski (New York: Farrar Straus Giroux, 1997), 8.

2. Like any artists at the mercy of the people, Komar and Melamid allowed themselves minor play with the material. None of the blue landscapes was executed en plein air; instead, the artists found a template for the ideal landscape based on the work of Italian painter Domenichino (1581–1641), betraying their old Soviet art historical interests. Moreover, the artists confessed their own improbable love for the blue landscape, which they discovered in spite of themselves. While painting on demand, they also depicted something like "a paradise within," a primordial dream of art and freedom and also an improbable blue-colored retreat for tired exiles that was nobody's native soil. When asked where they situate themselves in the "people's choice" project, Komar gave an ambivalent answer. He associates it with his "first encounter with Western civilization," which took place up in the air and in a toilet on board the Boeing that carried him to the United States. He visited the toilet, flushed, and saw the greatest surprise of his life—the dark blue liquid: the color of freedom and of the artificial heaven of consumer goods. A different kind of blue landscape flashed in front of the artist's eyes. It is from this perspective of refugees that Komar and Melamid search for "the people's choice" and a "universal language."

3. *Painting by Numbers: Komar and Melamid's Scientific Guide to Art*, 25.

4. Robert Skidelsky, *John Maynard Keynes, 1883–1946: Economist, Philosopher, Statesman* (New York: Penguin, 2003).

5. Lynn Hunt, *Inventing Human Rights: A History* (New York: W. W. Norton & Company, 2007).

6. David Rohde and Mohammed Khan, "Ex-Londoner's Diary of Jihad: A Portrait Sprinkled with Koran Verses and Epithets," *New York Times*, August 8, 2005.

7. The conversation continued about ads in the Russian newspapers looking for young women, aged 18–25, with good computer skills and "without hang-ups" (or "easygoing"), and whether this was a sign of liberation or a new kind of dependency, is a question I will skip for the moment.

8. There is a tragic irony in the fact that some American business partners of the Russian financiers, enthusiasts of the "wild East," ended up legitimizing the cunning use of the free market discourse to suppress democratic freedoms. The American businessman considered this to be a part of the Russian character, which proved to be an uncanny self-fulfilling prophesy since he was subsequently thrown out of Russia, in the process losing much of his profit.

9. I am indebted to Professor Jacques Rupnik for his comparative discussion of the 1968 in Prague and in Paris, winter 2008.

10. Orlando Patterson, *Freedom in the Making of Western Culture* ([New York]: Basic Books, 1991), 43. See also his discussion of the Bangkok Declaration in "Freedom, Slavery and Modern Construction of Rights" in *Historical Change and Human Rights. The Oxford Amnesty Lectures*, ed. Olwen Hufton (NY: Basic Books, 1994).

11. Amartya Kumar Sen, *Development as Freedom* (Oxford: Oxford University Press, 1999), 235–238.

12. Since I am not a specialist in Chinese intellectual history, I have relied on various secondary sources, including David Kelly's insightful essay "The Chinese Quest for Freedom as a Universal Value," presented at the conference. Among various intellectual contributions to the debate on freedom one could distinguish Lao-Zhuang's doctrine of inner spiritual freedom in imperial times feeding into various countercultures, including an anarchist critique of rulers and the ruling Confucian ideology. Buddhist liberation; Republican liberalism (Yan Fu, Liang Qichao) that was in dialogue with the ideas of Rousseau and Mill; the qualified contemporary prodemocracy movement; aesthetic anarchism in dialogue with Nietzsche; "Hao han," a folk ideology of a sovereign; personal freedom close to antinomianism; the Chinese version of Marxist Hegelianism in many forms, among others.

INDEX